THE WORD MADE FLESH

Towards an Incarnational Missiology

Ross Langmead

University Press of America,® Inc.
Dallas · Lanham · Boulder · New York · Oxford

Copyright © 2004 by
University Press of America,® Inc.
4501 Forbes Boulevard
Suite 200
Lanham, Maryland 20706
UPA Acquisitions Department (301) 459-3366

PO Box 317
Oxford
OX2 9RU, UK

Copublished by arrangement with American Society of Missiology
and Dr. Ross Langmead

Library of Congress Control Number: 2004102717
ISBN 0-7618-2911-3 (paperback : alk. ppr.)
ISBN 0-7618-2910-5 (hardcover : alk. ppr.)

Like all good theology, the work on the incarnational understanding of mission and evangelism should be done modestly, critically and rigorously. But let it also be done joyfully, with the expectation that we will discover more of what the gospel means.

— Darrell L Guder, "Incarnation and the Church's Evangelistic Mission," *International Review of Mission* 83 (1994): 426.

CONTENTS

PART ONE
INCARNATION AND MISSION

PART TWO
CRITICAL SURVEY

PART THREE
CONTOURS OF AN INCARNATIONAL MISSIOLOGY

PREFACE

Incarnational approaches to mission are supported across a variety of Christian traditions. Few take exception to incarnational mission in its most general meaning—somehow embodying the message Christians want to share, just as Jesus embodied the Good News. Brief appeals to an incarnational approach to mission pepper the literature of mission.

Incarnational missiology, however, varies dramatically in shape between Christian traditions. It also comes under theological fire. Is it a form of exemplarism, simply trying to follow Jesus in our own strength? Is it arrogant for Christians to compare their mission with the incarnating mission of Jesus Christ? Going further back, is the doctrine of the incarnation still sustainable as a basis for mission today?

So common and yet so seldom examined in any depth, this approach to mission calls for analysis. This study is the first attempt, to my knowledge, to tease out the meanings attached to incarnational mission and to propose a theological framework that overcomes the potential weaknesses of an incarnational approach to mission.

This research was undertaken as part of doctoral studies at the Melbourne College of Divinity and, with minor editing, is published in its form as a dissertation.

I was privileged to have the wise and gracious guidance of Rev Dr Lawrence Nemer, SVD, as adviser and Rev Dr Frank Rees as co-adviser. I was also given support in many ways by the Principal (Rev Dr Ken Manley) and faculty of Whitley College, the Baptist College of Victoria

(Australia), in the years when I struggled to combine teaching and the writing of a dissertation.

My family, Alison, Benjamin and Kia, were totally supportive in this process, which meant more than I can express. Llew Evans, household member, now eighty-nine years young, and enthusiast for all theology that matters, has read and commented on everything I have written and is a valued co-traveler in the adventure of incarnational mission. I am deeply grateful to many other good friends who also read sections or drafts at various times.

In the text all alterations in quotations, such as the insertion of inclusive language, are indicated by the use of square brackets. Biblical quotations are from the New Revised Standard Version (NRSV).

Few scholars are able to explore a topic that burns like a fire in the belly, allows them to read across a whole discipline, prods their spiritual growth, and leaves them eager to explore further in practice what they have tried to express in a disciplined, scholarly manner. I am deeply grateful.

Ross Langmead
April 2003

LIST OF ABBREVIATIONS

AG	*Ad Gentes* (1965, Vatican II document)
CELAM	The Latin American Episcopal Council
CLADE III	Third Latin American Congress on Evangelism (1992)
CWME	Commission on World Mission and Evangelism (of the WCC, since 1961)
EN	*Evangelii Nuntiandi* (1975, Pope Paul VI)
GS	*Gaudium et Spes* (1965, Vatican II document)
IMC	International Missionary Council (1910-1961)
LC	Lausanne Covenant (1974)
LG	*Lumen Gentium* (1964, Vatican II document)
ME	*Mission and Evangelism* (1982, WCC publication)
RM	*Redemptoris Missio* (1991, Pope John Paul II)
SEDOS	Servizio Documentazione e Studi (Research Centre for Missionary Institutes)
UR	*Unitatis Redintegratio* (1964, Vatican II document)
WCC	World Council of Churches

PART ONE

INCARNATION AND MISSION

CHAPTER 1

INTRODUCTION

This study explores the contours of an adequate incarnational approach to mission in the light of the strengths and limitations of incarnational approaches from a variety of Christian traditions.

It is common for Christians to say that mission ought to be incarnational, meaning that in some sense it involves embodying the good news that Christians proclaim. In fact "incarnational mission" has become a buzz-word in some Christian circles: impressive to the listener, warm in feel, and yet elastic in meaning.[1] Frequently, writers briefly appeal to the incarnation when discussing mission but then move on without clarifying what they mean. Christians are often called to follow Jesus as the pattern in mission, but what exactly are they to follow? In Jesus the divine is understood to have been somehow enfleshed in human form, but how does this notion apply to ordinary Christians?[2] Incarnational mission is a widely used notion begging for some careful analysis. This is the reason for, and the significance of, this study.

Genesis of the Study

There is a case for saying that all theology is closely linked to biography, meaning that in trying to talk about God all Christians do theology out of their ongoing personal journey and context.[3] This study is no exception.

This study was triggered by a single challenging comment made to me by Raymond Fung, formerly the Secretary for Evangelism in the Commission on World Mission and Evangelism of the World Council of Churches. Fung remarked in a lecture on evangelism in 1993 that incarnational mission (by which he meant mission modeled on the life of Jesus) has a certain pride about it, because it says in effect, "Look at us and you will see Jesus." In conversation afterwards he said that he did not espouse incarnational missiology because the church can never even remotely resemble Christ, and needs constantly to point beyond itself to Jesus.

In later correspondence, Fung elaborated by saying that there is only one Incarnation, with a capital "I," the unique Incarnation of God. He writes: "There are no others with a small 'i.' Speaking theologically and precisely, incarnation is not a methodology. It is not an adjective [such as 'incarnational']."[4] To Fung it is a noun with a definite article: "the Incarnation." He is critical of "incarnational mission" because he feels the term is used in a casual and pious way which leads to a neglect of verbal evangelism.[5] He would join others in preferring that the term be dropped because of terminal ambiguity and theological imprecision.[6]

Fung's views prompted me to question my strong commitment to a certain sort of incarnational mission. It had developed under the influences of conservative evangelicalism, the holiness movement and the radical discipleship movement, all of which urged strong links between Christian faith and a committed discipleship which issues in mission after the pattern of Jesus. Each of these groups assumed that Christians are called to incarnational mission (understood as following Jesus as our example). Now, however, several troubling questions which had caused difficulty for some time came to the surface. We will consider them more fully throughout the study, but they can be summarized here.

First, what exactly do Christians mean by mission being "incarnational"? Perhaps they refer to a style of mission (imitating Jesus), or maybe mission which is founded on the incarnate presence of Jesus Christ, once human and now present as the risen Christ.

How are Christians meant to attain this noble ideal? There are strong dangers of perfectionism in an approach to mission that encourages ordinary humans to aspire after Jesus the Son of God. There is also the danger of legalism, where outward behavior is even the criterion for whether people are considered Christian. This can become "works-righteousness," excluding the role of grace and forgiveness. Incarnational mission, so understood, can be immensely burdensome, joyless and crushing to the spirit.

Further, if the incarnation is distinguished from the cross and resurrection, as is common, incarnational mission is only part of the story. What is the good news in the mere fact of Jesus being human and divine? Where is the atonement? Is this a celebration of Christmas without Good Friday or Easter? Is Jesus' humanity the central fact, or is his resurrection important in interpreting who he was? A balance seemed to be missing.

Finally, exclusively incarnational talk seems to be too human-centered. How does incarnational mission relate to the whole creation, or bring hope for the environment, if it does at all? Is there a link between creation and redemption, between the cosmos and Jesus of Nazareth?

Fung's comment acted as a catalyst for this study. The research was begun without assuming that incarnational mission would be defensible. All that was clear was that the incarnational motif is widely and variously used across many Christian traditions and seldom given careful scrutiny. On that basis the study was conducted.

After critically surveying the dominant understandings of incarnational mission and gleaning insight from them, this study does defend incarnational mission, but only with a broad definition and care to avoid certain theological dangers. Among the findings we will elaborate are that (1) the incarnational motif is pervasive in the theology of mission; (2) there is a growing consensus on its importance and meaning; (3) it contains several dimensions, all of which are necessary in a balanced understanding of the incarnational approach; (4) the incarnation needs to be seen to include Jesus' birth, life, death and resurrection; (5) the incarnation is properly a central shaping and enabling factor in mission; (6) God's incarnating dynamic is the ultimate framework in which the unique event of the incarnation occurred; (7) in fact, overall, mission ought to be incarnational in character; and (8) its theological dangers can be avoided.

Methodology

This study is a venture in the theology of mission. This means, first, that its method is broadly **theological**. Missiology, the discipline of mission studies, is wider than the theology of mission. It uses other disciplines as well, such as the social sciences, because mission involves strategic questions as well as theological ones. In this study, however, we will mainly be using broadly theological disciplines such as biblical studies, historical theology and systematic theology. The criteria for good theology are broad and sometimes difficult to apply, but we will ask our incarnational missiology to (1) faithfully interpret the Christian tradition, (2) address contemporary human existence, (3) articulate Christian experience, (4) lead to transforming action, and (5) be intelligible and coherent.[7]

Second, the method of the study is strongly **missiological**. Despite being theological, a comprehensive and systematic theology is not its primary concern. We need only to address those questions directly related to mission. Further, the reason missiology explores those questions is directly to enhance authentic and effective ways of engaging in mission. All theology ought to be practical in orientation,[8] but not every theological exercise needs to be as practical as missiology generally is.

Having said we do not need to address all areas of theology, we will find, nevertheless, that theological doctrines are deeply interrelated. To explore the meaning of the incarnation not only involves doctrines such as the person and work of Jesus Christ, the cross and the resurrection, but also doctrines such as the trinity, creation, the human person, sin, grace, discipleship, the church, the nature of mission, the environment, and ultimate Christian hope.

Assumptions

This study proceeds on the basis of some assumptions, all of them commanding a wide consensus in contemporary missiology: (1) the basic truth of the Christian gospel, (2) the missionary nature of the church, (3) the urgency of Christian unity in Christian mission, and (4) the interrelationship of theory and practice. They are not only assumptions, but together they are motivating and shaping factors. Speaking personally, they make this research not only an academic exercise but a labor of love and hope. Consider each briefly.

The **basic truth of the Christian gospel** is nearly always an assumption in missiology, which is the most confessional of all theological disciplines. Missiology begins with committed faith and asks what it means to share it. Reflecting on the mission of God in history, missiology explores the ways Christians can become co-workers with God. This is not to say that one version of Christian faith is assumed; missiology is alive with debate about what salvation is, who Jesus Christ is and so on. Nor is it to say that mission excludes dialogue and genuine learning. What is assumed in missiology, however, is the basic truth of God's outgoing love in Jesus Christ, the reality of the risen Christ today, and the sense of grateful overflow and urgency which is the spring of all Christian mission. It is in this context that missiology explores its theological questions.

That **the church is missionary in nature** is a basic understanding of missiology,[9] even though it is a recent rediscovery for some traditions.[10] This means that the Christian revelation is believed to contain ultimate truth of universal importance, and is therefore actively to be shared in the best ways possible.[11] Christianity intrinsically desires the fullness of God's gracious rule, not only in human lives but also in society and in all of creation. Further, we assume that mission is properly the task of every Christian (not just the leadership) and the whole church (not just in individual witness).

The importance and **urgency of Christian unity** in mission is not as widely assumed in missiology as the previous points, but is basic to this study. We consider it obvious that disunity hinders mission, especially when proclaiming Christ as reconciler. John's Gospel portrays Jesus praying that his disciples may be one, just as he was one with the Father, so that the world will know God's love (Jn 17:20-23). In the context of this study, we have assumed that missiology ought to be done ecumenically, that is, in the respectful company of Christians of a variety of traditions. With such a methodological commitment, understanding is likely to deepen and differences are likely to be lessened. It is this assumption that has led to the detailed survey which forms the center of the study.

The final foundation, the **interrelationship of theory and practice**, is only assumed in the weak sense that all theology is practical in orientation, as mentioned above. The stronger claim that theory and practice are inseparably bound in a dialectical manner will be argued separately throughout the study.[12] This way of engaging in reflective practice, often labeled "praxis," binds together missiology (reflection on mission) and mission (becoming co-workers in the transforming work of God in history).[13]

Structure

The study consists of three parts, in which the ground is prepared, a critical and detailed survey is made, and contours of an incarnational missiology are drawn on the basis of the survey.

Incarnation and Mission

The first part (chapters 2 and 3) prepares the ground by making proposals concerning the use of terms, incarnational christology, and a framework for classifying the variety of uses of "incarnational mission."

A distinction is made between "incarnation" as a process and "the incarnation" as an event, but both are considered important in incarnational mission.

Most missiologists assume the truth and coherence of the doctrine of the incarnation. Here we go back a step and attempt to show that missiology, in drawing on the incarnation, is on solid ground in making that assumption, despite recent christological controversies. We argue that an **incarnational christology** is still viable. We defend a view of Jesus Christ as the Word of God incarnate, without, however, using the terms of the Council of Chalcedon in the year 451. We suggest seven requirements for a contemporary incarnational christology, that is, a way of understanding Jesus Christ as God-become-human.

In preparation for the survey of various uses of **incarnational mission**, we suggest three groups of meanings. Incarnational mission can be seen as (1) following Jesus as the pattern for mission, (2) participating in Christ's risen presence as the power for mission, and (3) joining God's cosmic mission of enfleshment in which God's self-embodying dynamic is evident from the beginning of creation.

A Critical Survey of Incarnational Missiologies

The second part (chapters 4 to 9) is a critical survey of incarnational missiology as it occurs in the missiological literature of a wide variety of selected Christian traditions. Not all traditions are represented, but a majority of them are. They are chosen because incarnational mission figures significantly in their literature. They are grouped very loosely according to the dimension they emphasize most strongly, while recognizing that other dimensions are also represented in their thinking.

The **Anabaptist** tradition, including both its sixteenth century origins and contemporary Mennonite expression, is considered first (chapter 4). It is followed by **radical evangelicalism** (chapter 5), which is strongly influenced by the Anabaptist vision. **Liberation theology**, particularly in its Latin American guise, is examined next (chapter 6). The traditions in these three chapters tend to emphasize Jesus as the pattern for mission, though other emphases are also found.

Jürgen Moltmann's missiology is considered next because his thought acts as a bridge between the first and third groups (chapter 7). His strong emphasis on participation in Christ best articulates the second group. His distinctive contribution is the reason he is included as an individual whereas the other chapters in the survey are given to Christian traditions.

We continue the survey with a third group, including **Roman Catholicism** and **Anglo-Catholicism** (chapter 8), the **ecumenical movement** and **Eastern Orthodoxy** (chapter 9). In the case of Anglo-Catholicism we look back a hundred years in history because of the significance of the book *Lux Mundi*.[14] This group tends (roughly speaking) to emphasize the third dimension of incarnational mission, the incarnating dynamic of God.

Contours of an Incarnational Missiology

The third part of the study (chapters 10 and 11) draws together conclusions from the survey and develops the three-dimensional framework for classifying incarnational mission, arguing that none of the dimensions should be neglected and that they are mutually interpretive. The central argument of the study is that God's embodiment in creation, pre-eminently in Jesus Christ, is the ultimate framework of Christian mission and also the central shaping and empowering factor. Christianity is "incarnational"; this adjective refers both to the reality of God's saving action and its manner. Christian mission, similarly, is incarnational in both senses: bodily experiencing a new reality in Christ and sharing it through embodiment as Jesus did.

This approach leads to emphases such as "self-emptying," integration of words and deeds, the "practice of Christ" ("christopraxis"), Good News to the poor, a theology of the cross, the church as the body of Christ, the presence of Christ, the affirmation of creation, and the importance of the gospel assuming different cultural expressions.

The study concludes by commenting on the particular appropriateness of incarnational mission in Australia, which is a skeptical, post-Christian and postmodern society (chapter 11).

Scope

A Selective Survey

This study does not claim to have surveyed all the major Christian traditions or approaches to theology, not even all those fruitful for our purpose. The limitations of space have, unfortunately, made difficult choices necessary. We selected those traditions which draw most often on the incarnation and which contribute a distinct perspective. There are several notable omissions from the traditions surveyed, namely feminism, evangelicalism and the Lutheran and Reformed traditions.

It would have been illuminating to consider the use that **feminist** missiology makes of incarnational mission, but, to our knowledge, direct consideration of the incarnational theme in feminist missiology is rare.[15] Sallie McFague is one writer who has developed the idea of God's embodiment in creation, related it to the incarnation, and briefly discussed what it means for mission.[16]

On the one hand, one can understand the reluctance of feminists to call Christians to pattern their mission on that of Jesus when it has been consistently interpreted in a patriarchal manner.[17]

On the other hand, feminist theologians have developed some incarnational themes. They have helped to recover the feminine aspect of the Word as Divine Wisdom, softening the maleness of incarnational christology.[18] The themes of liberative praxis and solidarity with the poor and oppressed (including women), common in incarnational mission, are common in feminism. Feminists make an important contribution when pointing out that to call for "self-emptying" and "servanthood" in mission may be radical and liberating for men, but is not necessarily so for women, who may be caught in these roles already.[19] Although only indirectly connected to our concern here, there are also promising links between the incarnation (which affirms human bodiliness) and the inclusion of women (who have been excluded through much of Christian history partly on the basis of an anti-physical tradition).[20]

A feminist approach to incarnational mission would be a good project on its own, exploring the themes of embodiment and bodiliness in ways that are beyond the scope of this study.

We have not considered **evangelicalism** (as distinct from radical evangelicalism) on its own, apart from the writing of John Stott, who is briefly considered,[21] and the Lausanne Movement,[22] which largely matches his perspective. The call for incarnational mission occurs most where evangelicals have sympathy for radical evangelicalism, and tends to be expressed accordingly. Radical evangelicalism is the wing of evangelicalism which provides the most fertile ground for examining incarnational mission, and so has been chosen for study. We do make some comparisons between the radical evangelical and mainstream evangelical approaches to incarnational mission.[23] As with feminism, however, a consideration of evangelical uses of the incarnation in mission would make a valuable study on its own, given the complexity and variety of the evangelical scene.

Due to the limitations of space the **Lutheran** and **Reformed** traditions are also not considered separately.[24] The Reformation was in part a reaction against what it considered an unhealthy emphasis on what Christians need to do to be saved, and its major themes were faith and grace in contrast to works or Christian behavior, though it must be said that the priesthood of all believers and the role of all Christians as "Christs" to their neighbors was also important to Martin Luther.[25] The Reformation also reacted against the idea of the church as the continuing incarnation, the divinely guaranteed earthly form of Christ.[26] Lutheranism understandably countered the prevailing emphasis on the work of the church with an emphasis on anticipating God's activity in the coming of the kingdom, but in the process perhaps missed some of the missionary thrust of Luther's own writings.[27]

Although these emphases might make the Lutheran and Reformed traditions seem unlikely sources for incarnational missiology, at least in their classical forms, recent Lutheran and Reformed missiology has swung back to the "center," we might say, as illustrated in the work of Lutheran missiologist James Scherer.[28] Although Moltmann is studied in chapter 7 not primarily as a representative of the Reformed tradition but for his own distinctive voice, many of his emphases reflect the Reformed contribution to Christian thought, particularly his insistence that it is God who takes the initiative and Christ who constitutes the church. Moltmann's contribution to incarnational mission comes from maintaining *both* these emphases *and* a stress on engaged discipleship and the "doing of the word."[29] Darrell Guder, whose work we draw on in this study, is another Reformed theologian who demonstrates the swing of the pendulum by articulating more thoroughly than any other missiologist the importance and nature of incarnational mission,[30] and the work of Presbyterian urban missiologist Robert Linthicum is a further example.[31]

Relationship to Theology of Embodiment

As well as not covering the use of incarnational mission in all traditions, the scope of this study does not extend to the theology of embodiment, which explores the connections between the incarnation and human bodiliness or sexuality.[32] This is a topic in its own right, which also draws on the incarnation, but with a different interest. James Nelson summarizes the concerns of a body theology in this way:

> God is uniquely known to us through human presence, and human presence is always embodied presence. Thus body language is inescapably the material of Christian theology, and bodies are always sexual bodies, and our sexuality is basic to our capacity to know and to experience God.[33]

What incarnational missiology shares with a theology of bodiliness is the conviction that embodiment is theologically significant. Given the goodness of creation, God's indwelling in it, the divine incarnation, the promise of human wholeness, the eucharist as the body and blood of Christ, and the church as the body of Christ, Christian theology "ought to have an immensely positive bias toward embodiment."[34] Instead, the church has a history of denigrating the body and overvaluing abstract and disembodied reasoning. Nevertheless, the current theological interest in embodiment "recalls the distinctive feature of Christianity, that God became body and in so doing has confirmed and healed all our bodily nature."[35] Consistent with much of modern thought, there is a recovery in theology of a sense of place, history, culture and bodily self. This leads to affirming the theological value of a wide range of things: the material world, the environment, the human person, history, sexuality, cultural diversity, narrative, marginalized voices, and, of particular interest to us, exhibiting in our bodies the life of Christ. Theology of embodiment illustrates the turn from the abstract and universal to the concrete and particular. Both incarnational missiology and theology of embodiment see in God's "enfleshment" a great deal to explore.

Throughout the study, then, "embodiment" will be used in an ordinary-language sense as a synonym for "incarnation" (without being limited to "the incarnation"). To embody something is to "enflesh" or "put body on" an idea, quality, or spirit.

The central question in this study is what it means for *the Christian church* to embody Christ in its mission. We will be able to probe this idea but not to exhaust it, as the relationship of the human to the divine is a mystery.

We will also speak of *God* as the subject of embodiment ("God being embodied"), whether in creation, in Jesus, in the eucharist, or in a church carrying on the mission of Jesus. This is an even deeper mystery than human embodiment, but in speaking this way we try to express the Christian experience of God.

Here at the beginning we do well to note the irreducible element of mystery not only in trying to understand the divine-human relationship but in all of our theological enquiry. When we have arranged and polished our words to our best ability they will barely begin to even point in the right direction. To the extent that they do, it is as likely due to imagination or courage as to knowledge; and even then it is gift.

CHAPTER 2

THE WORD BECOMES FLESH:
INCARNATION AND THE INCARNATION

Because the doctrine of the incarnation has been central to Christianity for most of its two thousand years it has a rich history of interpretation. In asserting that God became human in Jesus Christ for the sake of humanity, the doctrine of the incarnation is closely interrelated with many other Christian doctrines including the understanding of God, Jesus Christ, the Holy Spirit, the trinity, creation, the human person, sin, atonement, salvation, the end times, the church and non-Christian religions. Karl Barth says that "God with us" is the central reality of the Christian message in terms of which the rest of theology is to be worked out.[1] Therefore it is not surprising that various Christian theologies understand the incarnation in widely different ways. In some circles the term "incarnation" is unproblematic, while in others it is a metaphor past its useful life. It is a slippery theological term which calls for any who use it in theological discussion to spell out the meaning it has for them.[2]

Our first task, then, in this chapter and the next, is to discuss the meaning of the doctrine of the incarnation, the nature of Christian mission and some of the ways in which the incarnation may be important for mission. This framework will provide a background for the central part of the study, which will examine how various Christian traditions have invoked the incarnation in mission and mission theology.

Incarnation and the Incarnation:
Linguistic Considerations

Because the wide variety of meanings of "incarnation" is one of the central issues in its use, we need to set out how we intend to use terms such as "incarnation," "the incarnation," "incarnating dynamic" and "to incarnate." We begin this with some linguistic considerations.

The Terms "Incarnation" and "the Incarnation"

The English word "incarnation" derives from the Old French word *incarnatio* which in turn came from the Latin *incarnatus*, the past participle of the verb "to incarnate," literally meaning to "enflesh," "take flesh" or "clothe with flesh."[3] It was coined in the first two or three centuries of the Christian church as a technical theological term to express the meaning of the Greek phrase in John 1:14, *sarx egeneto*, which says that the Word "became flesh," or "became human" (we will discuss later its precise meaning in the Johannine context). It is used in theology both of the *process* of embodiment (which becomes important later in our analysis) and the *state* of "being enfleshed."

Used without the definite article, the idea of "incarnation" occurs in religions other than Christianity as well, referring generally to the assumption of human or material form by divine beings.

One notable example is the Hindu belief that the god Vishnu makes numerous divine descents (*avataras*) in human, animal and other forms, the most famous being the appearances of Krishna, who plays out the roles of charioteer and cowherd, among others.[4] We find another example in Mahayana Buddhism, where the Buddha is seen to have delayed his own entry to extinct-bliss (*nirvana*), choosing out of boundless love to remain a *bodhisattva* (someone on the very point of total enlightenment) and reincarnating as a human many times, for the sake of the enlightenment of all humanity, most recently as Gautama Buddha.

The Hindu doctrine differs from the Christian doctrine in that it (1) focuses more on theophany than enfleshment, (2) involves multiple descents, (3) is an outworking of cosmic laws, (4) results in a variety of forms including hybrid figures, (5) entails the view that the material universe is a flimsy veil and ultimately unreal, (6) and is based on a concept of cyclical time.[5]

The Buddhist doctrine is less about an incarnation than the repeated reincarnation of a person who simultaneously has cosmic and human bodies of varying types. The Buddha is not a supreme deity but a highly enlightened person who incarnates himself hundreds of times.[6]

While the notion of incarnation is not unique to Christianity it takes a unique form in classical Christian belief: the supreme divinity fully assuming lowly human flesh in a once-for-all self-revelation for the sake of restoring a broken relationship between humanity and God.

"Incarnation" can have an even wider meaning in the study of religion, referring to "the act or state of assuming a physical body (as a person, an animal, a plant, or even an entire cosmos) by a nonphysical entity such as the soul, the spirit, the self, or the divine being."[7] This demonstrates incarnation's root meaning as the process of embodiment or "enfleshment." We will use this wider meaning when arguing later that God by nature tends to embody Godself in creation and is always-outgoing-in-love, thus uniting creation and redemption. Taiwanese liberation theologian Choan-Seng Song, for example, uses "incarnation" in this broadest of ways when he says that John's Gospel shows incarnation not to be an isolated historical event involving Jesus of Nazareth, but a process that reaches back beyond time as the incarnating tendency of the Word, a tendency which reaches its greatest focus in Jesus Christ.[8]

Whenever **"incarnation"** is used without the definite article throughout this study the emphasis will be on the *process* of embodiment, even if the context makes it clear that the once-for-all incarnation of Jesus Christ is the instance of embodiment under consideration.

Used with the definite article, **"the incarnation"** has classically referred to the central mystery of Christianity, that is, the event in which, for the salvation of the world and without ceasing to be fully divine, God became fully human uniquely in Jesus Christ.[9] Throughout this study "the incarnation" will always refer to this *event*.

The Scope of the Event of the Incarnation

Determining the boundaries of this "event" leads us straight into one of many christological debates. There is a consensus that the incarnation was an event with historical dimensions (that is, Jesus was not "merely" mythical or legendary), making Christianity a strongly historical religion, but scholars vary widely in their understanding of the scope of the incarnation.

Some see the incarnation as **Jesus' birth** (or perhaps conception), the actual assumption of humanity by God the Son, the "*in*-carnation" or "*en*-fleshing." This is common in Eastern Orthodox theology, for example, which emphasizes Christ's pre-existence and his condescension in leaving glory to become human. In some theological discussions the incarnation refers almost a-historically to the mere fact of Christ's divine-human union.[10] It is also common in Anglo-Catholic thinking, which sees the incarnation as evidence of God's solidarity with creation and God's sanctifying of the material and cultural world. We see it as well in some forms of popular Christianity which make much of Christmas at the expense of Lent and Easter. They celebrate the wonder of God-come-among-us as an innocent child. It is not surprising that a term which refers to the assumption of humanity by God should often refer to the precise moment of assumption (whether conception or birth), and we are not arguing that "the incarnation as birth" is an illegitimate use of the term. As we will see, however, when used in a more intentional theological way this creation-affirming incarnational view is theologically inadequate because of its one-sidedness. It emphasizes creation at the expense of redemption, and incarnation without the cross and resurrection. It implies that the saving purpose of the incarnation is accomplished simply by God becoming human, regardless of what happened next. This notion of "flesh redeemed by being assumed," however, is not found in the New Testament, where for the greater part the decisive saving moment is found in Jesus' death and resurrection.[11] An incarnational mission based on such a truncated view of the incarnation will similarly be one-sided and distorted. Jean Daniélou points out that incarnational mission based on "getting alongside" and "identifying" has only taken the first step; it also needs to bring good news, challenge others and lead to transformation.[12]

Others see the incarnation as **Jesus' birth, life and teaching**, and emphasize the life of Jesus, particularly his siding with the poor, as a model for mission. David Bosch, in taking various saving events in the New Testament as lenses through which to view mission, sees the incarnation in this way, talking of "the incarnate Christ" and for the purposes of discussion excluding the cross and the resurrection. Bosch appreciates this lens because it helps Christians to keep in focus the humanity and simplicity of Jesus Christ, to bleed with victims of oppression, and to engage freshly with the "practice of Jesus."[13] Although the trajectory of Jesus' life reveals much of his saving purpose, it must be said that the same one-sidedness applies here as to "the incarnation as Jesus' birth." We must insist that Jesus' death and resurrection are an integral part of the meaning of his life.

For this reason others see the incarnation as including **Jesus' birth, life, death and resurrection,**[14] and this is the meaning given to the term in this study. These aspects are mutually related and interpret each other, in that the incarnation is usually seen to speak of God's self-communication, affirmation of the material universe, revelation in the life and teaching of Jesus, saving action in the death of Jesus, and victory over evil and death in the resurrection—all part of one sweeping movement of cosmic and universal significance.

A common synonym for "the incarnation" is "the Christ-event," which gathers his birth, life, death and resurrection as a unified event.[15] Some writers use the term "Christ-event" to indicate that the incarnation did not occur in isolation but is linked in a myriad of ways in every direction: to Christ's pre-existence, the culture into which Jesus was born, the impact he had on people, and their impact on others down to this day.[16] While it is important to recognize that the incarnation is in some way intertwined with the new humanity it inaugurated, notably the church as the "body of Christ," the boundaries of the "Christ-event" are very difficult to draw in theological discussion. For example, Rudolf Bultmann has used the idea of the "Christ-event" to include all occasions on which the Word is faithfully preached, thus effectively fusing together the ideas of the incarnation and the presence of Christ through the Holy Spirit.[17] In view of these ambiguities we will avoid the use of the term "Christ-event" and will use "the incarnation" in the ways already defined.[18]

Primary and Secondary Subjects of Incarnation

Continuing our discussion of terminology, it is worth noting that, strictly speaking, only God (or some other divine entity who is not already materially embodied) can be the subject of incarnation. In the classical Christian context, only God, or the Word of God (the Logos), or God the Son can "íncarnáte" (intransitive verb) or become "incárnate" (adjective).[19] The very idea of incarnation involves an implied contrast between divinity and humanity, a striking difference which is overcome by God. For this reason there is an oddness about saying that Jesus of Nazareth "incarnated himself" which is parallel to the oddness of saying that "Jesus resurrected himself." Strictly speaking it is even odder to say that the church can become incarnate among people, because it already has fleshly existence. Any sense it does have (and it is a powerful way of speaking) is secondary and derivative from "the incarnation." The primary use of "incarnation" and "the incarnation" in theology is reserved for the action of God; in this study we argue that God is incarnate in certain ways in creation but most fully in Jesus. No matter how important incarnational talk is in mission, it is only in a secondary and metaphorical way that we can speak of the church's mission being "incarnational" (adjective) or "to incarnate the gospel" (a transitive verb, in a novel usage).[20] Having said that, we need to acknowledge how powerful such metaphors can be in shaping and motivating Christian mission. Even more strongly, we will argue that because a "discarnate" (non-incarnational) gospel message is a contradiction, "incarnational mission" is not only a powerful metaphor but an essential ingredient in any proper model of Christian mission.

An Incarnating God

Another secondary use which is more obviously metaphorical than talk of "the incarnation," is talk of God's "**incarnating dynamic,**" in which the unique event of the incarnation is generalized backwards and forwards into the character of God. It is more obviously metaphorical because it refers to God's self-communication through the material universe and through historical events without implying that God continually becomes human, the usual meaning of "the incarnation" in Christian theology. Again, this is a powerful picture of God's creative, loving and self-giving nature.

To speak of God's incarnating dynamic is to have a form of **incarnational theology**, a theology which understands God to be dynamically immanent in creation as well as transcending it. This claims more than **incarnational christology**, which is any understanding of Jesus which claims that in him God was in some way incarnate (we will discuss the various understandings below). To illustrate the difference, it is possible to hold that God was incarnate in Jesus Christ but that this was a unique and unprecedented movement by an almost wholly transcendent God. Such a position would be an example of an incarnational christology, but not of an incarnational theology, which would extend the incarnational process to God's relationship with all creation.

We would argue for some form of incarnational theology, not just incarnational christology, both because it integrates our understanding of God as creator and redeemer, and because it articulates well the human experience of God's relationship to creation. Consider each briefly.

First, incarnational theology highlights the link between God's creative self-pouring in creating the material universe and God's self-pouring in the redemptive act of becoming flesh in Jesus Christ. It sees creation, reconciliation and consummation, not as three successive activities of God but as "three moments in God's great unitary action."[21] In the terms of process theology, Jesus Christ was "the unique focus for a universal presence and operation."[22] As both Justin Martyr and Athanasius argued in the second and fourth centuries respectively, God's Word, the Logos, has always been embodied in the world, and its incarnation in Jesus was simply a new and decisive revelation in a process which has gone on since creation.[23] From a quite different standpoint modern perspectives echo this Patristic view on the material nature of the word. Hans-Georg Gadamer, for example, argues that the human word is essentially material, always iconic, and fundamental for human meaning. A "discarnate word," that is, one which is not spoken or written into the material world by a speaker or writer, is meaningless.[24] Building on this, William Gray argues persuasively that for similar reasons the Logos is essentially incarnate in that by nature it seeks embodiment and audibility or visibility. Therefore "incarnation constitutes the very core, the very heart, the very being, of God."[25] On this view embodiment is not restricted to the unique act of incarnation in Jesus Christ but is part of the nature of God. It argues that meaning is only possible when it comes in bodily form.[26] This view of God and reality is plainly of great consequence for Christian mission. In particular, it implies that any "Word" that is not incarnate is not the Word.

The second reason for holding an incarnational theology is the history of the human experience of God's "transcendent immanence."[27] This perspective sees God's transcendence not as "absoluteness," or "distance" from us, but as a dynamic process of overflow,[28] or self-surpassing,[29] in which God reaches out in creation and redemption, seeking embodiment, identifying lovingly with the world, indwelling God's material universe, always incarnate as Spirit within humanity,[30] and always going out of Godself to become embodied in particular historical persons and events.[31] God is creative, reconciling love. Creation and incarnation are therefore intrinsically related through God's mission of enfleshment or incarnation.[32]

As a final comment on the "incarnation" family of words, we simply note that there is a broad, secular use of "to incarnate" which simply means "to take shape" or "put down roots." When used in missiology with a similarly broad meaning, such a verb is enriched by its association with the incarnation without being tied closely to it.

Linguistic considerations help us to clarify the use of terms, but they raise the question of the origin and meaning of the doctrine of the incarnation. What is the biblical witness to it, and what was the writer of John's Gospel claiming when he wrote that the "Word became flesh"?

The Incarnation: Some Biblical Considerations

For the purposes of this study it is not necessary to examine in detail the New Testament witness to the doctrine of the incarnation. This task has been undertaken notably by James Dunn in his careful study *Christology in the making: An inquiry into the origins of the doctrine of the incarnation.*[33]

As a background to understanding the incarnation and its relevance to mission, however, it will be useful briefly to (1) summarize the biblical evidence which gave rise to the classical doctrine of the incarnation, noting the centrality of John's Gospel in this, (2) ask what "becoming flesh" means in the Fourth Evangelist's writing, and (3) note the significance for mission of biblical incarnational christology.[34]

The Biblical Roots of Incarnational Christology

That God should become human was almost unthinkable in Israelite faith because God was seen in such strongly transcendent and monotheistic terms. Therefore we cannot find the doctrine of the incarnation in the Hebrew Bible, other than hints of a context for it, in God's positive evaluation of creation, God's image being found in humanity, God's acting through God's word/Word, God's Spirit at work in certain humans and at certain times, and God's saving promises.[35]

The terms "incarnation" and "incarnate" do not appear in the New Testament, though the concept of incarnation appears indisputably in the Prologue to John's Gospel and in varying degrees of clarity and ambiguity in other passages (such as Phil 2:6-11, Col 1:15-20, 2:9, Gal 4:4, 1 Cor 1:24, 15:47, 2 Cor 8:9, Rom 8:3, Mt 1:23, 11:19, 25-30, 18:18-20, 28:18-20, Heb 1:1-3, 7:3, 9:26, 2 Tim 1:9-10, 1 Pet 1:20, 1 Jn 1:3, 4:2-3). Dunn, in *Christology in the making*, shows that the doctrine of the incarnation developed fairly quickly, over a few decades, in the early church.[36] Although there has been vigorous debate about Dunn's conclusions, usually by scholars claiming more than Dunn does,[37] the broad outlines of his argument have been largely accepted and are accepted here.

Dunn's conclusions, in summary, are as follows. It is John's Word-christology (along with the letter to the Hebrews[38]) which most clearly points to the pre-existence and incarnation of the Son of God. A complex set of meanings surrounds the New Testament use of christological titles or ideas such as the Son of God, the son of man, the second Adam, a man filled with God's Spirit, a messenger from God, and the Wisdom of God. Some passages are popularly understood to imply the incarnation but, Dunn argues, are not fully developed in that they do not explicitly involve Christ's personal pre-existence.[39] In pre-Johannine Christian thought the incarnation did not necessarily mean that Jesus was some heavenly figure come to earth, but a fully-human person who revealed the action of *God*. Dunn says, "'Incarnation' means initially that *God's* love and power had been experienced in fullest measure in, through and as this man Jesus, that Christ had been experienced as God's self-expression, the Christ-event as the effective, re-creative power of God."[40] Some passages do speak of Christ's pre-existence (such as Jn 1:1-18, 1 Cor 8:5-6, Col 1:15-17, Heb 1:1-3 and Mt 11:27-30), and were heavily influenced by Jewish talk of Wisdom personified.[41] There is also evidence that the contemporary Hellenistic Jewish philosopher Philo saw the Logos as "God in the mode of self revelation."[42] Nevertheless, the Christian idea of the Word incarnate, while drawing on these influences, is quite new.[43] We can see it grow from the earlier writings to later writings in the New Testament. First, the content of Jesus' message is seen as the Word of God; then Jesus is equated with that Word; his pre-existence is hinted at and perhaps assumed without being explicit; and finally in John's Gospel Jesus Christ is seen as the incarnation of the pre-existent Word.[44] More so than in later dogmatic formulations, the New Testament always ties the incarnation to the cross and resurrection; the decisive act of salvation was not the "enfleshment" but Christ's death for humanity.[45]

Dunn argues that the Johannine church developed this full-blown incarnational christology by the end of the first century, ransacking available philosophies for ways in which to express it but driven primarily by the impetus of Jesus' life, teaching, death and resurrection.

John's Gospel, with its talk of a pre-existent Word becoming flesh, has been the rock on which incarnational christology has built ever since. Classical christology, defended by Millard Erickson, for example, has taken

John's Prologue to mean that God the Son existed as a person within the Godhead.[46]

Some biblical scholars, however, are more cautious metaphysically. C. H. Dodd sees John as saying, in effect, "let us assume that the cosmos exhibits a divine meaning which constitutes its reality. I will tell you what that meaning is: it was embodied in the life of Jesus, which I will now describe.'[47]

Dunn also is cautious. He wants to qualify his conclusion that John is proposing a pre-existent Son of God, a heavenly being who comes to earth. This is hard to deny, he says, but should be taken as an adventure in language. John ventures to combine divine sonship, seen in terms of relationship to God the Father, with the pre-existent but previously impersonal divine Word, without the later theological notions of oneness of substance or being eternally "begotten."[48] John was wrestling with the age-old tension in Jewish thought between God's transcendence and immanence, using categories at hand and hazarding much to achieve much.[49] So successful was John that much of christology since has been the elaboration of his incarnational approach.[50] Dunn is aware that John's concepts stretch and strain at both language and acceptable Jewish-Christian belief. Implicitly anticipating the metaphorical approach to theology we will argue for later, Dunn suggests that

> We honor him most highly when we follow his example and mould the language and conceptualizations in transition today into a gospel which conveys the divine, revelatory and saving significance of Christ to our day as effectively as he did to his.[51]

Not only should we recognize John's Logos-christology to be at least partly culture-bound, concludes Dunn, but we should also remember the many other ways of expressing the New Testament affirmation that God was in Christ reconciling the world (2 Cor 5:19). Dunn's careful final conclusion is as follows:

> If all this has any normative significance for modern christology it is that christology should not be narrowly confined to one particular assessment of Christ, nor should it play one off against another, nor should it insist on squeezing all the different NT conceptualizations into one particular "shape," but it should recognize that from the first the significance of Christ could only be apprehended by a diversity of formulations which

though not always strictly compatible with each other were not regarded as rendering each other invalid.[52]

We agree with Dunn that models other than the incarnation are present in the New Testament and are needed to understand Jesus' significance. (We will later argue for a metaphorical approach which calls for multiple models.)[53] We also share Dunn's metaphysical caution. Nevertheless, incarnational thinking has been central to Christianity, however it is expressed. In some sense the polarity between divinity and humanity has been overcome in Jesus of Nazareth. It is to the idea of God becoming "flesh" that we now turn.

The Meaning of "Becoming Flesh"

We have noted that we find the clearest expression of incarnational christology in John 1:14:

And the Word became flesh and lived among us, and we have seen his glory, the glory as of a father's only son, full of grace and truth.

It is also clear in 1 John, which twice emphasizes that the eternal word of life has come among us as flesh and blood in the person Jesus Christ (1 Jn 1:1-3, 4:2-3).

We also suggested that "becoming flesh" means "becoming human."[54] If we try to take quite literally the assertion "The Word became flesh," it is nonsense. If "the Word" means Meaning, Wisdom, the divine structure of reality or God's self-expression, it defies imagination to see it as literally clothed in flesh or enclosed in a physical body.[55] This would be to imagine the Word as the vivifying principle of Jesus' actual flesh, where "flesh" is seen as only part of a person. This is a crude mythical way of thinking, an approach which the Council of Constantinople in 381 condemned (attributing it, perhaps inaccurately, to Apollinarius).[56]

In contrast the writer of John's Gospel shows great subtlety of thought and a love of symbolic language. He employs vivid imagery such as Jesus being the "light of the world" (Jn 1:3, 3:19, 8:12, etc.), "the Lamb of God" (1:29), "living water" (4:10-14), "the bread of life" (6:35, 48), "the gate for the sheep" (10:7), "the good shepherd" (10:11; 21:15-17), "the way, the truth and the life" (14:6), and "the true vine" (15:1). He uses such metaphors and even paradox to express things that, perhaps, cannot be directly expressed.[57] Consequently we must interpret the "Word becoming flesh," a highly paradoxical phrase, to mean "being embodied in a human person" in some manner. We should no more take it to mean literal enfleshment than we should analyse how Jesus could literally become light.

It may well have been more accurate, therefore, for the early church not to have chosen the term "incarnation," enfleshment, but to have coined a term translating the Greek word *enanthropesis*, "becoming human."[58] The central idea, whichever term is used, is divine embodiment in a human person.

Not only does talk of the Word becoming flesh need to be taken metaphorically, but given the negative connotations of "flesh" in much Christian theology, we need to look a little more carefully at the phrase *sarx egeneto*, "became flesh," in the Johannine context.

The noun *sarx* is a common New Testament word[59] with three meanings: (1) literal flesh, as in meat or the human body, (2) the entire human person or humankind, with an emphasis on "bodiliness," mere earthly existence or transitoriness (this is similar to *soma*, "body," a neutral way of referring to human corporeality), and (3) humanity's sinful mode of existence in which "carnality" rules.[60] It is mainly Paul who uses *sarx* in this third way. He regularly contrasts human existence "built on flesh" and human existence in the Spirit. It is not our physical flesh which is sinful; rather, it is our mode of existence in which we reject God's Spirit rather than respond to the gift of life in Christ.[61]

John's Gospel does not generally use "flesh" in this distinctively Pauline way. In fact, the Prologue uses it positively, in the astonishing claim that while the Word is an eternal reality, the Word became flesh and lived among us, thus dignifying humanity and bringing together God and humanity. There is an implied contrast between the divine and the human, a polarity which is overcome in Jesus Christ.

Because the Prologue has the structure of a distinct unit, some say it is a prelude to, but not an integral part of, John's gospel. Nevertheless, we would agree with those who argue that it announces the controlling ideas of the Gospel, in the way that the prologue of a Greek tragedy signals its themes.[62] The use of *sarx* illustrates this. John 1:14 suggests that the divine and human realms, despite being vastly different, are united in Jesus. The way *sarx* is used throughout John only strengthens this perspective by underlining the contrast between the divine and human realms and calling attention to the significance of Jesus' divinity expressed in natural, human life. Most occurrences use *sarx* simply to mean what is human and natural

(Jn 1:13; 3:6; 17:2; 8:15). If "human flesh" rejects the Spirit (Jn 6:63, 3:6) then, as in Paul, flesh carries the connotation of opposition to God. God's redeeming action in Jesus, however, involves existence in the flesh, and a particular kind of life in which Jesus gives his flesh for the world (Jn 6:51-58).[63] Despite the obviously eucharistic overtones of Jesus' talk of eating his flesh and drinking his blood, the context is one in which Jesus calls people not simply to drink some elixir for eternal life but to enter a relationship with his Father (6:47) and follow in his path (6:27). In summary, "flesh" in John 1:14 stands for the whole person; the Word of God is now intimately bound up with human history.[64]

Therefore we would not agree with Ernst Käsemann's description of Jesus as "the God who walks on the face of the earth,"[65] his estimate of John's christology as "naïve docetism"[66] nor his view that "incarnation for John is really epiphany."[67] Käsemann's perspective derives from seeing the whole Gospel through the lenses of the seventeenth chapter and the phrase "and we have seen his glory" (Jn 1:14).[68]

Rudolf Bultmann is closer to the mark in saying that "the Word became flesh" means that God has been revealed in this human and worldly sphere in contrast to the divine, and not as humankind in general but as a definite human being in history, Jesus of Nazareth.[69] The paradox John presents, according to Bultmann, is that God's glory is to be seen, not alongside or through the humanity of Jesus, but *in* his humanity, with a certain hiddenness.[70] We would add, as Bultmann does not, that this humanity is not a "mere fact" but includes the life and teaching of Jesus (Bultmann's well-known view is that John presents only the fact and not the content of the revelation).[71]

We have seen that "becoming flesh" means "becoming human," and implies that God overcomes the polarity between the divine and human in the mystery of the incarnation; God's nature is revealed within the sphere of history in Jesus Christ. A comment on the connection between the incarnation, God's mission and Christian mission will conclude this brief sketch of biblical incarnational christology.

Word-Christology and Mission

We have noted that the biblical doctrine of the incarnation developed fairly rapidly in the early church to be fully stated in the later documents of the New Testament, particularly the Johannine literature. What makes it remarkable is that there were no parallels in Hellenism for a divine being (alongside or within God) who becomes human. What is more, the monotheistic faith of Judaism strongly resisted the notion of God embodied in a human person. It was clearly the impetus of the life, death and resurrection of Jesus which led to the doctrine, despite these obstacles.[72]

The clear doctrine of the incarnation in John's Gospel is the central reason for rejecting the view that the Gospel's christology is docetic or gnostic.[73] That the Word "became flesh," that is, genuinely a human being, would have been offensive and unthinkable to gnostically-oriented Hellenists, for whom the material world was inherently evil.[74] A second reason is the importance of Jesus' death in John's Gospel. Docetic theology sought to deny that Jesus really died a human death, but for John, paradoxically, the glory of Jesus was to be seen in his passion, death and resurrection. The Gospel points forward to Jesus' death throughout.[75] A third reason for seeing the Johannine Jesus as fully human is John's deliberate citing of Jesus' hunger, thirst, grief, anguish and love for friends (Jn 4:6-7, 11:33, 35, 12:27, 13:21, 19:26, 28).[76]

An anti-docetic or anti-gnostic polemic, however, is not the central thrust of John's Gospel;[77] rather, the Gospel (in its own measured and theological way) has a missionary thrust. John writes so that readers might come to believe that Jesus is the Messiah, the Son of God, and that through believing they might have life in his name (Jn 20:31). Marianne Thompson argues persuasively that John's doctrine of the incarnation is not primarily insisting on the fact of Jesus' humanity but saying to unbelievers that the Jesus who had lived a few decades before is the eternal and saving Word. The mere fact of Jesus' humanity is not the central claim; rather, "to know the incarnate Word, one must look at the peculiar path which he treads, which culminates in his death."[78] In Jn 17:18 and Jn 20:21 we find the incarnation set firmly in the context of mission: "As the Father has sent me, so I send you." Metaphysics is not John's only concern. He wants to establish as inseparable the life, death and resurrection of Jesus and its link with the church's mission.

The biblical doctrine of the incarnation, then, particularly in its clearest expression in John's Gospel is centrally about overcoming in saving action the gap between divinity and humanity. Not only is God revealed in Jesus Christ but God's redeeming action takes place in and through a human person (flesh), in birth, life, death and resurrection. Word-christology, as Dunn suggests, is an adventurous attempt by the writer of John's Gospel to express the divine, revealing and saving significance of Jesus Christ.[79]

We accept Dunn's conclusion that the doctrine of the incarnation is only one particular assessment of Christ and needs to be complemented by a diversity of formulations. Nothing in this study is meant to imply that incarnational christology is the only lens through which to view Jesus, his mission and the mission of the church. It is clear that to some extent we will need to find new ways of expressing the significance of Jesus today, with a fresh translation of biblical images or even using new metaphors that speak to our own cultures.

The idea that the divine meaning of the cosmos was embodied in the life of Jesus, however, has played a remarkably central part in the history of Christian belief, so much so that Christianity can be characterized as the religion of the incarnation. It is our argument that, while it may need restating for the contemporary context, the doctrine of the incarnation still remains central and powerfully expresses a Christian understanding of the way God acts savingly, with deep implications for the way Christians are to follow in mission.

Incarnational Christology:
Some Theological Considerations

Biblical notions of the incarnation, despite culminating in John's Word-christology, were still undeveloped, and left room for a great deal of theological interpretation throughout the history of the church.

To trace the many trajectories of this history is a task well beyond the scope of this study. What does lie within our scope is to discuss briefly some of the central theological issues of incarnational christology in order to suggest some possible contemporary expressions of it.

The central issues were clear by 451, at the Council of Chalcedon which has become a touchstone for Western orthodox christology. The same issues, raised as a result of Enlightenment thinking, are starkly presented in the recent debate on whether the incarnation is "merely" a myth. Without suggesting that these are the only important developments in the history of christology, we will use them in order to discuss the central issues of incarnational christology, albeit briefly.

We will classify various contemporary approaches to the incarnation, indicate which approach we take here, and argue (in the next chapter) that an adequate contemporary incarnational christology will have certain characteristics, grouped under seven headings.

Seven Senses of the Incarnation

There is a vigorous current debate and extensive literature on incarnational christology. Let us begin by clarifying the various meanings writers have in mind when they speak of their christology as incarnational.

Sarah Coakley usefully suggests six senses of incarnational christology, each position claiming less than the previous ones.[80] The list can be summarized as follows (the numbers are changed to take account of a suggestion to follow):

1. Jesus had two natures, in the "substance" terms of the Chalcedonian formulation.
2. Jesus is the only divine incarnation, absolute and final, a revelation "qualitatively" superior to all others.
3. Jesus is God's fully given self-gift. The revelation is "quantitatively" superior to all others, and Jesus is fully God and fully human.
4. Christ pre-existed in some divine form, e.g. the Logos.
6. God was involved in Jesus' life in a special and powerful way. Jesus' exceptional relationship with God has universal significance.
7. God is involved in human life, e.g. being present in time and history, being "God with us." This is claimed by all Christian theologies, and is more an incarnational theology than an incarnational christology.

Coakley's list requires one addition. It is possible to have a seventh sense, which fits best after her fourth. In this extra position, held notably by Geoffrey Lampe, for example, Jesus' pre-existence is not supposed (position 4) but he is seen as filled by the Spirit of God in a total or absolute way (more strongly than in position 6).[81] We might express it as follows:

5. Jesus Christ was fully human, and his divinity consists in his total transparency and obedience to the Spirit of God.

To simplify things further, we can group these into three types of current incarnational christologies, although the boundaries are sometimes indistinct:

i   Those which subscribe to the Chalcedonian definition (affirming position 1).

ii   Those, on the other extreme, which are unclear about or deny Jesus' divinity and therefore can be called non-incarnational (positions 6 and 7).

iii   Those, in between, which want to express the incarnation in different terms while affirming the divinity of Jesus (positions 2 to 5).

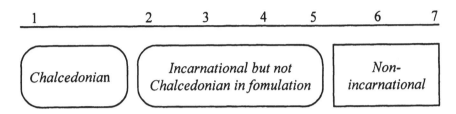

The Chalcedonian Definition

There are still many theologians who hold to the Chalcedonian definition, insisting that departures from Chalcedon fail to express adequately orthodox christology. Some recent examples are Gerald O'Collins,[82] Brian Hebblethwaite,[83] D M MacKinnon,[84] Alister McGrath,[85] Norman Anderson,[86] George Carey,[87] Stephen Davis,[88] Millard Erickson,[89] Vernon White[90] and James Moulder.[91]

We cannot here recount the christological controversies which dominated the first few centuries of the church as it was forced to articulate its faith under pressure from adventurous formulations, many of which were pronounced heretical. The process culminated in the confession of faith agreed upon at the general council at Chalcedon in 451.

Chalcedon was at pains to affirm the full humanity and full divinity of Jesus Christ, and attempted to express in a balanced way both his duality and his unity. It spoke of Jesus Christ as like us in all things except sin; as being of one substance (*homoousios*) with the Father as far as his divinity was concerned and of one substance with us as far as his humanity was concerned; as having two-natures, neither merged nor separate, but having one subsistence (*hupostasis*).[92]

The council chose its terms carefully for politico-theological reasons, to placate and unite the Alexandrian and Antiochene theological wings of the church.

Many have said that Chalcedon was a doctrinal triumph, and Karl Barth has argued that Chalcedon's formulation is normative for all subsequent development in christology.[93] Certainly, after a few further centuries of controversy, both the Eastern and Western wings of the church generally defended it in official places.[94]

Nevertheless it is hard to see why Christian understanding of the incarnation should be frozen at one point in the fifth century, in terms which are foreign to scripture, highly paradoxical in formulation, and highly dependent on the Neo-Platonist philosophy of the time (using nuanced Greek terms such as *ousia* [substantial reality], *phusis* [nature], *prosopon* [person] and *hupostasis* [subsistence]).[95]

We would have to agree with those who believe that its strong phrases merely paper over the difficulties inherent within them. Without entering the often technical debate about Chalcedon and its metaphysics, we can list a few problems.

First, to stress the duality of the person of Jesus Christ is to be in grave danger of picturing him as neither God nor human but the only representative of a third species, "God-human."[96] On the other hand, if Jesus' unity is stressed over his duality, the danger becomes that of docetism, the tendency to see Jesus' humanity as apparent rather than real.[97] Furthermore, as Friedrich Schleiermacher argued, there is a real question about the intelligibility and coherence of a formula that says one person has two natures, using "nature" in a similar way for both God and a human.[98] Even further, it is difficult to continue to use the language of substance and nature when its underlying philosophical framework is no longer tenable and we express our view of the human person in much more dynamic terms today, whether in the language of process, transcendence or narrative.[99] Finally, any description of the person of Christ is deficient if it fails even to mention outgoing love as constitutive of his relationship to God and makes it possible to construct a christology which is separated from ethics.[100]

Non-incarnational Christology

Reacting to the metaphysics of Chalcedon, the second group of theologians effectively holds to a non-incarnational christology, believing that the incarnation is a myth we should reject or "merely" a metaphor without ontological implications. If they use the term "incarnation" at all, they limit its meaning to the sixth sense in our list of meanings above, namely that God was merely involved in the life of Jesus in a special and powerful way.[101]

The group includes John Hick,[102] Maurice Wiles,[103] Michael Goulder,[104] Don Cupitt,[105] Dennis Nineham[106] and John Bowden.[107] Most of these were contributors to the famous book *The myth of God incarnate*, edited by John Hick.[108]

The publication of *The myth of God incarnate* in 1977 caused a furore in Britain.[109] This was partly because in it Anglican theologians rejected the incarnation so much loved by Anglicans and partly because of the provocative title and style of the book.

Although its contributors differed on some points, they all argued that the incarnation is only one interpretation of the significance of Jesus of Nazareth, one which they claim has never been justified or stated intelligibly.[110] They sought to show that the majority of critical biblical scholarship does not think that Jesus ever believed himself to be divine.[111] They argued that early christology grew rapidly in a setting where exceptional people were readily granted divine honors and where God's supernatural intervention was a natural way of thinking.[112] They argued that metaphysical assertions that Jesus Christ was both man and God not only used a philosophical framework we no longer accept, but struggled to be coherent even at the time the church formulated and accepted the claims.[113] They suggested that "incarnation" still has a use as a metaphor or myth, meaning that Jesus was a human person who "embodied God's self-giving love,"[114] but they denied that the incarnation has any literal meaning or metaphysical reference.[115] So, we would argue, they were in the main prepared to espouse a non-incarnational Christianity.

This non-incarnational view of Jesus Christ raises important questions, but in our opinion fails in its theological imagination by seeing only two routes open for a modern christology, either subscribing to the Chalcedonian definition or abandoning any talk of the incarnation which affirms Jesus Christ's humanity and divinity.

Briefly we would argue (1) that the non-incarnationalists are dismissive of the role of metaphor and myth; (2) that they ignore modern anthropologies which allow for ways of expressing the "immanence of transcendence" and therefore new understandings of the divine acting within the human; (3) that to begin christology "from below," with the historical Jesus, is not to exclude any expression of what might be happening "from above"; (4) that in rejecting supernatural intervention the non-incarnational view is weak in its suggestions of how or even whether God acts in history and within humans; (5) that it fails to explain how Jesus acted for our salvation, tending towards a weak model of atonement in which Jesus is merely our example; and as a result of all this, (6) that it fails to provide an adequate basis for, or understanding of, Christian mission.

We will deal with these points more fully in the next chapter when we suggest in positive terms what shape a contemporary incarnational christology needs to take.

Incarnational but not Chalcedonian in Formulation

If we cannot follow Chalcedon and yet do not want to abandon a belief in the incarnation which entails God's action in the fully human and divine Jesus Christ, it becomes necessary to reformulate the doctrine in new terms. Many contemporary theologians are engaged in this task, and the extent to which they depart from the Chalcedonian definition varies greatly.

Some theologians distance themselves from the exact terms used by Chalcedon while saying with varying enthusiasm that its intention (guarding Christ's full humanity, full divinity, unity and duality) was a worthy one and its wording fitting for its time. In this group we could include writers such as Karl Rahner,[116] Leonardo Boff,[117] Edward Schillebeeckx,[118] Hans Küng,[119] Walter Kasper,[120] and Brian McDermott[121] (all of whom are Roman Catholics, who must at least nod in the direction of Chalcedon because it is part of the magisterium).

Others vary in their assessment of Chalcedon's success in the fifth century but are clear that we need to reject it as quite unworkable today. They include Jürgen Moltmann,[122] Wolfhart Pannenberg,[123] John Macquarrie,[124] Norman Pittenger,[125] John Cobb,[126] Donald Baillie,[127] Geoffrey Lampe[128] and John Robinson.[129]

These writers all want to speak of the incarnation, but not in classical terms. We will draw on many of them as we outline in the next chapter what we will argue are the essential elements of an adequate contemporary incarnational christology. We will then go on to indicate the main ways in which such an incarnational understanding shapes Christian mission.

CHAPTER 3

INCARNATIONAL CHRISTOLOGY AND INCARNATIONAL MISSION

In the last chapter we teased out the various meanings of "incarnation" and "the incarnation," looked at the biblical roots of the concept, and raised some of the central theological issues which have been at the heart of the doctrine of the incarnation. We concluded that in understanding the incarnation our choice is not restricted to either using the "substance" terms of Chalcedon or treating the incarnation as "mere myth." There are ways forward for contemporary incarnational christology which both speak to the modern mind and express the classical Christian claim that Jesus was fully human and yet also divine. The way we understand the incarnation is critical for Christian mission. As we will show, God's incarnating nature and its expression in the incarnation of Jesus Christ together provide the basis for mission, the motivation and enabling power for mission, and the model for mission.

In the following pages we will outline the parameters of an incarnational christology. This outline draws upon the group of theologians mentioned at the end of the last chapter, those who seek a strong formulation of incarnational christology in non-Chalcedonian terms. Nevertheless, we are not following the approach of any one source, nor are we specifying one particular incarnational christology. Rather, we will outline and argue for a number of major directions in the understanding of the incarnation which we believe are essential in *any* adequate contemporary incarnational christology.

Contemporary Incarnational Christology

In our judgement an adequate contemporary incarnational christology needs to be metaphorical (in a fuller sense than John Hick's), to be relational in its anthropology, to start "from below" but speak of God's actions as well, to be pneumatological, to be trinitarian, to be soteriological to the core, and to issue naturally in "incarnational" mission. Let us consider these seven requirements in turn.

Metaphorical

We will first outline very briefly what it means to hold a metaphorical theology and why we should acknowledge the metaphorical nature of our understanding of God. Then we will consider what it means to view the incarnation as a metaphor.

A metaphor is a "figure of speech whereby we speak about one thing in terms which are seen to be suggestive of another."[1] Metaphors saturate language. They are irreducible to literal speech because of the interaction that occurs between elements within them.[2] Although they usually involve a comparison between a better-known and a lesser-known element, as illustrated in "The Lord is my shepherd," they are not fully translatable into other words. In nearly all lively communication and exploration of abstract or religious ideas metaphor plays a central part, not just colorful and untranslatable, but pointing in evocative ways to a reality which cannot be captured in literal speech.[3]

Metaphorical theology adopts a "critical realist" stance, which takes language to describe the world in terms that are true or false (realism) but acknowledges the creativity of the human mind in imposing order on the world and constructing pictures to more or less adequately give an account of it (this makes the realism "critical"). Critical realism sits between "naïve realism" at one extreme, the simple belief that our language literally describes how things are, and "fictionalism," or instrumentalism, at the other, the belief that we have no true or false understanding of the world, only more or less useful fictitious constructions of it.[4] Therefore critical realism relies heavily on metaphors and models.[5]

Critical realism is prepared to talk about the truth or falsity of models, but prefers terms such as "adequacy," "appropriateness" or "coherence." It takes its models very seriously but not literally. It does make tentative ontological claims, that is, claims about what is and is not true about Jesus and God.[6] Even metaphors, less systematically developed or integrated into a world-view than models, can be subjected to critical scrutiny and be judged "cognitive, informative and ontologically illuminating."[7] In metaphorical theology, "the theist can reasonably take his [or her] talk of God, bound as it is within a wheel of images, as being reality depicting, while at the same time acknowledging its inadequacy as description."[8] Such an approach refuses to choose between (on the one hand) the extremes of mystical silence or (on the other) confidence that we can talk easily of God.

We need to acknowledge that we cannot divide language neatly into the literal and the metaphorical, because it lies on a continuum between more literal statements and more strongly metaphorical expressions. Many seemingly literal expressions, such as "the arm of a chair," are actually dead metaphors. Many other seemingly literal expressions, such as "By raising his hand the police officer stopped the traffic," are not simply literal on reflection.

This pervasive presence of metaphor is especially noticeable when reaching for ways to express new or religious ideas. Suzanne Langer writes, "Every new experience, or new idea about things, evokes first of all some metaphorical expression. As the idea becomes familiar, this expression 'fades' to a new literal use of the once metaphorical predicate, a more general use than it had before."[9] Both science and theology resort to metaphors to capture new understandings, but theology has a particular need for metaphor because ordinary language is inadequate to express religious experience and articulate an understanding of God.[10] Janet Soskice sums up her book *Metaphor and religious language* by saying that theology involves an attempt to refer to reality, but also an awareness that reality cannot be fully captured. She says, "In our stammering after a transcendent God we must speak, for the most part, metaphorically or not at all."[11]

If we take this approach to religious language, how are we to understand the incarnation?

John Macquarrie sums up the metaphorical perspective boldly when he writes (as noted in the last chapter):

The Word was made flesh. How can we understand this? If we try to understand it literally, it is nonsense. The Word is Meaning, and Meaning cannot be transformed into the biological tissue we call flesh. The word "flesh" is being used in a figurative sense for the realm of the human, the empirical, the historical.[12]

In a metaphorical incarnational christology the incarnation is taken as a **model** for picturing the relationship between God and Jesus Christ. That is, the assertion that Jesus embodied the fullness of God is a way of framing our understanding of Jesus' birth, life, death and resurrection. It makes tentative ontological claims about Jesus without pretending to explain exactly how God can be present in a person. It frames our Christian experience because it asserts that this is the most adequate explanation for what the disciples and early church experienced and we experience today.

We could equally say that "The Word became flesh" is a **metaphor**, but given its development as a central Christian doctrine it is probably more appropriate to refer to the incarnation as a model.

If we define a myth to be a model in story form, we can also call the incarnation a **myth**, the story of the Word being involved in creation, descending from heaven, revealing God in human form, and returning to be with the Father. It is doubtful, however, whether this word is helpful, given its common usage as "mere myth" in *The myth of God incarnate* and the variety of other meanings it carries in the extensive literature on myth.[13] Hick, for example, has used the term "myth" to mean that the incarnation is "only a story," in which claims to Jesus' uniqueness and divinity are not taken seriously. (It is noteworthy that in recent writing, Hick now calls the idea of God incarnate "a metaphor," with more neutral overtones. Nevertheless, he still dismisses it as "devoid of literal meaning" and therefore only metaphorical, as if it was similar to saying that Joan of Arc incarnated the spirit of a resurgent France in 1429.[14])

Several features of metaphorical thinking are helpful, not only in understanding the incarnation but also in understanding its power for Christian mission.

First, metaphorical thinking accepts the need for more than one model. A Spirit christology (God's Spirit "dwelt" in a human), for example, can be seen to complement an incarnational christology (God "became" human) rather than to be opposed to it. In fact, it can be seen either as complementary to the incarnation (on the same level as a model), or as a way of understanding the incarnation (a model for making a more abstract model accessible).[15] This does not have to eliminate critical comparison and judgements about which way of thinking adequately accounts both for the biblical evidence and contemporary ways of thinking about the human person.

Second, models retain the tension built into metaphors, which express both similarity and difference ("It is and it is not"),[16] so a certain degree of agnosticism is seen as natural and necessary. On this view the language of the incarnation of the divine Word is powerfully evocative, but need not lead to bitter disputation about exactly how God became human, as if we are battling for the literal truth in describing the inner workings of God. Language can only partly express the depth of religious experience and the awe of Christian worship.

Third, models have great emotive power, including the power to order experience and interpret the world. They can result from reflecting on the stories we live by, and, like belief in the incarnation, can be critically analysed and evaluated. They are less than literal pictures of reality and yet more than useful fictions. Ian Barbour's summary of the role of religious models points us towards the power of the incarnation in Christian life. (He defines myth neutrally as a model in narrative form.)

> Models embodied in myths evoke commitment to ethical norms and policies of action. Like metaphors, religious models elicit emotional and valuational responses. Like parables, they encourage decision and personal involvement. Like myths, they offer ways of life and patterns of behavior.[17]

The fourth comment is directly related to mission. A metaphor usually changes our perception of both (or all) elements in it. Indeed, the Christian belief that God became human has permanently changed and enriched our understanding of both God and humanity. It was the incarnation that led to a trinitarian understanding of God, and it was the incarnation that led to the hope that humans could participate in divinity through their own humanity.[18] The model of the incarnation is not "just a metaphor" but is a powerful, open-ended image which makes ontological claims and is still capable of motivating and sustaining Christians as they frame the mystery of God's saving action in the terms of God becoming human in Jesus.

Using Relational Categories to
Understand Humanity

Chalcedon described Jesus' humanity and divinity in terms of his essence or substance. What made Jesus divine was sharing in the divine substance. He was paradoxically of one substance (*homoousios*) with God and with humanity. Contemporary christologies, however, have other ways of conceiving of the human person.

Process theology, for example, sees humanity as "becoming" rather than "being," and defines God's presence in terms of God's loving action.[19] Humans can respond to love and thereby reach their full potential. Sin is defined as humanity failing to respond in love to God the Cosmic Lover.[20] Norman Pittenger's way of describing the incarnation is to say that in Jesus God uniquely focused loving energy and Jesus responded in freedom, so that human and divine activity coincided.[21]

John Cobb, somewhat more philosophically, also presents a christology in which there is no conflict between Jesus' humanity and divinity. He points out that when we think in terms of substances two things cannot be in the same place at the same time, so there is a problem in understanding Jesus as having both divine and human "substances" present in his person at once. When we think in terms of experience, event and choice, however, many influences can be present in the one person and the one process, enabling the Logos as the "transcendent ground of order" to operate within a human life without "confusion, separation or division," to use the Chalcedonian terms.[22] "God's constitutive presence in Jesus' selfhood in no way reduced his humanity. On the contrary it perfected it." [23]

There are difficulties in process christology, though we cannot expand on these at any length here. The welcome news in process christology for Christians on mission, namely that God's incarnational activity is universal and continues in the church,[24] also creates some difficulty in articulating the uniqueness of Jesus Christ. Debate continues on the adequacy of the process view of God and the extent to which process theology is a biblical theology. Nonetheless, our point here is that process christology illustrates one approach in understanding humanity and its relationship to God in dynamic terms.

There are other contemporary ways of understanding the human person. Macquarrie argues that "human transcendence" has in recent times left behind its static connotations (permanent superiority over the world) to take on a more dynamic sense (moving beyond horizons without limit, tasting the infinite). If a principle of transcendence is built into our understanding of humanity, we may be able to understand Jesus Christ as fully human and yet so "transcending" in his humanity that we see him to be divine as well.[25]

An incarnational christology that uses dynamic and relational categories to understand humanity is highly conducive to the idea that God can act within the church in a way similar to the incarnation. There is potential for reducing the gap between the incarnation (which we can still see as unique in its fullness and God's revealing intention) and God's activity within Christians. We will draw on this in understanding incarnational mission, seen as mission that is empowered by the incarnation.

"From Below" but Also "From Above"

Nearly all contemporary christologies begin their study of Jesus Christ with Jesus of Nazareth rather than the incarnation of the divine Logos. This is called christology "from below" rather than "from above." This methodological choice emphasizes Jesus' full humanity, the importance of history to the modern mind, the identity of Jesus and the Christ, the actual content of Jesus' life and teaching as a basis for all doctrine, and the primacy of the practice-of-Christ (christopraxis) in developing an understanding-of-Christ (christology).

Some theologians then set "ascending christology" against "descending christology," defining incarnational christology solely in terms of "descending christology."[26] Despite their implication, however, christology "from below" is not necessarily non-incarnational. Neither is a christology incarnational because it starts "from above." It can be incarnational when it concludes after studying Jesus of Nazareth that in him God became human.

Christology "from below" need not end up as a low christology. (A low christology is one that asserts only one or two of the seven senses of incarnation listed above, or takes an adoptionist position, which takes Jesus to have been an ordinary human adopted as God's Son at a point of his life such as at his baptism.) This is because a christology's starting point does not limit what it eventually claims ontologically, about (for example) Christ's pre-existence or identity with the divine Logos. Christology "from below" is an epistemological label, that is, referring to the way we come to know and interpret Jesus Christ.

In asking where the incarnation fits when christology starts "from below," we must say that it is the answer to the question raised by examining the life, death and resurrection of Jesus of Nazareth.

Christology "from below" and christology "from above" really complement each other. The question, "How can we understand Jesus' humanity in such a way that we can also call him divine?" must lead to the complementary question, "How can we understand God taking on a genuinely human way of being?."[27] A christology "from below" has the correct starting point but is only half the story, inviting us also to ask what God's place is in the story of Jesus.[28]

As an example, Macquarrie argues that the two most common theories about the person of Christ are not opposing but complementary ways of seeing things. Deification, on one hand, sees Jesus growing so fully into transcendent humanity that we call him divine. "In-humanization," on the other hand, sees the divine Word becoming human.[29] To call Jesus the God-man is to speak on at least two complementary levels. It is to say that in Jesus human transcendence has grown to the point where it is united with the divine life, so much so that he merits the title of "divine." It is also to say that all this is from God and that one of the mysteries of God is that there is a humanity within God which qualifies God's otherness and is a bridge between God and humanity.[30]

Most christologies which begin "from below" go on to try to articulate the sense in which we can speak of the "humanizing of the divine" as well as the "divinizing of the human." For example, Wolfhart Pannenberg, who is explicit in starting "from below," affirms the doctrine of the incarnation but insists that many of the problems of christology stem from beginning with that doctrine (as Barth does) rather than culminating in it as a concluding statement.[31]

A theology which *begins* with the incarnation can struggle to speak to the modern mind. For this reason consideration of the incarnation is often the "second moment" of contemporary christologies, a way of answering the second question ("What is God doing in this?," following "How is this human remarkable?"). If it proceeds in this way, christology "from below" is not necessarily anti-incarnational; rather, in dealing with the relationship between God and humanity it begins with Jesus' humanity and, most would argue, leads us to beliefs about God becoming human, or fully dwelling as Spirit in Jesus of Nazareth.

Perhaps it is even more complicated than that. The study of Jesus may be able to peel back layers and try to begin with Jesus of Nazareth, but as

Christians we actually start with our tradition, already interpreted. It is not that we begin with history and end up with theology, or begin with Jesus the carpenter and end up with Jesus the divine Word made flesh. Rather, we come to know and understand Jesus Christ through what was remembered and passed on in the early church (already theologically laden). This in turn interacts in a dialectical way with our own experience.[32] It is on these grounds that Jürgen Moltmann, whose christology fits neither of the labels "from below" and "from above," recommends that we abandon them.[33] Nevertheless, our consideration of the benefits of these approaches has enabled us to see where the emphases need to be placed in developing a contemporary incarnational christology.

An important contribution of the doctrine of the incarnation is its insistence that God has taken the initiative in becoming part of humanity. It says that while we should accept Jesus' humanity without reservation, something more was going on in the life of Jesus, and that-something-more is the very presence and embodiment of God, as astonishing as it is to say this. The doctrine of the incarnation safeguards the "from above" dimension of christology at a time when it is tempting for Christian theology to water down its claims and, having begun "from below," to forget the classical Christian belief that the birth, life, death and resurrection of Jesus Christ was an expression of the very nature of God.

Pneumatological

There are two main reasons for insisting that a contemporary incarnational christology be based on the activity of the Holy Spirit, or God as Spirit. First, the New Testament witness to Jesus repeatedly speaks of the Spirit at work in Jesus.[34] Second, the activity of God as Spirit in Jesus is one very good way of understanding what incarnation might mean. "Inspiration" (being "in-spirited") has often been distinguished from "incarnation" on the grounds that inspiration is temporary and the product of an impersonal influence. Spirit christologies reject this and see incarnation in terms of inspiration.[35] They claim that God "indwelt" Jesus Christ in a permanent, personal and unique "infilling," "God-possession" (*enthousiasmos*) or inspiration. This would be hard to distinguish phenomenologically from incarnation.[36]

Several Spirit christologies have been put forward.[37] Geoffrey Lampe, for example, sees the Spirit as God's personal and active presence in God's creation.[38] God has always been "incarnated" in men and women, forming their spirits from within and revealing Godself to them. Creation and redemption are one movement as God has pointed us forward toward full relationship with our creator. In Jesus the incarnate presence of God evoked a full and constant response of the human spirit. This personal union can be called deification or sonship. Jesus acts as representative, perfection, exemplar and enabler, and is the source of our ability to enter a similar relationship with God.[39]

All proponents of Spirit christology argue that inspiration is the most appropriate way to understand incarnation[40] (though ironically Hick uses Lampe's and Robinson's perspectives to support his own non-incarnational conclusions and dismisses their claims to the uniqueness of Jesus).[41] Most Spirit christologies are trinitarian too,[42] with only Lampe arguing that the trinity makes no sense and preferring "the unifying concept of God as Spirit." [43]

Moltmann takes an alternative approach, criticizing all "anthropological" christologies such as those we have just considered, in which humanity reaches its perfection through divine inspiration. Like them he calls for a pneumatological christology, but insists that it apply to more than the inner-person. Christology must be cosmic, historical and social, so that the salvation Jesus brings stems from his trinitarian history and affects people, societies, history and eventually the whole universe, on an eschatological horizon.[44] Moltmann sees the divine Spirit as involved in every way in the mystery of Jesus, and so, in a different framework, espouses a thoroughly pneumatological christology.[45]

The role of the Spirit is central in any attempt to express the action of God in Jesus Christ. In addition to Moltmann and the Spirit christologies mentioned, other approaches also stress the importance of the Spirit in Jesus' life and mission. These include process theology (which has some remarkable parallels) and the theology of Rahner (with his transcendental anthropology). Incarnational christology does not lead to a binitarian theology of Fatherhood and Sonship, but has to take account of the repeated New Testament emphasis on the work of the Spirit. This leads us to the next point.

Trinitarian

While it is not our intention here to outline a doctrine of the trinity, we would argue that an incarnational christology needs to be trinitarian due to the Christian experience of God's self-revelation. Talk of God's unity has to co-exist paradoxically with talk of God's tri-une being, however conceived. Every way of expressing the trinity is metaphorical, including the Chalcedonian talk of three persons and one substance. Examples include Augustine's analogies of the trinity as mind, knowledge and love, or as memory, understanding and will.[46] Further examples are God above us, God alongside us and God within us (Pittenger, Hans Küng),[47] or God as an egalitarian and mutually interpenetrating fellowship of love (the "social trinitarianism" of Moltmann).[48]

The incarnation necessitates the trinity. Belief in the incarnation was historically the central factor in the development of the doctrine of the trinity, because the early Christians experienced Jesus Christ in ways which led them to affirm his divinity. This forced modifications to their strong monotheism, and their experience of salvation soon came to be expressed in trinitarian terms:

> For the structure of Christianity is the mediation of God to human beings in history through Jesus and the continued experience of God as Spirit in the world which is also identified by Jesus. This is the essential structure of the Christian movement, and it is enshrined in the New Testament.[49]

Trinitarian thought guards against Jesus being seen as "merely" human. It is also the ground of incarnational thought, the framework which makes incarnational talk possible. Moreover, it speaks of the Holy Spirit as the means through which God continues the mission of Jesus in the world today, therefore linking the Spirit-centered incarnation with a Spirit-centered Christian mission.

Soteriological

The incarnation is the "central event and fact of salvation history, and the central content of the Christian message."[50] For Christians it is God's supreme self-communication.[51] This means that it is fundamentally soteriological, the pivotal saving event in the mission of God, whether seen as a single new event or as the culmination of God's incarnating processes. So, to use traditional categories, all talk of Jesus Christ's *person* must take place in the light of his *work*. Every christology needs to be soteriological, that is, oriented to the gracious, saving work of God in Jesus Christ.[52] Indeed, there can be no understanding of his divinity and humanity, or his uniqueness, without attending to his mission. An adequate doctrine of the incarnation must continually point us to the Good News brought by Jesus and remind us of God's overflowing love and grace and the cost of God's involvement in the transformation of the world.

Learning from the past, recent christology has emphasized the inseparability of "who Christ is" and "what Jesus' purpose was." [53]

There was a tendency in patristic christology to over-emphasize the person of Christ, elaborating in great detail the nature of his divinity and humanity and insisting on both. In defense of the early Fathers, we must say that they often hammered this out in the context of interpreting Christianity against other religions and sects. Further, they made expert use of the philosophies of the time. Nevertheless, a certain flexibility of christological interpretation was one of the casualties of the christological controversies of the first four centuries, as some who made important contributions leaned too far one way or the other and were declared heretics.

The pendulum swung and there was a tendency in medieval and Reformation christology to concentrate on Christ's work: the atonement, penal substitution, justification and the benefits of salvation. Luther's colleague Philip Melancthon, in a famous comment, wrote that "to know Christ means to know his benefits and not ... to reflect upon his natures and the modes of his incarnation,"[54] an illustration of a soteriology in reaction against christology. As a result of this swing there was often a concentration on the suprahistorical fact of the cross as if the atonement was some sort of cosmic transaction focused solely on Jesus' death, without regard for the life which led to that death and even at times neglecting the resurrection.

On the one hand, the incarnation reminds those who underplay the metaphysical questions of who Jesus was that God was in Christ reconciling the world. On the other hand, the incarnation also reminds those who see the problems of christology primarily to be concerned with the doctrine of the person of Christ that christology must be centrally about soteriology. The soteriological thrust of the incarnation leads directly to our next point, which is that an adequate incarnational christology must point to and shape the mission of the church.

Issuing Naturally in Incarnational Mission

We have outlined a perspective in which the incarnation is a model for understanding the mystery of God's saving presence in Jesus Christ. This central saving event is the culmination and unique focus of the incarnating dynamic of God, who, though transcendent, is also immanent in creation and by the very nature of love seeks to relate to all humanity and be embodied in a new order. The mission of God is to encompass all creation in the gracious and transforming presence of God (the "kingdom of God'). The Good News of the kingdom came in the person of Jesus, who embodied all he proclaimed. For this reason the incarnation is the crux of the mission of God.

This is the crucial link for mission. Incarnation is both the event of salvation and the way in which God's saving purposes are accomplished.[55] God chose to identify with humanity, becoming one of us and in Jesus living a life of radical and transforming love. As Darrell Guder puts it, the incarnation is the "what" and "how" of God's saving action.[56] The adjective "incarnational" draws attention to the way God acts in the incarnation for us and our salvation. It emphasizes the congruence between God's message and method.[57] A *message* of world-transforming love was demonstrated through a *life* of world-transforming love. The significance of the cross is that God in Jesus challenged the powers of sin and death and paid the price for it, in apparent failure. The significance of the resurrection, a new act of God beyond our full understanding, is that it is God's validation of the mission of Jesus, experienced in power among the first disciples and appropriated ever since in the lives of many.

The next link for mission is the call by Jesus to follow him as disciples, that is, as those who learn from him how to live. The church is called to continue the mission of Jesus. To take up the cross, to follow Jesus, is to join the same cause Jesus had, in his risen power through the Holy Spirit.

This is what leads us to say, along with representatives from across all Christian traditions, that the incarnation is fundamental for Christian mission. For example, the evangelical writer John Stott writes that "all authentic mission is incarnational mission."[58] From a different tradition, in Bible studies sent out in preparation for the World Council of Churches Conference on World Mission and Evangelism held in Melbourne in 1980, we find the claim: "The incarnational mission of Christ is thus the only model of mission." [59]

At this point we have to recognize that the nature of incarnational mission has not been discussed. In what ways are incarnation and *the* incarnation important for mission?

Incarnation and Mission

We have argued that incarnational christology is still central to Christian faith and that it is the basis and inspiration for mission. We now begin to tease out the various ways in which the incarnation appropriately inspires and governs mission, using some of the dimensions of contemporary incarnational christology as our guide.

Christian mission is incarnational in three basic ways, each of which has a strong governing influence on the way in which we are to understand and practice mission. We will now outline them, listing some of the possible implications for mission and very briefly signaling possible dangers of each way of understanding incarnational mission. This will give us a framework with which to approach the second part of the study, a critical survey of the way in which a variety of traditions and theologians use the incarnation in their missiology. Building on this framework and the survey, the third part of the study will attempt to outline the contours of an adequate model of incarnational mission.

Using the approach of metaphorical theology we have argued that the incarnation is a model which articulates the Christian experience of the way God's overflowing love and tendency to be present in creation reaches a climax in the birth, life, teaching, death and resurrection of Jesus Christ. This framework sees *incarnation* as a movement of God, evident in the processes of creation and redemption, and with the incarnation as its prime example. The doctrine of *the incarnation* asserts that God has acted in Jesus for the salvation of humanity. The whole incarnational direction of God's activity is "missional" to the core. The call to discipleship includes the call to an *incarnational style* in mission, following the pattern of Jesus' own mission. Incarnational missiology takes into account these three dimensions of incarnation. To see God's action and Christian mission incarnationally is not only to see embodiment as a motif, a governing idea, and a way of framing experience in the past, present and future. It is also to see God's presence in the risen Christ as the enabling power for mission.

The three basic ways in which incarnation and *the* incarnation shape Christian mission are, simply put, (1) seeing Jesus as the pattern for mission, (2) experiencing the continuing presence of Christ in the church as the body of Christ, and (3) understanding the activity of God in a sacramental/incarnational framework.

There is a case for presenting these three meanings of incarnational mission in reverse order, with God's mission first, then the power for mission second, and an incarnational style of mission in response, third. I have chosen, however, to follow the sequence in the order in which my personal journey has raised the questions, as mentioned in the introduction: trying to follow Jesus, realizing the centrality of the presence of the risen Christ, and situating this in an overall framework of God's incarnating dynamic.

Incarnational Mission as Following Jesus

Taking seriously the call to discipleship as spelt out repeatedly in the Gospels leads inescapably to an incarnational style of mission. Incarnational mission begins with Jesus of Nazareth and attempts to translate for today his call to follow him. Each of the Gospels, for example, makes it clear that Jesus demanded a radical and whole-of-life response in discipleship. The Gospel writers wrote with the double intention of telling the story of Jesus and interpreting his call for the early church. They see the invitation to the first disciples to follow Jesus of Nazareth as an invitation to the early church to continue the mission of Jesus. According to the Gospels, following Jesus is costly, requires a new attitude to possessions, occurs in community, includes the poor and the religiously excluded, involves trust and prayer, and is made possible by the grace and love of Jesus.[60]

Discipleship involves both the benefits of being part of the kingdom of God and the responsibility to be part of the continuing mission of Jesus.[61] Paradoxically, its grace is costly, as Dietrich Bonhoeffer put it.[62]

This vision of discipleship is wider, more behavior-oriented, more concrete, and more public than a view of discipleship as "the imitation of Christ," the interior quest to become more like Jesus in one's "spirit" or attitudes.

Quite a few aspects of Christian mission can be labelled as "incarnational" in the sense of following Jesus as our pattern, or doing mission "in Christ's way." Here we will do little more than simply list them, as we will discuss them in more detail as we encounter them in our critical survey of Christian traditions.

The integration of word and deed: There is a scholarly consensus that the central message of Jesus was the imminence of the kingdom of God, a vision in which God's love is extended to all, particularly outcasts and sinners. His life demonstrated the values he preached, so that "in both his words and deeds, Jesus became the personification of this loving, saving presence of God in the world."[63] His embodiment of his own message, christology affirms, represents something deeper than the mere congruence of a person's life and beliefs; it reflects the way in which God's self-communication took shape. The mission of the church in following Jesus, therefore, is to "flesh out" the Good News of God's gracious love and reconciling action in Christ. This is part of what is meant by an incarnational model of mission.

This means that evangelism (involving at least "saying the gospel") and social involvement (involving at least "doing the gospel") are part of the one integrated mission of making visible the Good News in our lives and spoken testimony. As the Lukan Jesus puts it: "You will be my witnesses" (Acts 1:8). *"Being* a witness and *saying* the witness are inseparable aspects of the same calling"[64]

Mission as christopraxis: Flowing out of the last point, to follow Jesus Christ is to follow his liberative praxis (which we will define, following Karl Marx, as a deliberate program of humanizing action which interacts dialectically with reflection).[65] Christology needs to be christopraxic. To put it another way, our faith in Christ only makes sense as a walk of faith in which we are experiencing liberation and contributing to the liberation of others.

In this way incarnational mission affirms (differing from some contemporary Christian ethicists) that Christian ethics is more than a vague commitment to loving our neighbour. Although its content is not determined in detail, neither is it indistinct from non-Christian ethical systems. Jesus preached and lived a radical alternative vision of social and personal relationships. In following Jesus, Christian lifestyle and ethics are of great importance.

Good News to the poor: Another point of scholarly consensus is that Jesus, among other things, was a social prophet with an alternative vision which radically included those who were excluded, particularly the economically poor, the religiously impure, notorious sinners, Gentiles, women and children.[66] Incarnational mission is usually passionate about this dimension of discipleship; indeed, some writers define incarnational mission as mission among the poor.[67] Liberation theologians Leonardo and Clodovis Boff include in their list of key notions of liberation theology: *"Incarnation* among and *solidarity* with the outcast."[68] The metaphor of "incarnation among the poor" here stems directly from seeing Jesus as the pattern for mission.[69]

Vulnerable love: A range of personal qualities is often attributed to Jesus, and the whole range is used to justify emphases in Christian mission. For example, it is common in the evangelical tradition to emphasize spiritual obedience, dependence on God and our merely-delegated missionary authority (our "sentness" mirroring Jesus' "sentness"), rather than, say, Jesus' concern for the poor.[70] Obviously some discernment is necessary. For example, Christians are not called to emulate Jesus' masculinity or personality type. Incarnational mission requires Christians to link Jesus' personal qualities with the message he proclaimed, and discern on that basis the ways in which he ought to be seen as an example.

There are substantial historical difficulties in establishing what Jesus said and did, and discovering his internal attitudes would seem to be even more difficult, if not impossible. Nevertheless, among the most widely accepted personal qualities attributed to Jesus are that he embodied love for others, was radically open in his friendship and showed a remarkable combination of humility and certainty of purpose. There is a broad consensus that Jesus was the "man for others,"[71] showing through vulnerable love the nature of God, even to the point of death.

The way of the cross: As the Gospels make plain, to follow Jesus is to take up the cross and follow Jesus in conflict, suffering and possible loss of life for his sake (Mk 8:27-9:8, Mt 16:24-28, Lk 9:23-27, Jn 12:23-26). It is tempting for Christians to point instead to the resurrection and emphasize discipleship as living in the power of the risen Lord. The criterion for discipleship, however, is the crucified and risen Lord, which "calls for a life of discipleship in which it is existentially manifested that the risen Lord makes himself known under the shadow of the cross." [72]

John Yoder argues that this is the only way in which Jesus is the pattern for Christian mission, but then sees many implications in it:

> Only at one point, only on one subject—but then consistently, univer-
> sally—is Jesus our example: in his cross.... The believer's cross must be,
> like his [or her] Lord's, the price of his [or her] social nonconformity....
> [It] is the social reality of representing in an unwilling world the Order to
> come.[73]

The list above summarizes the main ways in which Jesus can be understood as the pattern for mission. It also raises questions about whether it is adequate to think only in terms of Jesus as pattern. We would argue that it is not, for two specific reasons, which lead us to fill out our understanding of incarnational mission in the two ways which follow.

First, Christianity is not primarily about the imitation of an outstanding founder; it is about the "power of God for salvation" (Rom 1:16). What this means is that the continuing transforming power of the incarnation is central in Christian mission, and that incarnational mission is more than the imitation of Christ. "'Transformation' needs 'following,' and 'following' needs 'transformation.'"[74] This was hinted at in Bonhoeffer's famous discussion of "costly grace." Mission in Christ's way emphasizes the cost; mission in Christ's presence emphasizes the grace. Therefore we need to balance any emphasis on the cost of following Jesus on the road of discipleship with an emphasis on the new life of grace and liberation which empowers, motivates and sustains that journey.

Second, the focus on Jesus of Nazareth can unintentionally eclipse the christological affirmation that *God* was in Christ reconciling the world (2 Cor 5:19). Most of the above emphases of mission-as-following-*Jesus* can also be phrased in terms of *God's* qualities as revealed in Jesus Christ, which is precisely our third way of understanding incarnational mission.

For example, as we hinted in the list above, to say that Jesus was characterized by embodying his message is also to say that God is characterized by embodying outgoing love by means of incarnation. Similarly, Jesus' particular care for the poor is often linked to the self-emptying motif we find in Philippians 2—so the self-emptying of God the Son was a double kenosis, becoming human and becoming an ordinary Jewish person who lived among the poor. As a further example, Jesus' vulnerable love and path to the cross are, in ways we struggle to understand, reflective of the very nature of God and God's action for the transformation of humanity. What we learn from Jesus also teaches us about the nature of God.

Incarnational Mission as Participation in Christ

The second way in which mission can be understood as incarnational is to see mission as enabled and guided by the continuing presence of

Christ through the Holy Spirit. In other words, Christ is present and "becomes flesh" wherever his mission is being continued.

Paul's image of the church as the body of Christ (Rom 12:5, 12:27, Eph 1:23, 2:16, 4:4, 12, 16, 5:23, Col 1:18, 24, 2:19, 3:15), while at times emphasising co-operation and unity, and at times Christ's headship, often suggests that the church is a "body" for Christ's continuing presence. Luke records Jesus promising the disciples that whoever listens to them listens to him (Lk 10:16, cf. Jn 13:20). Matthew concludes his Gospel with Jesus commissioning the disciples and promising his presence: "And remember, I am with you always, to the end of the age" (Mt 28:20). John's famous passage, "As the Father has sent me, so I send you" (Jn 20:21), promises the fullness of the Spirit to the church.

This is a necessary corrective to incarnational mission as merely following the pattern of Jesus, for the Christian life is not so much a life like that of Jesus as a life in Christ.[75] Frank Rees argues that how the church acts must follow "what the church is." He sees the mission of the church as flowing from the nature of the church:

> [The church] is His Body, the concrete expression of His spiritual being-in-the-world. The Church exists in an *inherent continuity* with the historical ministry of Jesus: for the Crucified One is risen and has poured out His life into the world.[76]

The strongest way of expressing this understanding of incarnational mission is to see **the church as the continuing incarnation**, a view found in the Catholic, Anglo-Catholic and Eastern Orthodox churches.

If we keep the metaphorical nature of language in mind and leave room for the church to be self-critical, this image is useful in reminding the church of the mystery of its very being and of Christ's presence in the church. This extends to eucharistic language in which "participating in Christ" is a rich concept. The Eastern Orthodox church makes a particular contribution here in seeing the incarnation as the center of a whole world view in which Christ is present through the eucharist and the worshipping presence of the church, radiating out to the world and gathering people into the body of Christ.

If, however, talk of the church as the extension of the incarnation lacks the safeguards mentioned there is a danger that the church will become unchallengeable as the mystique of divine authority grows. There needs to be dialectical awareness of the divine and human basis of the church, an institution which both reveals and yet obscures Christ in its daily life. Talk of the church as the perpetuation of the incarnation also tends to limit the presence of Christ in the world to the church.

A related theme is the idea of **theosis**, or divinization, strong in Eastern Orthodox Christianity but muted in Western Christianity. The doctrine affirms that God became human so that humans may become divine. Mission is incarnational in the sense that we are caught up in a double movement of God in assuming human flesh in order to "catch us up," in restoration and transformation, into the likeness of Christ. In its stronger forms, this is a bold doctrine, but contemporary Orthodox theologians are aware of the metaphorical dimensions of the language of theosis, and use it as a vivid image of finding true humanity in Christ and recovering the "likeness" of God in humanity.

There are a variety of ways of expressing incarnational mission as the experience of the presence of Christ. The role of **grace** in enabling our human response is one way. Another is the role of **the Holy Spirit**, who is also the Spirit of Christ, as guide, inspiration and awakener of our response in faith and mission. A third is to use phrases such as "**conformity to Christ**," "participation in Christ" and "solidarity in Christ" to interpret the idea of discipleship as the "following of Christ"; each of these three phrases is meant to point to Christ as an active force in the Christian life.

Incarnational mission as the experience of the presence of Christ uses a dialectical approach to understand the relationship between grace and "works." We simultaneously have faith and are grasped by faith. We strive and yet we let go. We follow Jesus, which at the same time is a participation in Christ. If the emphasis on grace were disconnected from discipleship, this form of incarnational mission would be one-sided, but this is seldom a danger in writing on incarnational mission.

This understanding of incarnational mission is not in tension with following the pattern of Jesus but rather fills it out, emphasizing the unity between the power for mission and its unfolding in concrete embodiment. The radical evangelicals at the Lausanne Congress on World Evangelism in 1974 expressed the charismatic nature of mission well in their manifesto on the sharing of the gospel:

> [It] is Good News of a new creation of a new humanity, a new birth through him by his life-giving Spirit; of the gifts of the messianic reign contained in Jesus and mediated through him by his Spirit; of the charismatic community empowered to embody his reign of shalom here

and now before the whole creation and make his Good News seen and known.[77]

This is incarnational mission understood as *at the one time* experiencing the transforming presence of Christ *and* following Jesus in embodying it in Christian community and mission.

We may note here that the idea of the church as the continuing incarnation in some ways sits halfway between the second and third dimensions of incarnational mission, because it calls attention both to the presence of Christ in the believer and to the ongoing incarnating activity of God. To this latter dimension we now turn.

Incarnational Mission as Joining God's Incarnating Mission

The third way of understanding incarnational mission is to see it as cooperating with God's "incarnating" activity from creation, throughout history, climactically demonstrated in the incarnation of Jesus Christ and continuing as the mission of God today. It involves a panentheistic view of God in which God continually and by very nature reaches out to the universe, not remaining fully transcendent but indwelling creation and becoming embodied in it, particularly in the life of humanity. As Sallie McFague puts it, the doctrine of the incarnation ought to be radicalized beyond Jesus of Nazareth to include all matter. "God is incarnated in the world."[78]

Incarnation can therefore be seen as the process of divine embodiment. Taken as generally as this, the incarnational and sacramental views of the world are similar. In both cases we discern the divine in the material or human. In both cases also, a material object or person bears to us the presence or power of God. Further, in both cases we experience God as entering historical and material reality by means of embodiment in what functions as a symbol, pointing beyond itself and participating in the power of the transcendent.

As we will discuss when distinguishing between incarnational and sacramental perspectives, *the* incarnation is the supreme example of a sacrament.[79] As Leonardo Boff argues, the sacramental/incarnational perspective has strong implications for mission because it sees the divine as suffusing the human in many ways, seeking embodiment and "concretization." Hence the mission of the church is to demonstrate the structure of life (particularly human life) as revealed in Christ.[80] It is to join God in God's mission of enfleshment.[81]

This perspective closely links creation and redemption, just as the Prologue to John's Gospel does when it identifies the divine creative Word with Jesus Christ the Word who "became flesh and lived among us' (Jn 1:14). It takes the structure of the incarnation (which is embodiment and enfleshment) and reads it back into the heart of God. Our human experience of God, then, can be interpreted as "incarnation," the transformation of the present by the creative and powerful force which is God creating and re-creating humanity through the mystery of Christ.[82]

There are three emphases which flow from this dimension of incarnational mission: the affirmation of this world, mission as self-emptying, and incarnation as the basis for inculturation.

Affirming creation and the whole of life: To stress the movement of God towards immanence is to affirm creation, the material world, culture and the value of humanity. Incarnational mission of this type, particularly as seen in Catholicism, Anglo-Catholicism, and the ecumenical movement, emphasizes the role of Christian mission in all areas of life, whether politics, economics, the arts, education or recreation. It tends to look for the best in culture and begin by affirming it, perhaps speaking of Christ "completing" or transforming it, rather than upturning it. Incarnational mission of the "immanentist" type reminds us that creation is good and that the Creator wants us to work for transformation in all of life, not separating the spiritual from the material. It is fertile for developing Christian mission to include ecological renewal and a cosmic vision.

There are dangers in over-emphasizing "incarnation" as solidarity with creation if the movement to come-alongside is the only accent. Without the cross and resurrection, this baptizes culture without challenging it, as we will later discuss. Incarnational mission in the first major sense, following the radical prophet Jesus, is an important corrective to any potential one-sidedness in seeing incarnation as immanence.

Incarnational mission as self-emptying: In discussing discipleship we mentioned Jesus' solidarity with the poor, seeing it in terms of Jesus of Nazareth, "from below." We can also speak of the action of God ("from above") in self-emptying (or kenosis). Here we are not espousing kenotic christology, a theory which sees God as shedding attributes of omnipotence, omniscience, and omnipresence to become human for a while.[83]

Rather, the language of Philippians 2 is taken as a vivid metaphor which points to something important in our experience of God. It says that Christ Jesus, though in the form of God, did not exploit his glory but "emptied himself, taking the form of a slave, being born in human likeness.... [He] humbled himself and became obedient to the point of death—even death on a cross" (Phil 2:6-8).

At the heart of the mystery of the incarnation is God's condescension and God's going-out-of-Godself, engaging in mission not from a position of glory or power but from weakness, poverty and nakedness.[84] If we are invited to join God's mission of enfleshment, this is a costly and at times paradoxical aspect of the journey.

Part of the paradox is that self-emptying is something one can do only when one has a certain fullness, status, self-esteem, dignity, wealth or power, and these things are often not present as initial conditions among the poor or oppressed. It is not necessarily good news to call a landless peasant to "take the form of a slave" or invite a woman who has only ever known a life of service to embrace "servanthood." This is something of which liberation theology, particular feminist theology, has reminded us well. Without completely removing the paradox, we may say that the Good News is both the gift of liberation (empowerment, joy, strength, dignity, fullness) and at the same time the call to humbly share what we have (in self-emptying, solidarity and hospitality). Without the first, there cannot be the call to the second.

The incarnation as the basis for inculturation: We will define "inculturation," or "contextualization," to mean the two-way, critical, dynamic and in-depth interaction between the gospel and culture necessary for the Good News to take genuine root within a culture. The view that the incarnation provides a missiological basis for the process of inculturation is one of the least controversial aspects of incarnational mission.

Darrell Whiteman puts the argument succinctly, arguing that Jesus is the appearance or embodiment of God in terms humans can understand:

> In our discussion and practice of contextualization, we must take our cues from the incarnation. In the same way that Jesus emptied himself and dwelt among us, we must be willing to do likewise as we enter another culture with the Gospel. The incarnation is our model for contextualization.[85]

In this section we have argued that the various ways in which incarnation and *the* incarnation shape mission can be gathered in three groups, those which reflect (1) Jesus as the pattern for mission, (2) participation in the presence of Christ, and (3) joining God's mission of enfleshment.

This three-fold understanding is loosely trinitarian, stressing the activity of God the Son, God the Spirit and God the Father (or Creator).

Put in another way, we have discussed the incarnation as (1) the model for mission, (2) the power for mission and (3) the ultimate basis for mission.

Or again, our understanding of God's incarnating activity throughout history and in Jesus Christ leads us to (1) the pattern of mission, (2) the ability to engage in mission, and (3) the whole framework for mission.

We also find an echo of this structure (in reverse order) in the account of Pentecost in Acts 2. The mysterious movement of God is evident first in the rushing of wind (2:2). Then come the tongues of fire, gifts to each person of the Holy Spirit's power (2:3). Finally, there follows powerful verbal witness and lives so radically changed that many are converted to belief in Jesus Christ (2:4-47).[86] There are echoes here of God's incarnating dynamic, the power of God for mission, and radical lifestyle changes patterned on the life of Jesus.

The three-pronged perspective we have outlined provides a lens through which to examine now a variety of Christian traditions and theologians to uncover carefully the way "incarnation" and "the incarnation" are used in missiology.

In our survey we will group the traditions loosely according to their main (though not exclusive) emphasis. First, we find in Anabaptism, radical evangelicalism, and liberation theology a strong emphasis on Jesus as our pattern for mission (chapters 4, 5 and 6). Then we find in the writing of Jürgen Moltmann a strong emphasis on participation in Christ (chapter 7). Moltmann is included as a significant individual theologian because his perspective acts as a bridge between the first and third groups. Third, we find in Catholicism, the ecumenical movement, and Eastern Orthodoxy a strong emphasis on God's ongoing incarnating mission, at times centered in the church (chapters 8 and 9). In each case we will discover not only their main thrust but also the way they treat other dimensions of incarnational mission.

PART TWO

CRITICAL SURVEY

CHAPTER 4

MISSION AS DISCIPLESHIP: ANABAPTISM

The first three traditions we will examine (Anabaptism, radical evangelicalism, and liberation theology) all stress the role of Jesus as the pattern for mission. In the Anabaptist tradition Christians are gripped by the concept of incarnational mission arising from discipleship. No other Christian tradition has emphasized as much the following of Jesus in daily life. Anabaptists see mission as incarnational in a double sense. First, and most importantly, faith is a matter of following Jesus in committed discipleship, which involves taking Jesus as our pattern. Moreover, we live in solidarity with Christ, thus making visible the pattern of Jesus in the world. The Anabaptist vision of radical discipleship is an inspiring source for understanding incarnational mission.

The Anabaptist tradition so clearly insists that Jesus is the pattern for Christian mission that it sharply raises many of the major questions of incarnational mission. What is it to follow Jesus in committed discipleship? In what sense, if any, is the Christian life the imitation of Christ? Can Christians even hope to live in the way Jesus did? How important is God's enabling work in the Christian life? What is it to live "in Christ"? What is the meaning and role of grace? In what way is Jesus normative for Christians? What does it mean for Christians to "take up the cross" in following Jesus? Is incarnational mission particularly good news to the poor? In anticipating a new society should Christians basically withdraw from existing societies or work within them to change them?

Our treatment of the Anabaptist view of incarnational mission will be used to open up these questions and set the stage for our encounter with them in other traditions, and therefore will be more extensive than it might otherwise have been.

In this chapter we will briefly describe Anabaptism; outline its approach to incarnational mission, examining at some length the dimensions of Anabaptist discipleship; and offer an appreciation and critique of the Anabaptist approach to incarnational mission.

Who Were and Are the Anabaptists?

The Anabaptist movement began as a decentralized collection of radical sixteenth-century Christian groups who emerged in Europe during the Reformation but were rejected by Catholics and Protestants alike.[1] Appealing to the New Testament, the Anabaptist groups insisted that membership of the church belongs only to adults who choose baptism as believers. They dismissed infant baptism as invalid and therefore did not see themselves as carrying out re-baptism (the meaning of "Anabaptism"), a heretical practice carrying the death penalty in canon law.[2] As well as being "believers' churches," challenging the state control and monopoly of religion, Anabaptist groups became known (generally though not without exception) for the "centrality of the Bible, an apolitical stance, nonresistance to evil and refusal to participate in military operations, a stress on ethics defined in terms of discipleship or following the example of Jesus, and a visible church preserved through systematic discipline." [3]

After beginning with radical intensity and facing a great deal of persecution, including martyrdom and exile, the surviving Anabaptist groups later adopted a much quieter existence, often in rural and communal settings. Today the Mennonites, Amish, Hutterites and some Brethren groups trace their ancestry directly to the Anabaptists. Baptists can claim indirect links going back to visits by General Baptist founder John Smyth to the Dutch Mennonites in Amsterdam in about 1608.[4] The Mennonites are the largest twentieth-century Anabaptist group, and Mennonite scholarship provides the most vigorous discussion of the meaning of Anabaptism today.[5]

For centuries Anabaptist history was written by its enemies, and the radical reformers were vilified as heretics and fanatics. They have been identified almost completely with the peasants' uprising of 1525 and the violent apocalypticism of the Anabaptist leaders in Münster which led to a massacre in 1535.[6]

A significant turning point occurred in 1943 when Mennonite historian Harold S Bender gave a paper called *The Anabaptist vision* which presented Anabaptism as

> the culmination of the Reformation, the fulfillment of the original vision of Luther and Zwingli, and thus ... a consistent evangelical Protestantism seeking to recreate without compromise the original New Testament church.[7]

This vision saw the essence of Christianity in terms of discipleship, the church as a committed voluntary community, and the ethic of love and nonresistance. It was a lofty argument for discipleship. It has inspired a generation of Mennonites to try to live a "life patterned after the teaching and example of Christ," to use Bender's words,[8] and so undergirds the dominant Anabaptist view of incarnational mission.

The essence of Anabaptism has since been shown to be more complicated than this. To distill his vision Bender had selected one strand of Anabaptism (which began in Switzerland), and called it "Anabaptism proper,"[9] dismissing the sects on its periphery.[10] Since about 1975 scholars have shown there were several independent origins of Anabaptism in Switzerland, South Germany and the Netherlands.[11] Modern Anabaptists now face a more complicated interpretive task in applying sixteenth-century Anabaptist principles. There is no easy way to decide what should be considered central to Anabaptist traditions because a wide variety existed, from pacifist to militant, from politically engaged to withdrawn, and positioned on nearly all points of the theological spectrum on many major doctrines. John Howard Yoder says there was no "univocal Anabaptism" in the sixteenth century, and as a result of many influences on the Anabaptist tradition, there are even more voices today.[12]

Nevertheless, "for all the variants ... all the Anabaptists can be seen as an entity," a "pan-European phenomenon," argues George Williams in his detailed history of the Radical Reformation.[13] Walter Klaassen argues that after the movement crystallized by about 1540, one can hazard some themes held in common, namely salvation involving both divine and human cooperation, the baptism and "priesthood" of all believers, and a view of

Christianity as gathered congregational community rather than clericalized and territorial churches.[14]

J A Oosterbaan also sees an underlying unity. He surveys a variety of claims for the uniqueness of Anabaptism, and argues that the Anabaptists fused the form and content of faith in a "faith gestalt."[15] They did not emphasize faith's content, the objective, doctrinal, revealed side of faith, as did Luther and Calvin, and (much later) Barth. Nor did they simply emphasize faith's form, our existential human response in discipleship. They held the two in one, seeing faith as conforming in Christ to Christ. Faith was "a walk with Christ in obedience, trust, love and discipleship."[16]

From a survey of what twenty-five leading Mennonite scholars say is the essence of Anabaptism, Calvin Redekop concludes that a workable definition of Anabaptism does not yet exist,[17] but his own results show this conclusion to be rather pessimistic. They show that Anabaptists today see Anabaptist perspectives clustered around the idea of the church being different from the world, separate and living out its new life in discipleship under the authority of Jesus as seen in the New Testament. A communal approach and pacifism are also important elements in the tradition.[18]

As our brief summary of Anabaptism shows, it is remarkable for taking seriously the expectation that Christians should live in a quite different way from those around them. Mission flows from living as Christ lived. At the start of our survey, Anabaptism provides a very clear example of the first understanding of incarnational mission, that of Jesus as the pattern for mission.

It is early Anabaptism and recent Mennonite missiology which will provide us with the richest material for analysis. In their enthusiasm for evangelism the early Anabaptists foreshadowed the modern missionary movement by over two hundred years. For a variety of reasons, however, such as persecution and the growth of separatist and exclusivist theology, the Anabaptists soon lost their missionary zeal and settled down to try and remain faithful and pure, becoming known as the "quiet in the land."[19] Modern Mennonite missiology has recovered the vision somewhat, and is vigorously interpreting the best of early Anabaptist approaches to mission for Christians today.

The Anabaptist Vision of Incarnational Mission

Several Anabaptist themes are linked directly to incarnational mission. Incarnational mission as discipleship is the most important emphasis, raising closely related issues such as the imitation of Christ, participation in Christ, the role of grace, and the way in which Christ is normative for Christian life. To discuss these issues we will give more attention to discipleship than to other themes. Other Anabaptist missiological themes related to incarnational mission are the theology of the cross, an emphasis on going to the margins of society, and the importance of Christian community in mission.

Discipleship as Incarnational Mission

There is no question that Anabaptist mission and discipleship are one; that is, mission is a natural dimension of the lives of ordinary believers in the course of following Jesus.[20]

This was true of the early Anabaptists, who saw every disciple as a missionary, in the sense that all were called to live out the gospel and to bear witness to its power in their lives.[21] There was no organized mission program, only the spontaneous and effective expression of the Christian message by educated and uneducated alike, in spoken word and in daily life.[22] In this they were consciously attempting to restore the vitality of the New Testament church, which also spread rapidly through the enthusiasm and lives of ordinary Christians.[23] Because they saw the call of Jesus as a call to committed discipleship, they expected their faith to make a radical difference in daily life. Their discipleship, many sources indicate, led to high standards in behavior and a concrete difference in their day to day ethics and approach to life.[24]

Discipleship and mission are also one in the contemporary Anabaptist-Mennonite view.[25] Anabaptist discipleship is to be distinguished from a discipleship of interior attitudes, pursued in an ascetic or mystical tradition. Denny Weaver writes:

> Discipleship is an assumption that one who accepts Jesus Christ will use Jesus' life and teachings as the norm within which to shape the Christian life. While those assumptions seem obvious, they are not the assumptions of the majority Christian theological tradition.[26]

Bender, in his influential restatement of the Anabaptist vision in 1943 interpreted discipleship in an inspiring way. Discipleship, he said, meant the transformation of the entire way of life of both believer and society, shaped after the teachings and example of Christ. Anabaptists, he said, demanded an outward expression of the inner experience (though we could chide Bender for even suggesting that they would allow these dualistic terms). The whole of life was to be brought under the lordship of Christ in a covenant of discipleship.[27] Christian life was to focus not so much on the inner experience of grace as on the outer application of that grace in the "Christianization of all human relationships."[28] The key phrase of the Anabaptists was not "faith in Christ" but "following Christ" ("*nachfolge Christi*" in German), with baptism as the pledge of total commitment to obey Christ.[29] They aimed to create a new life based on divine principles.[30]

This is a fully-fledged view of Christian existence as embodiment in daily life of the incarnate Christ, as plainly an incarnational model as we could imagine, with a clear missiological thrust.

In fact it is so strongly expressed that it is too optimistic about the possibility of such a life, and, we would argue, shows some theological naivety.

Lawrence Burkholder, in sympathetically interpreting the vision of his friend and colleague Bender, went even further. He wrote that *nachfolge Christi* is a life which is externally patterned after the New Testament.[31] "Christianity is the concrete and realistic 'imitation' of Christ's life and work in the context of the kingdom of God."[32] It is in this framework that mission occurs; Christ's message becomes the message of the disciple. Burkholder goes on to argue that this refers to Jesus' ministry of preaching and service, his rejection of social and political structures, his freedom from cultural attachments, his eschatological outlook, and his ethic of love and non-resistance.[33]

We note in Burkholder at least some awareness of the impossibility of copying Jesus in every detail: "The life and teachings of Christ are to be duplicated in principle and in many cases the principle determines the form."[34] Nevertheless, he is not tentative in outlining the principles and forms we should follow. There is a confident ring in his belief that the New Testament church was uniformly faithful in interpreting Jesus, and that as the earliest form it was "therefore the normative form of Christianity." [35]

The vision of discipleship we find in Bender and Burkholder is rather overwhelming, seeming to emphasize our human response to Jesus Christ, our imitation of him. In Oosterbaan's terms this is a concentration on the form of faith at the expense of its content,[36] which raises questions about whether incarnational mission in the Anabaptist tradition is an impossible dream. Our discussion of Anabaptist discipleship, then, is largely about whether incarnational mission, so understood, is even possible. It invites a brief analysis of the Anabaptist handling of the "imitation of Christ."

The "imitation of Christ" tradition: Views on what the imitation of Christ means for Christian life have varied greatly in the history of the church, ranging from a detailed copying of Jesus' life to following one or two of Jesus' attitudes such as obedience. On another axis, interpretations have also varied between those which emphasize human efforts in imitating Christ, and those which emphasize God's initiative in "conforming us to Christ." Imitation terminology seems to have been used both positively and negatively across all traditions, with a variety of meanings. John Elliott likens it to a fog which persistently wafts over the theological trenches.[37]

We will use the phrase "**the imitation of Christ**" (often found in its Latin form, *imitatio Christi*) to refer to the discipleship tradition where emphasis is put on following Christ as our model in some sense. We can visualize a spectrum of views on how we become more christlike in our Christian growth. On one extreme is "It's up to us to imitate Jesus," while on the other is "It's all God's action." We can use "the imitation of Christ" for the whole of the first half, from extreme exemplarism (at one pole) to a balance (near the center) between divine initiative and human response; always there is emphasis on our response in following Jesus Christ in daily life.

Ways of Understanding Discipleship

Imitation of Christ   Conformity to Christ

|_____|_____|

Exemplarism   A balance of God's action and ours   It is all grace

We will use the terms "**exemplarism**," "mere imitation," "external copying," or the Greek term *mimesis* (copying, imitation) to designate the belief that Jesus was our example, and that by his example we are enabled to follow in imitation. The pejorative tone of most of these terms reflects their general use by theologians.

"Conformity to Christ" will refer to the process of Christian growth towards christlikeness (however conceived) with an emphasis on God's initiative rather than human response. This covers the other half of the spectrum, ranging from a balance in the middle (where divine initiative and human response are both seen as important) to the extreme (where humans are seen to contribute nothing to the process of sanctification, seen as wholly the work of the Spirit).

The strong bias in modern Protestant theology against the imitation of Christ partly stems from the German Reformation when "Imitation of Christ piety" (*Imitatio-Christi Frömmigkeit*) became a polemical slogan hurled against any sort of "moralism, merit, monkery [and] mysticism."[38] Luther was at first influenced by writers such as Bernard of Clairvaux and Thomas á Kempis, but later he turned against imitation piety. For a start he felt the idea implied a doctrine of works. Then some of the Anabaptist groups disgusted Luther when old people played with hoops on the street in obedience to Jesus' saying that we must be like little children in order to enter the kingdom of God.[39] This animus is evident in both Protestant and Roman Catholic contemporary scholarship.[40]

There are several understandable reasons for caution towards the imitation tradition, which can be summarized under the headings of Plato, popular pietism, Pelagianism and perfectionism.

First, there has been a general desire to distance Christian discipleship from the **Platonic notion of mimesis.**[41] Alister McGrath, for example, argues that imitation "brings in its wake a whole range of ideas and attitudes that are profoundly hostile to the gospel of grace," and names the Platonic idea of *mimesis* as suggesting that we externally imitate an example, dependent on our own efforts to look like Christ.[42] For Plato, imitation was uncreative copying, as inferior as the phenomena of this world are to the ideal forms which lie behind them.[43]

Second, imitation has been associated with vulgar **piety** and attempts to imitate Jesus literally or in self-mortification, divorced from the whole idea of mission. This was particularly true in the medieval church. Bernard of Clairvaux (1090-1153) developed a mystical style of imitation, meditating systematically on each biblical scene from the life of Jesus.[44] Francis of Assisi (1181-1226) also tried to copy the life of Jesus in his itinerancy, his dress, and even the manner of his burial.[45]

Thomas á Kempis (c.1380-1471), in his classic work *The imitation of Christ*,[46] encouraged Christians to strive for perfection through discipline and a focus on the spiritual rather than the material and sensual.[47] He commended following Jesus by mortifying the flesh and building up the personal virtues of meekness, poverty of spirit, humility, purity, sorrow for sin, and peace and joy in persecution.[48] He wrote, "The stricter you are with yourself, the greater is your spiritual progress." [49]

In 1896 the American Congregational pastor Charles Sheldon wrote the devotional classic *In his steps*,[50] a book which has gone on like *The imitation of Christ* to become one of the religious best-sellers of all time.[51] Sheldon tells a fictitious story in which the reader is invited to imagine what would happen if Christians asked in every situation, "What would Jesus do?." Its title is based on a phrase from 1 Pet 2:21 (not taken in context, it must be said), a verse which follows encouragement to endure suffering and says:

> For to this you were called, because Christ also suffered for you, leaving you an example, so that you should follow in his steps.

In his steps is widely regarded as an oversimplified approach to ethics, a work of popular piety, and an unworkable model for discipleship if taken literally and alone.[52] Among ethicists *In his steps* gives the imitation of Christ a bad name due to its naivety and emphasis on "mere imitation." [53]

The third understandable reason for caution towards imitation of Christ is the danger of it being **Pelagian** in its tendency to emphasize human effort and the possibility of Christians achieving spiritual goals simply by striving.[54] Christian theology has been on the alert to this danger since the early church declared the views of Pelagius (late 4th and early 5th century) to be heretical. The debate on Pelagianism was less about Christian growth and discipleship than about human ability to take the first crucial steps towards salvation, but the links are obvious.[55] Pelagius stood clearly in the imitation tradition, suggesting that the radical demands of Jesus should be obeyed literally.[56]

The fourth understandable reason for caution is the danger of **perfectionism**. It is a small step from wanting to do one's best to feeling one has always to try even harder and aim for perfection.

Discipleship more than imitation: Set against this context of suspicion of the imitation tradition, the Anabaptist insistence on discipleship as following Jesus is distinctive. We referred above to the simple statements of Bender and Burkholder which, as they stand, seem to urge mere imitation. Are they rightly correcting a neglect of discipleship or popularizing a theologically inadequate form of imitation of Christ? It seems that in trying to do the former they have done the latter.

In fairness to Bender, in his essay *The Anabaptist vision* he says that it is by grace that we are enabled to walk the path of discipleship.[57] Bender's Christianity was never reducible to behavior and the indwelling presence of Christ was crucial to him.[58]

Nevertheless, these assumptions receive little focus in *The Anabaptist vision*. Its influence has been great in Mennonite circles for fifty years, so much so that a whole generation of Mennonite scholars has subsequently emphasized a behavioral concept of discipleship as imitation, giving only passing attention to the work of Christ and of the Spirit in transforming Christians.[59]

A vigorous debate in Mennonite circles began in 1992 with a brief article by Stephen Dintaman suggesting that this emphasis has led to a spiritual poverty among Mennonites.[60] He argued that the vision gives little insight into human behavior, appeals only to strong people who are basically in control of their lives, and says little to those who are wounded or trapped in life. He urged Mennonites to recover their awareness of the liberating work of God through Jesus' life and resurrection and in Jesus' presence today through the Holy Spirit. Dintaman cuttingly labelled the "Anabaptist vision" as "pre-pentecostal discipleship."[61] He wrote:

> There is a growing realization that the kind of heroic discipleship we espouse is meaningless to people whose lives are so chaotic that the basics of family life and moral order are not possible, let alone a life of Mennonite virtue; and that the rhetoric of heroic discipleship can and does mask the fact that many in our Mennonite communities are deeply in need of grace and healing in their own personal lives.[62]

As we suggested earlier, this debate on Mennonite identity is all about the very possibility of incarnational mission in the discipleship tradition. The question being asked is, "How can ordinary people ever hope to live heroic lives of discipleship if Christianity is merely an ideal to be fol- lowed?." If Jesus is only our example, the ideals will crush us and set us up for failure. The call is for an emphasis on the transforming power of the gospel, and for a recovery of the work of the Spirit within the lives of believers.

In terms of the spectrum in our diagram above, Mennonites are currently moving back toward the center, though still clearly located on the "imitation" side. Some Mennonite scholars have argued that this was the position of the early Anabaptists anyway. The early Anabaptists spoke often of the presence of Christ and of the church living in Christ.

For the sixteenth-century Anabaptists the Good News was the real possibility of holiness in life due not to the example of Jesus but to "the work of Christ who sets people free to respond to him."[63] Cornelius Dyck illustrates this particularly from the writings of Pilgram Marpeck, Balthasar Hubmaier and Dirk Philips. He shows that for them grace was "God coming to people in Spirit and in power."[64] The imitation of Christ was enabled by life-changing grace restoring the image of God through divine power in the lives of Christians. These Anabaptists clearly avoided saying that discipleship is imitation by human effort alone.

It is more common these days in Mennonite theology to talk of Christ's presence through the Holy Spirit, whose role is central. The Spirit draws us to God, transforms us, and begins to "make us right" in reality, and not just before God. Such an emphasis more clearly meets the pneumatological requirements for an adequate incarnational christology, as outlined in chapter 3. John Driver suggests that in conversion and discipleship our change of allegiance from the spirit of the age to the Spirit of Christ is a fundamental change of energizing power and is what it means to put on Christ, and to live in Christ.[65] The importance of the Holy Spirit is also at the center of the debate sparked by Dintaman on the Anabaptist vision.[66]

Alan Kreider, in an article on Anabaptists and suffering, demonstrates that the suffering and martyrdom of the Anabaptists was due to a vivid sense of participation in the living Christ who was transforming their lives from within but nevertheless demanded outward obedience in the form of discipleship even at the cost of suffering and death.[67] His use of "participation in Christ" leads us to consider this idea in more detail, as it occurs in the theology of Denny Weaver and John Howard Yoder, two major contemporary Mennonite theologians. It is an important way of expressing the presence of Christ in the lives of believers. Our question in looking at Yoder and Weaver is to what extent incarnational mission as the presence of Christ is woven successfully with the obvious and dominant idea of incarnational mission as following the pattern of Jesus.

Discipleship as participation in Christ: Yoder: John Howard Yoder was a Mennonite who taught theology at the (Catholic) University of Notre Dame in Indiana. He is well-known for his book *The politics of Jesus* but published extensively in the areas of peace, ecumenism and Anabaptist history.[68] He is known for seeing the church as a community which stands as a counter-sign, or prophetic alternative, to the established social order.[69]

The politics of Jesus urges the relevance of the incarnation for the social and political stances of Jesus' disciples today. It was written to use existing conclusions in biblical studies to press the point that Jesus was a model of radical political action and is relevant to, indeed normative for, modern Christian ethics.[70]

Yoder says that discipleship is a call to an ethic marked by the cross, seen as the cost of social non-conformity.[71] This cross is the only point on which we are to imitate Jesus: "Only at one point, only on one subject—but then consistently, universally—is Jesus our example: in his cross." [72]

Yoder sees in Paul's writings no concept of imitation as a general guideline which would lead us to copy Jesus' actual lifestyle of celibacy or manual work, for example.[73] Instead Yoder demonstrates the prevalence in New Testament ethics of a "participation-imitation" tradition (my compound). New Testament writers repeatedly say that the attitude or behavior of believers is to correspond to that of Jesus, or reflect or partake in it.[74]

Participating in Christ is not a loose or general concept, however. A thorough list of gospel passages shows ways in which the disciple is to share in the way of Jesus, ways such as: love of God, forgiving, loving indiscriminately, mystically living in Christ, giving oneself, serving others, subordination, condescension, suffering servanthood, innocent suffering and death as victory.[75] For Yoder these dimensions of discipleship have a strong missiological thrust because the voluntary subjection of the church will have a missionary impact on the world.[76] In Yoder's scheme, incarnational mission is to follow Jesus in a peaceful path of self-giving, reconciliation and revolutionary voluntary subordination. He sums up his comments on the ethics of Jesus as follows:

> There is thus but one realm in which the concept of imitation holds ... this is at the point of the concrete social meaning of the cross in its relation to enmity and power. Servanthood replaces dominion, forgiveness absorbs hostility. Thus—and only thus—are we bound by New Testament thought to "be like Jesus." [77]

Revising his book with comments for the second edition, Yoder discusses recent work on imitation (by A T Hanson and A E Harvey) and a passage from Bonaventure, before summing up again with crystal clarity:

None of these writers, contemporary or classic, seems to have been attending to the quite evident distinction between a naïve outward ("franciscan') replicating of the shape of Jesus' life (barefoot itinerancy, celibacy and manual labor), which never arises in the apostolic writings, and vulnerable enemy love and renunciation of dominion in the real world, which is omnipresent. The latter is far more concrete than a "broad pattern of self-giving love," [a quotation from Harvey] and the former is a red herring. Thus mainstream interpreters, even when intending to take seriously the originality and radicality of Jesus' teaching in the original setting (as Harvey certainly does at the outset) wind up eviscerating or platonizing the concreteness of the ethic of the gospel.[78]

Yoder makes it clear that his book is a corrective exercise, and he comments in the second edition that some readers seemed to have missed the paragraph near the end where he says that to emphasize Jesus' role as teacher and example is not to downplay Jesus' role as sacrifice and the believer's inward experience of forgiveness and transformation.[79]

Yet it must be said that although Yoder distances himself from imitation as copying, he is not as successful in distancing himself from discipleship as a human response to an example. There is little mention of the resurrection, of the Holy Spirit, and of the nature of the mystical element of participation in Christ. Even given his purpose, there seems to be an overstatement of the social and political nature of the new community without sufficiently addressing how we actually achieve this radical self-giving and reconciliation. Without more talk of the power of the risen Christ Yoder is in danger of simply advocating heroic discipleship. In interpreting classic Pauline passages about justification by faith almost purely in terms of removing the social barriers between Jew and Gentile, Yoder is in danger of overlooking the barriers between humans and God which are also broken by the incarnation.

Discipleship as solidarity in Christ: Weaver: J Denny Weaver teaches theology and ethics at Bluffton College, a Mennonite college in Ohio, and has written extensively on Anabaptist distinctives in general and Anabaptist christology in particular.[80]

In his widely read book *Becoming Anabaptist: The origin and significance of sixteenth-century Anabaptism*, Weaver strongly emphasizes discipleship in terms of following the ethical example of Jesus.[81] While he acknowledges that there was diversity among sixteenth-century Anabaptists he shows that crucial among the themes common to the several Anabaptist groups was "the idea of discipleship or following of Jesus, or a Christocentrism which made both the life and teaching of Jesus normative for the community of the church."[82] In so doing he gives only passing attention to the work of Christ in enabling Christians to experience new life.[83] On the spectrum we defined above, Weaver seems in *Becoming Anabaptist* to be close to the left end, emphasizing human response at the expense of the enabling role of Jesus Christ. As an example of Weaver's strong statements consider this passage:

> Discipleship means that the essence of Christianity is following Jesus, that is, obeying his teaching and following his example.... Jesus' teaching and example become the standards for those who would be part of the kingdom of God. Those who fail to accept this standard thereby demonstrate that they do not belong to the kingdom of God or acknowledge Jesus as Lord.[84]

Elsewhere, however, Weaver pays much more attention to the work of Christ in discipleship. He persuasively argues that despite the diversity of early Anabaptism the idea of discipleship as solidarity in Christ unites much of the radical reformation, and is seen in the work of Hans Denck, Michael Sattler, Conrad Grebel and Balthasar Hubmaier.

> The solidarity principle includes the ideas of discipleship and imitatio christi, but is also broader than these. The principle assumes not only that believers will follow the model of Jesus' teaching and acts, as Bender said, but also that believers participate in his work and he in theirs, if they are to be counted as members of Christ's body. The solidarity principle thus also includes, in some form, the idea of the present body of Christ as an extension of the incarnation of its head.[85]

For example, Denck tried to preserve both human freedom and divine initiative, referring to Paul's words: "It is no longer I who live, but it is Christ who lives in me" (Gal 2:20), and "I worked harder than any of them—though it was not I, but the grace of God that is with me" (1 Cor 15:10). For Denck grace was central as the means for turning to God.[86] Denck is often quoted in modern Anabaptist writings as insisting that we cannot know Christ except in discipleship. This is only part of what he wrote. The sentence following the famous passage is equally important, insisting as it does that the Christ who calls us also empowers us to respond. The two sentences together read as follows:

The Means to God however is Christ, whom no one may know unless [one] follow after him with [one's] life. And no one may follow after him except as [one] already knows him.[87]

There is a case for this simple but profound statement being considered the high point of the Anabaptist understanding of incarnational mission. It locks together the two dimensions of Jesus as pattern for mission and Christ as empowering presence in mission.

In reminding us of the balance in Denck's writing, Weaver illustrates a contemporary Anabaptist emphasis on solidarity in Christ, a phrase which seems to have a similar meaning to "participation in Christ." In other writings he repeatedly argues for the re-uniting of christology and ethics, which he sees as separated by the ontological approach of the Chalcedonian formulation.[88] While Weaver is more often found arguing for the importance of obedience and discipleship, he always acknowledges that Jesus is the "agent of salvation," "instigator of our new life" and "agent of forgiveness."[89] In this way he is arguing for a fusing of soteriology and ethics as well; ethics and salvation coincide.[90]

Discipleship and grace: Both Yoder and Weaver are more concerned to argue for the centrality of discipleship and obedience than to explain in detail the other side of the coin, the gift of grace in enabling Christians to live this new transformed life. This leads us to consider the role that grace plays in Anabaptist thought. James Moffatt once wrote that "the truth of grace forms an acid test for all moralistic interpretations of the Christian religion."[91] Does the Anabaptist-Mennonite tradition pass this acid test, or is its incarnational approach fatally flawed by an over-emphasis on human efforts to follow Jesus?

"Grace" is traditionally used in theology to refer to God's free giving towards humanity, and is usually connected to the undeserved enabling of a transformed relationship between God and humanity through the work of Jesus Christ. It is one of the most widely used Christian terms, and yet is one of the hardest to define.[92] Although we often use "grace" to refer to a particular action of God, and it has developed a number of technical and secondary meanings, it generally refers to the gratuitous quality of God's love in all of God's dealings with humanity.[93] It has the two dimensions of forgiveness, emphasized by Protestantism, and transformation of our lives, emphasized by Orthodoxy and Catholicism; these two are often labelled justifying grace and sanctifying grace.[94]

The context in which Anabaptism developed was, of course, Luther's insistence on grace as central to Christian faith. For Luther grace was like a favor, the free gift of salvation totally independent of the merit of the recipient. It was justifying grace, changing our status before God but, following Augustine's interpretation of Paul, not changing our essential human condition, so leaving us, in Luther's famous phrase, simultaneously justified and yet sinners (*simul justus et peccator*).

The early Anabaptists protested strongly against this "forensic" view of justification, which seemed to treat conversion as a mere change of legal status before God, a change from being guilty to being undeservedly declared blameless. They charged the Reformers with being antinomian, that is, emphasizing pure grace so much that they ignored the call to live differently.[95] Denck wrote sarcastically: "Isn't it a shame that we wish to learn to know Christ and nevertheless retain our old godless nature?"[96] Hubmaier also wrote:

> As soon as one says to them, "It is written: Leave evil and do good," Ps.37:27, they answer, "We can do no good. Everything happens out of the providence of God and from necessity." They imagine that by that they are permitted to sin.[97]

The second charge was that of "cheap grace." Anticipating the critique of Dietrich Bonhoeffer by over four hundred years, Menno Simons accused the Reformers of turning the "grace of God into lasciviousness' by preaching only what the people wanted to hear and using our inability to do anything of our own volition as an excuse for remaining in our sinful life.[98]

The early Anabaptists related grace to discipleship much more than to salvation. They emphasized the enabling power of grace in daily Christian life, but grace was integrally involved in both conversion and subsequent Christian living. Grace as enabling power both awakened faith and transformed the new Christian. The Anabaptists were therefore similar to and yet different from both Catholicism and Protestantism. They shared with Catholicism an emphasis on sanctifying grace, but felt that Catholicism tolerated a lowest common denominator in Christian behavior, expecting only monks to pursue a genuinely committed Christian life. They shared with Protestantism its emphasis on the freedom of personal forgiveness but saw Protestantism as almost exclusively linking grace to personal forgiveness, at the expense of a transformed life.

Alvin Beachy, in a landmark study on the concept of grace in the Radical Reformation, defends the Anabaptists from the Reformers' charges that they were "works-righteousness people" who did not know the meaning of grace.[99] He demonstrates with many passages from early Anabaptist writing that grace was seen as the action of God in working an ontological change in Christian believers, that is, a real metaphysical change within human nature. He concludes:

> Grace is God's act whereby [God] renews the divine image in [us] through the Holy Spirit and makes the believer a participant in the divine nature. The Radicals did not think that this grace could be earned through any meritorious work. It came as a sheer gift from God.[100]

Anabaptists saw in varying ways the ontological change which takes place through grace, but placed the accent on the activity of God, and maintained the distinction between the once-and-for-all character of Jesus and our Spirit-enabled attempts to follow him. Moreover, there was no talk of Christians attaining sinlessness or perfection on earth.[101] Menno Simons wrote that all Christians "daily sigh over their poor unsatisfactory evil flesh, the manifest errors and faults of their weak lives."[102] We can see the Anabaptists were careful in their talk of the divinization of Christians not to imply that we follow by our own efforts, become fully divine or attain perfection on the pilgrimage. They saw the Holy Spirit "both as *enabling grace* and *motivating power* within the new life of the Christian." [103]

The emphasis on grace as God's initiating activity, God's free gift, the application in our lives of Christ's atoning work, and the enabling power of the Holy Spirit, is found widely in contemporary Mennonite scholars, though in varying degrees. Among the scholars surveyed above, Harold Bender, Denny Weaver and John Yoder represent those who strongly stress obedience and discipleship while at least acknowledging the importance of grace. We could also include John Driver[104] and Norman Kraus.[105] Others, such as Alvin Beachy, Cornelius Dyck,[106] Robert Friedmann,[107] Walter Klaassen,[108] Arnold Snyder,[109] and J C Wenger[110] echo more clearly the early Anabaptist emphasis on grace as both enabling and transforming, involving both God's initiative in Christ and our response in discipleship. The current debate on Anabaptist spirituality sparked off by Dintaman's article on the poverty of the Anabaptist vision indicates that this issue of the role of grace in discipleship is a central one for the identity of Mennonites today.[111]

None of this discussion of grace suggests that the Anabaptists and Mennonites are guilty of the charge of works-righteousness, taken to mean that they believe that salvation can be won by human effort. Christian theology has always struggled to say exactly how God is at work in us while we are nevertheless responsible for our actions. The Anabaptist-Mennonite tradition falls within the broad parameters of classical Christian thought, which in various ways asserts both sides of the tension, that it is the Spirit of God who awakens us with the Good News and enables us to respond, and yet that we have the freedom to respond or not, and as we turn to Christ in discipleship we have some part to play in daily Christian living. The Anabaptist-Mennonite expression of this balance, in insisting on the indissolubility of grace and response, of faith and works, and of belief and action, undoubtedly emphasizes discipleship and obedience, but in general does not fall into the theological traps of exemplarism and perfectionism. It is, therefore, an example of incarnational mission which emphasizes Jesus as a pattern for mission but without totally neglecting Christ as enabling presence in mission.

Discipleship: What are disciples to follow? We noted above that the discipleship tradition accepts Jesus' life and teaching as the norm which shapes the Christian's life; it finds it hard to understand why this seemingly obvious assumption is not held by the majority of Christians.[112] This raises the question of what it is that Christians should follow in the example of Jesus. If Jesus is the pattern for incarnational mission, what is the shape of that pattern?

John Howard Yoder is the clearest in outlining what is normative in the life of Jesus. We have noted his insistence that Christians are not called to imitate Jesus except in one thing, and that is to take up the cross daily. The cross has a concrete social meaning in relation to overcoming enmity and domination.[113]

By working through many biblical passages which give direction to followers of Jesus, Yoder reminds readers of the extremes to which Jesus calls his followers. We are called to be pure and holy, forgive others, love our enemies, live as Christ lived, die and be raised with Christ, love one another, serve as Jesus did, share his sufferings, and even surrender our lives as Jesus did.[114] A close reading of the Synoptic Gospels by Donald Kraybill yields a similar picture, in which we experience the gracious presence of God among us as an upside-down kingdom, a new order of things that is radical, revolutionary, and full of social as well as religious implications.[115]

Yoder summarizes a great variety of biblical passages by saying that the big themes are (1) renunciation of power and domination, (2) the abandonment of earthly security, (3) the challenge Jesus poses to worldly powers, and (4) the likely antagonism of the world. The social implications of taking up the cross are clear and sometimes costly. The issues of power, violence and the dignity of people were central in Jesus' time and are again central issues for Christian discipleship.[116]

Anabaptists argue that not only the style of Jesus' life but also his teaching call us clearly towards a non-violent stance, a non-hierarchical (or perhaps inverse-hierarchical) perspective on status and power, the practice of Christian discipleship as a voluntary and serious commitment, and Christian community as a clear alternative to the ways of the world. This comes through repeatedly in Anabaptist writing, both from the sixteenth and twentieth centuries. Jesus is seen as both model for our behavior and the means of our transformation.[117]

We would argue for some caution in drawing ethical lines directly from the life of Jesus to our own context. It is not straightforward for several reasons. (1) We simply do not have a clear picture of the historical Jesus to use as a template even if that were the right way to tackle ethical issues. (2) There are serious hermeneutical issues, that is, issues of interpretation, involved in using biblical passages, located as they are in a variety of situations and perspectives in the first century. (3) We all tend to emphasize some passages and neglect others in forming our overall picture of the gospel or the life of Jesus. (4) Two thousand years of Christian ethics informs us and complicates the picture. (5) Finally, many ethical issues are either situated in a totally new social context or did not exist in biblical times.

There are times when due recognition of this complexity in Christian ethics is given in Anabaptist writing. For example, Yoder writes in *The politics of Jesus* that although his central purpose is to show the relevance of the ethic of Jesus for modern disciples, he is "not affirming a specific biblical ethical content for modern questions."[118] He shows awareness of the role of theological interpretation and the importance of context in interpreting scripture for another time.[119]

There are other times, however, when Anabaptists seem to say without qualification that Jesus is the norm for our daily life, as if the specifics are obvious, and as if the difficult work of hermeneutics and Christian ethics is not needed. The danger here is that incarnational mission seen as following Jesus as pattern is made to sound straightforward in principle. The task of discerning how Jesus is normative in daily life is, on the contrary, a demanding, ambiguous, and ongoing one.

The positive contribution of the Anabaptist call to regard Jesus as normative is to present a radical alternative to other schools of Christian ethics. It challenges those perspectives which regard Christianity as calling us to "be human," as if Jesus were part of God's call to all people to grow into a full humanity already discernible within the human spirit.[120] The Anabaptist vision is a radical one, based on the new and seemingly "upside-down" values of Jesus, which are bound to cause a clash with the world around us. Incarnational mission for the Anabaptists, mission which both follows and participates in Jesus Christ, is always going to be distinctive, critical of culture, vulnerable, and servant-like, and therefore perhaps destined to be a minority while the present order lasts.

We have examined Anabaptist views of discipleship at length because Anabaptist mission has always occurred as a natural result of committed discipleship, seen as the concrete following of Jesus in daily life. It has led us to consider the imitation of Christ and the writings of Yoder and Weaver, and to conclude that Anabaptism emphasizes imitation but recognizes the work of God in enabling Christian response. We have also considered the relationship of grace and works, and (briefly) the way in which Jesus is normative for Christian ethics. Most of the dimensions of Anabaptist incarnational mission have thus been raised already.

We now turn to consider more briefly three other themes, namely the Anabaptist theology of the cross, Good News to the poor, and the Christian community as a sign of the kingdom.

Mission is Shaped by the Cross

The early Anabaptists knew from experience that the life of discipleship may involve suffering, rejection and even death. Yoder unpacks the meaning of the cross in these terms, which are representative of many Anabaptist theologians, even if more political in tone than some:

The believer's cross must be, like his [or her] Lord's, the price of ... social nonconformity. It is not, like sickness or catastrophe, an inexplicable, unpredictable suffering; it is the end of a path freely chosen after counting the cost. It is not, like Luther's or Thomas Müntzer's or Zinzendorf's or Kierkegaard's cross ..., an inward wrestling of the sensitive soul with self and sin; it is the social reality of representing in an unwilling world the Order to come.[121]

The Anabaptists share this emphasis on the cruciform nature of incarnational mission with many missiologists, particularly Bonhoeffer, Moltmann and the liberation theologians, all of whom remind us of the costly nature of this path.[122]

In light of this emphasis on the cross, it might be argued that the resurrection is not given sufficient weight in some contemporary Mennonite missiology. To take some notable examples, Yoder hardly mentions the resurrection in *The politics of Jesus* and John Driver gives almost no attention to the resurrection in his *Understanding the atonement for the mission of the church*.[123] On the other hand, the resurrection gets attention in Kraus's *Jesus Christ our Lord* and in *The transfiguration of mission*, a collection edited by Shenk.[124]

The balance between the cross and the resurrection is perhaps found in the language of the "crucified and risen Christ." The resurrection is the basis of our experience of the risen presence of Christ, but the Christ we know is the crucified Christ. The resurrection, writes Thorwald Lorenzen,

reveals that in and with the death of Jesus, God has continued in a decisive way what Jesus began during his life—to struggle against the forces of sin, evil and death—and from this struggle God has emerged as the victor. That is the triumph of the resurrection of the crucified Christ.[125]

The Anabaptists remind us, however, that our experience as disciples, even though perhaps suffused with resurrection presence and joy, will generally be a costly and demanding commitment, as the kingdom is not yet fully present. While the poor remain poor and the lost remain lost, disciples can expect suffering and rejection, and mission takes the shape of the mission of Jesus: that of the cross. Jesus calls us, nevertheless, to gain life by losing it, and the paradox of the cross-and-resurrection is found in such a perspective. Incarnational mission, on this view, is costly and in various ways leads to suffering.

Incarnational Mission Means Going to the Margins

Anabaptism shares with liberation theology not only a focus on the life and teaching of Jesus, but also (as a consequence) a special concern for the poor, outcast and oppressed. This view of the incarnation emphasizes the double significance of the life of Jesus: Jesus expresses God's solidarity with humankind, and also expresses God's particular solidarity with the voiceless and the powerless. If discipleship is central in mission, then solidarity with the poor is central too. The social location and social and economic teachings of Jesus are part of our understanding of who he is and what our mission is. As José Míguez Bonino says, in outlining what liberation theology and Anabaptist missiology have in common:

> Jesus' option for the poor and his identification with the helpless and defenseless belong now to the heart of any authentic theology. Christ did not *also* do that: he *was* that ... and so his disciple![126]

The early Anabaptists did not articulate this much; they just lived it out. As with liberation theology and its practice, Anabaptism grew largely from the peasant classes, despite enjoying some educated leadership.[127]

Illustrating the liberationist argument that what you can see depends largely on where you stand, early Anabaptists, mostly poor, turned to the Bible to find in their plain reading of it that Jesus was born into a simple working-class family, lived among the ordinary people, showed sympathy to the socially excluded, harshly criticized the rich and respectable, and taught that all humans should love and care for each other.[128] Sebastian Lotzer, representative of the ideas of other Anabaptist peasant writings, wrote a tract in 1523 expressing socially radical ideas.[129] "God almighty has always given and announced his holy Word only to simple, pious and unaffected people, as when he was about to be born, it was announced to the shepherds, not to the learned men and Pharisees," he wrote.[130]

Much of the good news to the poor in early Anabaptism stemmed less from a theology of special concern for the poor than from practices such as the priesthood of all believers, the rejection of the magistracy and other hierarchical social structures, the sharing of goods, the acceptance that the Holy Spirit could speak through all regardless of social rank, and the insistence that Christians match in their lives the biblical injunctions to love each other and see Christ in the poor and imprisoned.

There were a few strands of thought which emphasized the rights of the poor in society, from reformist tendencies in early Swiss Anabaptism to the violent and unsuccessful revolt of the peasants of Münster. Unfortunately the Anabaptists soon sharply distinguished between the fellowship of believers, in which radical sharing should take place, and the world outside, where God's laws could not be expected to work. In this way the egalitarianism and communalism which was such good news for the Anabaptist poor was not extended to social action for the poor in wider society.[131]

Contemporary Mennonite missiology is much clearer in articulating the significance of the life of Jesus for action on behalf of the poor. Few church traditions are as clear and consistent in enabling us to understand the biblical material on God's interest in the poor.[132]

For example, John Driver argues forcefully that in the person of Jesus the gospel comes to us from socio-economic and political weakness rather than from human power. It comes, in social and political terms, from below rather than from above. Driver lists the same biblical material as do the radical evangelicals and liberation theologians: Galilee as the periphery of Judaism; Jesus' emphasis on the disenfranchised such as the Samaritans, the poor, the prostitutes, the publicans, those with leprosy, foreigners, women and children; his revolutionary social teaching; and so on.[133] Driver urges us to shape our mission according to the keys we find in Jesus' life, death and resurrection, in which we discover God's saving presence in the world.[134]

A second example is found in Linford Stutzman's *With Jesus in the world: Mission in modern, affluent societies*, which recommends a particular social strategy for incarnational mission.[135]

Stutzman identifies social location as a key missiological issue. Where we choose to live and work, that is, the incarnational choice we make, ultimately determines the impact our mission will have.[136] This is Stutzman's definition of the incarnational approach to mission, then: the deliberate choice of social position out of which to witness.[137]

He sketches a sociological model of modern, affluent societies in which there are three groups: the establishment at one end, the marginalized at the other, and the middle-class majority in the middle.[138] When analysed in terms of power and hope, the majority falls into two groups. One, which Stutzman calls Majority B, tries to gain power through aligning with the establishment and pins its hopes on attaining a better share of benefits in the status quo. The other, called Majority A, arises from the marginalized end of the majority group. Its members tend be more aware of the plight of the marginalized, motivated by hope for a better world, gripped by belief in the possibility of change and prepared to take personal risks to achieve those ideals. Put simply, social action often arises from the marginalized end of the middle-class, those with sufficient power and hope to act, and yet sufficiently close to the periphery for a social vision to be kindled.

Stutzman's main argument is that "Jesus incarnated and preached the good news of the kingdom from social position A within the social spectrum ... raising the hope of the marginalized from a position of proximity to them."[139] He argues in some detail that the early church emerged from a similar social position, even though there were many members from all parts of the social spectrum. So did the Anabaptist movement.[140]

His understanding of incarnational mission as "being in society the way Jesus was' is very clear, and his call strong, when he summarizes his critique of the modern Western church:

> The fact is that churches which consistently proclaim and live out the gospel message, visibly demonstrating the radical hope of the coming kingdom after the manner of Jesus and the early church, are the exception. Churches with a message counter to the tired values of the establishment in modern affluent societies are rare. Churches which are in society in the way Jesus was in his are a tiny minority indeed.[141]

Without suggesting that they will necessarily be always effective, Stutzman offers several ways for a missionary in an affluent society to be incarnational in mission: contextualizing the gospel; working slowly through personal relationships, networks and alliances towards social change; seeking out those who are both "insiders" and social critics; and eating and drinking with the non-Christians all about us.[142]

The two examples we have considered, those of Driver and Stutzman, illustrate two views, the liberationist perspective as found within Mennonitism-Anabaptism, and a more sociologically nuanced argument situating incarnational mission between the middle-class and the totally marginalized.

Like all Christian traditions, Anabaptism does not always live up to its own vision. Writing as "one of the family," and as the founder of Evangelicals for Social Action in the United States, Ronald Sider suggests that the big question to Anabaptism from liberation theology is whether "the wealthy Mennonite church in North America and Western Europe has any intention of living what the Bible teaches about the poor." [143]

An Alternative Community

The Anabaptists share with the whole believers' church tradition an ecclesiology closely linked to missiology. That is, what it is to be the church is inseparable from what it is to be on mission. The church is seen as a covenant community of committed believers living as a sign in the midst of the world. The label "believers' church" has only been used widely since a conference on the theme in Kentucky in 1967 and the publication of a book by that title the following year. [144] The conference definition reflected Anabaptist emphases in defining the believers' church in mission terms:

> The congregation is called out of the wider society for a communal existence within and for, yet distinct from, the structures and values of the rest of the world. This distinctness from the world is the presupposition of a missionary and servant ministry to the world. At times it demands costly opposition to the world. [145]

This approach is based on the biblical material which talks of reconciliation as the making of a new creation (2 Cor 5:17), a new humanity (Eph 2:10, 15) and the bringing of a new peace (Eph 2:14-17, Col 1:20). It reflects the biblical theme of the new community, which together is the body of Christ. The missionary structure of this community lies in its provisional nature as an instrument of God's intention to establish shalom for all people in ways that will transcend the church and even history as we know it. [146]

Incarnational mission, seen from this angle, is essentially communal. It is the partial embodiment of the "kingdom presence" of God. It is the church as sign of the kingdom. It requires that the church actually represent an alternative piety, alternative politics, alternative set of relationships, alternative society, alternative approach to possessions, and so on. This is the meaning of the slogan by Hans Kasdorf: "As the believers' church is Christocentric, so its mission is ecclesiocentric." [147]

Larry Miller illustrates typical Anabaptist idealism when he writes provocatively:

> Is it unreasonable to believe that only churches with this particular identity—alternative, voluntary, missionary, pacifist microsocieties—can be instruments of Messiah's transfigured mission? ... Only churches which are alternative societies, transformed in relation to existing society because they are already conformed to Messiah's vision of the future, can demonstrate the nature of life in the coming kingdom.[148]

Other traditions may find Miller's uncompromising language difficult to take. Yet the way Anabaptists stress the witness of the Christian community in incarnational mission is echoed in different ways across the Christian traditions. Incarnational mission implies that the gospel must become visible (flesh) in the lives of Christians if its power is to be felt by others. The corporate nature of Christian witness is an important dimension of this vision.

Our survey of Anabaptist emphases in mission shows that incarnational mission, seen dominantly as a style of mission and yet also as participation in the incarnational presence of Christ in authentic mission, is a central aspect of Anabaptist thinking.

Anabaptist writing is full of references to the incarnation as the strategy of mission used by God and therefore to be used by us.[149] Wilbert Shenk writes, "The fundamental missionary stance is that of the servant. The strategy is the incarnation. The sign marking the way of mission is the cross."[150] In contrast to the way many conservative evangelicals almost exclusively emphasize the atoning work of Jesus as if his whole life were geared toward one cosmic transaction, Anabaptists see the whole of Jesus' life, his death and his resurrection being of a piece. What Jesus did, how it led to his death, and the significance of the resurrection as God's seal on Jesus' obedience are all fundamental to the nature of our mission. "The salvation of God's community depends on the life, death, and resurrection of Christ in their entirety." [151]

As Shenk puts it, incarnational missiology will always be "missiology enroute," continually tested and applied as the Christian community "witnesses to the world of its own experience of being transformed through encounter with the Messiah."[152] The strengths of Anabaptist missiology have come through clearly. It remains to offer some evaluative comments on some of the potential weaknesses in the Anabaptist set of perspectives and practices.

Evaluative Comments

We have noted, in discussing Anabaptist emphases in mission, how its incarnational approach, based both on the life and teaching of Jesus and participation in Christ, has led at its best to a vigorous holding together of christology, ecclesiology and missiology, in which there is a unity of faith and action, a clear call to an alternative social reality, a preparedness to suffer and face rejection in following the way of the cross, an emphasis on all believers and their daily life, and a clear commitment to the poor. In terms of the criteria we listed for an adequate theology, we can say broadly that it faithfully interprets the Christian tradition, addresses contemporary human existence, articulates Christian experience, leads to transforming action and is intelligible and coherent.[153] It also reflects the relevant requirements of an adequate contemporary incarnational christology, particularly in being trinitarian, acknowledging the role of the Spirit, salvation-oriented, and (notably) issuing naturally in incarnational mission.[154]

It should be clear that we are in basic sympathy with the Anabaptist vision. Nevertheless, there are several aspects of it which deserve critique, or at least some caution about their inherent dangers.

Withdrawal from the World

The language of the Schleitheim Confession, a significant early Anabaptist document arising from a conference of Anabaptist leaders at Schleitheim, Switzerland in 1527, is startling to the modern ear. The fourth of its seven articles declares that the Anabaptists will have nothing to do with the wicked world. There are only the opposite realms of light and darkness, Christ and the devil, discipleship and unbelief, and the two opposites will have no part with the other.[155] Earlier we applauded the clear alternative offered to the world by a committed community of discipleship. Now we see the less helpful side of providing an alternative, namely withdrawal as a mission strategy. It is muted and even disavowed in Mennonite missiology today, but has been a dominant theme in Anabaptism from the start.

The early Anabaptists drew a thick line between what was of Christ (and therefore within Anabaptist fellowships!) and the rest of the world, which was of Satan.[156] This reflected a strongly dualistic view of reality.[157]

The liberation theologian Bonino strongly objects to this view. He argues convincingly that Christians cannot simply withdraw and ignore the world as if it is full of falsehood, oppression and death. The reality of the world is ambiguous; it is also the cosmos and the humanity that God created and cares about. Bonino acknowledges that modern Anabaptists moderate the extent of withdrawal and dualism, talking instead of counter-cultural communities, standing as parables, testifying to an alternative way which God wills for all humanity. Nevertheless, this still over-emphasizes God the Redeemer and a futuristic eschatology at the expense of God the Creator (evident in the goodness of all creation) and God the Holy Spirit (evident working in the world today).[158]

Moltmann puts the same critique, suggesting that it is only in apocalyptic times that the Christian community has had to stand in such opposition to the world,[159] implying perhaps that while there might have been justification for such a stance in the turbulent, corrupt and dangerous times of the European Reformation, the opportunity for engagement in modern democratic societies is much greater.

Charles Scriven, a Seventh Day Adventist with strong Anabaptist leanings, offers a constructive middle way between the rhetoric of non-engagement and the call for total engagement. In a bold and fascinating study of H Richard Niebuhr's ethics Scriven argues that if Niebuhr had been consistent he would have moved in an Anabaptist direction. Scriven suggests that Niebuhr's famous phrase "Christ against culture," applied by Niebuhr to Anabaptists,[160] is nonsense, because all people are part of culture and cannot be "against culture."[161] He outlines in some detail an approach which starts from the classic Anabaptist position of living out an alternative, but develops it in the direction of Niebuhr's favored type, called "Christ the transformer of culture."[162] Scriven argues:

> The church serves the surrounding culture by being an alternative society and a transformative example. In this way it is, under God, an agent of social conversion, midwiving a world whose form is Christ.
>
> For what the radical heritage holds up before us is nothing less than the prospect of social change through the witness of small groups—cells of

Christians, if you please, who by their solidarity with Christ remake the world.[163]

The question of the extent to which Christians ought to be involved in the world around us is not one which can be solved in general terms but needs to be wrestled with in each situation. Scriven at the least offers a model which occupies the middle ground, between the tendency of Anabaptist missiology to speak of withdrawal from the world, and the opposite tendency, where the danger is that the church loses its identity in service to the world.

Lack of Social Responsibility

The second reservation worth expressing about the Anabaptist approach to mission follows from the first and concerns the difficulty of developing a sustained program of social responsibility in a vision which often criticizes social structures trenchantly "from outside" and sustains a rhetoric of withdrawal, "alternative society," or "kingdom communities." There is a danger that Anabaptist groups will only be able to speak practically on personal and communal ethics within discipleship communities, while being unable to engage in the compromise and cut-and-thrust of real-world politics, economics, and social policy-making.

In his study of early Anabaptists Alvin Beachy concluded that while there were positive sides to the idea of a voluntary and separate church, the negative side was its inability to take part in government and the administration of justice.[164] Some Anabaptists said the state was necessary; they just could not take part in it. Following the example of Jesus, they felt they could not use force in maintaining law and order, swear oaths, and subscribe to capital punishment. Their eschatological sense was keen and they did not fit in an ongoing society occupied with what Bonhoeffer later called "penultimate things."[165] This has remained an element of the Anabaptist-Mennonite tradition. "Yet," asks Beachy, "one must ask whether the disciple who admits the need for the state has any right to unload the whole burden of social responsibility upon the shoulders of others."[166]

As early as 1957, Burkholder put the dilemma eloquently, speaking as a committed Anabaptist. He asks why the church as a whole has rejected the Anabaptist notion of discipleship and mission:

> The answer seems to lie in the area of social responsibility. The church has not known how to correlate the demands of the kingdom with the demands of world order.... The church has not known how to face the problems of culture, the complexities of economic life, and the prevention of social chaos with the Gospel ethic alone. It has never known how to correlate the social responsibilities of a Christian majority with the ethic of complete love. It has not been able to translate the personal ethics of discipleship into a social ethic embracing the structures of human society.[167]

Burkholder identifies a potential weakness in the Anabaptist perspective on incarnational mission. It tends to see things in absolute terms, in such a way that the ambiguities of political and economical life are difficult to handle. It provides few tools with which positively to relate "Christ's ethical absolutism" to the world.[168] Another danger of such ethical absolutism is the perfectionism we have already mentioned.

He also identifies a tendency to be unable to correlate the shape of the kingdom with society here on earth. Although Anabaptists see radical communities as pointing toward the kingdom, we may ask what shape that kingdom has if all approximations to it in government and wider society fall so short that Christians must always seek a minority alternative. Perhaps in the minds of some Anabaptists the goal of incarnational mission is really eschatological in the sense of being in the distant future and other-worldly.

In fairness to contemporary Anabaptism we must acknowledge that despite Anabaptist thought pointing clearly in the direction of withdrawal from society or setting up alternative social structures, the current practice of many Mennonites tells a different story. There are many examples of Mennonites contributing to specific improvements in social policy and practice, such as peacemaking activities, conciliation structures in the state corrections area and mediation in the legal area, to mention just a few.

An Ethical Christianity for Heroic Disciples

The third and final reservation about the Anabaptist approach to discipleship has been discussed above. There is a danger (and it is only a danger) that the Anabaptist vision will be reduced to an ethical one, the call for Christian disciples to walk a heroic path in trying to follow Jesus, who reached heights we can never reach. Such a reduced vision lacks grace and is a crushing one.[169]

The holding together of believing and doing is a central Anabaptist tenet, but can prove difficult to handle. "Once doing became a part of faith, the tendency was to concentrate on human action at the expense of trusting solely in God's grace."[170] This was the basis on which Luther rejected Anabaptism without qualification, believing it to be works-righteousness, without a sense of dependence on God.

We have noted the way various Anabaptist theologians handle the combination of grace and obedience, particularly through the use of phrases such as "participation in Christ" and "solidarity in Christ."[171] Nevertheless, we have also noted that some Anabaptists strongly emphasize our human response to Jesus' example, at the expense of talk about the initiative of the Holy Spirit in awakening and sustaining our response.[172] We also drew attention to the current controversy among Mennonites, started by an article by Stephen Dintaman in which he pointed to the spiritual poverty of the dominant interpretation of Bender's *The Anabaptist vision*.[173] Dintaman is critical of what he calls the theological reductionism of casting the language of faith into exclusively sociological and activist frameworks.[174]

We have seen that it is possible for Anabaptists to express the unity of faith and action in a way that appropriately acknowledges the role of grace and the work of the Holy Spirit. Dintaman may simply have hit a nerve and prompted a restatement of the Anabaptist vision for twenty-first century Mennonitism. If so, the danger we see may not be a problem.

Summary

In the Anabaptist idea of discipleship, or the following of Christ, we have a full-bodied expression of incarnational mission. At times it seems that the Anabaptist idea of incarnational mission is reduced to the imitation of Christ, or less literally, radical obedience to Christ, with a strong emphasis on our human response. At other times expressions such as "participation in Christ" and "solidarity in Christ" serve to emphasize the gracious and active presence of Christ in the discipleship community, enabling response and transforming the daily lives of those who follow. The Anabaptist vision is radical, committed and communal, and is seen to apply to all Christians and their mission in daily life. It is closely linked to the crucified and risen Christ, and allows incarnational mission to be shaped by the way of the cross. As a result of its focus on the life and teaching of Jesus it has a special concern for the poor. Despite potential dangers in its withdrawing from the world, at its best it carries the vision of transforming the world through living out incarnationally a clear alternative which points, as did the mission of Jesus, to the kingdom of God.

In the next chapter we turn to consider a tradition which self-consciously owes a great deal to the Anabaptists, radical evangelicalism.

CHAPTER 5

A HOLISTIC KINGDOM THEOLOGY: RADICAL EVANGELICALISM

The group which most uses the term "incarnational mission" in missiological literature is undoubtedly the left wing of evangelicalism, those loosely known as the radical evangelicals. Consider a typical example of the use of the term by one of the leading exponents of radical evangelicalism, Orlando Costas, in a passage outlining the missiological implications of the incarnation. (Costas uses "incarnation" here to mean Jesus' birth and life.)

> [It] was out of the mystery of the incarnation, to which Jesus' resurrection and death bear witness, that the early Christian community began to understand its mission as participation in the continuing mission of Jesus Christ. The church is to follow the pattern of the incarnation because it is the body of Christ indwelled by his Spirit: the new people of the God whose Son became flesh in Jesus of Nazareth by the power of the Holy Spirit.[1]

In this chapter we will first briefly identify radical evangelicalism. Then we will examine the meaning of incarnational mission in radical evangelical literature. This will lead us to examine the role of Jesus as pattern for mission and as presence in mission, and then to look briefly at seven major themes of radical evangelical mission, each of which points to an aspect of incarnational mission: kingdom theology, the lordship of Christ, discipleship, holistic mission, good news to the poor, community and contextualization. We will conclude with some evaluative comments.

The Radical Evangelicals

The Group

As a self-conscious movement radical evangelicalism grew from the spontaneous gathering of a group of radically minded delegates at the Lausanne Congress on World Evangelization in 1974 who responded to presentations by René Padilla, Samuel Escobar and Costas. A group of about two hundred delegates ("the Radical Discipleship group") met and drew up a document called "Response to Lausanne," published in the official volume of papers as "Theology and implications of radical discipleship."[2] Partly due to its origins and partly due to its concern for the poor the movement has a strong Third World focus, though radical evangelicals are found all over the world.[3]

Let us list some of those who have published in English in a radical evangelical vein. Those with Latin American roots or teaching positions include Costas, Escobar and Padilla as well as Guillermo Cook,[4] Emilio Núñez[5] and John Driver.[6] From India but now in Oxford are Vinay Samuel (Indian) and Christopher Sugden (British missionary to India).[7] Some from North America are Jim Wallis,[8] Donald Kraybill,[9] Richard Mouw,[10] George Williamson[11] and Wes Michaelson.[12] Many Asian and African evangelical theologians hold radical evangelical views.[13] Among those with Australian and New Zealand links can be counted Athol Gill,[14] Thorwald Lorenzen,[15] John Smith,[16] Charles Ringma,[17] Dave Andrews,[18] Martyn Newman,[19] Viv Grigg,[20] Michael Duncan,[21] Dorothy Harris[22] and Christopher Marshall.[23] Among the British are Colin Marchant,[24] John Gladwin,[25] David Sheppard,[26] Jim Punton,[27] Pat Dearnley and Pete Broadbent.[28] The journals in this tradition include *Sojourners* (perhaps the flagship for the movement) and *The Other Side* (both from the United States), and *Transformation* and *Third Way* (both from the United Kingdom).

Related Groups

There is no clear boundary between radical evangelicals and their wider parent group, the **evangelicals**, so several prominent writers can be classified one way or the other, illustrating that radicality admits of degrees and is partly in the eye of the beholder. We need not define evangelicalism in its great variety; we may simply say that evangelicals have a strong evangelistic emphasis, a high view of the historical reliability of the Bible, and a focus on the atoning work of Jesus Christ appropriated in the life of the individual believer.[29]

As an example of the unclear boundary, Ronald Sider, founder of Evangelicals for Social Action, is known for his longstanding and passionate advocacy of social justice and concern for the poor, and many would consider him to be a radical. He clearly argues that a biblical proclamation of the Good News calls for radical discipleship.[30] Nevertheless, he carefully distinguishes himself from prominent radical evangelicals (Costas, Richard Mouw and Vinay Samuel), whom he labels as a sub-type of the "dominant ecumenical model" of mission. Sider regards them as theologically dangerous and criticizes them for considering socio-political transformation to be a part of the meaning of salvation.[31] Unlike most radical evangelicals and like most other evangelicals Sider maintains a strong distinction between evangelism and social action and argues that evangelism is primary.[32]

Conversely, John Stott's views are classically evangelical and he would seldom be classified as a radical. Yet he attended the Radical Discipleship gathering at the Lausanne Congress, signed the manifesto produced, and presented it to the Congress with his backing. He has been a leader in the recovery of evangelical social concern, and uses terms such as "holistic mission" and "incarnational mission" in his recent writing,[33] though ultimately agreeing with Sider about evangelism and social action. We will consider his use of "incarnational mission" later in this chapter.

In a similar vein there are no clear boundaries between radical evangelicalism and the "**radical discipleship movement**," illustrating that not only radicalism but evangelicalism also admits of degrees. In fact radical evangelicalism and the radical discipleship movement are virtually indistinguishable.

The discipleship movement is gripped by the same emphases, but includes many who are not clearly evangelicals.[34] In his introduction to *Who will roll away the stone?* Ched Myers names a long list of European-American theologians who espouse radical Christianity, including well-known people such as James McClendon, Robert McAfee Brown, Douglas John Hall, Daniel and Philip Berrigan, and Richard Shaull.[35] Drawing on earlier figures, we could include those as diverse as Dorothy Day, William

Stringfellow, Martin Luther King and Dietrich Bonhoeffer in the radical discipleship tradition.[36]

This list reminds us that the vision of radical Christianity also overlaps with that of **liberation theology**. Radical evangelicals and radical disciples clearly have liberationist concerns, although they typically quibble with liberation theology on minor matters.[37] Radical disciples in first-world situations are often those who attempt to understand what a liberationist approach, a theology from "underneath," might mean for Christians who find themselves in the *locus imperii* (situation of empire), to use one of Myers' central interpretive categories.[38]

Finally, many **Mennonites** hold views which are substantially the same as those of radical evangelicalism, though with less emphasis on direct social engagement and a stronger emphasis on non-violent resistance. Writers such as John Howard Yoder, Wilbert Shenk, Donald Kraybill, John Driver, Norman Kraus, James Metzler, Willard Swartley, Linford Stutzman and Ronald Sider come to mind. Radical evangelicals are usually more than willing to acknowledge the Anabaptist contribution to their perspective.[39]

Self-definitions

How do radical evangelicals define their perspective? It is essentially a recovery, from a critical evangelical framework, of the social dimensions of the gospel.[40] It expects to see both personal and social changes taking place as the kingdom of God begins here and now.

Costas puts the lordship of Christ at the very center, in a statement which is typical of the radical evangelical view. His perspective, he says,

> implies an understanding of the Lordship of Christ from the specific angle of radical evangelical Christianity, which seeks to derive its knowledge of Christ from the witness of the canonical Scriptures, through the hermeneutical mediation of exegesis, historical studies, and the social sciences, motivated by a personal encounter with him and verified in a life of radical discipleship amid the struggles of history.[41]

There is a distinct ethos in this statement by Costas. We notice a greater use of the social sciences than we find in Anabaptism, more emphasis on social transformation than in evangelicalism, and a stronger accent on personal faith than in most forms of liberation theology.

Elsewhere Costas argues that the radical evangelical tradition is a socially-engaged stream within evangelicalism evident in the Wesleyan movement, the mission of William Carey, the eighteenth-century Moravian missions, the anti-slavery movement, early feminism, the Social Gospel movement and the civil rights movement. While accepting the evangelical doctrines of scripture as a rule of faith, salvation by grace through faith, and conversion as a distinct faith experience, it emphasizes the demonstration of the transformed life.[42] Drawing on the Anabaptist tradition, the holiness movement and other sources, the radical evangelical tradition has stressed the "praxis of faith," "a faith that becomes flesh, that is spiritually energizing and, therefore, historically transformative."[43] We can already see how central the incarnational theme is to the radical evangelical concept of mission.

What drives radical evangelicalism is a biblically-oriented perspective of discipleship involving the whole of life, in a way that allows for biblical and socio-political insights to be integrated. Myers writes that "discipleship is not an otherworldly journey but a following of Jesus in the vicissitudes of history." [44]

The radicalism of the Latin Americans, such as Costas, Padilla and Escobar, arises naturally from their social location on the "underside of history," seeing things from among the dissenfranchized and oppressed.[45] The radicalism of those located among power and wealth is a more deliberate choice, an attempt to find a non-imperial tradition while doing theology in Pharaoh's household, as Myers puts it.[46]

The word "radical," as used by this group, refers to a cluster of ideas including: going to the root of things in our analysis;[47] a renunciation of everything for Jesus;[48] a total commitment involving every area of life;[49] discipleship involving a total social realignment;[50] an unconditional and all-embracing response;[51] costly and compassionate identification with the poor;[52] and allowing commitment to God to shape all other decisions.[53] The radical vision is an urgent one, fueled by a desire to see the existing order of things overturned. It seeks to build from the roots again, and has a comprehensive vision of the re-ordering of society and religion, beginning with an unconditional commitment on the part of Christian disciples which involves the practical re-ordering of personal priorities according to the call of Jesus.

Incarnational Mission in Radical Evangelicalism

For radical evangelicals mission is essentially incarnational, both in following Jesus as our pattern and in experiencing the continuing presence of Jesus in mission. The group frequently invokes the incarnation, insisting that the way Jesus lived is the way we are to carry out Christian mission today. Consider just two examples from conference statements.

The Radical Discipleship statement from the Lausanne Congress lamented that evangelicals have "failed to incarnate the Gospel."

> Methods in evangelization must center in Jesus Christ who took our humanity, our frailty, our death and gave himself in suffering servanthood for others. He sends his community into the world, as the Father sent him, to identify and agonize with [people], to renounce status and demonic power, and to give itself in selfless service of others for God.... We must allow God to make visible in the new humanity the quality of life that reflects Christ and demonstrates his reign.[54]

We find a similar and even clearer call to incarnational mission in the statement of the Third Latin American Congress on Evangelism (CLADE III) in 1992. Under the heading "The incarnational pattern for mission," it says:

> The incarnation is the model for the mission of the church. In his incarnation Jesus identified himself with sinful people, shared their aspirations, anguish, and weaknesses, and dignified them as creatures made in the image of God. The church is called to approach its mission in this way.[55]

In order to examine the dimensions of incarnational mission in radical evangelical perspective we will first look at the ways in which this group sees both the pattern of Jesus and the presence of Jesus as important in mission. We will then examine how incarnational mission is either implied or clearly called for in each of seven other dimensions of radical evangelical missiology: kingdom theology, the lordship of Christ, discipleship, holistic mission, going to the margins, community and contextualization.

Jesus Is the Pattern for Mission

As we would expect from a radical discipleship tradition there is a repeated emphasis on following in the footsteps of Jesus. Escobar is representative:

> Jesus Christ, our model of missionary, was not only the carrier of a message, but he himself was the message, by his way of being among [people], by the qualities of his character, by his compassion and his readiness to come close to [people] in their need. The New Testament is clear in the demand for the Christian and the church to be also a living expression of the message, "living letters" as Paul put it in 1 Cor 3:1-3.[56]

That Jesus is the model for mission is seldom argued because it is seen as self-evident.[57] The following of Jesus in mission is usually taken together with the following of Jesus in discipleship, because the life of discipleship and mission is seen as a unity.[58] Gladwin, for example, says that "Jesus' way is the true pattern for human life,"[59] and links Christian mission to that of Jesus: living for the kingdom of God in the strength of God in the normal patterns of human life, particularly in society, politics and material issues.[60] Gladwin is careful to say that unlike Jesus we are not "incarnated" (in the classical theological sense of the divine becoming human) because we are a part of the world to begin with. Nevertheless, "enfleshment in human history" is the way God speaks and is therefore the way we should engage in mission.[61]

Like the Anabaptists, the radical evangelicals clearly want the life and teaching of Jesus of Nazareth (as far as we can discern them through the witness of the Gospels) to be normative in Christian discipleship and mission. Jesus is the controlling criterion, the test of our identity, the lord of our entire lives, the foundation of the church.[62]

Yet this is not generally a position of simple exemplarism, where Christians are called to imitate Jesus literally.[63] There tends to be an awareness in radical evangelical writing that it is a big jump from what Jesus did to what we are to do, one which requires some hermeneutics.

Costas acknowledges that although obedience to all of Jesus' teachings is the ultimate goal, those teachings are dynamic, not totally defined in scripture, and above all, to be seen in context. The central principle for Costas is that of the love of Jesus, and the Holy Spirit plays an important role in guiding us in our understanding and application of this very general criterion.[64] There are many strategies open to modern disciples; most of the Christian agenda, says Kraybill, will be to question the dominant paradigms and encourage clusters of alternatives, rather than to propose a blueprint for the kingdom.[65]

The faith to which Jesus calls Christians is more a lifestyle than a creed, and not even one particular lifestyle but a range of lifestyles with certain basic qualities.[66] Gill is very aware of the layers of formation of the Jesus tradition in the Gospels, and recognizes that we need to interpret the life and teachings of Jesus just as the Gospel writers did: "[These] stories of Jesus and his disciples may be reinterpreted into our situations with the basic trajectories of the Jesus tradition providing the fundamental direction for the way that we might live as Christians today."[67] One of the missiological implications of the incarnation is that Jesus of Nazareth is the criterion by which we test for truth and authenticity in mission.[68]

For radical evangelicals Jesus is the pattern for mission because he is the foundation and life of the church. The church has its identity in Jesus because Christ created the church and is its life. "It is *his* church; the church is on *his* mission. The crucified and risen Christ must be the criterion for everything the church tries to be and do."[69] This leads us to consider just what this means in the radical evangelical perspective.

Incarnational Mission Reflects Christ's Transforming Presence

Compared to many in the Anabaptist tradition, radical evangelicals are generally more aware of the gracious and transforming presence of God in Christian mission, and its importance as the foundation and meaning of incarnational mission. Consider part of the first main paragraph of the Radical Discipleship statement at Lausanne, which describes the gospel of Jesus Christ:

> [It] is Good News of a new creation of a new humanity, a new birth through him by his life-giving Spirit; of the gifts of the messianic reign contained in Jesus and mediated through him by his Spirit; of the charismatic community empowered to embody his reign of shalom here and now before the whole creation and make his Good News seen and known.[70]

For radical evangelicals incarnational mission is the mission of a trinitarian God; it is the continuing mission of God in Jesus Christ who lives today and works within us through the Holy Spirit. God is still being embodied in history. The incarnation is neither merely history nor merely an existential framework for life today. Because it is the crucified and risen Jesus who lives today and calls us into a new reality through a response of faith, we are transformed by our practice of discipleship.[71] Our obedience and discipleship is enabled by God's grace, and thus our "good works" gain what Lorenzen calls a theological dignity. They have a proclamatory and missionary function because they are grounded in the saving and enabling grace of God.[72]

Incarnational mission in this sense is the presence of the risen Christ in the life of the believing community.[73] To the extent that the church faithfully responds it is the body of Christ, "the community through which Christ wants to encounter the world as savior and liberator," and through which "Christ can share his life with the world."[74] Christ is not simply incarnate in the church as a matter of right; Christ invites the church make real the gift of his incarnate presence by the way the church engages in mission.

Costas repeatedly emphasizes the role of the Spirit as Christ's presence in incarnational mission. The following three statements are examples of this emphasis:

> The church is to follow the pattern of the incarnation because it is the body of Christ indwelled by his Spirit: the new people of the God whose Son became flesh in Jesus of Nazareth by the power of the Holy Spirit.[75]

> To incarnate Christ in our world is to manifest the transforming presence of God's kingdom among the victims of sin and evil.... Christ's transforming power is mediated by the work of the Spirit in the life and witness of the church.[76]

> The proclamation of the kingdom is not a matter of words or deeds, but of words and deeds *empowered* by the liberating presence of the Spirit.[77]

Radical evangelicals at their best seem to be able to hold works and grace in a healthy tension. They balance their urgent call for all Christians to become involved in costly and practical mission with an acknowledgement that it is only through the gift of the transforming power of Christ that we are able to participate at all in the ongoing mission of Jesus.

Living as a Sign of the Kingdom of God

The combination of call and gift we have just mentioned is characteristic of the kingdom of God, one of the dominant themes of radical evangelical writing. We find it as a key concept in the writing of nearly every representative of radical evangelicalism, and it is understood in a distinctive way. With respect to evangelicalism this is a recovery of the kingdom, particularly in its social dimensions here-and-now. To liberal Protestantism the emphasis on a future consummation of the kingdom may well seem naïve.

Evangelicalism, drawing on its Protestant roots, has usually focused more on the personal dimensions of forgiveness and grace than on the social dimensions of Jesus' proclamation. Particularly in the twentieth century, many evangelicals have not believed that the kingdom of God includes a "coming social and political reality to which the church is now to be a sign." [78]

Radical evangelicalism, on the other hand, has been enthusiastic about a broader concept of the kingdom of God as transformative at both personal and social levels, both now and in a future consummation. This view of the kingdom is closely tied to the incarnation and its implications for mission. Kingdom theology speaks broadly of God's gracious rule. The transforming reign of God is embodied in Jesus and is to take shape in the life and mission of the church according to the pattern of Jesus.

Costas, for example, sees it as a new order of life:

> [Jesus] did not suffer and die to leave things as they were but, rather, to bring a new order of *life*. He both proclaimed and embodied the kingdom of God, the new order of love, freedom, justice, and peace which aims at the total transformation of history and demands a radical conversion as condition for participation in it. To incarnate Christ in our world is to manifest the transforming presence of God's kingdom among the victims of sin and evil. It is to make possible a process of transformation from personal sin and corporate evil to personal and collective freedom, justice, and well-being. [79]

Christopher Marshall, as another example, summarizes a study of the kingdom of God in the teaching of Jesus by saying that the church is to

heal the sick, to restore the lost to relationship with God, to incarnate an alternative way of life under the lordship of Christ, and to pray for and work towards the transformation of human society in the name of the coming reign of God. All this is implied in bearing witness to the gospel of the kingdom.[80]

As a further example, Kraybill puts the radical evangelical view very clearly when he characterises the kingdom of God in dynamic terms as the rule of God in the lives of people. It is always becoming, spreading, growing. It is present wherever people submit their lives to God's authority. "Kingdom living is fundamentally social," actualized when God rules in people's hearts *and* relationships.[81] Kraybill is aware of the scholarly debate on the meaning of the kingdom of God. He sees the idea as a general symbol, pointing beyond itself to multiple meanings which incorporate the Old Testament longing for it, Jesus' inauguration of it, its power at Pentecost, its presence in the lives of believers through the centuries, and its final consummation.[82] For most of his book *The upside-down kingdom*, he unravels the social implications of the kingdom in Jesus' time and attempts to find directions for today. Again, we find that the link between the kingdom of God and incarnational mission is strong. The rule of God in human lives is also the shaping presence of the crucified and risen Christ. Kraybill argues that for God there is no division between the spiritual and the social. "In the incarnation, the spiritual became social."[83] Word and deed become one in the incarnation, and so the Good News is a "single, integrated gospel of the kingdom." [84]

This gospel of the kingdom, for radical evangelicals, is characterized by a stronger sense of involvement in the world than we find among Anabaptists and Evangelicals, but a clearer separation of church and world than is found in many ecumenical circles. The incarnation, for radicals, implies that God's way is to be alongside, to suffer with humanity and not just for it.[85] As Mortimer Arias points out, any tension in the incarnation between real identification and citizenship of another world, as illustrated by John 17:16 ("They do not belong to the world, just as I do not belong to the world"), must be seen against the backdrop of John 3:16 ("For God so loved the world that he gave his only Son").[86] The incarnation is seen by radical evangelicals as an affirmation of God's presence in creation; this rules out any form of Christianity which draws Christians out of the world and abandons it to the forces of evil. Rather, kingdom theology drives the church into the world and alongside humanity.

The Lordship of Christ

Radical evangelicals emphasize the lordship of Christ so strongly that the call to acknowledge Jesus not only as savior but also as lord of all life is sometimes used as the defining characteristic of radical evangelicalism.[87] Costas reminds us that "Jesus is lord" is one of the earliest confessions of faith (1 Cor 12:3, Rom 10:9).[88] In the early church the lordship of Christ was at the same time the motivation and the content of mission.[89]

As with kingdom theology, this is an emphasis which evangelicals have largely neglected until recent decades. Where it has played a part it has often referred to inner submission to Christ the lord.

In the Lausanne Congress Radical Discipleship statement, however, the lordship of Christ is a rallying cry. The first section on the good news of Jesus Christ's lordship of the entire universe finishes with the assertion, "Jesus is Lord! Alleluia! Let the earth hear his voice!"[90] Although the statement is less than three pages long the lordship of Jesus Christ is mentioned nine times. In particular the statement confesses that evangelicals have failed in their obedience to the lordship of Christ in refusing to submit to his Word, and have often "separated Jesus Christ the Savior from Jesus Christ the Lord." [91]

The first dimension of this affirmation is **the worthiness of Christ** to be called lord of all life. Radical evangelicals do not hesitate to use the premodern metaphor of "lord," despite criticism of it in some recent theology,[92] because Jesus himself subverts the hierarchical overtones of the metaphor with his "upside down" social and political framework. Jesus is, paradoxically, the servant lord, humble and poor and yet, as Christ, to be worshipped as divine.

The second dimension of Christ's lordship is its applicability to **all of human life** and its demand for total commitment. In discussing the radical nature of Christian conversion Costas writes: "No area of life may be left out. The whole of it must come under Jesus Christ's lordship."[93] Discipleship is the working out of the implications of following Christ in every aspect of life, physical and spiritual, individual and social.[94] We will discuss this further when discussing discipleship in the next section.

A third dimension of the lordship of Christ is its **gracious and liberating** nature. Gill makes this a continual theme. The call of Jesus is a call of grace and love, which evokes, demands and makes possible the trustful obedience which is the radical response of discipleship.[95] In calling us to turn our lives around it liberates us. The Radical Discipleship statement talks of the gospel as good news of liberation, wholeness and restoration.[96] The lordship of Christ differs from the way earthly lords operate in that it is based on vulnerable love rather than military power. It is creative and liberating, communal and fraternal. It facilitates a new community, paradoxically demanding absolute allegiance but at the same time returning to us freedom and maturity.[97]

A fourth dimension of Christ's lordship in radical evangelicalism is its **cosmic** nature. The Radical Discipleship statement speaks of the lordship of Jesus Christ over the entire universe, and speaks of the cosmic nature of salvation. This does not receive much attention elsewhere in evangelicalism, despite its acceptance of the cosmic christology of passages in the New Testament such as Philippians 2 and Colossians 1.

What these four dimensions of the lordship of Christ amount to is a call to acknowledge Christ's lordship. Christian mission brings into actuality the lordship of Christ being proclaimed. In a sense it is claiming times, places and situations for Christ as Lord. Christ's presence is found where his lordship is welcomed. In being part of "enfleshing" the proclaimed Word, Christian mission is "incarnating" Christ's lordship. This leads us to discuss our response in discipleship and obedience.

Discipleship: The Following of Jesus

As we noted above, radical evangelicalism is sometimes called the radical discipleship movement, with little distinguishing the two. Discipleship is seen by radical evangelicals as following Jesus in costly, concrete ways, travelling a path of mission which involves the way of the cross. The perspective owes much to the Anabaptist view of discipleship. Through discipleship the mission of Jesus is "made flesh," taking shape in the whole of life. Discipleship is obedience to Christ the lord of all life.

It was at the Lausanne Congress, from the Radical Discipleship group, that many first heard articulated the link between the lordship of Christ and a radical kind of discipleship with concrete implications for lifestyle and daily practice.[98]

As we noted above, the combination of "radical" and "discipleship" implies a total commitment in following Jesus, both rooted and disciplined.[99] The first call of the gospel, writes Tom Sine, is a "more radically biblical form of discipleship that will re-order our entire lives."[100] It is part of a praxis-oriented perspective, in which the proper response to the gospel is not one simply of belief but of repentance and obedience, in other words, of discipleship. Costas expresses this in terms which make the link between discipleship and incarnational mission clear. For the gospel to transform us, he argues, it must "become incarnated," take root and become praxis, and the only way for this to happen is in the process of effective discipleship, seen as a personal relationship which shapes our entire lives. Costas sees discipleship not as the passing on of knowledge but the soaking down of a new way of being, deeply incorporated into our lives.[101]

Discipleship is centrally the following of Jesus in the way of the cross, that is, challenging the old order at the risk of suffering, persecution and death. Myers wryly calls radical discipleship "a dying prospect."[102] Jim Wallis says that "the cross of Christ is both the symbol of our atonement and the pattern for our discipleship."[103]

Discipleship is also seen as a life of servanthood and a life of solidarity with the poor.[104] We will comment further on this later.

The most extensive reflections on the nature of discipleship are found in Gill's writing, in which he pays close attention to the Synoptic Gospels. He continually emphasizes that it is a costly and yet a gracious call, both demanding and liberating. It has to do with "specific acts of self-sacrifice in concrete situations,"[105] and has implications for relationships, power and material possessions. It involves welcoming those whom Jesus welcomed. Traveling with Jesus sets us free. Gill does not suggest that Jesus calls us to one particular lifestyle. He does show from the Gospels, however, that Jesus calls his disciples at least to freedom from attachment to possessions, life in community, mission, renunciation of power and privilege, an inward journey of prayer and trust in God, and the living of life as a gift from God.[106]

Holistic Mission: Words and Deeds Integrated

The radical evangelical emphasis on holistic mission follows naturally from kingdom theology, the lordship of Christ and discipleship, all of which point in the direction of the multi-dimensional good news of God's concern for the whole person.

Holism (sometimes spelt "wholism" but with no observable distinction) is the view that the perspective of the whole, seen to be more than the sum of its parts, is central to understanding reality.[107] In science and philosophy holism is close to the ecological view, which pays attention to the organic interrelationship of the parts to the whole. In missiology the term has been widely used in recent years by radical evangelicals, by some evangelical aid and development agencies such as TEAR Fund and World Vision, and otherwise notably by Stott.[108]

Terms with meanings similar to "holistic" include "integral," "whole" and "comprehensive." The term "integral," often used by Latin Americans, is a synonym for "holistic," and emphasizes the holding together of mission in one task without division.[109] The word "whole" is perhaps used by those who are shy of the more direct term. One of the themes of the Manila congress of the Lausanne movement was "calling the whole church to take the whole gospel to the whole world" ;[110] it hints at but does not specify a holistic perspective. The term "comprehensive" can simply mean "holistic," but also can mean that we merely include both evangelism and social action, without the integration implied by a holistic perspective.[111]

Radical evangelicals and evangelical aid agencies often use the term "holistic" without definition, but usually refer to a holistic view of either the gospel, the human person or mission. In fact, there is a strong interdependence between these three: the content of mission, those to whom mission is directed, and the desirable method of mission.

Alfred Krass says, for example, that the communication of a gospel that is holistic must itself be holistic.[112] Similarly, in his address to the Lausanne Congress, Padilla said that a holistic *method* of mission corresponds to a comprehensive view of *salvation* that addresses *people* in all aspects of their being.[113] Again, in the statement of the Third Latin American Congress on Evangelism (CLADE III) in 1992, the paragraph on "integral mission" holds the three together tightly. The Church should base its vision and mission on "the gospel which, when it is comprehended in its fullness, is proclaimed in word and deed and is directed to the entire human person."[114]

Holistic mission opposes the separation of evangelism and social action, and the separation of physical and social liberation from spiritual liberation. For many, the road to holism has had several stages. (1) At first many radical evangelicals spoke almost exclusively of social action, in order to redress the imbalance they saw in evangelicalism. In the context of evangelicalism this has earned radical evangelicals the reputation for being strongly socio-political in their view of the gospel. (2) Then many tried to emphasize both evangelism and social action. Some, like Sider and Stott, have remained at this position. It is for this reason that we can consider Sider to be on the edge of the circle of radical evangelicalism, with Stott a little further outside due to his moderation (tending to conservatism) in many ways. (3) Meanwhile radical evangelicals have gone on to insist that mission is one task, with several facets but still an integrated whole.

Let us unravel these last two stages a little more, because it confuses some that writers such as Stott and Sider use holistic language without having moved to the last stage.

In Stott's most recent book there is a chapter entitled "Holistic mission."[115] Stott sees evangelism and social action as in partnership, like marriage partners, or, to change metaphors, like two blades of a pair of scissors or the two wings of a bird. He strongly argues that they should be held together and that they are both parts of the Christian mission.[116] His theological reasons for holding them together are good as far as they go. God cares for humans in all our dimensions, physical, social and spiritual; Jesus integrated words and deeds in his teaching and healing; and we also need in our mission to "make the Word flesh," in a "similar integration of words and deeds."[117] The problem is that apart from the last phrase, which he quotes approvingly from the Manila Manifesto,[118] Stott's perspective is still ultimately dualistic. He calls evangelism and social action "natural twins."[119] Even though he makes every effort to hold them together, they are fundamentally different, and, what is more, only one of them is of eternal value to him.

Sider is in the same position. Using all the fashionable terms of radical evangelicalism, he calls his approach "wholistic mission as incarnational kingdom Christianity,"[120] and wants "wholistic revivals, wholistic apologetics, wholistic political engagement, and wholistic congregations."[121] Yet those who respond to his call to transcend one-sided Christianity using his perspective are presented with a two-sided Christianity, which includes both evangelism and social action, instead of a holistic view of the gospel.

Costas, on the other hand, illustrates a thoroughgoing holism in mission.

For Costas the wholeness of mission means that incarnational witness (which here means the presence of Christians living for Christ in the world) is an essential part of mission and not just a secondary means.[122] He concludes *The church and its mission* with a passionate plea. We are sent both to call people to enter new life through faith, and to

> proclaim, in word and deed, the good news of this new order of life *in* the multitudinous structures of society, ... [standing] as Christ did, in solidarity with the poor and the oppressed.... No dichotomies here: not a vertical vs. a horizontal emphasis of mission; not redemption vs. humanization—but a holistic vision of God's mission to the world and the church's role in it.[123]

Costas continued this theme in his next book, *The integrity of mission.* He stated that his purpose was to look at world mission as "a unitary, indivisible whole, in the hope of generating a wider vision and a stimulating and more effective missional involvement." [124]

A holistic approach to mission demands the integration of words and deeds, that is, a belief that the two are the expression of one mission and are needed to interpret each other. Radical evangelicals see a clear incarnational basis for this view of mission. Drawing on the Gospels' portrayals of Jesus, radical evangelicals continually urge Christians to allow the Word still to become flesh. The Good News is meant to be heard, seen and touched.[125] By the way we live and articulate our faith as the church we are meant to be an "embodied question mark," challenging the values of the world.[126]

Each of the six other incarnational themes we are considering in examining the radical evangelicals (kingdom theology, the lordship of Christ, discipleship, going to the margins, community and contextualization) involves this holding together of what Christians say and do, of word and deed, of proclamation and presence, of verbal witness and prophetic lifestyle, and of evangelism and social action. Mission is clearly seen as the integration of what is proclaimed and what is lived out.

There are times in the literature of radical evangelicalism, however, when incarnational mission does not imply this integration, but rather seems to refer merely to non-verbal witness or the demonstration of the gospel. Costas, for example, sometimes contrasts verbal witness to incarnational witness.[127] He never carefully defines incarnational mission, and often characterises it in terms such as involvement with the struggles of the people,[128] the life of orthopraxis (right living),[129] actualizing gospel truth in our personal and social relationships,[130] actualizing love and justice in social institutions,[131] and solidarity with the oppressed.[132] Costas tends overall to over-emphasize "deeds" at the expense of "words." In the terms of our three-stage road to holism, we could say that Costas reverts at times from the third stage (genuine holism) to the first stage (emphasizing social action) in response to a context in which a narrowly defined evangelism continues to be the dominant emphasis.[133]

The contribution of the radical evangelicals, then, on the relationship both between the spiritual and temporal dimensions of salvation and between evangelism and social action, has been to insist that the questions have been framed wrongly on the basis of dualism and that mission must be a holistic enterprise.

To the Margins, on the Way of the Cross

Radical evangelicals share with liberation theologians the conviction that the gospel is particularly good news to the poor. They often point out that the incarnation was not only a movement of God towards embodiment in a human person but also a significant statement about social location. Jesus was of humble birth, lived among the poor, sided with the oppressed and outcast, and died the death of a common criminal. To follow Jesus means to take the same path of solidarity with the poor and oppressed, risking the same marginalization and treatment.

There are many examples. Lorenzen is unambiguous: "The incarnational thrust of faith implies an inherent bias toward the marginal people."[134] Dearnley and Broadbent also put it strongly: "The incarnate Word came as a poor and oppressed first-century Jew, homeless and persecuted. Yet this was the way in which the God of the universe chose to express [Godself] in the world."[135] Costas calls this the first missiological implication of the incarnation, the discovery of "a new and fresh experience of Jesus Christ from within the harsh reality of the hurt, destitute, and marginated of the earth."[136] All these examples argue strongly that incarnational mission involves costly solidarity with the poor and that Christ's presence is found when we are alongside the poor.

Popular radical evangelical literature on mission can almost be defined by its emphasis on costly mission among the poor. Books by Dave Andrews,[137] Michael Duncan,[138] Viv Grigg,[139] Colin Marchant,[140] Jim Punton,[141] Charles Ringma,[142] Ronald Sider,[143] John Smith[144] and Jim

Wallis[145] (five of whom are from Australasia) are good examples. Dorothy Harris, Australian director of Viv Grigg's mission agency, Servants to Asia's Poor, actually entitles an article "Incarnation as relocation among the poor."[146] In it she argues, as does Viv Grigg elsewhere, that all Christians are called to incarnational mission, which always involves ministry with the poor, simplicity of living and patterns of renunciation, but not necessarily relocation among the poorest of the world, which is always a special vocation.[147] Many of the above are examples of urban missiology; the call to live alongside the poor and take up their interests is pervasive in the literature of urban mission.[148]

The central point here is that it is the incarnation which drives radical evangelicals to special concern for the poor. Many examples could be given. Church of England bishop and urban missioner David Sheppard writes that it is central and orthodox Christian doctrines such as the kingdom of God and the incarnation which compel him to argue that there is a divine bias to the poor.[149]

Radical evangelicals would generally agree with John Howard Yoder that to carry our cross is not only to endure the suffering that comes our way but to discern the concrete social meaning of the cross. It means freely chosen vulnerability, servant-love, power-in-weakness, innocent suffering and victory-in-death.[150] Radical evangelicals follow a missiology of the cross rather than a theology of the cross. In other words, it is for mission that Christians are called to live under the cross, following the path of Jesus. While affirming the importance and reality of the resurrection, the radicals draw from Paul's theology the understanding that the risen Christ differs significantly from Christian believers. While Jesus has already been raised from the dead, believers live in the promise and partial experience of resurrection. "Their present existence should be an existence marked by the cross." [151]

Community: Embodying the New Order

Radical evangelicals continually speak of life together in the messianic community. An important part of incarnational mission is the partial embodiment in community of the new order of relationships God intends for humanity. Incarnational mission here means living out a social alternative in the power of the gospel. The vision for a new community comes both from the Gospel accounts of the life and teaching of Jesus and his disciples, and from the life of the early church.

Gill, for example, organizes his second book around the themes of discipleship, community and mission, three of the central themes of the Gospels.[152]

Arias argues that Christians in the early church, though a motley lot, embodied and pointed to the new reality they proclaimed:

> [They] were living manifestations of the new life in the coming kingdom, not only as individuals but also as an integrated group in their life and witness: a base community committed to Jesus and his kingdom—an incarnational sign of the kingdom. Jesus' evangelization was ... an *incarnational evangelization.*[153]

Sine calls for a confessing community, arguing that "the first call of the gospel is neither to social activism nor to proclamation, but to *incarnation*, to fleshing out something of God's new order."[154] Incarnational mission involves more than certain actions; it is a way of being as well, which speaks in itself.

Radical evangelicals see community as important not only because it is the new reality to which Christians are called in the Gospels; community is also a prophetic and liberating alternative to the individualism of modern society. Furthermore, community is seen as a practical necessity if we are to challenge the old order with a new reality. We cannot do it alone.

Although among radical evangelicals concepts of community vary from the dilute (closer fellowship in churches) to the strong (radical communal experiments with a common purse), all radicals see discipleship as an essentially social concept involving much closer relationships with other Christians. Luther Smith investigates five radical Christian communities in the United States in his book *Intimacy and mission*, and finds that they are motivated by the desire to model a new society. Radical disciples, he concludes, make their devotion to God the priority which shapes all other decisions in life, including how they live together. They work for a fellowship of intimacy, where they support and care for each other, working through the conflicts that arise. They also work for a fellowship of mission, where the whole community is involved in social transformation.[155] These are all ways of making the gospel visible in life together. Put another way, these are all events in which Christ is to be found incarnated. On the one hand, his transforming and gracious presence is enfleshed wherever transforming community occurs. On the other, community is enabled as gift wherever Christ's presence is sought, welcomed and interpreted.

Incarnation as Contextualization

Some radical evangelicals, particularly Costas, see contextualization as an important dimension of incarnational mission. Costas argues that God speaks in the vernacular and addresses people in the particularity of their time and space. Jesus was firmly located as a first century Galilean Jew.[156] The good news is culturally clothed from the start. The incarnation tells us that the good news will always seek to be relevant to its context and to address each person in a "language" he or she can understand.

In fact, Padilla and Costas link incarnation and contextualization very closely, treating them almost as synonyms:

Wherever there is oppression, there is the Spirit of Christ incarnated in the *experience* of the oppressed; there is God contextualized in the present history of the nonpersons of society. (Costas)[157]

Contextualization and incarnation are basic to the Christian mission. (Costas)[158]

It may be said that God has contextualized [Godself] in Jesus Christ. The incarnation makes clear God's approach to the revelation of [Godself] and of [God's] purposes: God does not shout [God's] message from the heavens; God becomes present as a [person] among [people]. (Padilla)[159]

If the gospel is not contextualized, the Word of God will remain a *logos asarkos* (unincarnate word), a message that touches our lives only tangentially. (Padilla)[160]

It is not within the scope of this study to explore contextualization in detail. We can simply note that one of the reasons for the development of contextual theology is the close link between incarnational missiology and the principle of fleshing out Christian faith in particular cultural settings.

Evaluative Comments

We have seen that incarnational mission is central to radical evangelical missiology. What is also noteworthy is the way various theological emphases form an integrated perspective in which they are all important. We refer here to themes such as the kingdom of God, the lordship of Christ, holistic mission, discipleship, good news to the poor, the way of the cross, and community. Radical evangelicals, though they draw on traditions such as Anabaptist thought, liberation theology and evangelicalism, make a distinctive contribution to incarnational missiology.

The recovery of kingdom theology and the discipleship tradition have enabled a holistic perspective to be reintroduced into evangelicalism, despite resistance. The combination of the fervor of evangelicalism and the holism of radical discipleship, both firmly anchored in scripture, offers a vigorous and stimulating perspective in mission, which has also been very fruitful in missiology.

What is more, the radical wing of evangelicalism appears to offer evangelicals a far more critical and sophisticated use of scripture which is aware of how the text was formed, the varying perspectives found within the Bible, and the role of the reader in interpreting it. Writers such as Myers, Gill, Lorenzen, David Batstone, Arias and Kraybill are particularly careful in teasing out the different strands of biblical thought when interpreting scripture, whereas writers such as Costas sometimes appear overconfident about what we can know of Jesus of Nazareth.[161] Many of the radical writers are also aware of the difficulties of discerning ethical principles from the Gospels and translating them into our situation.

Although the cost and challenge of discipleship dominates the discussion, radical evangelicals do not simply talk of following Jesus as our model. They are generally aware of the need to talk both of following the example of Jesus (the first dimension of incarnational mission we outlined in chapter 3) *and* of living in the gracious presence of the risen Christ who enables Christians to follow (the second dimension outlined). Christ is found not only in the past, as model, nor only in the heavens as lord, but also in the present, as the gracious, enabling Spirit, wherever Christians seek to actualize Christ's lordship. With regard to our third dimension, while not emphasizing God's incarnating dynamic in creation to any extent, the emphasis on cosmic salvation lends itself to being developed in that direction.

The balance generally seen in radical evangelical incarnational missiology stems at least partly from the balance of their incarnational christology, which meets most of the criteria we suggested in chapter 3.[162] Their evangelical roots do not lead them to think metaphorically or use relational categories for understanding Christ's divinity. Nevertheless, their christology is solidly trinitarian, is soteriological and leads naturally to a strongly incarnational view of mission.

There is a difficulty at times in the tone of urgency and absolute commitment. If the language is taken plainly, one might wonder how ordinary people are meant to understand and respond to the radicality of the demands. There is a danger that guilt and perfectionism will creep in when absolutes are continually proclaimed. Often radical writing gives few clues on how the call to renounce worldly values, identify with the poor and walk the way of the cross is practically to be done. Burn out, conflict and disillusionment can occur as a result of high idealism untempered by realism and a "spirituality of the long haul." It seems as if something is missing in this prescription for maturity and freedom under Christ. Some radical evangelical writing which passes for missiology is actually sermonic, with a strong appeal to those whose consciences are the most tender. Despite stressing Christian community, there is sometimes an implicit individualism in the repeated call for the Christian disciple to walk the radical path. The acceptance by the Roman Catholic tradition of degrees of attainment and the need for confession and regular restitution contains some clues for modifying the intensity and heroism of radical evangelicalism. A stronger recognition of the grace which underlies the mission of Jesus is also important. Finally, to remember that Christian mission is God's mission, and that ultimate hope lies in God and not in Christian efforts, helps to make incarnational mission in the radical evangelical style lighter on the shoulders of Christians.

Nevertheless, the radical evangelical tradition elaborates many aspects of incarnational mission in a way that has the potential to inspire Christians to great commitment. It holds together several of the central themes in Christian discipleship and incarnational mission, and puts forward a clear call for Christians to take the incarnation seriously in community, discipleship and mission.

CHAPTER 6

LIBERATIVE PRAXIS:
LIBERATION THEOLOGY

Liberation theology begins with the social reality of oppression and sees the good news of the gospel largely in terms of liberation from that oppression. To be a Christian disciple in this framework is to engage in liberative practice, joining the struggle to make the kingdom of God visible in specific and socially critical ways. Though quite distinctive, liberation theology is our third example (following Anabaptism and radical evangelicalism) of a missiology where Jesus of Nazareth is central as the pattern for mission. Speaking of Latin America, Jon Sobrino sums it up in the following terms:

> Evangelizers must recapitulate Jesus' own incarnation, embracing it as a process that generates its own dynamics. Incarnate in the world of the poor, they must share their immense pain, this misery that cries to heaven, the protracted or sudden crucifixion of millions of human beings.[1]

Liberation theology takes several forms, but is generally a label for action-oriented theologies which strongly emphasize liberation from any type of human oppression, whether social, economic, political, racial or sexual.[2] Its main forms today are those concerned with the liberation of women, oppressed minorities (as in Afro-American theology) and the poor in Latin America, Asia and Africa. Latin American liberation theology has had the highest profile since its beginnings in the 1960s, but each member of the family of liberation theologies has developed its own distinctives, often quite independently of the other types.

To sample the way liberation theologians use the theme of incarnation and the incarnation in mission we will select two representative theologians from Latin America who have written substantial christologies with a missiological thrust, Leonardo Boff (from Brazil) and Jon Sobrino (from El Salvador). A briefer consideration of the liberation theology of Taiwanese theologian Choan-Seng Song, who has also developed an incarnational approach, will provide an East Asian perspective as well. (Until we come to Song's perspective we will use the term "liberation theology" to refer to Latin American liberation theology.)[3]

Boff wrote the first Latin American liberationist christology, *Jesus Christ liberator* (1972), and Sobrino has written two significant books on christology, *Christology at the crossroads* (1976) and *Jesus the liberator* (1991).[4] Each explains with clarity and urgency how an incarnational approach to the following of Jesus in concrete ways is central to the Christian life. Most commentators group their work together and see it as representative and important.[5]

Leonardo Boff was born in Brazil in 1938 and did his doctoral study in München. He was Professor of Systematic Theology in Petrópolis, Brazil, from 1970 to 1992. Ordained a Franciscan priest, he came under sustained scrutiny from the Vatican in the 1980s for his writings critical of the institutional church, and resigned from the priesthood and the Franciscan order in 1992. He is national adviser to base communities in Brazil.[6]

Jon Sobrino was born in Spain in 1938, studied in the US and did his doctoral study in Frankfurt. He has lived mainly in El Salvador since 1957. A Jesuit priest, he is Professor of Philosophy and Theology at the University of Central America in San Salvador. He narrowly escaped assassination in 1989 when right wing gunmen killed six of his colleagues on the university campus in his absence, and has commented that he writes in the middle of war, threats, conflict and persecution.[7]

The major themes of liberation theology from a Latin American perspective are well known. It sees theology as rightly preceded by Christian practice, the two related by a rhythm of action and reflection. It begins with an analysis of the social situation and a commitment to the poor. It sees Christian faith as involving not just devotion or piety but practical solidarity with the poor. The living God sides with the oppressed, and the kingdom of God is God's project in history and eternity. Jesus led the way in obedience to God and identification with the helpless and defenseless. Discipleship consists of following Jesus with our lives, empowered by the Spirit. The mission of the church is to be a sign and instrument of liberating evangelization. It will entail conflict and persecution and even, possibly, martyrdom.[8] Central to many of these themes is mission as embodying the love of God we see patterned in Jesus of Nazareth.

Incarnational Mission in Latin American Liberation Theology

Following Jesus in Liberative Praxis

For liberation theology Christian faith is a liberative practice, a discipleship which builds the reign of God here in history by overcoming oppression and working for fullness of life for all, but particularly the poor.

Liberation theologians agree with the Anabaptists that faith and discipleship are the same reality.[9] Boff says that the key element of a christological faith is "following Jesus and his cause."[10] Sobrino says that the following of Jesus is "a summons to collaborate with the kingdom of God."[11] "Christian life as a whole can be described as the following of Jesus. That is the most original and all-embracing reality, far more so than cultic worship and orthodoxy."[12] The liberation theologians echo the Old Testament prophets in declaring that the worship of God is worthless unless it is accompanied by justice. Boff asserts the primacy of orthopraxis (correct acting) over orthodoxy (correct thinking).[13] Francisco Moreno Rejón puts it more carefully and is probably closer to the Old Testament prophets when he says that orthopraxis is not the criterion of orthodoxy, but does function as a touchstone for it.[14]

The idea of "**praxis**' occurs frequently. Sometimes it seems to be a synonym for "practice," but liberation theologians usually follow the more technical use introduced by Karl Marx.[15] In Marxism praxis is humanizing action which interacts with reflection, seeking to transform human existence, and emphasizing that we are makers of our own history. It is never mere theory, but neither is it mere practice, the two being related critically and dialectically in a context of commitment to the poor.[16] Christian praxis, then, refers to "the concrete expression in life of the historical impact of faith."[17] All these dimensions just mentioned are present in terms such as "orthopraxis," "christopraxis' and "the praxiological" import of Jesus' message.

Christian praxis, for Sobrino, is the same as discipleship.[18] Christians cannot profess Christ without following Jesus in history. There is "no *spiritual* life without actual, historical *life*. It is impossible to live *with spirit* unless that spirit *becomes flesh*."[19] This incarnational theme continually recurs in liberation theology. There is a passion to actualize the reign of God in people's lives, in society and in history. One can feel Sobrino's frustration with Christian indifference to this awareness when he writes:

> The good news cannot be proclaimed as God's word unless it has to some degree become a good reality, at least in those who proclaim it.... [In] the Church as a body ... this embodiment of the good news in Christian living cannot be lacking. Such a failure would amount to saying that God has good news for the world but unfortunately it cannot become a reality. Then we would no longer be dealing with the effective word of God, which is what we want to transmit.[20]

For Sobrino, clearly, embodying the reality being proclaimed as part of a process of growing towards the praxis of Jesus is an essential ingredient of evangelization.[21]

Liberation theologians give three reasons for the importance of living out the praxis of Christian faith: the crying need of the poor, the call of Jesus, and the need to follow Jesus to understand God.

In Latin America the overwhelming and heart-rending **reality of poverty** is the context in which Christian liberative practice, and then liberation theology, was born. As Leonardo and Clodovis Boff say of the people among whom they work, "They are hungry, they are poor, they are exploited, and they die young."[22] The Boffs tell a story from their experience of a village where the Christian base community literally struggles to meet because the people are starving.[23] Liberation theologians continually remind us that what we see depends on where we stand, and the place from which they do their theology is among the poor. From that perspective a faith that does not embody justice and hope is worthless. Incarnational faith, which really transforms and which tackles concrete obstacles to life, is essential. Sobrino quotes Oscar Romero's words:

Living as we do in a world in such evident need of social transformation, how shall we not ask Christians to incarnate the justice of Christianity, to live it in their homes and in their lives, to strive to be agents of change, to strive to be new human beings?[24]

The call of Jesus is the second reason given for discipleship as praxis. The fundamental task of Jesus, according to Boff and Sobrino, was to serve and inaugurate the reign of God, making God present in his life. His call to his disciples was to join him in this mission. He called for both personal conversion, which involves a new mode of existing before God, and social transformation, which involves re-modeling society according to the law of love.[25] "The following of Jesus is the *totality* of the Christian life," argues Sobrino.[26]

The need to follow Jesus in order to understand God is the third reason given. Boff argues that it is only by following Jesus, trying to live what he lived, that we begin to grasp the mystery of who he is.[27] Sobrino expresses it more technically, saying that discipleship is an epistemological principle.[28] That is, we only understand Jesus in the light of our committed practice. We can only know by "doing." He goes as far as saying that "access to God is only possible in a liberative praxis based on following Jesus," a claim which, on the surface, would seem to leave out the role of grace altogether and make the Christian life a result of merely human endeavor.[29]

Grace, however, is important to the perspective of liberation theology. Boff's *Liberating grace* is an outstanding example of theology which is both orthodox and liberationist at the same time. Boff defines grace as the most basic and original Christian experience, consisting of both the encounter with the God-who-gives and the encounter with human beings who open up to love and give in return.[30] Grace seeks embodiment in historical situations and invites humans to respond.[31] It is not grace unless it is liberating grace. Grace, for Boff, is the fundamental experience of gift, but one which evokes a response in concrete terms. It is an attachment to the risen Christ which moves us into a new reality and allows Christ to act in us.[32] We note here the fusing of the first dimension of incarnational mission (following Jesus) and the second (being shaped by the reality of the risen Christ).

Sobrino also speaks of grace, though not at length. Citing 1 John 4:19 ("We love because God first loved us"), he calls grace the "gratuity of God" which graces human beings and allows us to practice liberation with generosity and humility.[33] Sobrino devotes a book to the *Spirituality of liberation*, but radically reinterprets the experience of God as something that amounts to liberative practice in history.[34] He speaks of "spirit" as equivalent to "life" and rigorously translates talk of the spirit into talk of kinship with God through collaboration in establishing the reign of God.[35]

It is difficult to know whether the program of "cashing" all mystical or "spiritual" talk in terms of liberative action ultimately reduces the reality of experienced grace. Perhaps in Sobrino's stress on praxis he overdoes the anchoring of grace and spirituality to visible action. This certainly seems true when we search in his writing for references to the term "grace" or for passages where the emphasis is not on Christians building the kingdom through their own historical involvement. René Padilla is correct to warn of the danger in Sobrino of seeing the kingdom of God as "a utopia to be fashioned by [humans] rather than as a gift to be received in faith." [36]

In Latin American liberation theology the following of Jesus as we have outlined it is the central metaphor for both the Christian life and evangelization. Under this heading we have already raised most of the other aspects of liberation theology which relate to an incarnational approach to mission. To some of these others we now turn.

Starting with the Historical Jesus

Liberation theology stresses the historical Jesus rather than the Christ of faith: Jesus of Nazareth, his life and teaching, and the path he took to the cross.[37] Boff affirms the mystery of the incarnation (God becoming human) but reminds us to fill that concept with the historical and human elements that made up the life of Jesus, and not to see it as merely a divine transaction.[38] Boff gives five reasons for Latin American liberation theology emphasizing the historical Jesus. (1) It sees a similar situation to that of Latin America applying in Jesus' time. (2) Attending to Jesus' life shows us something of the liberative program we are to follow. (3) It points up the conflict we are likely to face. (4) His life reminds us that following is the response he calls for. (5) Finally, Jesus shows us the way to the Father through conversion and practical change.[39]

Boff seems to be aware that we do not have ready access to Jesus of Nazareth because the Gospel writers selected, re-arranged and highlighted elements of Jesus' life, writing not a history but a response to Jesus.[40] Although he thinks that the message of Jesus and the faith of the early

Christians can never be adequately separated Boff argues they can be distinguished. He thereby places himself among those scholars, such as Ernst Käsemann, who are concerned with what has been known as the "new quest" for the historical Jesus. They tend to be less confident about details than those who pursued the now discredited "old quest," but hopeful nevertheless about discerning broad outlines of Jesus' ministry and message.[41]

Although starting with the historical Jesus, Boff sees the hermeneutical key as approaching Jesus through commitment to him, as did the early church and the authors of the New Testament, and as the church has done in varying degrees throughout history. Hence not everything hangs on our knowledge of the historical Jesus. God has been revealed not only in the historical Jesus, but in the living Christ, mainly but not only in the church. "The incarnation of Christ ... is a process that began one day in Nazareth and that has not yet arrived at its final destination because Christ has not yet Christianized all of reality."[42] As part of this process, God is revealed in the communal opening of scripture, where Christians read it in "liberating perspective."[43] The crucified Christ is also discovered and known particularly among the poor. In these ways the historical Jesus does not remain a figure from the past but a living reality still being discovered in the church. Here the incarnation functions as an integrating concept covering not only the presence of God in Jesus of Nazareth but also the unfolding of the incarnating process ever since, including the mission of the church.

Sobrino speaks in similar terms, stating at the outset of *Christology at the crossroads* that his starting point is the historical Jesus (his person, teaching, attitudes and deeds) and not the Chalcedonian formula, nor christological titles, nor Christ's presence in the liturgy, nor the resurrection, nor the preached Christ of the early church, nor even Jesus' teaching taken alone.[44] What he means is that "it is the historical Jesus who is the key providing access to the total Christ." [45]

For liberation theologians the historical Jesus is important not as a historical figure to be understood but as a person to whom to respond. Here is the clearly incarnational element. Sobrino argues that what makes Jesus "historical" is his lived life and practice, and Jesus invites Christians to continue that practice. This, Sobrino says, we must safeguard above all.[46]

Incarnation as Transparency
Between Divine and Human

Boff has a fascinating way of integrating the incarnation, transcendence, immanence, the nature of Christ, sacramentalism, and, flowing out of all of this, mission. He makes a simple suggestion, acknowledging that he is trying to conceptualize what is essentially mystery. It is a view similar to the one we earlier called the incarnating dynamic of God, and bears similarities to the way John Macquarrie expresses his understanding of transcendence.[47]

The incarnation, argues Boff, is not just a central doctrine, but also the key to a new incarnational understanding of reality. It points to the mutual presence of the divine and the human, the eternal and the historical. Transcendence and immanence are the terms we usually reach for to explain God's otherness and presence-among-us respectively, but to relate them we need the idea of transparency. The more transparent a human is to the divine, the more the transcendent God is immanent.[48] Incarnation, therefore, is the process of the transcendent God becoming historical in events and people who are transparent to God, that is, transformed, liberated and "divinized."[49] The whole of reality can become transparent and sacramental. Humans are capable of self-transcendence and self-communication, relating to others and to God. Jesus, fully human, did this in an absolute way and in this consists his divinity.[50]

In his more recent work Boff shows remarkable optimism, given his social context, as he expounds this holistic and ecological view of reality which he believes will lead to both justice for the poor and restoration of the planet:

> The divine shines in and forth from everything.... Religious experience makes everything sacramental, because it is penetrated by and suffused with the presence of the divine.... The divine is not something added to human experience from outside. It is manifested through all experience.[51]

Put in missiological terms, incarnation is the process of God becoming transparent in temporal and historical ways, above all through Jesus but also through the continuing process in which "the divine penetrates the human and the human enters into the divine."[52] Without equating the church to Jesus Christ himself,[53] Boff argues that "Christianity can be understood as a prolongation of God's incarnation process. Just as the Son took everything upon himself in order to liberate everything, so the Christian faith seeks to become incarnate in everything in order to transfigure everything." [54]

Here Boff refers to incarnation more than *the* incarnation, meaning a process reflecting the very nature of God and extending throughout history (this is the third dimension of incarnational mission suggested in chapter 3). The mission of the church is to demonstrate the incarnational structure of human life as revealed in the incarnation of Jesus Christ.[55]

Some Elements of "Following Jesus"

Some of the major elements of following Jesus, according to liberation theology, are commitment to the poor; a critical socio-analytical program; conflict, suffering and possible martyrdom; and Christian community.

Commitment to the poor is one of the starting points of liberation theology. Boff and Sobrino repeatedly ground this commitment in the incarnation. Boff argues, for example, that God has not become incarnate in Caesar on his throne, or in priests at the altar, but in the shape of the oppressed and excluded who are sent outside the city to be crucified.[56] "His incarnation is taken 'to the hilt.'"[57] Sobrino often refers to what he calls the double kenosis of Christ: becoming human and also becoming weak and in solidarity with the poor.[58] Leonardo and Clodovis Boff include in their list of key notions of liberation theology: "*Incarnation* among and *solidarity* with the outcast."[59] The simple argument is that because Jesus did it, as his followers so should we.[60]

Sobrino argues eloquently that the church should point to Christ by being "incarnated" in the weakness of this world and being a church of the poor:

> I don't know what other way of being church can take seriously the fact that its mission—like God's own mission and that of God's Christ, Jesus—is to put truth where there are lies; freedom where there is oppression; justice where there is inhuman poverty; community where there is indignity; mercy, love, justice, life where there is suffering, torture, murder, disappeared persons, in a word death.[61]

The difficult thing for the church, argues Sobrino, is not how to understand Jesus but to embody its faith where it ought to be—among the poor and in the unlovely reality of poverty. The song "Were you there when they crucified my Lord?" is worth more than a thousand pages of ecclesiology, he says.[62] The mission of the church must be incarnational in the sense of following God's "downward journey." Evangelizers have no option but to demonstrate with their lives the basic fact that God loves people "in the lowest abysses of poverty and misery" by drawing near in solidarity.[63]

A second element of following Jesus is a **critical socio-analytical program**, in other words, a praxis for human liberation. This follows and makes effective our commitment to the poor. We do not need to develop this in detail here. Although at times liberation theologians claim that Jesus' liberative praxis challenged the social and political structures of his day,[64] they just as often base the need for such a political program on a social analysis of the current situation, whether informed by Marxism or other sources.[65] At one point Leonardo Boff actually cites sustained political strategies as an example of something we cannot derive from Jesus, because Jesus' intense apocalyptic hopes precluded it and he neither claimed to be a political messiah nor spoke clearly against the Romans.[66] The project of Jesus, according to Boff, included political implications but was deeper and liberative in a multi-dimensional way.

The third element of following Jesus is **conflict, suffering and possible martyrdom**. For liberation theology this is a significant aspect of an incarnational approach to mission. Following Jesus is a path of costly and painful discipleship, because a central part of following Jesus is to challenge the powerful forces which keep the poor in poverty and the powerless from participation and dignity.[67] It also involves a call for the church to renounce its worldly wealth and power, operating not in a coalition of church and state but in a critical relationship to the government and other powerful groups.

This is not a glorification of suffering. Nor is it primarily a theology of the cross. Rather the focus on the cross is a by-product of a theology of discipleship, a broader idea which includes an expectation of suffering but also the expectation and experience of resurrection.[68] Sobrino says there should be no Christian mystique of the cross. "The cross is the outcome of Jesus' historical path.... Incarnation situated in a concrete context comes before the cross."[69] "What God encourages is real incarnation in history, because only in this way will history be saved, *even though* this leads to the cross." [70]

It is also something the church should face together. It is not an individual call to a suffering discipleship, but a call corporately to be the body of Christ. In accepting that Christ was crucified, we should ask how this crucified body is made present in history. Latin American liberation theologians, operating in a context of people who are both Christian and oppressed, insist that as well as speaking of Jesus as the "crucified God" we must speak of those who are crushed by poverty, institutional violence and early death as "crucified peoples."[71] Archbishop Romero, before his assassination in 1980, showed in provocative terms that he understood the leadership role required of the church as a body:

> I rejoice, my brothers and sisters, that our church is persecuted for its efforts of incarnation in the interests of the poor.... It would be a sad situation if, in a country where such horrible murders are being committed, we had no priests among the victims. They are witnesses of a church incarnate in the problems of the people.[72]

In recent decades Latin America has seen many martyrs (taken in the broad sense of being killed as a direct result of their faith), from Archbishop Oscar Romero and the six Jesuit theologians to many unknown peasant farmers and members of the urban poor. Sobrino argues that martyrdom is "the fullest, most integral expression of the incarnation that takes place in concrete Latin American reality."[73] This is a deeply sobering thought for those who would embrace an incarnational approach to mission.

The fourth element of discipleship, again following from the one before, is **Christian community**, expressed in Latin America in base Christian communities. Boff argues that base communities are the church at the grass roots. They represent a new birth of the church (an "ecclesiogenesis") and a growth of hope and faith among the poor, meeting in small, informal groups and concretizing their following of Jesus. This embodiment of faith interweaves the gospel with life. In the context of base communities, often-uneducated Christians come to know Christ through reading the scriptures and encountering in their lives together the Word-made-flesh in historical struggle and new birth. Boff suggests that as they organize for their own liberation and experience evangelization in their own lives they then evangelize others and the whole church.[74] Base communities are primary ecclesial structures of incarnational mission.[75]

The Incarnating Process and
Continued Incarnation

As Roman Catholic theologians, Boff and Sobrino work in a framework where the idea of the church as the continuing incarnation of Jesus Christ is generally accepted. Yet by seeing the idea in a different perspective and taking a more critical stance towards the record of the church they radically recast the notion of the church perpetuating the presence of the incarnate Christ. Two differences from the standard interpretation are noticeable: a view of incarnation as a process (held by Boff), and treating the identity between Jesus and the church as metaphorical and based on an identity of mission. These are both powerful visions of the incarnation as the foundation and spring of mission.

Boff suggests that **an incarnating process exists.** While Boff's christology generally emphasizes Jesus' humanity, and partially defines Jesus' divinity in terms of his radically fulfilled humanity, Boff also speaks of a complementary process in which God by very nature "becomes' and creates history and is revealed most fully in Jesus of Nazareth. The incarnation is an "eruption" in the dynamic incarnating process of the divine reality. Yet even "the incarnation" should not be limited to the birth, life and death of Jesus, but should be understood in the light of the resurrection, which inspired Paul to say of Christ "He is everything and in everything" (Col 3:11).[76] Because Jesus touches all humanity and makes possible our liberation at all levels, "the Incarnation contains a message that concerns not only Jesus Christ but also the nature and destiny of every person."[77] We are all destined to be images and likenesses of Jesus Christ. The incarnation points to the human capacity through Jesus to identify with the Infinite, to open ourselves to God and neighbour so that "we can be the fulness of divine and human communication like Christ."[78] These are lofty ideas indeed, and perhaps, taken in isolation, too rosy in their view of human nature. Their context, however, is a framework in which the incarnation is working itself out in history and the church, as part of a cosmic unfolding which is incarnational in character, and will not be complete until Christ has Christianized all of reality.[79] We note here how Boff's view of incarnational mission includes all three dimensions we outlined in chapter 3, Jesus as pattern, Christ as enabling power, and God's incarnating dynamic.

Liberation theologians see the identity between the church and Christ **in metaphorical terms and as an identity of mission.** Although Boff and Sobrino both use terms such as the church "continuing" the incarnation, "prolonging" it and "perpetuating" it, they tend to use them in a strongly metaphorical sense, illustrating the metaphorical approach to theology we argued for in outlining (in chapter 3) the directions of an adequate incarnational christology. Boff quotes Pius XII's statement that "the Church is Christ" and comments that we should not take it literally, because the church is at the same time saint and sinner, always in need of conversion and reform. The continuity is one of function and not of nature or essence. Boff says, "Just as Christ achieved salvation for all persons, the Church must prolong that mission throughout the centuries. It has the same mission as Christ. Yet traditional theology has taken Jesus Christ as the model for understanding the whole church." [80]

Rather radically, Boff suggests that the church is not based on the incarnation of the Word (created by God, we might say) but was born of a decision by the apostles to respond in the Holy Spirit to the risen Christ and his program (created by our faith through the Spirit), and it will continue to exist only as long as Christians "continually renew this decision and incarnate the Church in ever new situations." [81] He puts a twist on the common use of "prolongation" by saying that the church's existence is founded on "the prolongation of Jesus' service to all women and men, particularly to the humiliated." [82] If the church serves others, then it prolongs the incarnation of Jesus Christ. Apart from Christ, nothing is guaranteed to be a sacrament of salvation; the church can be grace or "ungrace" according to whether it is aligned with the liberating praxis of Jesus. [83]

Sobrino follows Boff in arguing that the "real body of Christ in history" (the continuation of the incarnation, speaking metaphorically) is the church when incarnated in the weakness and poverty of this world, thus making Christ visible, in a limited way. When this happens, and only then, "whoever sees the church sees Christ (a little or a lot of Christ)." [84]

Holistic Evangelization

Latin American liberation theology sees the whole of corporate Christian life as evangelization. To be a sign and instrument of the Good

News is the reason for the church.[85] This is a profoundly incarnational vision.

The term "evangelization" needs clarification here. First, liberation theologians broaden it to encompass the whole of "mission," including announcing and embodying all that the reign of God entails. Second, Boff and Sobrino want to insist that even in a so-called Christian society there is more good news to announce, embody and hope for. The poor are evangelized when they are liberated; they evangelize the rest of the church when they show the signs of Christ risen; and the church evangelizes the world when the Good News has at least to some extent become a reality in its life.[86] Setting what some would consider a nearly impossible task, Sobrino argues that evangelization consists of rendering God present and initiating the reign of God.[87]

Difficult though it may be, this vision of integrating faith and practice and combining words and deeds, in the manner of Jesus, is central to the liberationist perspective.[88] Priscilla Pope-Levison studies ten Latin American liberation theologians, Catholic and Protestant, and concludes that the liberationist model of evangelization to which they all aspire is holistic:

> A wholistic evangelization seeks to go beyond the boundaries of horizontal/vertical, spiritual/secular, personal/social, and individual/structural.... Examples of this wholistic approach are the integration of evangelization and social justice, evangelization and liberation, proclamation and action, annunciation and denunciation, conversion in the individual and corporate spheres, and sin in the individual and corporate spheres.[89]

Incarnation as Inculturation

In common with other Catholic theologians Boff and Sobrino sometimes use the terms "incarnation," "to incarnate," "to become incarnated," and "to take flesh" to refer to taking shape in a specific cultural setting, that is, to the process of inculturation or contextualization.[90] We will discuss this further in our consideration of Catholic approaches to incarnational mission (in chapter 8).

In summary, Latin American liberation theology, particularly as articulated by Boff and Sobrino, is strongly incarnational in each of its facets: following the liberating praxis of Jesus; costly solidarity with the poor; facing conflict, suffering and even martyrdom; embodying the Good News in our lives; experiencing God's incarnating activity in history; inculturating the gospel in a variety of cultures; and integrating word and deed holistically. It remains to evaluate briefly their approach in the light of two common criticisms.

Evaluative Comments

The main critical questions put to liberation theology concerning its incarnational view of mission are: Can we know the historical Jesus we are being challenged to follow? Even if we know, are we able to follow just because Jesus led?[91]

The first question is **whether we can know the historical Jesus** as well as the liberation theologians suggest. Several commentators have suggested that the basic weakness in the christologies of Boff and Sobrino is that they claim too much about the historical Jesus without sufficient evidence.[92]

For example, the "Galilean crisis' that Sobrino argues (in his earlier work) happened to Jesus of Nazareth[93] is more likely shaped by Mark as part of his narrative strategy.[94] Some of Sobrino's "historical" statements sound more like kerygmatic statements; for example, "The liberation of the Hebrews from Egypt can be taken as a historical statement about God."[95] Also, Boff sometimes sounds over-confident in making claims for Jesus of Nazareth from the Gospels.

Nevertheless, Boff directly addresses the hermeneutical question of how we can know Christ. He explicitly acknowledges that Jesus' history and message were radically amalgamated with the history of the faith in the early church, but argues (along with much of New Testament scholarship) that we can assume at least some continuity between what Jesus did and what the early church remembered and wrote down.[96]

Also, in more recent writing we find Sobrino responding to criticisms that the quest for the historical Jesus is doomed to failure. To start with the historical Jesus is not to see him as an object of investigation, but to emphasize his full humanity. It is also to focus on the relationship between his action in history and the response of Christian community, through whom we now interpret him. It is to see the overall practice and spirit of Jesus as a criterion of discipleship. Our response to Jesus is what matters most.[97]

The second question put to liberation theologians is **whether Christians are able to follow Jesus simply because he has led the way**. In a detailed critique, Todd Speidell argues that liberation theologians merely advocate following Jesus as a pattern for mission, a form of exemplarism. He says that if we take the path of liberation theology our following of Christ will ultimately fail, "for we are left with our own following of Jesus' following." [98]

We can say in reply that although liberation theologians overwhelmingly emphasize faith proven in action, largely in reaction to a more passive and "interior" faith, they are also aware of the enabling power of Christ. Boff reminds us that the following of Jesus is not a merely moral demand to copy Jesus but an attachment to the risen Christ which projects us into a new reality and allows Christ to act in us. [99] Sobrino says that a Christian life of love is only possible because of the sheer grace of God loving us first. [100] Similarly, Ignacio Ellacuría says that Christ does not just show us the way but is the very being of God with us and for us. [101]

The two criticisms amount to the question of who Jesus is and where Jesus is to be found. In reply the liberationist approach to incarnational mission insists that Jesus is not only a pattern, found in the *past*; he is also *present* whenever there is engagement in liberating praxis, especially among the poor. An interactive hermeneutic enables knowledge of the historical Jesus *and* enables the praxis. Christ is discovered as liberating and empowering presence, that is, as incarnate.

In our consideration of Latin American liberation theology, particularly of Boff and Sobrino, we have found incarnation to be central. In a similar way to the Anabaptists and radical evangelicals, liberation theologians contribute to missiology a clear perspective on the following of Jesus in daily life as the essence of Christian faith. There is a strong emphasis on the incarnation as the pattern for mission, and yet also an emphasis both on the incarnation as the presence of Christ in mission and incarnation as the ongoing activity of God. This last emphasis is developed well in the work of Choan-Seng Song, to which we now turn.

An East Asian Perspective:
Choan-Seng Song

Taiwanese theologian Choan-Seng Song merits consideration partly because he gives an East Asian liberationist perspective, partly because he illustrates an ecumenical Protestant approach to liberation theology, and partly because he develops in some detail an explicitly incarnational approach to mission which links creation and salvation. We could discuss him equally well in this chapter with liberation theologians or in our chapter on ecumenical approaches to incarnational mission. Of all missiologists he most clearly develops what we have called the third dimension of incarnational mission, joining the incarnating dynamic of God.

Song (born 1929) has been Principal of the Tainan Theological College in Taiwan, has served for a period as Associate Director of the Faith and Order Commission of the World Council of Churches, and is now Professor of Theology and Asian Cultures at the Pacific School of Religion, Berkeley, and Regional Professor of Theology at the South East Asia Graduate School of Theology in Singapore and Hong Kong.[102] Among his better known books are *Third-eye theology: Theology in formation in Asian settings*, suggesting a more heart-based and intuitive "Asian" approach to theology, and *Tell us our names: Story theology from an Asian perspective.*[103] He has recently completed a three-part christology under the title *The cross in the lotus world.*[104] Of particular interest for incarnational mission are his *Christian mission in reconstruction: An Asian analysis* (1977) and an article on a Taiwanese theology of the incarnation (1976).[105]

Song believes that Christian mission is by nature incarnationally shaped, that is, an eternal process of God going out of Godself to become embodied in history.[106] This is such a strong principle that, for Song, any act that reflects God's mission of enfleshment is Christian mission, and any act that does not is not mission.[107] His reflections on the importance of the incarnation for mission are rich and varied. We will consider first his central understanding of mission as reflecting God's mission of enfleshment, and then gather under several other points some of the implications of this view.

God's Mission Is Enfleshment

For Song, the Prologue of John's Gospel points to the deep mystery that God is both the creative God and the incarnating God. Both aspects of God are intertwined, so that from the very beginning both creation and incarnation have been eternal activities of God. In a chapter entitled "Mission of enfleshment" Song points to the identity of the creative Word and the incarnate Word.[108] It is the nature of God to "become," to be embodied, to incarnate.[109] Hence Song uses "incarnation" both with and without the definite article. It can refer to an eternal process called "incarnation" or its consummation in Jesus, called "the incarnation." In the incarnation the Word became flesh. That is, God the Creator became God the "Incarnator." [110]

The implications for Christian mission are clear:

> Since God's mission in creation and incarnation is that of enfleshment, that of imparting [Godself], Christian mission as witness to God's mission should be that of imparting to others one's own self as grasped by the love of God in Jesus Christ. In the last analysis, the mission of Christians is to *be with* this world, or more concretely, to be one with the agony and joy of this world with the transforming power of God's love. Jesus Christ is God's being with this world.[111]

In intertwining creation and incarnation Song has a very broad view of what constitutes the incarnating dynamic of God. Incarnation is the "immediate presence of the Eternal One in the midst of the temporal and transient," both creatively and redemptively. As our lives become invaded by God's incarnation which is eternally present as a powerful creative force, the present moment is transformed, despair gives way to hope and our lives become "incarnational events."[112] Incarnational theology is concerned with what happens between God and humans in particular times and places, creating and re-creating humanity in a process of humanization through the mystery of Christ.[113] Incarnation has little to do with the ontological categories of the Latin and Greek christological controversies and much more to do with an existential dynamic, a process in which the church allows God to become embodied in its life and enfleshed in creation.[114] This is the basis for Song's lifelong project of finding Asian expressions of the gospel.

The basic meaning of incarnational mission, then, flows from Song's Logos-theology. It is that God's eternal enfleshment, experienced both as creation and redemption, is to be reflected in Christian mission, by "being with this world." The essence of mission is to give oneself for others by rejoicing with those who rejoice and weeping with those who weep.[115] Hence Song is critical of Western missionaries to China in the first half of this century, some of whom were distinguished by their "disembodiment," proclaiming their message without acting for justice and the liberation of those under tyranny at the time.[116]

Several implications unfold from this understanding of God's incarnating dynamic.

Risking Loss of Identity

Song sees God's becoming incarnate in Jesus Christ as becoming "what-God-was-not," at the risk of losing God's own identity. This is the heart of the paradox of Christian faith: the divine embodied in the human. "It should also constitute the heart of Christian mission."[117] Song interprets in two ways this going out from ourselves and taking another shape.

First, it is **a mission of self-emptying**. Song explores the meaning of Christ "emptying himself" (Phil 2:7) and being stripped bare. This mission begins in weakness, poverty, and (metaphorical and literal) nakedness. Its costliness and renunciation are overwhelming. Paradoxically God's nakedness in assuming human flesh is the salvation of humanity. In its apparent weakness it is a rich and redeeming "nakedness." Song is highly critical of foreign missionaries and Christian churches in Asia, who often speak from relative wealth, power and security. Incarnational mission must begin differently, and Song sees few who will take up the challenge.[118]

> As long as the church is preoccupied with her own endowments, welfare and security, she only pays lip-service to Christ's mission of self-emptying. And according to Bonhoeffer, for the church to exist for others, she must first divest herself of what she already has.[119]

Risking our identity in becoming what-we-are-not has a second meaning for Song, that of abandoning our own identity in cross-cultural mission and risking **the inculturation of the gospel**. Mission must face what he calls historical pluralism, and instead of Christianizing the world, must aim to renew civilizations deeply rooted in other religions. It aims to be contextual and expects new ways of responding to the love and justice of God. It attempts the difficult task of ensuring that it is Christ-centered rather than church-centered.[120]

Becoming Available, Being "There for Others"

"God's mission of enfleshment means that God has now become available to [humanity]. Jesus Christ is this availability of God."[121] Song is referring here to Christ's role as partner, brother, friend and the one who is present at every critical moment of our lives. In the life of Jesus of Nazareth this availability unfolded in radically unconventional ways, breaking barriers between people and God and including those who had been excluded by religion. Song is sharply critical of what he calls the "compound Christianity" of many missionaries, and argues that incarnational mission involves removing walls, denying ourselves, and going beyond "us-and-them" in a search for an inclusive "we." Song feels that much of Christian mission bears only a faint echo of the vulnerable availability that we see in God's mission of enfleshment.[122]

The Sacramental Nature of Christian Mission

Song has a radical interpretation of the sacrament of the Lord's Supper, arguing that it does not need to be observed in a liturgical context as much as acted out in a missionary context.

> Each act of mission undertaken to make visible the saving love of God is a sacramental act.... [The Lord's Supper] does not need to be held, observed or celebrated. The Lord's Supper happens.... The healing of bodily disorder, restoration of broken relationships, elimination of social injustice, working for peace among men [and women], in a word, becoming witness to the reality of God in the world, are all literally the sacrament of the Lord's Supper. The Lord's Supper, therefore, is an action and not a ceremony.[123]

The last meal Jesus had with his disciples was not only the culmination of Jesus' ministry but also the launch of the new ministry of his disciples. Song calls it "the consummation of the mission of enfleshment."[124] The Christian re-enactment of it remembers and partakes in Christ's body broken for all.

Song sees Jesus Christ (including his life, teaching, death and resurrection) as the primary sacrament, because as the Word made flesh, he supremely exemplifies the spiritual visible in the material. Nevertheless, Jesus and the churchly sacraments are not the only sacraments. Affirming a type of sacramentalism, Song sees anything as sacramental insofar as it makes Christ's redemptive presence real in the world. Mission is sacramental when "its words take form in action."[125] The incarnational approach to mission, it seems, ties together the missionary and the sacramental dimensions of the church.[126]

In putting his case, Song is probably unfair to sacramentalism in characterizing it as the view that in the sacraments themselves there is an inherent saving power, as if magical.[127] It is this definition which leads him to say that sacramentalism is a theologically untenable position.

Yet Song's argument is strong in what it affirms, which is both a missionary sacramentalism and a sacramental missiology. The link between the eucharist and participation in the mission of Jesus is one worth recovering and emphasizing, on the grounds Song uses: What the Lord's Supper means has to be enacted daily in mission.

Incarnation Points to Humanization
as the Goal of Salvation

The incarnation provides the theological grounds for humanization to be the central concern of mission, according to Song. God entered humanity, thereby affirming it, dignifying it and enabling its fullness. God's mission has its beginning with humanization (the incarnation) and its end in humanization (the full humanity of all people). In fact, Song prefers "the humanization of God" to the term "the incarnation," suggesting that although they mean the same thing humanization reminds us of the process involved, of the "becoming" in "The Word became flesh." [128]

This perspective is important to Song in the Asian context, because in China the church has found it difficult to relate the spiritual reconstruction of the individual to the reconstruction of society (we might say that this is true not only of China). The reason, he suggests, is an abstract view of the incarnation as the meeting of divinity and humanity. This has not touched the Chinese mind deeply enough to take root and "become flesh" in social as well as individual ways. The deeper meaning of the incarnation is God's humanization, that is, a transformative meeting of God's humanity and our distorted humanity. This transformation is a gift from the creator and savior God and touches us deeply at all levels, spiritual and material, individual and social.[129] It involves justice and reconciliation as well. It is a transfiguration in the stuff of history.[130] With an eye to critics of ecumenical programs for humanization, Song says it is a full and deep view of humanization that we must pursue in mission. Not only must we deepen humanization with a proper view of the incarnation. We must also fill out the incarnational approach to mission with this dynamic theology of humanization.[131]

"Jesus, the Crucified People"

Following a direction explored by Moltmann, Song argues in his book *Jesus, the crucified people* that those who, in the pain of the world, find God absent are looking in the wrong place.[132] The incarnation strengthens the meaning of Immanuel, "God with us."

> God as Immanuel is not just God-*with*-Jesus, but God *is Jesus*. God as Immanuel is not only God-*with*-suffering-human-persons, but God *is* suffering human persons. This is the decisive meaning of the incarnation.[133]

Song goes on by means of stories of pain and hope, and meditations which theologize in a deceptively indirect manner. He tells one story from the novel *The samurai*, by Japanese Catholic writer Shusaku Endo, set in the seventeenth century and following the world travels of a samurai who becomes a Christian on his epic journey.[134] In Mexico the samurai comes upon a Japanese Christian monk estranged from the church and living and working among the poor and oppressed Indians. The monk has a roughly carved wooden cross outside his small hut, with an Indian Christ on it, pug-nosed and with pigtails. When asked by the samurai whether he will return to Japan, he says:

> "I'm too old to return." The renegade monk lowered his eyes to the ground. "I ... wherever the Indians go, I shall go; where they stay, I shall stay. They need someone like me to wipe off their sweat when they are ill, to hold their hands at the moment of death. The Indians and I—we are both without a home...." [135]

Song comments that the monk knew that the Indians needed him to share their pain. "This at least he knew. But is there anything else more important than this to know? Is this not the heart of what is called 'theology of the incarnation' in Christian theology?"[136]

In this way Song pushes to the limits the perspective that Jesus *is* the crucified people. Theology often says that to know God we must know Jesus, but we must go further and say that to know Jesus we must know people, the sort of flesh-and-blood people Jesus knew: those who are exploited and poor, who are nobodies in the world.[137] Because the way of Jesus inevitably confronts the kingdoms of this world, "the way of Jesus has, then, to be the way of the cross."[138] Elsewhere Song suggests that "to be a church of this crucified God is to be a crucified church. It is a suffering church that can give witness to the crucified God.'[139]

We can see that, for Song, incarnational mission means (among other things) that, guided by a liberative reading of scripture, we are both to find Jesus among the suffering and to love in concrete ways those who are being crushed. It is a costly road with the potential for the church on mission to be "crucified" itself.

Song develops incarnational missiology in several important ways, as we have seen, particularly in linking creation and redemption as aspects of God's mission of enfleshment (illustrating better than most the third dimension of incarnational mission, the incarnating dynamic of God). He links this in concrete ways to self-emptying, availability and suffering in mission. He develops sacramentalism in a missionary direction, wanting the Lord's Supper, or its healing at least, to take place in daily life. Finally, he links the "humanity of God" with the possibility of full humanity for broken and crushed people.

In evaluating Song's contribution, it is the last point which leads to our main criticism of his thought. While it is not novel to put humanity at the center of the Christian vision of salvation, Song tends to be anthropocentric to the virtual exclusion of any cosmic vision. This anthropocentrism was almost universal among theologians in the 1960s and 1970s as many rediscovered justice and liberation as a central part of the gospel. Song, however, remains wedded to his Christian humanism in his more recent publications, at the expense of integrating an environmental perspective into his missiology. The irony is that in uniting creation and redemption his theology is particularly fertile for an environmental perspective, and yet the focus remains on humanity alone.

Nevertheless, Song makes a distinctive contribution. He shares the basic orientation of liberation theologians, but with an Asian perspective. This perspective is evident in his intuitive approach, his story telling, the influence of eastern religions, and his awareness of the minority status of Christianity in his context. In Song's case this perspective is enriched by a systematic theological approach. His fascination with incarnation and *the* incarnation, and their importance for mission, is obvious at many points of his writing. He sums it up when commenting, as he often does, on John 1:14. "What a mystery is packed into this brief statement! ... To learn to say the Word-become-flesh in one breath with crescendo reaching the climax at the 'flesh' is a theological adventure we wish to embark on."[140]

Overall, we have seen in the three chosen representatives of liberation theology a sustained argument for incarnational mission. Liberation theology certainly meets all the requirements suggested for an adequate incarnational christology. We see it in starting "from below," with the historical Jesus, while making strong statements about God's action ("from above"). We see it in a metaphorical approach and in the relational terms through which humanity is related to divinity (especially in Boff's talk of transparency and transcendence).[141] Finally, we see it in the trinitarian framework, the role of the Holy Spirit and the strong soteriological emphasis directed towards incarnational mission.

We found that the Latin American theologians' emphasis on discipleship (like that of the Anabaptists and radical evangelicals) accords with the biblical vision and leads to a vigorous and compassionate missiology. In the writing of Boff, Sobrino and Song we found a variety of dimensions of incarnational missiology, including God's incarnating dynamic, a sacramental vision, commitment to the poor, the integration of word and action, an expectation of suffering and persecution, and incarnation as inculturation. We noted that in Boff's writing in particular all three dimensions of incarnational mission suggested in chapter 3 were present in a balanced and interactive way.

We have found in the last three chapters (examining Anabaptism, radical evangelicalism and liberation theology) a powerful emphasis on mission as the following of Jesus in daily life. This challenges nominal Christianity and evangelism seen as proclamation alone. Mission is shaped by the pattern of Jesus, with all the risks and costs that may be involved. We have also found, nevertheless, that with varying degrees of success, each of these traditions also draws on other dimensions of incarnational mission, namely mission as acting in the enabling power of the risen Christ, and mission as joining the incarnating mission of God.

CHAPTER 7

CHRIST'S ANTICIPATORY PRESENCE: JÜRGEN MOLTMANN

The perspective of Jürgen Moltmann serves as a bridge between the strong emphasis on incarnational mission as following the pattern of Jesus (surveyed in chapters 4 to 6) and the emphasis on God's incarnating dynamic and continuing incarnation in the church (to be surveyed in chapters 8 and 9).

In Anabaptism, radical evangelicalism and liberation theology, the clear call to discipleship (the first dimension of incarnational mission) is complemented by other dimensions of incarnational mission (participation in Christ and joining God's incarnating mission). Similarly, in Catholicism, Anglo-Catholicism, ecumenical literature and Eastern Orthodoxy we will find all three dimensions, even though a view of incarnation as an expression of God's nature (the third dimension) is particularly strong. In Moltmann as well, we find the three dimensions, but what he contributes most distinctively is an emphasis on God's initiative in making incarnational mission possible through the saving and empowering presence of Christ (the second dimension).

Moltmann's bridging role comes from the way he so strongly and effectively ties the presence of Christ both to discipleship and to the continuing incarnating mission of God. He is tempted neither to advocate mere imitation, as if we can succeed in incarnational mission by virtue of our human efforts, nor to suggest that as the continuing incarnation of Christ the church will succeed in incarnational mission because of the guaranteed presence of Christ in the church.

It is, therefore, Moltmann's significance in articulating a view of incarnational mission in terms of conformity to Christ as both criterion and power for mission that justifies his inclusion as an individual theologian in the middle of a survey which otherwise examines Christian traditions.

Moltmann (born 1926) has been Professor of Systematic Theology in the Protestant faculty at Tübingen for most of his career. No other contemporary writer is as influential in putting forward a missiologically-oriented theology with a strong christocentric focus. He is arguably the most influential German Protestant theologian writing today. A theologian in the Reformed tradition, he is in intellectual conversation with liberation theology, Anabaptism, Catholicism, Eastern Orthodoxy and the ecumenical movement.[1]

On the surface Moltmann's writing does not seem to be worth mining for insight into incarnational mission. A survey of over fifty of his books and articles, including all of his major works, reveals no occurrence of the term at all.

Nevertheless, in digging a little deeper into Moltmann's ecclesiology and christology we find that although Moltmann uses other terms, his missiology points clearly in the direction of incarnational mission understood as participation in Christ. In this chapter we will briefly sketch the outlines of Moltmann's missiology, list some themes pointing to incarnational mission and assess the contribution of Moltmann's incarnational missiology.

Moltmann's Messianic Missiology

It is not necessary to attempt to summarize Moltmann's theological project. Nor is it necessary to give a detailed exposition of his missiology, which is so pervasive in his theology as to make that task also too large. It will be useful, however, to indicate some of the contours of his approach and how they determine for Moltmann the nature of Christian mission.

Moltmann has published his most substantial work in two series of books. The first series was a trilogy,[2] in which he looked at the whole of theology through the lens, first, of hope, then of suffering, and then of the church.[3] The second series is more like a systematic theology, although open-ended by design and (in sympathy with our times) simply called "contributions to theology."[4] The main topics of this series are the doctrine of God, creation, christology, pneumatology and eschatology[5] Although Moltmann has changed and grown in his views, there is a basic consistency in his approach which allows us to take a view of his theology as a whole.[6] As we would expect, it is in Moltmann's books on christology and ecclesiology that we find the theology that is most fertile for incarnational missiology.[7]

Moltmann's starting point was the **theology of hope**. He sees God's revelation as an unfolding series of promises which point strongly to fulfillment in the ultimate future or *eschaton*.[8] Although he outlines philosophical reasons for acknowledging the power of hope and the primacy of the future in human experience, Moltmann grounds his Christian hope in the resurrection of the crucified Christ.[9] His whole theology, his whole vision of hope, is a resurrection faith. Defining eschatology as the doctrine of Christian hope, he argues that "from first to last ... Christianity is eschatology, is hope, is forward looking and forward moving, and therefore also revolutionizing and transforming the present."[10] In later works he continually emphasizes the messianic nature of Jesus Christ and the church's expectation. A messianic framework is one in which promise repeatedly leads to expectation, then an unfolding of God's revelation, and ultimately, fulfillment.[11] It is the future which interprets the present, and we live in anticipation of the coming God.

In *The crucified God* Moltmann presented the other side of the dialectic between the resurrection and the cross, that is, between a future-oriented hope of God and **God's present identification** with suffering and lost humanity.[12] God is revealed definitively in the suffering of Jesus Christ, the promised one (Messiah), who anticipates in his suffering and resurrection the fulfillment of God's promised future of freedom.[13] Moltmann places the cross at the center of theology, and sees it as the criterion for the church, with strong implications for social involvement alongside the poor and the oppressed.[14] He pushes to the very limit the idea that the cross represents death within God, and unveils a mutuality of giving by God the Father and submission in God the Son. His talk of godforsakenness in the death of Jesus Christ makes sense only in the context of his doctrine of the Holy Trinity.[15]

Moltmann describes the **trinity** as a community of relationships between Father, Son and Holy Spirit. He argues that the Bible tells the story of Jesus in a framework that demands an understanding of God simultaneously as sending-Father, sent-Son, and Spirit drawing people into the fellowship of the Son with the Father.[16] He develops a doctrine of the trinity as a free and loving community-in-divinity, with no dominance or subordination.[17] Jesus reveals to us this trinitarian foundation of reality and hope. Jesus discloses God's solidarity with us through suffering and crucifixion, overcoming death through the vulnerable power of love, and inviting us into God's open and transforming fellowship.

Moltmann's "social trinitarianism" has enabled him to develop an **ecological theology** in which God's involvement with the world resembles the mutuality within God.[18] The Spirit of God is a Spirit of Life, not confined to the Christian community but promising cosmic renewal and a "redemption of nature which will again make her God's creation and the home country for human beings." [19]

Moltmann's theology, then, can bear several labels. Once calling it "theology of hope," Moltmann now calls it a messianic theology, because it sits so squarely on God's promise and Christianity's future orientation, grounded historically in the incarnation (including the cross and resurrection).[20] It is also an *"eschatologia crucis,"* a cross-centered ultimate hope, in which the resurrection of the crucified Jesus issues in an ultimate hope for all of God's creatures.[21] Moltmann also labels it a political theology, because of its clear commitment to address suffering and oppression, issuing directly out of Moltmann's theology of the cross.[22]

Because it is structured on promise and hope, Moltmann's whole theology **points towards mission**. "In the contradiction between the word of promise and the experiential reality of suffering and death, faith takes its stand on hope and ... strains after the future," he wrote in *Theology of hope*.[23] He sees in the resurrected Christ the future of the humanity for which he died.

> Those who hope in Christ can no longer put up with reality as it is, but begin to suffer under it, to contradict it.... [The] goad of the promised future stabs inexorably into the flesh of every unfulfilled present.... [This hope] makes the Christian Church the source of continual new impulses towards the realization of the promised future that is to come.[24]

Moltmann links the two words "promise" and "mission," pointing to their common etymological base: "The *promissio* of the universal future leads of necessity to the universal *missio* of the Church to all nations."[25]

The order is that God's promise leads to mission, which leads to the church as a sign of God's coming kingdom. Thus Moltmann can say that mission "does not come from the church; it is from mission and in the light of mission that the church has to be understood."[26]

If we ask what this mission is, we are led directly to the incarnational nature of mission in Moltmann's thought.

Incarnational Mission in Moltmann's View

Moltmann's missiology is based on the resurrection and God's promised future, with a call for the church to respond by opening itself to this new reality in Christ. So (1) the lordship of Christ is central, calling Christians to follow Jesus as pattern and to live in his "sphere of influence." (2) Moltmann calls Christians to find the anticipatory presence of Christ in the church and among the poor, pointing forward to his presence in glory. (3) We are to "conform to Christ," taking on his shape. (4) This involves the practice of Christ (christopraxis) in the whole of life and especially (5) in solidarity with the poor, (6) all in a holistic and ecological framework. (7) Throughout, the emphasis is on God's action in history, rather than our human response. We will briefly consider each of these incarnational themes.

Christ the Criterion of the Church's Mission

Moltmann sees the question "What is mission?" to be the same as "What is the nature and task of the church?"[27] The answer for him is that the lordship of Christ is the church's sole determining factor.[28] Christology ought to be the dominant theme of ecclesiology.[29] In other words, the "all-embracing messianic mission of the whole church corresponds to Christ's messianic mission and to the charismatic sending of the Spirit 'which shall be poured out on all flesh.'"[30] Moltmann's missiology is deeply incarnational; he argues that the church is actually constituted by continuing Christ's mission in the presence and under the lordship of Christ. All aspects of Moltmann's missiology reflect this central understanding.

He spells out this lordship in several ways, each of which is an aspect of discipleship. We will return to expand some of them below.

First, the messianic mission of Jesus proclaimed good news to the poor and called people to repentance, a message of joy, liberation and solidarity with the poor and weak.[31]

Second, Jesus calls us to follow him on the way of the cross, a way of self-surrender and public suffering. This mission is incarnational in that the life of Christ is to be embodied and made transparent in our lives. Moltmann says the church is called to a "public apostleship" and "public intervention on behalf of the lost and the despised," in what amounts to a "worldly, bodily and hence also a political Christ-mysticism. How else should the life of Jesus, the life of the one who is risen, be manifest 'in our mortal flesh'?" [32]

Third, our messianic mission is to acknowledge Christ as lord through testimony, fellowship, and living with a passion for life. "Christian existence is new life in Christ's sphere of influence."[33] Moltmann presses this point, arguing that the church exists only to the extent that it reflects this new life, in its internal relationships, and in its public stance.[34]

Fourth, messianic mission has an aesthetic dimension in that Jesus is beauty, freedom, song and laughter, and the church is to live in the new reality as a feast without end.[35] This is an important corrective to excessively ethical approaches to Jesus' lordship. Moltmann cautions the Western church against making Jesus the new law-giver.[36] Any incarnational missiology which emphasizes the imitation of Christ in an ethical sense needs to take this into account. To take Jesus as our pattern for mission includes eating, drinking, and dancing. To live in the kingdom of God is to be guests at the feast of God.

Fifth, Jesus calls us to open and public friendship. Complementing the titles of Jesus which emphasize his uniqueness and difference from us, calling Jesus our friend emphasizes his acceptance of us and solidarity with the unrighteous and despised. It is open and inclusive, and it is public and political rather than private and intimate.[37]

These five dimensions of the lordship of Christ speak of the ways in which the church becomes the true church, amounting to living "in Christ's sphere of influence." We should note that Moltmann's image here implies a power or influence emanating from the risen, living Christ. The resurrection is the basis for the new life and lifestyle of the church. Moltmann's metaphor suggests that Christian faith consists of simply moving into range. Even though the various dimensions of obedience to Christ as lord amount to a life of costly discipleship, Moltmann consistently reminds us that this life comes as joy, liberation, and a gift of grace. Christ's presence, or sphere of influence, is what animates Christian mission and makes it incarnational. In the terms we defined when discussing Anabaptism, Moltmann emphasizes conformity to Christ rather than the imitation of Christ, that is, God's initiative rather than human effort.[38]

If the church is constituted by Christ's mission and Christ's presence, this raises the question of where in particular we find the presence of Christ.

Christ's Anticipatory Incarnation

To what extent can we say that Christ takes initiative and is present among us, identifying with us or even incarnating himself today in our world?

Moltmann argues that Christ is present in three main ways:

i   By virtue of his promises to identify with us, Christ is present in word, sacrament and Christian fellowship. This is an identification with active mission. In effect: "He who hears you hears me" (Jn 20:21-23, Mt 28:18-20).

ii By virtue of his promises to identify with them, Christ is also present among the poor (Mt 25:31-46). This is an identification with suffering expectation: "Whoever visits you visits me."

iii By virtue of his promises, Christ is present as himself in his parousia, that is, his future presence in glory.[39]

In other words, Christ is present in the church and its mission, among the poor, and in hope.

The balance between all three modes of presence is important.[40] If we were to live only according to Christ's presence in the church, there would be a focus on the present, on the church possessing the truth, and on the risen Lord to the exclusion of the crucified Christ. If we were to live only aware of Christ's presence in those who suffer, there would be a focus on the distant future and on God as ultimate avenger of the oppressed.[41] Ideally the first mode opens out beyond itself to the second so that the church lives in the tension of the "already" and the "not yet," anticipating the fullness of the presence of Christ already partially experienced (this anticipation of fullness being the third mode).[42]

Interestingly, in referring to the poor Moltmann talks of Christ's "anticipatory incarnation in them."[43] It is one of the rare instances, if not the only case, where Moltmann speaks in terms of Christ becoming incarnate in humans.

For Christ to be present in the church in his "anticipatory incarnation," the church must be where Christ was and is, living out a new reality particularly among those who are powerless, excluded, and suffering. This is not simply an ethical direction which it is proper for Christians to follow. This is to say that the church is only the church when it enters into the ongoing incarnating activity of God by embodying the lordship of Christ. It is, as Moltmann says, a matter of ecclesiology as much as missiology.[44] It is the crucified and risen Christ who determines the nature of the church and the shape of its mission.

We note that Christ's presence is crucial to mission just as being on Christ's mission is the way to be assured of Christ's presence. Incarnational mission here is discovering the ways in which Christ has taken the initiative in being present in the missionary church and among the poor.

Embodying Christ and Taking His Way

In his book *God in creation*, Moltmann talks of Christians conforming to Christ, or taking on the shape of Christ. Humans are made in the image of God, but how are we to fulfill our potential in this regard?

> Since [Jesus] is the messianic *imago Dei* [image of God], believers become *imago Christi* [image of Christ], and through this enter upon the path which will make them *gloria Dei* [glory of God] on earth. According to Romans 8:29, they will become "conformed to the image of the Son" and, through their discipleship, grow into the messianic form of Jesus.[45]

Moltmann calls this the messianic calling of human beings, and points out that becoming like God through Christ is "both gift and charge, indicative and imperative."[46] The indicative (we might call it "becoming what we are') is as important as the imperative (to "become what we ought to be"). It is also a process, *becoming* human rather than *being* human. Further, it takes place in community and involves soul and body undivided.[47]

This process of being conformed to the likeness of Christ, or "embody-ing" Christ, is for Moltmann just a small part of the total process of God's involvement in creation, in which embodiment is the goal. In creation God proceeds from resolve to word, and then to the creation of material and bodily forms. Humans are God's image on earth not just in their spirituality but in their total bodily existence. They become aware that their spiritual paths and their words all end in the lived form of their bodies, alive and in society.[48]

Embodiment, or incarnation, is not only the goal of creation but also the mode and goal of God's reconciling work. Moltmann's way of expressing this suggests how incarnational mission might proceed:

> According to the biblical traditions, embodiment is also the end of God's work of reconciliation: "The Word became flesh...." By becoming flesh, the reconciling God assumes the sinful, sick and mortal flesh of human beings and heals it in community with [Godself]. God's eternal Logos becomes a human body, a child in the manger, a savior of the sick, a tortured human body on Golgotha. It is in this bodily form of Christ's that God brings about the reconciliation of the world (Rom 8:3). In his taking flesh, exploited, sick and shattered human bodies experience their healing and their indestructible dignity.[49]

In his recent work Moltmann adds to this theme of the spiritual importance of God's own embodiment in reconciliation. Discussing "crea-tures" rather than the "Creator," he expresses a strong and positive emphasis on human bodily life, which is "ensouled," passionate, vulnera-ble, and to be celebrated. Bodily life expresses the energies of the life-giving and embodying Spirit of God (as well as God's vulnerability and openness to loving and dying).[50]

For Moltmann, therefore, not only does our call to identify with the risen and crucified Christ issue from the nature of the church but also from the very nature of God, who in eternal history is always reaching out in self-giving, becoming embodied in creation, then in incarnation, and ultimately in the new earth, the transfigured embodiment which will fulfill redemption.[51] Like Choan-Seng Song, Moltmann sees incarnational mission to be based not only on the initiative of Christ, but the initiative of God in creation and reconciliation.

Christopraxis: The Stamp of Christ
on the Whole of Life

How do we understand the relationship between believing in Christ and following Christ in ethical and lifestyle terms?

Perhaps the simplest way to state Moltmann's answer is to say that belief and obedient response always go together. Moltmann named his recent volume on christology *The way of Jesus Christ* partly to underline the invitational nature of christology:

> A way is something to be followed. "The way of Jesus Christ" is not merely a Christological category. It is an ethical category too. Anyone who enters upon Christ's way will discover who Jesus really is; and anyone who really believes in Jesus as the Christ of God will follow him along the way he himself took. Christology and christopraxis find one another in the full and completed knowledge of Christ. In this christology I have linked dogmatics and ethics in closer detail than in previous volumes.[52]

Moltmann is saying, then, that believing and following are interwoven inextricably. He refuses to say that either believing or following is more important. Discipleship (christopraxis[53]) is not the practice which applies the theory (christology). The two are related in a dialectical and complex fashion. The practice already involves cognitive content and christological belief already involves a response in obedience and freedom. "Christology and Christian ethics cannot be separated."[54] For disciples what unites both is learning who Jesus is, "with all their senses, acting and suffering, in work and prayer,"[55] and showing the same compassion for the poor that characterized Jesus' ministry:

> Christology emerges from Christian living and leads into Christian living.... Christological theory has to point beyond itself, and paradoxically away from itself, to the doing of God's will, in which "knowing Jesus as the Lord really becomes whole and entire.[56]

Moltmann refers to the current debate on whether there can be a Christian ethics[57] and argues that if there is no specifically Christian ethic then the whole messiahship of Jesus is called into question. Christian ethics challenge us as to "how far the way of Jesus is to be taken seriously."[58] His approach, also taken by the Anabaptists, is one that was neglected by the Reformation, and only Dietrich Bonhoeffer has taken it up among modern German theologians.[59] Moltmann's remarks on this are powerful:

> The recognition that Christ alone is the Redeemer and Lord cannot be restricted to faith. It must take in the whole of life.... The *solus Christus* [Christ alone] of the Reformers ... also means *totus Christus*—the whole Christ for the whole of life, as the second thesis of the Barmen Theological Declaration of 1934 says. But this means that christology and christopraxis become one, so that a total, holistic knowledge of Christ puts its stamp not only on the mind and the heart, but on the whole of life in the community of Christ; and it also means that Christ is *perceived and known* not only with mind and heart, but through experience and practice of the whole of life.[60]

We can see that although Moltmann doesn't use the phrase "incarnational mission" he continually argues forcefully for the church to embody the saving freedom of Jesus Christ in anticipation of God's full salvation. In this last passage he firmly links belief and the practice of discipleship in daily life, arguing that only in the "practice of Christ" can we say we believe in Christ. This passage also makes clear that for Moltmann Christ is actually known through experience and practice. Here Christ is more than an example in the past or an anticipated future presence, in that the promised hope reaches into the present and is incarnated in missionary faith and practice.

Incarnational Missiology in Trinitarian Context

Moltmann's theology is systematic in temper. He does not speak of creation without implying the fulfillment of the end times. He does not speak of the cross without speaking also of the birth, life, resurrection, ascension and coming in glory of Jesus. Ecclesiology is intimately linked to missiology, and, for similar reasons, to christology.[61] Because he has an overarching vision (not complete, he freely admits) of the nature and activity of God in history and in Jesus Christ, he sees how the doctrines of the Christian faith are always intertwined. This feature of his theology is strengthened by his explicitly relational and ecological framework, worked out in detail in *God in creation*, but evident earlier and applied since.[62]

Nowhere are the links more obvious than in his argument for a solidly trinitarian view of God. As we outlined briefly earlier in the chapter, Moltmann sees Jesus Christ as part of the self-giving, suffering, infinitely loving and free mutual community which is the triune God. The meaning of Jesus' life and suffering and death only becomes clear when seen against the horizon of God's creative and self-giving love, always moving towards embodiment, always redemptive in direction, and now uniquely disclosed in Jesus, who fulfills and redefines messianic hopes.

There is an implicit critique here of any incarnational mission which is exclusively christocentric, concentrating all of its focus on Jesus Christ. Such a view is in danger of underplaying the role of the Spirit in mission. It can also easily forget that the mission of God is directed towards shalom in all of creation. A third danger is found in some evangelical perspectives, in which a distant and demanding God is implicitly set against the passive and sacrificial Jesus, in an ill-fitting virtual bi-theism. In such a perspective Jesus can often be paradoxically portrayed as less than fully divine and yet not quite human.[63] A fourth danger is the moralism that can result from an excessive focus on the historical Jesus and the kingdom as God's present rule;[64] against this, Moltmann emphasizes that salvation is holistic and has a novel future as well.

Moltmann's trinitarian view keeps the various dimensions of the incarnation firmly within an overall vision of the God of hope and fulfillment. Moltmann therefore keeps incarnational mission in a trinitarian context. He is not in danger of merely emphasizing Jesus as our pattern for mission. He continually emphasizes as well the presence of Christ through the Spirit, and relates incarnation to the tendency of God the creator to become embodied in creation. All three basic dimensions of incarnational mission are kept in view in Moltmann's trinitarian framework.

Before leaving discussion of Moltmann's view of the trinity, it is worth noting that some critics have accused him of holding to a form of tritheism, in which God consists of three distinct persons.[65] This is a relevant issue because his missiology draws heavily on inner-trinitarian dynamics. Moltmann's trinity is a community of Father, Son and Spirit "whose unity is constituted by mutual indwelling and reciprocal interpenetration."[66] There are three persons, each a subject who takes initiative.[67] Do we not have three gods here?

Moltmann answers by saying that our very definition of personhood involves relationality, so in the Godhead there are not three autonomous persons; there is ultimately one, a unity of mutuality which will be fully unified in the eschatological future.[68] He also counter-attacks by charging with modalism (in which God is essentially one, appearing in three modes) those such as Schleiermacher, Barth and Rahner who in the end emphasize God's unity over God's trinity.[69] William Placher argues persuasively that Moltmann's relational model of personhood leads not so much to three independent persons in the Godhead but to three mutually-dependent-and-loving "persons" whose will is one.[70] Although Moltmann has been a leading voice in the recent renewal of interest in the social view of the trinity, he is drawing upon a tradition going back to the Cappadocian Fathers and today stands with Colin Gunton,[71] Catherine Lacugna,[72] Wolfhart Pannenberg,[73] Leonardo Boff,[74] Cornelius Plantinga, Jr,[75] David Brown,[76] Daniel Migliore[77] and many others. We would argue, against his critics, that Moltmann is articulating a genuine trinity which gives weight to both the "threeness" and the "oneness" of God.[78]

The Incarnation as Solidarity with the Suffering and the Poor

One can hardly open to a page of Moltmann's writing without finding mention of God's identification, through the incarnation, with the poor, the excluded, and the suffering. To identify with the crucified Christ means to identify with the suffering and misery of the poor and oppressed.[79] Moltmann sees this as the very nature of the trinitarian God, not just a feature of the life of the historical Jesus. "The theology of the cross [in which the crucified Christ identifies with the abandoned] is a critical and liberating theory of God and [humanity]."[80] The implication of this approach is clear. Incarnational missiology is particularly good news to the poor. In mission it will always take the option for the poor.

Moltmann adds to the christological titles in the New Testament the title of friend and writes an eloquent defense of its appropriateness for Jesus, the friend of sinners (Lk 7:34) and the one who declared his friendship towards his disciples and laid down his life for his friends (Jn 15:13-14).[81] Reminding us that friendship has nearly always been a public concept rather than a private and intimate one, Moltmann makes a case for seeing open friendship as the spirit of the kingdom of God, shown both in God's approach to us and our response to God and to others.[82]

Open and public friendship, or simple solidarity, then, is an important element of incarnational mission for Moltmann. Jesus calls us his friends if we follow him in friendship of the poor and the excluded, welcoming them literally and figuratively to our table.[83] This inclusive approach and Jesus' reputation for eating, drinking and celebrating with "the wrong types' is an integral part of the pattern of the incarnation which is determinative for incarnational mission. Friendship, at the same time a simple idea and yet a costly path, is a key aspect of taking the way of Jesus Christ.

Holistic and Relational

Moltmann explicitly grounds the reality of the person (whether divine or human) in relationship rather than in substance, and endeavors to think in terms of networks, interconnections, and mutuality of relationship.[84] It is an ecological approach, cosmic in its breadth and holistic in its perspective, particularly in his more recent work.[85]

His holistic approach is supportive of incarnational mission's insistence that an integral approach to proclamation and lifestyle witness is necessary for Christian discipleship. Whereas evangelicalism, for example, tends to separate evangelism and social action and then struggles to put the two back together, Moltmann argues that a messianic lifestyle concerns the "whole of life." [86]

His relational approach challenges us to act in Christian community, because alone we are not fully human, and the call to freedom is a call to community.[87] Incarnational mission always proceeds in community, aware that it is part of salvation to experience restored relationships, aware of the team that Jesus drew around him and aware that resistance and solidarity require mutuality to survive.

The relationships involved in this open friendship and life in community are not always "restored" but include conflict, failure and awareness of our handicaps, as well as suffering. The community is a scarred and broken body which lives not only in the reality of Christ's healing presence but also in hope of full restoration in the future.

The Gift of God's Initiative

We suggested at the beginning of the chapter that Moltmann serves as a bridge between those who emphasize discipleship and those who emphasize God's assured incarnational presence in the world and the church. We suggested that Moltmann reminds us that it is God who takes the initiative, and that a central dimension of incarnational mission is the presence and power of Christ in Christian mission.

Standing clearly in the Reformed tradition, Moltmann emphasizes our human inability to bring about salvation and our complete dependence on the free and powerful initiative of God. Christopher Morse summarizes very well Moltmann's implicit views on incarnational mission:

> No human agency can produce or control the promise that initiates liberation in history.... Human beings do signify the Scripture through their words and actions, but only God can make these words and actions significant to faith as God's own promise. Only God determines when our words and acts come to be God's Word.[88]

Evaluative Comments

We have noted his reminders along the way, but can now draw them together. Moltmann's eschatological perspective emphasizes the action of God in history towards the ultimate victory of vulnerable love, and leads to a trinitarian perspective in which it is God, as Father, Son and Spirit, who acts incarnationally for the reconciliation of all. We also noted Moltmann's image of discipleship as living in Christ's "sphere of influence." He espouses a sort of Christ-mysticism in expecting to find Christ present not only in the word and sacraments but also in the poor and in the church's political existence for justice. He speaks of being conformed to Christ, a process which is as much "becoming what we are" as "trying to become what we ought to be." He unites the experience of Christ and the practice of Christ.

We can avoid two important dangers if we clearly hear Moltmann's emphasis.

The first is the temptation to rely on our own efforts to be christlike, as if by simply trying we could mold ourselves in the shape of Christ and thereby point others to Jesus. Some uses of "incarnational mission" carry the sense that discipleship is a matter of *Christians* changing our lifestyles in order to follow Jesus (as we saw when considering the Anabaptists).[89] Seen this way, the whole incarnational project of the church lays too great a burden of good works upon Christians.

In the face of this temptation Moltmann reminds us that although we need to respond, response is the second moment in the Christian dynamic. God's liberating action in grace is always the first moment. Although belief in Christ is inseparable from obedience to Christ, our obedience is at the same time an opening up to the invitation of Christ to live in freedom and joy.

The second danger Moltmann helps us to avoid is that of dissolving christology into ecclesiology through imagining that the church incarnates Christ here and now.

The main reason for Moltmann's reluctance to talk in terms of Christ's incarnation in the church is that it blurs the distinction between the limited church and the fullness and otherness of Christ. He points to the important difference between the incarnation of the Logos and the indwelling of the Spirit in the church. Christ incarnate has a freedom, an otherness, a mission, an atoning death and a future for the church and for the whole of creation. He has a critical and liberating relationship with the church as its head or fount-of-freedom.[90] Christ is not to be totally identified with either the church or the Spirit at work in the church. Even Moltmann's talk of the presence of Christ in the church (a weaker expression than any talk of the church "incarnating" Christ) is heavily and precisely qualified. It is only by virtue of Christ's unilateral, indirect and limited identification that our proclamation and existence can bear Christ's presence.[91] It is unilateral in that it issues freely from Christ's promises to be with us; it is indirect in that it is through the Spirit that Christ indwells the church; and it is limited in that Christ is present only insofar as the church takes the form of Christ in its bodily existence.[92] This falls well short of easy talk of the church "incarnating Christ" for our age.

It is on these grounds that Moltmann rejects the idea of the church as the continuation of the incarnation. He traces the concept back to Augustine, and finds it in Pope Pius XII's *Mystici Corporis Christi* of 1943: "[Christ] upholds the Church and so, after a certain manner, lives in the Church that she may be said to be another Christ."[93] In other words the church is the body of Christ and the body and the head together are Christ. In this view "Christ is therefore only Christ in the full sense together with the church."[94] The problem, however, is that the qualitative difference between Christ and the church is lost.[95] Christology is dissolved into ecclesiology because talk of Christ becomes talk of the church, a claim too bold altogether.

Moltmann's emphases on the freedom and otherness of Christ and the centrality of God's initiative are, as we have shown, distinctive and important for incarnational missiology.

Although it is not our task to give an overall assessment of Moltmann's missiology some critical comments are also appropriate.

First, the strong future-orientation of his theology leaves some wondering what can be expected now. The unity of God, for example, is only an eschatological unity (yet to be achieved), and it might be argued that Christ's atonement is incomplete because its consummation awaits the *eschaton*. It may be true that overall Moltmann's theology is rather one-sided in its future-orientation. Nevertheless, Christian faith, for Moltmann, is not all directed towards the future because it is founded on the resurrection, a feature which is developed in much of his work. Thus future hope is balanced by the presence of the risen Christ, a crucial factor for incarnational mission.[96] It is Moltmann's deep sensitivity to pain and suffering which makes it impossible for him to construct a theology of glory-in-the-present rather than a theology of hope.

This last comment makes the second common criticism surprising. Liberation theologians criticize Moltmann for detachment from concrete political statements.[97] We would agree with Bauckham that Moltmann is relatively lacking in specific proposals,[98] but our brief outline of Moltmann's incarnational missiology has shown that the directions of Christian mission are abundantly clear and involve solidarity with the poor, the excluded and the suffering. It seems reasonable that in each context Christians must work out their own form of social and political involvement.

Third, there are features of Moltmann's approach which make it difficult both to assess and understand, as some reviewers have pointed out.[99] In the boldness and breadth of his theological vision he pushes ideas to the limit without it always being clear (at least to this writer) how they fit his theological system. Some of this may be due to the European theological style, and some due to his preparedness to "remythologise" theology in reaction to Bultmann's demythologizing project.[100] We might mention as examples the tension between God's unity and tri-unity;[101] the tension between Jesus Christ being one with God and yet thoroughly forsaken by God on the cross;[102] and the difficulty of making clear connections between the importance of the church as the messianic community and his more recent universal vision of salvation.

Nevertheless, Moltmann, more clearly than most, provides a christology which nourishes missiology in a balanced manner. Note how much his incarnational christology satisfies the requirements suggested in chapter 3. Moltmann uses *relational* terms to understand both God and humanity, in doing so demonstrating a *metaphorical* approach in his talk of the "social trinity." He is clearly *trinitarian* and the role of the *Spirit* is crucial. His whole theological structure is *soteriological*, and, most importantly in this context, issues naturally in *incarnational mission*.[103] Let us expand this last point.

We have shown that Moltmann uses several phrases which are very similar in import to "incarnational mission." He talks of embodiment being the mode of God's reconciling work, including the whole creation.[104] He talks of christopraxis, which is none other than the Christian practice of discipleship.[105] He calls his recent christology *The way of Jesus Christ*, explaining that belief in Christ is inseparable from certain ethical imperatives, and that to be a Christian is to travel on the way that Jesus took.[106] He also speaks of the whole Christ in the whole of life.[107] He rivals liberation theologians in his insistence that to follow the crucified Christ is to live in solidarity with those who claimed Jesus' particular attention, the poor and oppressed. Moltmann's missiology urgently presses Christian disciples along the road to mission in Christ's way. Even more distinctively, we have seen that Moltmann sees incarnational mission also in terms of the presence and power of Christ in mission. Mission is not just the following of Christ but choosing to respond to Christ's invitation to live in his sphere of influence, animated by forgiveness and the joy of liberation.

Moltmann's thought has acted as a bridge in reminding us that incarnational mission is not only about trying to follow the pattern of Jesus (a strong theme of chapters 4 to 6) but also responding to the power and presence of Christ and joining his mission. In chapters 8 and 9 this understanding opens out further in an emphasis on the ongoing process of divine incarnation as the ultimate framework for mission. This brings us to the third of the three dimensions of incarnational mission outlined in chapter 3.

CHAPTER 8

INCARNATION AS SACRAMENT: CATHOLICISM

I n this chapter and the next we turn to traditions strong in the third dimension of incarnational mission, which sees the church as joining God's incarnating activity in history.[108] We begin with a study of Catholic approaches to mission, in which incarnation has been a significant theme.

The terms "Catholic" and "Catholicism" refer not only to the Roman Catholic church, the global Christian community in communion with Rome, but also to traditions with a similar style of Christianity, such as Anglo-Catholicism.[109] It is continuity with Peter and not the importance of Rome that distinguishes the tradition.[110] It is also an ecclesial style, identified by Richard McBrien as a commitment in practice and belief to three distinguishing principles: sacramentality, mediation, and communion.[111]

The **sacramental** view of life finds the divine present in the human, in the material and in the everyday. Sacraments, in the wider sense, are any material objects or events through which the real presence of God is manifest. The principle of **mediation** affirms that sacraments not only reflect the presence of God, as Protestants have emphasized, but cause what they signify. Catholicism has always affirmed the importance of the priest in focusing and mediating the presence of God.[112] The principle of **communion** sees the way to God to be a communal, or "churchly," way. For Catholicism the individual's relationship to God is always set in a community of faith. The Bible is the testimony of the original faith of the church and is interpreted by the church. The church is of central importance, mediating salvation in the church's role as the sacrament of Christ. It is in this ecclesiology that the three principles of Catholicism come together as one.[113]

There are certain distinctive themes in Catholic incarnational missiology. We will show that both Roman Catholicism and Anglo-Catholicism emphasize that the incarnation will only be complete when the mission of God is fulfilled by Christ and the church together in drawing all nations to God. In this view the church is the **ongoing incarnation**, an understanding sometimes carefully nuanced and at other times stated more baldly. It is also common to see the incarnation in terms of God **assuming a cultural existence** in Jesus, bound to a time, place and culture. On this understanding the incarnation becomes the theological foundation for the ongoing process of inculturating faith in the various cultures of the world. A further common incarnational theme, as already mentioned, is the **sacramental** perspective. The incarnation is the greatest sacrament, and just as Jesus Christ is the sacrament of our encounter with God, so the church is the sacrament of our encounter with Jesus Christ.[114]

As well as emphasizing these distinctive themes, Catholic traditions share with others such incarnational themes as the fusing of word and deed in lived witness, the church as a sign of the kingdom, and a special concern for the poor. Mary Motte suggests that the increasing influence of the incarnation in the way Christians reach out in mission is a matter of consensus between Protestant and Catholic missiologists, a conclusion strongly backed by our survey of Christian traditions.[115]

To survey exhaustively the theology of mission in the Catholic tradition in one chapter would be an impossible task. It is worth noting that in considering Roman Catholic missiology in this chapter we are excluding liberation theology because we discussed it in chapter 6; it is not to imply that liberation theology has not been a strong influence in Roman Catholic thinking.

Our approach will involve examining three periods of recent Roman Catholic missiology, the times before, during and after the Second Vatican Council (1962-1965). We will limit ourselves to issues related to incarnational mission, and will analyse post-Vatican II emphases in more detail, with some evaluative comments. Then we will briefly examine and evaluate the Anglo-Catholic understanding of incarnational mission, using one of its classic texts, *Lux Mundi* (1889), to open up the issues for us.

The Pre-Vatican II Period

Background

Roman Catholic ecclesiology shows us immediately why incarnational mission, with its variety of meanings, is close to the center of Catholic missiology. For centuries Catholic theologians have been united in seeing the church as a continuation of the incarnation and, in a strong sense, the body of Christ, both human and divine.[116] Johann Adam Möhler, for example, wrote in 1844:

> The visible Church ... is the Son of God himself, everlastingly manifesting himself among men [and women] in a human form, perpetually renovated, and eternally young—the permanent incarnation of the same, as in Holy Writ, even the faithful are called the body of Christ.[117]

There was no comprehensive official statement of the doctrinal basis for Roman Catholic missionary activity until the Second Vatican Council.[118]

Vatican II was not the occasion of new thinking, however. It was the culmination of decades of new thinking in Roman Catholic missiological circles. French theologians such as Marie-Dominique Chenu, Yves Congar and Jean Daniélou were influential in the decades before Vatican II. They were significant in a ferment which involved a new interest in biblical studies, a reinterpretation of patristic sources, a renewal of the role of the laity, and a new awareness of the social sciences. The Catholic Action movement of the inter-war years proclaimed that mission should occur wherever lay people mixed with the masses of the world.[119] The worker-priest movement of the late 1940s, though soon suppressed, saw priests working in factories in the name of "incarnating the church" in the world, and developing the notion (expressed by Chenu in 1947) of the church being in a continual state of mission even in a so-called Christian society.[120]

The Vatican II documents took up many of the missiological emphases of this period, most of which see mission as shaped by the incarnation in some sense. In no-one were these emphases more evident than the eminent church historian, Cardinal Jean Daniélou (d. 1974).

Jean Daniélou

Daniélou's most notable contributions to incarnational missiology were in re-interpreting the idea of the church as the continuing incarnation, and outlining a spirituality of incarnation for Christian missionaries. Without disputing the Roman Catholic doctrine that **the church continues the incarnation of Christ**,[121] Daniélou re-framed it in missiological perspective. He insists that the church is missionary by its very existence, and that the incarnation is important in understanding how God works among us and how we should therefore work in mission. "The Incarnation of our Lord must be continued in the Church if she is to be a missionary and speak to all nations." [122]

Christian mission, the responsibility of both clergy and laity, continues the mission of God in the Word-becoming-flesh.[123] To base our mission on Christ is to live in utter dependence on God, imitating Jesus who claimed to do nothing of himself but only what the Father sent him to do.[124] For Daniélou incarnational mission is a life of self-emptying and dependence on God; we note that it is more a life of holiness lived in the rhythm of the sacraments than a life of engagement in the world.

While Daniélou's emphasis on the role of the whole church in mission was progressive, his confidence in the authority of the Roman Catholic church was more conservative. He speaks of the church possessing truth, authority and sanctity in an inalienable, incorruptible, and indefectible manner,[125] and sees the Roman Catholic church as an infallible institution, officially and exclusively appointed to carry out God's mission.[126]

Related to the church as the continuing incarnation is the idea that the church completes Christ as his fullness, or "pleroma." Daniélou argues that the spiritual life of the church is "a sharing in the divinized humanity assumed by the Word, whose body and pleroma it is."[127] The idea is restated in *Lumen Gentium* at Vatican II:

> [Christ] fills the Church, which is His Body and His fullness, with His divine gifts (cf. Eph. 1:22-23) so that she may grow and reach all the fullness of God (cf. Eph. 3:19). (LG#7)[128]

The idea of the church as the pleroma of Christ seems to complement that of the church as the continuing incarnation. Both talk of completing Christ's mission, the first as a spatial metaphor and the second a temporal one. The pleroma doctrine is not developed enough for it to be clear what metaphysical weight we should put on it. Taken literally, as with talk of the ongoing incarnation, it is a high claim indeed for the church.

In *The salvation of the nations* Daniélou discusses at length **incarnational spirituality in mission**.[129] He sees incarnational mission (1) as adaptation to cultures, (2) as only part of the missionary task leading to "transfiguration," and (3) as vulnerable suffering.

First, affirming what is now generally called "indigenization," or **adaptation to cultures**, Daniélou says the first missionary task is "to make Christianity incarnate in all that is good" in other religions and cultures, just as Christ was incarnate in the Jewish race[130] and early Christianity assumed Greek and Roman forms.[131] We must understand the cultures, espouse them, and treat them with sympathy.[132] He reflects the views of his times in not feeling challenged to re-evaluate the cultural clothing of his own faith. Daniélou writes:

> All is lost if, when we go out among [others], we become like them, instead of them becoming like us. In such cases, there is an incarnation; but without a transfiguration it is worthless.[133]

Second, as we can see from the quotation above, for Daniélou the incarnational movement in mission is **only the first step, properly leading to "transfiguration."** Assuming the thought forms of the people is only a means to an end.[134] The ultimate goal is to challenge culture with the gospel, and to transform people as they become participants in the divine life.[135] The spirituality of incarnation, therefore, needs to be complemented by a spirituality of redemption (an interior and spiritual journey of holiness and intercession) and by transfiguration (the goal of incarnational mission).

Daniélou's belief that incarnational mission is not enough on its own follows from his narrow understanding of the incarnation. He uses "the incarnation" to refer to the movement of God towards humans in assuming flesh, an event excluding Christ's death and resurrection. He writes: "The mystery of the Incarnation and the Passion is consummated in the mystery of the Resurrection and the Ascension." [136]

Even though we would argue for a fuller view of the incarnation, Daniélou reminds us appropriately that "getting alongside," "understanding" and "identifying" are only the first step in the fullness of mission.

Daniélou points out, as a third aspect of incarnational spirituality, that Christ's incarnation involved not only becoming human but also a process of self-emptying and **vulnerable suffering**, taking on the form of a slave by being a humble member of a humble culture. This renunciation and self-limitation is a part of incarnational mission.[137] Daniélou has in mind "evangelical poverty," where the Christian chooses to live simply, and even to suffer, for the sake of spreading the Good News.

In the process of making this point he also cautions Christians on mission not to affirm too naïvely, in view of the incarnation, the sacredness and beauty of the flesh. Asceticism still has its place, he argues, because we are sinful flesh. In our bodiliness we need purification and discipline.[138] St Francis sang the Canticle of the Sun, about nature leading him to God, only after he had received the stigmata, the wounds of Jesus felt miraculously in his own hands and feet. "We must not sing the Canticle of the Sun too soon. That would be incarnation in the evil sense of the word." [139]

This understanding of incarnational mission as potentially a dangerous glorification of the material or fleshly domain is not found anywhere else in missiological literature, to this writer's knowledge. It is surprising to find Daniélou using "incarnation" in this negative way. Perhaps it reflects a dualism of spirit and matter which is now much less common in theology. It certainly runs together two meanings of "flesh" discussed in chapter 2 above: "being human" (as in Jn 1:14) and "being ruled by sin and passion" (as in Gal 5:17-21 and other parts of Paul's writing).[140]

Whatever our views on evangelical poverty or asceticism, Daniélou makes the important point that the incarnational path involves absorption of pain and refusal to harden ourselves to suffering.[141] Jesus faced self-emptying and vulnerable suffering. Incarnational mission involves the same.

In developing Roman Catholic ecclesiology in a missiological direction and in outlining dimensions of an incarnational spirituality of mission, Daniélou was the most influential Roman Catholic voice for incarnational mission in the 1940s and 1950s.

At the Second Vatican Council currents such as those we have mentioned, which had been flowing for some time, gained acceptance at the official level. Theologians of mission who had been censured, such as Congar, found themselves sought out as Council advisers and members of drafting committees.[142] Congar was delighted to find that most of the things he had worked on, including new approaches to mission, were taken up at the Council.[143]

The Conciliar Documents

The Second Vatican Council of the Roman Catholic church was a series of four sessions held in Rome from 1962 to 1965, called by Pope John XXIII (1958-1963) and completed under Pope Paul VI (1963-1978). It issued sixteen main documents, of which three have direct relevance to incarnational mission: *Lumen Gentium* (Dogmatic Constitution on the Church) (generally abbreviated as LG), *Gaudium et Spes* (Pastoral Constitution on the Church in the Modern World) (GS), and *Ad Gentes* (Decree on the Church's Missionary Activity) (AG).[144]

We will now outline the main emphases of the conciliar documents relevant to incarnational mission.[145] We will return to some of them in discussing and evaluating post-conciliar trends.

The Church Is Missionary by Nature

"The pilgrim church is missionary by her very nature" (AG#2). Developed theologically in *Lumen Gentium* (LG#1-8) and then explicitly stated in *Ad Gentes*, this view puts the missionary activity of the church at its center rather than at the periphery. It is linked to the trinitarian mission of God, in creation, in the incarnation of Jesus Christ and in the calling and sending of the church through the Spirit (LG#2, 3, 4). The church is no longer the sender in mission but the sent; mission is no longer simply the work of the church but is the church at work.[146] It is the work of the whole church to the whole world. This radical change of perspective is favorable to an incarnational understanding of mission, in which the lives of Christians, rooted in a variety of cultures, assume central importance in mission. All Christians together in ministry and mission *are* the church.

Unfortunately *Ad Gentes* is unable to carry this insight through consistently. The first five sections are progressive and more theological, but their perspective is not reflected in the last two-thirds of the document (from section 6 onwards). Here we find mission dealt with in the old paradigm, in which missions are officially established from the center as overseas efforts by people with a full-time missionary vocation.[147] "The participation of the laity in mission is to be channelled by the hierarchy."[148]

Although the document contains new perspectives and opens the door to a new model of mission it then tries to bolster support for traditional missionary work.[149]

The Church Is God's Pilgrim People

A whole chapter of *Lumen Gentium* is given to the implications of calling the church the people of God (LG#9-17). This recovers a biblical image (e.g. Rom 9:25-26; 2 Cor 6:16; Eph 1:14; Heb 8:10, 11:25; 1 Pet 2:9-10; Rev 18:4) which implies that we are called by God, marked as God's, a fellowship of truth and love, a pilgrim people on the way to fullness in Christ, and a sign and instrument of God's mission to the world (LG#9). The whole church is the people of God, not only the priests or bishops. This strongly personal and communal image could almost be labelled as *the* image of the church in the central conciliar documents,[150] chosen in order to balance the institutional image the church had previously projected.[151]

The image of the church as pilgrim also softened previous emphases, in particular the holiness and perfection of the church. Being "on the way" acknowledges that the church groans in imperfection as part of humanity at the same time as it is the mystical body of Christ. The church's eschatological nature is the foundation of her pilgrimage towards the fullness of perfection in the end times (LG#6, 8, 9, 48-51). The very incompleteness of her present state is the impulse to engage in mission (AG#2, 7, 9). This is the theological basis for the statement quoted earlier that the pilgrim church is missionary by her very nature (AG#2). This image of the church as wanderer, called out of the world and sent back into it, and having no fixed abode on its journey to God's future, is a powerful correction to triumphalist images. It later helped to open the door for theologies which talked of the church of the poor. It was also part of the renewed emphasis at Vatican II on the reformability of the church: "Christ summons the Church, as she goes her pilgrim way, to that continual reformation of which she always has need" (UR#6, that is, *Unitatis Redintegratio* [Decree on Ecumenism], section 6).[152]

The Council directly urges incarnational mission when discussing the nature of pilgrimage as a hard life in a foreign land. In doing so, it calls the church to identify with the poor and oppressed:

Just as Christ carried out the work of redemption in poverty and under oppression, so the Church is called to follow the same path in communicating to men [and women] the fruits of salvation. (LG#8)

The Church Is Sacrament, Sign, and Instrument

Lumen Gentium, in its first section, calls the church a sacrament, sign, and instrument of union with God and the unity of humanity (LG#1), and the affirmation is echoed in *Ad Gentes* (AG#1). We should note that this priestly image is applied to the whole church in its role as carrier of (and pointer to) God's presence. It is not a reference to the churchly sacraments, nor to the role of priests. David Bosch points out that similar metaphors such as salt, light, yeast, servant, and prophet have also recently been recovered in both Protestant and Roman Catholic circles, with Vatican II as a catalyst.[153]

We have already noted that there are connections between a sacramental and an incarnational perspective on mission.[154] The incarnational approach is a special case of the sacramental approach. The church as sacrament is seen to be an embodiment of God's real and saving presence in the world, both a material sign and an agent. Similarly incarnational mission can be seen as that mode of Christian existence which embodies, as a concrete sign, the presence of Christ. We will return later to the relationship between these two approaches.[155]

The Church Is the Local Church in Variety Everywhere in the World

There was a marked shift in emphasis at Vatican II from universality to locality and (at least in theory) from uniformity to variety. Local churches, each under a bishop, are recognized and the universal church is explicitly seen as a collegial union of particular churches (LG#23).

The Council applies this perspective to mission by counseling local churches to witness effectively both locally and far away (AG#20). A feature of this witness is training in awareness of cultural variety, heralding what was to become a growing acknowledgement in Roman Catholic documents of the need to take account of cultural forms and diversity in the church's mission (AG#26, UR#16). This deeper engagement with culture was based theologically on the incarnation (GS#58), developing Daniélou's view that the incarnation is the foundation for espousing cultures. We find the clearest expressions in two well-known sections of *Ad Gentes*:

> The Church must become part of [non-Christian groups and cultures] for the same motive which led Christ to bind Himself, in virtue of His Incarnation, to the definite social and cultural conditions of those human beings among whom He dwelt. (AG#10)

> Thus in imitation of the plan of the Incarnation, the young Churches, rooted in Christ and built up on the foundation of the apostles, take to themselves in a wonderful exchange all the riches of the nations which were given to Christ as an inheritance.... As a result, avenues will be opened for a more profound adaptation in the whole area of Christian life. (AG#22)

This was only the beginning of a shift in emphasis, which was inconsistently expressed in the conciliar documents and, some say, has not been followed through since.[156] Despite expressing a new spirit of liberalization in the church, *Lumen Gentium* is still very careful to re-affirm the hierarchical and institutional controls which operate downwards from the pope to the bishops, priests, deacons and laity (LG#18-29).

The Church Is to Integrate Word and Deed

The view that incarnational mission embodies the Good News by the integration of word and deed is strong in the conciliar documents, which consistently affirm a congruence of faith and life (LG#33, 39, 42, AG#11, 20, 21). The "making visible" of the incarnate Son occurs through a mature and living faith which penetrates the entire life of believers, activating them to justice and love, especially towards the needy (AG#21). *Lumen Gentium* even defines evangelization at one point as the combination of a living testimony and the spoken word (LG#34). *Gaudium et Spes* condemns the heresy of splitting faith from daily life and urges lay people to be engaged in secular duties in a way which is synthesised with their religious values (GS#43). The document concludes with a call to remember Jesus' saying that others will know we are his disciples if we love one another (Jn 13:35); it enjoins Christians to love Christ in word and deed, and to endeavor to serve the people of the modern world ever more effectively (GS#93).

The mission of the laity, however, is rather indirect and often amounts to being good citizens in ways which "penetrate the world with a Christian spirit" (GS#43). Incarnational mission in this context means identifying with a community, finding one's social purpose and acquitting oneself with excellence, good social purpose, and a Christian spirit. Under the heading "The incarnate Word and human solidarity" *Gaudium et Spes* reads:

> The very Word made flesh willed to share in the human fellowship.... Willingly obeying the laws of his country, He sanctified those human ties, especially family ones, from which social relationships arise. He chose to lead the life proper to an artisan of His time and place. (GS#32)

This is a mission of sanctifying those elements of society that the gospel affirms, interpreted here in fairly conservative terms as civil obedience, the family, relationships, and gainful employment. Without a prophetic element this affirming approach to culture has some dangers, discussed below.[157] What is important here, however, is that the second Vatican Council again uses the incarnation as a theological foundation for mission.

There were, of course, other major themes of the documents of Vatican II. In addition to some of the themes we have considered, Avery Dulles mentions the modernization of the church, renewed attention to scripture, collegiality at all levels of leadership, religious freedom, the active role of the laity, ecumenism, dialogue with other religions, and the social mission of the church.[158] Nevertheless the new vision of mission (as distinct from "missions"), though incompletely articulated at the time, was a central theme in the sweeping changes of Vatican II. Robert Schreiter summarizes the revolution:

> Whereas previously missionary activity was the specialized and clearly defined task of winning converts and establishing the church, it now became the general task of all believers, involving a more complex combination of proclamation, witness, dialogue and service. It had become at once more fundamental and less well-defined.[159]

As our five points in this section have indicated, the new approach to mission, while trinitarian in outlook, was clearly based on the incarnation, leading to a new vision of the church as:

i   missionary in nature,
ii pilgrim-like in its "incarnational" identification with the homeless and poor,
iii a sacramental sign of God's presence, like Jesus the pre-eminent sacrament,
iv engaging with the meaning of the Good News in a variety of cultures, following the pattern of Jesus, and
v   seeking an integration of word and deed in mission.

Post-Conciliar Trends

We will use several significant events and documents since Vatican II (along with recent writings by selected missiologists) to chart some of the relevant post-conciliar trends.

One significant expression of collegiality to arise from Vatican II has been a three-yearly synod of bishops in Rome on different topics each time. The 1974 bishops' synod, on the topic of evangelization, was notable for the strident voices of Third World bishops, particularly from Africa. It was unable to resolve some of the differences of view, and asked Pope Paul VI to issue a statement on evangelization.[160] This apostolic exhortation was published in 1975 under the title of *Evangelii Nuntiandi*, or "On evangelization in the modern world" (commonly abbreviated as EN).[161]

Another result of Vatican II was the establishment of a Document and Research Center (Servizio Documentazione e Studi, known as SEDOS) for the combined missionary-sending Roman Catholic religious institutes. SEDOS has held several conferences, notably in 1969 and 1981.[162]

Meanwhile the Latin American Episcopal Council (CELAM) met for its second and third conferences in Medellín, Colombia, in 1968 and in Puebla, Mexico, in 1979, events where the themes of liberation theology were vigorously discussed.[163]

The World Council of Churches/Roman Catholic Church Joint Working Group, meeting from 1965 onwards, produced a document on common witness and proselytism in 1970, updated in 1981.[164]

Pope John Paul II issued an encyclical letter in 1991 entitled *Redemptoris Missio*, or "On the permanent validity of the Church's missionary mandate" (commonly abbreviated as RM).[165]

The themes we outlined in considering Vatican II have remained important in Roman Catholic missiology. The idea of the church as the ongoing incarnation continues to be central, for example, with the clearer recognition that came with Vatican II of the church's imperfection (EN#15). We will comment on three themes which have developed in importance in the post-conciliar period (inculturation, the integration of faith and life and solidarity with the poor) and briefly address a final theme with close links to incarnational mission, the sacramental perspective.

The Incarnation as the Basis for Inculturation

Inculturation has become a major theme in mission, particularly in Roman Catholic missiology. We can define it briefly as an ongoing process which involves two-way, critical, dynamic and in-depth interaction between gospel and culture not only in unevangelized countries but also within our own culture.[166] In its development since the early 1960s the notion of inculturation contains within it a critique of "adaptation," "indigenization" and "accommodation," which are now generally seen as shallower, Western in orientation and involving only peripheral changes in our presentation of the gospel to fit various cultures. We will use "inculturation" as an umbrella term for concepts such as "contextualization" (rare in Roman Catholic literature) and "interculturation."[167] It does carry different meanings. Aylward Shorter, for example, defines inculturation entirely without ethnocentric connotations, whereas Aloysius Pieris trenchantly criticizes inculturation precisely for assuming that Western Christians hold a trans-cultural gospel which can be clothed appropriately for other cultures.[168]

We will not enter the debate on exactly how Christian faith ought to engage with culture, to what extent we should go in adopting cultural forms, or what inculturation means in specific cultural situations. These are questions beyond the scope of this study. Nevertheless, inculturation is one of the central meanings given to incarnational mission in recent Roman Catholic thinking, and therefore deserves some more detailed critical discussion. (Throughout the study we have deferred such a discussion with the intention of conducting it in this chapter.)

A dominant theme in the literature: In the first flush of enthusiasm after Vatican II Enda McDonagh declared that the missionary practice of entering into another mentality is based most deeply in the central mystery of the incarnation:

Missionary activity is geared precisely to allow Jesus to be himself, Asian or African as well as Jewish or European. Unless the Church which embodies him and bears the responsibility for extending his incarnate presence in every people and culture enters fully and freely into these cultures it is confining the scope of the incarnation.[169]

Another significant passage from a SEDOS research seminar in 1981 read:

> Inculturation has its source and inspiration in the mystery of the incarnation. The Word was made flesh. Here flesh means the full concrete, human, and created reality that Jesus was. Inculturation, therefore, becomes another way of describing Christian mission. If proclamation sees mission in the perspective of the Word to be proclaimed, inculturation sees mission in the perspective of the flesh, or concrete embodiment, which the Word assumes in a particular individual, community, institution or culture.[170]

In both of these passages there are two ways in which inculturation is a form of incarnational mission. Inculturation is based on *the incarnation*; that is, we extend the mission of God in the incarnation. Inculturation is also based on *incarnation*; that is, embodiment and the embracing of cultural variety are styles of mission. The two are aspects of one argument, and together point towards an incarnational model for mission.

References to inculturation being based on the incarnation are found throughout Roman Catholic missiological literature since Vatican II. Despite Aylward Shorter's claim that the incarnational emphasis went out of vogue soon after Vatican II, a selection of examples can easily be found in sources spanning thirty years. Examples include sources such as Avery Dulles (in 1967),[171] Johannes Schütte (1972),[172] the 1973 Eastern African Bishops' conference (AMECEA),[173] the 1974 Synod of Bishops,[174] Walbert Bühlmann (1976, 1986),[175] the Puebla conference of CELAM (1980),[176] Donal Dorr (1982),[177] Anthony Gittins (1989),[178] and Robert Hardawiryana (1995).[179] A section of *Redemptoris Missio* (1991) is entitled "Incarnating the gospel in people's cultures," and John Paul II declares that "through inculturation the Church makes the Gospel incarnate in different cultures and at the same time introduces peoples, together with their cultures, into her own community" (RM#52).

A striking aspect of most of these references to incarnation as the basis for inculturation is how brief and undeveloped they are. Perhaps writers take for granted the centrality of the incarnation and consider our engagement with culture to be justified by a simple reminder that in Jesus God was focused in a person, a time, a place and a culture. "The incarnation," "the incarnational method" and the call to "incarnate the gospel" are often alluded to and quickly left behind, as if it is obvious what it is about incarnation that we are to emulate. As we can see from the analysis in this study, however, the concept of "incarnation" in mission raises many questions of meaning and method.

A broader view of incarnation desirable—Aylward Shorter: Aylward Shorter is one Roman Catholic missiologist who gives the term "incarnation" the analysis it deserves. He sees the Second Vatican Council's view that the incarnation is the basis for inculturation as one of its most creative insights.[180] Inculturation is analogous to God taking flesh, in the form of a human person in a culture. This analogy reminds us of several important and commonly acknowledged things, acknowledges Shorter. First, Jesus is the subject matter of inculturation. Second, cultural solidarity is a condition for communication. Third, Jesus was committed to the cross-cultural dynamic of his own day. Finally, Christ needs cultures in order to spread the universal Good News and the sharing of his life.[181]

Despite its strengths, Shorter sees shortcomings in the incarnational model as well, though we would not accept his arguments.

First, he says, it gives the impression that inculturation is a single event, happening only when the gospel is first addressed to a culture. The ongoing nature of inculturation is overlooked. Also, if incarnation is seen as the descent of a disembodied Word, it lends itself to talk of the essence of the gospel (EN#63), as if we can grasp it in its culturally disembodied state.[182] Shorter sees it this way because he takes the incarnation strictly to mean the one movement of God in becoming human in Jesus. Shorter calls for us to enlarge the idea of incarnation to take into account "the whole Christian mystery, the life, death and resurrection of Jesus Christ, and their consequences for humanity."[183] He admits many theologians do widen their idea of incarnation, and we have argued for such a view in chapter 2.[184] This seems to deal with his objection to the analogy.

Second, Shorter warns that too much emphasis on the extent to which Jesus assumed a cultural existence can lead to "culturalism," in which we forget how much he challenged his own culture. This argument is essentially the same as that of Daniélou in emphasizing transfiguration alongside incarnation.[185] Shorter rightly reminds us that Jesus had a role as stranger as well as an enculturated first-century Jew. Again, if our view of the incarnation is broad enough to include Jesus' religious and cultural challenge, his death and his resurrection, this objection is answered.

It is for these reasons, Shorter says, that "incarnation" was replaced in common use not long after Vatican II with the term "inculturation" (which, he points out, has its own shortcomings),[186] though we have noted the inaccuracy of this observation. With his basic point we are in agreement:

> All of these defects in the incarnation-model are remedied when a more inclusive approach is taken to the mystery of the Word made flesh. This is, in fact, the main theological criticism that has to be made of the analogy between Incarnation and inculturation. One cannot use only one aspect of the Christ-event to illuminate the dialogue between Gospel and culture. The whole mystery of Christ, passion, death and resurrection, has to be applied analogically to the process of inculturation.[187]

Incarnation as the Integration of Faith and Life

A survey of Roman Catholic missiology since Vatican II uncovers frequent references to incarnational mission understood as the fusion of lived and spoken testimony. It is interesting that the majority of the references are from the 1990s. It is perhaps not surprising that the majority of the authors write from Third World countries. This new emphasis on the integration of faith and life contrasts with the situation before Vatican II, when there was not a strong emphasis on the calling of lay Roman Catholics to live out their daily faith in radical obedience to Christ, apart from a few instances such as the Catholic Action movement. We noted earlier that in the conciliar documents themselves lay Christians were called to "penetrate the world with a Christian spirit" (GS#43), though even this was understood rather indirectly.

More recent writers see it as important for Christians to embody in Christian community the message they proclaim, and to combine the spoken word with credible lives which reflect the transformation promised in Christ (LG#34). Mission means "witness and a way of life that shines out to others" (RM#26). Shorter, for example, argues that the gospel is transmitted only by a living preaching, "by a life which is certainly not wordless or lacking explicitness, but primarily by a *life*, and one lived in a community which is a sign of the transformation being effected."[188] Implicit in all the references is an integral or holistic approach.[189]

Different terms are used to express this understanding. Robert Hardawiryana includes several dimensions of life when he speaks of making witness "truly incarnate" (particularly in Asia) by Christians being

> profoundly renewed in their concrete life-style, in their way of living in community with others, in relationships with sisters and brothers of other faiths, in their involvement in the common struggle for human dignity and rights, in their painstaking efforts for integral human development.[190]

Barbara Hendricks emphasizes the quality of Christian community, the "authentic following of Jesus Christ embodied in a local ecclesial community" marked by servanthood. She expresses an incarnational vision when she says, "Religious meaning is mediated most fully through persons who embody the message they preach."[191] There are echoes here of Bernard Lonergan's category of "incarnate meaning." He would join Hendricks in saying that incarnate meaning is meaning embodied in people, their way of life, their words and their deeds.[192] It combines all other carriers of meaning such as art, symbol and language, and is therefore the fullest and most effective means of communicating meaning.[193]

Most writers who stress the embodiment of faith in Christian lives relate it either indirectly or directly to the incarnation as a model for Christians. For example, Dulles argues that the church ought to imitate Jesus and be the visible extension of Christ in the world.[194] Under the heading "The mission: Incarnation of Christ," Johannes Schütte writes that in Christian communities Christ "is to become a living presence in a new incarnation."[195] Anthony Gittins refers to Christians "seeking to *live out* or *incarnate* the gospel simply and radically."[196] Finally, Jacob Kavunkal talks of the necessity of following the pattern of Jesus' life, actualizing it in a "contrast society" which re-enacts the ministry of Jesus.[197]

Most examples of incarnational mission as "word and deed integrated" are as brief and undeveloped as the examples of incarnational mission as inculturation. The terms are used loosely, speaking sometimes of "incarnating the gospel" and sometimes of "a new incarnation of Christ." At times one suspects that the valid insight that the integration of faith and life is important in mission is simply conveniently linked to the incarnation. The link is appropriate, but is often casually and loosely made.

Nevertheless, this understanding of incarnational mission is a recurring theme in recent Roman Catholic missiology, in common with all the traditions we survey in this study.

Incarnation as Solidarity with the Poor

There is a strong thread running through contemporary Roman Catholic missiology affirming the call to pay central attention to the poor. The Puebla conference of the Latin American Episcopal Council (CELAM) affirmed the radical conclusions of the Medellín conference eleven years earlier when it said: "We affirm the need for conversion on the part of the whole Church to a preferential option for the poor, an option aimed at their integral liberation."[198] It called for Christians to embark on a radical discipleship which gives a privileged place to the weak, the lowly and the poor. In this and many other ways Puebla represented the emphases of liberation theology (see chapter 6). These themes, however, have entered the discussion of mission across the whole of Roman Catholic missiology, so that not only those who could clearly be labelled liberation theologians are found espousing the cause of the poor and defining the call to follow Jesus in ways which include solidarity with the poor.[199]

The life and teaching of Jesus are the basis usually given for this path.[200] Mary Motte, for example, writes:

> God loves each one in a unique, concrete, existential way as evidenced in the Incarnation. The call to universal mission is a call to embody this message of good news especially for those who are least likely to hear it because of the conditions in which they live, for example, the poorest, the oppressed, those who live on the periphery of society.[201]

Several authors make the point that if real transformation is to take place among the powerless and suffering the church must follow the self-emptying path of Christ by emptying itself of power, wealth and status, and taking a stance of concrete solidarity with the poor.[202] This is a frequent model of incarnational mission, often linked directly to the mystery of the incarnation (RM#88).

For most, who interpret the kenosis of Christ in socio-political terms as well as metaphysical terms, the self-emptying of Christ was a double condescension (becoming human, becoming poor).[203] For Pieris, however, the first "condescension" is hardly a "come-down" because humanity is

God's finest creation, the fruit of love; too much talk of kenosis in God's becoming flesh demeans humanity and the flesh. Incarnational christology should not take John's Gospel to say simply that the Word became flesh. What type of person did Christ become? It is the second condescension, ignored by many theologians in the past, which Pieris insists is the real one, because slavery is ugly: "Incarnation cannot merely be the hypostatic union between divine and human natures, but the covenantal identification of God with the slaves of this earth." [204]

The Sacramental and the Incarnational Perspectives

In examining Roman Catholic missiology the relationship between the sacramental and the incarnational perspective requires comment because the two are closely related and bear strong similarities.

A sacramental perspective, as we indicated at the beginning of the chapter, is one that sees "the divine in the human, the infinite in the finite, the spiritual in the material, the transcendent in the immanent, the eternal in the historical." [205] In the widest sense any object or event or person can function as a sacrament. "The sacraments," on the other hand, refer more narrowly to the seven church-controlled sacraments which, according to Roman Catholicism, together celebrate and communicate the saving grace of God. [206] Our interest here is in the wider use of the terms "sacrament" or "sacramental."

Jesus Christ is considered the primal sacrament of God. [207] The divine was fully present in Jesus' humanity. This primacy of Jesus as sacrament has long been uncontroversial in Roman Catholic thought.

More recently, since the work of Henri de Lubac, Roman Catholic thought has also seen the church as the sacrament of Christ. [208] Edward Schillebeeckx has taken it up [209] as have several Vatican II documents, [210] the best known passage being one we mentioned earlier from *Lumen Gentium:* "By her relationship with Christ, the Church is a kind of sacrament or sign of intimate union with God, and of the unity of all [humankind]" (LG#1). [211]

At times it seems that Roman Catholic writers see the church's role as sacrament to be guaranteed due to her status as mediator between the individual Christian and Jesus Christ. [212] At other times, however, a critical principle is introduced. The church is then seen as a sacrament of Christ *insofar as* she actually does embody the new life God offers her. [213] Since

Vatican II there has been much more acknowledgement of the imperfection of the church and its need of continual purification.

There is substantial overlap between the sacramental and incarnational perspectives. In this context let us take an "incarnational" perspective to mean expecting to embody in Christian lives and words the presence of Christ which is being proclaimed. The incarnational perspective is sacramental because it expects God's presence to be made visible in earthly vessels, namely Christian lives. Often no distinction is made between the two perspectives. Timothy McCarthy, in commenting on the prominence at Vatican II of the church's sacramental role, explained that it meant the church must exemplify the gospel, practicing what it preaches and emulating the striking lifestyle of the early church.[214] Dulles writes that as sacrament the church must incarnate itself in every culture.[215]

To be more precise, we could say that the incarnational perspective is an example of the sacramental view, extending the sacramental perspective in the direction of discovering the presence of Christ in ordinary life. The sacramental perspective is assumed in the incarnational perspective; the incarnation is the prime instance of a sacrament, and the incarnating dynamic of God is evident in the way God is found in the material, tangible and mundane aspects of life. In terms of ethos, the incarnational perspective seems to allow a sharper and more prophetic tone, remembering the historical Jesus, whereas sacramentalism breathes a certain serenity and harmony.

There can be little disagreement with the sacramental perspective unless one holds to a dialectical theology where the divine-human gap is extremely wide and the incarnation itself is always a paradox. It is true that we might fall at different points on the spectrum between an immanentist and transcendent view of God, finding either the typically Roman Catholic analogical imagination or the typically Protestant dialectical imagination more congenial.[216] It is also true that if the sacramental perspective becomes a strong sacramentalism centered on the churchly sacraments it can lead to an under-emphasis on service to the world.[217] On the other hand, if Christians find themselves enabled by the churchly sacraments (particularly the eucharist) to go out and be sacraments themselves, these dangers are avoided; the sacramental presence of Christ is then properly linked to the mission of the incarnating church. It is only where the model of the church as sacrament is taken in isolation that an imbalance is likely, as

Dulles points out for each of the images he considers in *Models of the church*.[218]

Our analysis of recent Roman Catholic missiology has shown that it operates in a sacramental framework in which the incarnation is the primary sacrament and the church seeks to make the presence of Christ visible in its life and mission. We have found that the theme of incarnation as inculturation is very important for incarnational missiology, as is incarnation as the integration of word and deed, and incarnation as solidarity with the poor. These last two are perhaps more prominent than expected given that liberation theology was excluded for separate treatment. Throughout, we have been reminded that insofar as Christian mission is concerned it is the whole church that embodies Christ in the world and not the Christian individual. All of these emphases listed are important aspects of incarnational mission.

Roman Catholic missiology, in its variety, demonstrates all three dimensions of incarnational mission outlined in chapter 3, but makes its most creative contribution (in our judgment) to the third. The first dimension is found in increasingly frequent references to following Jesus, solidarity with the poor and the integration of word and deed. Roman Catholic liberation theologians are obviously influencing the whole church in its recognition of these themes. The second dimension, mission in the power of Christ's presence, is evident in the view that the church is the continuing incarnation and particularly in Catholic eucharistic theology. The third dimension includes the sacramental perspective, a positive attitude towards culture, and the use of the incarnation as a basis for inculturation. Roman Catholicism makes strong and distinctive contributions in each of these areas.

The dangers in the dominant Roman Catholic approach to incarnational mission, such as they are, apply to both Roman Catholicism and Anglo-Catholicism, so we will return to them after discussing Anglo-Catholic missiology in the next section.

Anglo-Catholicism

We found the idea of the church as the continuation of the incarnation to be strong in Roman Catholic missiology. The idea is also closely associated with Anglo-Catholicism, particularly with *Lux Mundi: A series of studies on the religion of the incarnation*, edited by Charles Gore and published in 1889.[219] The incarnational emphasis of *Lux Mundi*, whose title means "the light of the world," so dominated Anglicanism for fifty years after its publication that Anglicanism as a whole is sometimes said to be distinguished by being "the religion of the incarnation."[220] Some consider *Lux Mundi* to embody the true spirit of Anglicanism and many claim Gore remained the pre-eminent Anglican theologian until the time of William Temple.[221] Therefore we will examine Anglo-Catholicism's incarnational emphasis largely through *Lux Mundi* and responses to it.

Lux Mundi brought Anglo-Catholicism (as the high-church movement had been known since the 1830s) to dominance in Anglicanism.[222] Bearing the marks of the high-church movement and the Christian Social Movement, *Lux Mundi* also crystallized a new liberal Catholicism within the Anglican church, attempting to restore the balance between the head and the heart (as against the Tractarians),[223] between the incarnation and the atonement (as against the evangelicals),[224] and between tradition and criticism (as against liberal biblical scholars).[225]

> [Lux Mundi] marked the recasting of Anglican theology in an incarnational mold, *Christus consummator* [Christ the fulfiller] rather than *Christus redemptor* [Christ the redeemer], inductive rather than deductive in character, and welcoming of historical criticism, scientific advance, and an awareness of development. It was a church theology, a prayed theology, and a theology with clear social implications.[226]

Anglo-Catholicism is a style of Anglicanism distinguished by (1) a claim to be Catholic (that is, part of the historic, world-wide church), (2) a taste for ritual and beauty in worship, (3) a strong sacramentalism, (4) its strongly incarnational faith, (5) a world-affirming temper, and (6) a high doctrine of the church.[227] The last four are of particular interest for incarnational mission. We will not discuss sacramentalism because what has been said about Roman Catholic sacramentalism applies to Anglo-Catholicism. The last three we will examine more carefully.

The Incarnation as the Climax of God's Immanence in Creation

Liberal Anglo-Catholicism has been called "incarnationalism" because of its belief that the incarnation is the climax of a long, saving process at work through God's presence in creation in his Word, the Logos.[228] Gore and his colleagues tended to see the incarnation in terms of Jesus' birth, life and teaching. Placing less emphasis on the cross and judgement, they reflected nineteenth century optimism by holding to a christocentric cosmic humanism which was also to be the hallmark of the writing of Pierre Teilhard de Chardin fifty years later.[229] Aubrey Moore, in *Lux Mundi*, appeals to both Athanasius and Augustine in arguing for the immanence of God as the eternal Energy of the cosmos and the underlying reason within things, everywhere present but beyond the material universe as well.[230] J R Illingworth, also in *Lux Mundi*, puts a similar view, appealing to Thomas Aquinas, who wrote that the incarnation is the "exaltation of human nature and consummation of the Universe." [231]

Seeing the incarnation as the climax to God's incarnating dynamic led to three emphases in the contributors to *Lux Mundi*. First, they remind us that Jesus' life is as important as his sacrificial death and our mission must respond to the challenges Jesus threw out in his life and teaching. The incarnation is important, among other reasons, for its social and moral implications.[232] Second, they remind us that God's identification with humanity is foundational to mission; to say "God is with us" is a strong affirmation of human worth and an adequate basis for Christian humanism. Finally, they remind us that to focus on the cross alone is to be in danger of reducing the gospel to a matter of personal forgiveness and to neglect other dimensions of the kingdom of God. *Lux Mundi* was critical of the tendency of popular theology, particularly evangelicalism, to emphasize the atonement in isolation from other aspects of Christian doctrine.[233]

Anglo-Catholic incarnationalism could easily adopt the slogan "God with us," but it would emphasize that God is always and increasingly with us, not just in the life of Jesus. It provides a cosmic framework in which God's incarnating dynamic is evident in creation and all dimensions of human culture, as well as in the church and in the interior life of the Christian. This incarnationalism also expands our view of mission, because God's revealing presence is consistently broadened beyond the limits of the life, death and resurrection of Jesus.

However, as several commentators have pointed out, in trying to redress the balance between the incarnation (as the immanence of God in Jesus' birth and life) and the cross, *Lux Mundi* probably neglects the cross.[234] The crucified Christ recedes in this vision, so it is in danger of being a one-sided view of life, where the cry of the oppressed is not heard because Christians look past the harshness of human experience to a serene and immanent God. Alistair Heron puts it powerfully:

> The road back to *Lux Mundi*'s vision of a world suffused by the light of the divine immanence is barred for us by an angel with a flaming sword— and the flames are not those of the transfiguration but of Auschwitz and Hiroshima, of Vietnam and Afghanistan.... For those who have ears to hear, the cry of desolation uttered by Christ on the cross is as essential a key to understanding our human predicament as the Prologue to the Fourth Gospel. It is also essential to realizing who and what God is.[235]

A This-worldly and Life-affirming Faith

A major feature of the immanentist view of God is the value it places on the material, the cultural and the human. In fact, Illingworth argues that the incarnation "reconsecrated earth, for the Word was made Flesh and dwelt among us."[236] The only adequate Christianity, he suggests, is one which bears on ordinary people in their ordinary moments and in their occupations, interests, enthusiasms, and amusements. Through the incarnation the human body acquires a new meaning and new graces, and as a result, so do the family, society, the state, the arts, and the sciences.

Anglo-Catholicism has always shared the Catholic tendency to celebrate life and be world affirming, seeing classic Protestantism as in danger of being dull, dreary, and focused on the future life. George Carey defines incarnational faith in earthy and life-affirming terms, quoting with a light touch the Roman Catholic writer Hilaire Belloc:

> Where'er the Catholic sun doth shine,
> There's music and laughter and good red wine.
> At least I've always found it so—
> Benedicamus Domino! [Blessed be the Lord!][237]

This positive outlook extends to the Anglo-Catholic view of the human person; it sees the incarnation as the basis for a Christian humanism.[238] J K

Mozley, writing on the incarnation in 1936 from within the Anglo-Catholic tradition, noted that since the Oxford Movement and the Christian Social Movement (coalescing in Liberal Anglo-Catholicism) in the nineteenth century, theology has been more aware of the difference that the incarnation makes to our feeling for the value of human life. Because the Son of God has shared in our common life, human nature has been "exalted to the right hand of God."[239] Perhaps this is as close as Western Christianity comes to expressing the notion of theosis, or divinization. Anglo-Catholics use the incarnation to counter notions of the total depravity of humanity. They have argued strenuously for human dignity and the possibility of the kingdom of God being this-worldly in nature.[240] These views on the incarnation mean that Anglo-Catholicism approaches mission actively expecting to find God already at work in people.

The positive value Anglo-Catholicism places on wider society means that mission begins by consciously affirming and endeavoring to add to the truth known to all. Anglo-Catholics tend to see God already involved in the human achievements of civilization, and see their mission partly as the restoration of the divine image in humanity by molding, purifying and supplementing social systems.[241] Christianity is meant to "appropriate and hallow" all dimensions of human endeavor.[242] This view in *Lux Mundi* includes support for an established church and the belief that the state has a divine sanction.[243]

The strong social commitment of Anglo-Catholicism sometimes leads to a more critical and prophetic role for the church. The influence of the Christian Social Movement is felt throughout Anglo-Catholicism.[244] Gore specifically urges his readers to bear the burdens of the poor, live selflessly, turn from wealth and self-aggrandizement, and sound a prophetic note in society.[245]

Writing in 1994, Episcopalian Mellick Belshaw sounds the same note, arguing that the incarnational perspective of *Lux Mundi* is still the ground for the church's presence and ministry among the poor.[246] He argues that the incarnation lies at the heart of mission, that the church often has to do battle with the dominant culture, and that Jesus' manifesto at the synagogue as recorded in Luke 4 sets the agenda for all who follow Jesus in mission.[247] Belshaw's critical stance comes from supplementing Anglo-Catholic incarnationalism with a theology of the cross, which shows us that God's power is revealed in weakness and that this insight is always found most keenly among the poor.[248] Mission among the marginalized, he concludes, "brings us to the very heart of the incarnation." [249]

Nevertheless, Belshaw's voice stands out as rare in contemporary Anglo-Catholic literature. Although Gore's incarnational emphasis has served for a century as the basis for Anglicanism's social and political involvement, that social critique and engagement has dimmed somewhat, with hardly any interest in social and economic theory among Anglo-Catholics today.[250] In founding the Community of the Resurrection at Mirfield, Yorkshire, Gore himself seemed to set the direction more towards monasticism than fully engaged social action.

Perhaps this is partly because the social optimism which made it possible to suggest such a cosy relationship between church and state has dissipated in the century since the publication of *Lux Mundi*.[251]

It is also partly due to the theological inadequacy of a vision of "cultural Christianity." Illingworth valued secular civilization so highly that he saw it as "nothing less than the providential correlative and counterpart of the Incarnation."[252] H Richard Niebuhr, however, suggested that we cannot affirm Jesus as the Christ of culture unless we affirm much more than that.[253] He points out that Jesus' commandments were much more radical than a call to lift culture to a higher plane by sifting and purifying.[254]

The contribution of the world-affirming aspect of the Anglo-Catholic approach to mission is to remind the church of God's activity in human affairs and to call the church to social and political commitment on the grounds that the incarnation "reconsecrates earth," to use Illingworth's phrase.[255]

Its limitation lies in its too-positive estimation of wider human society as an approximation to and locus of the kingdom of God. We should not completely reject this optimism, some of which is due to a certain Anglican inclusiveness and the strongly world-affirming temper of Catholic traditions. Such optimism, however, reflects a nineteenth century perspective which is no longer widely shared.

The Church as the Continuing Incarnation

Possibly the best known dimension of the Anglo-Catholic view of the incarnation is the belief that the church is in a very strong sense the body of Christ. Echoing traditional Roman Catholic teaching, Gore popularized among Anglicans the idea that the church is the extension or the continuation of the incarnation:

> What was realized once for all in Jesus, is perpetuated in the world. The Church is the body of Christ. It is the extension and perpetuation of the Incarnation in the world. It is this, because it embodies the same principle, and lives by the same life.... The Church exists to perpetuate in every age the life of Jesus, the union of [humanity] with Godhood.[256]

This passage shows us that, in Gore's thought, the incarnation is foundational to mission. The incarnation includes an inherent dynamic of unfolding or reaching out which is realized in the response of the church.

The distinction between the Anglo-Catholic expression of the presence of Christ in the church and more modest ecclesiologies is a matter of degree. The divide seems to be the confidence with which Anglo-Catholicism (with Roman Catholicism and Eastern Orthodoxy) asserts that the church, for all its faults, is divinely ordained and given a guarantee that through history it will always embody the life of Christ and exercise his functions through the Spirit. Those with a lower ecclesiology will use the language of the "body of Christ" more metaphorically and will sometimes distinguish the visible church from the invisible church, making greater allowance for the possibility of apostasy within the church.

The high view of the church in Anglo-Catholicism naturally leads to a church-centered model of mission, with several strengths. It reminds us that as the body of Christ the church lives by embodying Christ to the world. A high ecclesiology also rightly emphasizes the corporate and historical nature of the church in its mission. Furthermore, in its emphasis on worship it provides a strong eucharistic and worshipful context for experiencing the transforming work of God in the lives of Christians.

This view has its limitations, however. Overall Anglo-Catholicism has been disappointing in carrying through its comprehensive incarnational vision for mission emanating from the worshipping life of the church. Anglo-Catholicism seems to have a rather inward-looking style of mission which was not what Gore had in mind when he urged Christians to be deeply and critically involved in society. Its emphasis on worship and ritual seems to have taken much of its energy.

In briefly outlining the Anglo-Catholic emphases on the cosmic significance of incarnation, a world-affirming faith, and the church as the continuing incarnation, we have noted along the way the contributions Anglo-Catholicism makes to incarnational mission. In particular it provides a cosmic framework for the immanence of God and God's incarnating dynamic reaching its climax in Jesus Christ. It grounds Christian humanism in the incarnation. It also contributes a positive and celebratory note in affirming the material world on the basis of the incarnation.

We also noted some dangers or disappointments of the Anglo-Catholic approach, namely its neglect of the cross, its serene optimism, its cultural Christianity and, over the years, its dimmed social conscience and inward-looking stance. This leads us to several evaluative comments which apply to both Anglo-Catholic and Roman Catholic missiology.

Evaluative Comments on Catholic Missiologies

While recognizing the variety we find in Catholic missiology (including the Roman Catholic and Anglo-Catholic wings) its general directions allow us to make some brief critical and appreciative comments. The main dangers in the Catholic approach to incarnational mission (without suggesting that Catholic missiologists necessarily succumb to them) are those of one-sidedness: (1) a complacent view of the church as the divinely-guaranteed perpetuation of the incarnation, (2) a world-affirming but insufficiently challenging sacramental perspective, and (3) an inward-looking church-centered mission. Consider each briefly.

First, the view of the church as bearer of the **continuing incarnation** can easily neglect the keen anticipation of something new and far better than what has already been.[257] A radically incarnational and ecclesiocentric vision can be the most conservative model of eschatology possible, because in it the significant saving events have already happened and are simply unfolding in the church.[258] There can be complacency in seeing the church as extending and fulfilling Jesus' incarnation. The kingdom of God can easily be identified with the church. The church can come to see its role as guarding the treasures it has been given, instead of straining towards the future as the people of God, in full awareness of its imperfection.

It is a high claim to speak of the church as the literal embodiment of Jesus Christ, or his extension in time. A more modest way of speaking befits the nature and role of the church. We may certainly speak of the work of the Spirit in the church, the presence of Christ in the church, the image of the church as the body of Christ, the church as divinely ordained and the church as both human and yet divinely inspired. Nevertheless, as we were reminded by Moltmann, we need to remember that the church draws its life from Christ its head and its criterion.[259] The theological danger of equating the church to the incarnate Christ is that of conflating christology and ecclesiology.

Another danger for a sacramental and strongly world-affirming perspective is that of **losing a prophetic voice**. Sacramentalism can simply find God in the world rather than struggle to change the world. A one-sided sacramentalism may find it difficult to account for radical evil; in finding God in many places, it can be serene when it should be troubled, and attuned to beauty at the expense of hearing pain. We argued above that an incarnational perspective needs to remember the prophetic edge of Jesus. We quoted Heron's claim that the road back to the serene worldview of *Lux Mundi* is barred to us by Auschwitz and Hiroshima. As the liberation theologians and radical evangelicals powerfully remind us, the seeming absence of God in history needs to be expressed at times, as well as the presence of God in the world.

Third, there is a danger in the Catholic perspective of an **inward-looking church-centered mission**. We do not generally see Gore succumbing to this, nor Roman Catholic missionary orders, for example. Nevertheless, there can be a tendency for Catholic mission to focus on worship and the eucharist as the central locus of mission, and to focus on the activities of the organized church, at the expense of service in the world or the daily life of its lay members.

Notwithstanding these comments, we have shown Catholic missiology to contribute several distinctives which need to be remembered in a balanced approach to incarnational mission. They tend to cluster in the third dimension of incarnational mission, that of mission as co-operation with God's overall incarnating purposes in creation. In Catholic missiology there is a comprehensive sacramental and sometimes immanentist perspective in which God's incarnating dynamic is evident in creation, redemption and the ongoing mission of God by means of the Holy Spirit operating particularly through the church. All of this adds up to a clear expectation that just as in Jesus the divine was revealed in the human, so today in the mission of the church we ought to expect to see Christ revealed. This is the central Catholic view of incarnational mission. With it goes a clear emphasis on the incarnation as the basis for inculturation and as the ground for affirming and engaging culture.

In the ecumenical movement and Eastern Orthodoxy, we find a related, but different, cluster of incarnational perspectives from the third dimension of incarnational mission, and to those two traditions we now turn.

CHAPTER 9

THE INCARNATING GOD:
THE WCC AND EASTERN ORTHODOXY

In different but related ways, the ecumenical movement and the Eastern Orthodox churches conceive of mission in broad terms as the mission of the trinitarian God with which the church is invited to co-operate. In ecumenical statements we find the term *missio Dei* (the mission of God), referring to God's action in the world and not only through the church. In Eastern Orthodox theology, although the church is the channel through which God is seen to work, we see the same trinitarian framework. God the creator makes Christ's redemptive presence present in the eucharist through the Holy Spirit, inviting humanity to participate in the mystical and ethical process of divinization. As in Catholicism, these views illustrate the third dimension of incarnational mission we outlined in chapter 3, the ongoing incarnating dynamic of God, and (in Eastern Orthodoxy) the church as the ongoing incarnation.

In common with other streams of Christianity these two traditions also see incarnational mission in terms of holistic mission (integrating word and deed), quality of "presence," Good News to the poor, and inculturation.

We will take the World Council of Churches (WCC) as representative of ecumenical Christian thinking, and will mainly use the WCC's official documents to discern its approaches to incarnational mission, acknowledging the inevitable diversity of a world grouping of Christian churches.

"Orthodoxy" generally includes two groups. The Oriental Orthodox churches, consisting of the Coptic, Syrian, Armenian, Ethiopian and (Indian) Malankara churches, are those who did not accept the theology of the council of Chalcedon in 451. The Eastern Orthodox churches, the "Greek" rather than the "Latin" wing of early Christianity, diverged from the perspective of Rome over several centuries, resulting in a schism between the two in 1054, with the patriarch of Constantinople challenging Rome's claim to universal jurisdiction.[1] The largest of them (in order of estimated size) are the Russian, Romanian, Serbian and Greek Orthodox churches.[2]

The World Council of Churches

A survey of reports on WCC assemblies and on conferences of its Commission on World Mission and Evangelism (CWME) does not reveal very many direct references to incarnational mission. It is difficult to hazard a guess at the reasons for this paucity in general reports. Perhaps greater attention has been paid to the social and political realities of the world than to the theological underpinnings of mission. Perhaps also (in recent decades) a developing interest in inter-religious dialogue has led to kingdom-centered and theocentric theology in preference to incarnational emphases. Whatever the reasons, although an incarnational form of mission is usually assumed, references in WCC reports are for the most part indirect or fleeting, as we will see below.

The exceptions, documents which often directly appeal to incarnational mission, are the 1982 WCC publication on mission, *Mission and evangelism: An ecumenical affirmation*, and *The San Antonio Report* of the 1989 CWME conference.[3] Other material issued in preparation for WCC events or appearing in the WCC journal *International Review of Mission* supplements these references.

Combining both direct and indirect references, we can be more positive. There is "a broadening ecumenical consensus about the relationship between the incarnation—the actual way in which the Word became flesh or the model of Jesus' life—and the way in which the church goes about its mission." [4]

The order of the following points is roughly parallel to the chronological order of their emphasis within the WCC.

Missio Dei: Wider than the Church

From the formation of the WCC in 1948 there was a growing emphasis, through the phrase *missio Dei*, on mission being God's initiative (rather than that of the church). WCC literature tended to distinguish the kingdom of God carefully from the church and see the world as the place where mission occurs, beyond the activity of the visible, institutional church. To be part of God's mission means to join in God's movement towards people, what we earlier called "God's incarnating dynamic." Incarnational mission in these terms is not a march of victory, however; it is to join with the incarnate and crucified Christ.[5] These trends surfaced at the International Missionary Council (IMC)[6] conference at Willingen in 1952 and were clearest between 1961 and 1975.[7] A trinitarian missiology has prevailed ever since in ecumenical thought.

At the time this involved a dethronement of the church from the center of mission. J C Hoekendijk wrote an influential article in preparation for the Willingen conference arguing that the kingdom of God, and not the church, ought to be central in mission. He criticized the church-oriented theme of the conference and suggested that church-centered missionary thinking distorted and narrowed the missionary enterprise.[8] The conference divided over how central the church is in mission. There was a clash between the views of Hoekendijk and the Anglicans, who argued for a much stronger ontological view of the church as the extension of the incarnation.[9]

Analysing the Willingen conference soon afterwards, Wilhelm Anderson articulated the reasons for a trinitarian basis for mission rather than an ecclesiocentric incarnational basis. First, a theology of mission must go back beyond the church's missionary obligation, to the "self-revelation of the triune God in Jesus Christ."[10] Strictly speaking it is God who carries out the mission and the church is the church inasmuch as it co-operates with that mission.[11] Second, and relatedly, mission needs to be seen not only in the light of the incarnation (here taken as the birth and life of Jesus) but also in the light of the cross and the resurrection. "It is only when these three aspects are taken together that they constitute the witness of the triune God."[12] Third, the incarnational view, as expressed at the conference, carries too high a view of the church.[13] It draws a line too directly from the incarnation to the church as its extension.[14]

Although Anderson did not go as far as Hoekendijk in dismissing the role of the church, he supported the critique of the church-centered incarnational approach to mission and contributed to a strong swing in ecumenical missiology.

This pendulum swing was so strong in the period from 1961 to about 1975 that some felt that ecumenical missiology almost lost sight of the church while listening to the agenda of the world, leading to debate on whether *missio Dei* was being twisted to serve a secular and reductionist version of mission. It was not until the CWME conferences in Melbourne (1980) and San Antonio (1989) and the publication of *Mission and evangelism: An ecumenical affirmation* (1982) that mission again found its home in ecclesiology and the one-sided worldly orientation was balanced by seeing the church as having an important role in the mission of God.[15]

Holistic Mission and Participation
in the Whole of Life

The ecumenical movement's commitment to a holistic view of mission (or evangelism), in which verbal proclamation and living witness are integrated in the one task, stands out as one of its most prominent emphases. (Note that in WCC documents the terms "mission" and "witness' are used interchangeably with the term "evangelism." [16]) Tracing the occurrence of "evangelism" in WCC documents from 1961 to 1991, Priscilla Pope-Levison says, "The essential key to ecumenical evangelism … is that it is holistic—the "whole church" brings the "whole Gospel" to the "whole world,"—and comprehensive—involving both word and deed." [17]

Critics of the WCC often argue that its official statements do not sufficiently address those who are "lost" as well as those who are oppressed.[18] It is difficult to say how frequently verbal evangelism and personal conversion would need to be mentioned to constitute balance and what level of infrequency would constitute neglect of that dimension.

Consider the Bangkok CWME conference in 1973, which some say illustrates an excessively this-worldly and socio-political view of salvation today, focusing almost exclusively on salvation as social and political liberation.[19] One of its statements begins, "Within the comprehensive notion of salvation, we see the saving work in four social dimensions …," and goes on to outline the struggle for economic justice, human rights, solidarity against alienation between people, and hope in personal life.[20]

This seems to indicate that when the WCC spells out what salvation means it uses entirely this-worldly terms, and that deeds rather than words are the appropriate way to engage in mission.

In defense of the Bangkok statement we must say that this section is specifically about social justice and yet still contains a strong statement on how comprehensive salvation is, encompassing body and soul, society and the individual, justification and justice, and so on.[21] It emphasizes that in doing its job of relating salvation to social justice it in no way denies the personal and eternal dimensions of salvation; in fact it regards the dimensions as inseparable.[22] It does not neglect the eschatological dimension.[23] All of these factors form the context in which the struggle for liberation is set.

An overview of WCC mission theology does, however, support the contention that it has been uneven in its efforts to express an integral and balanced view of mission. In the years from the integration of the IMC into the WCC in 1961 to about 1975, increasing attention was paid to social action as an integral part of mission. Partly in response to criticism of the WCC's one-sidedness, proclamation was emphasized more at the Nairobi assembly in 1975. Retaining the liberationist perspective of the Bangkok CWME conference (1973), a theology of Good News to the poor was articulated at the Melbourne CWME conference (1980). A carefully nuanced balance was achieved in *Mission and evangelism: An ecumenical affirmation* (1982), perhaps the high point in articulating a holistic view of mission. The San Antonio CWME conference (1989) was more open about proclamation but was unable to integrate it well into an overall view of mission. The Canberra assembly (1991) showed tensions and differences as the issues of syncretism and dialogue clamoured for attention at the expense of articulating again a holistic view of mission. The Salvador CWME conference (1996), where gospel and culture themes dominated, was similar.

Nevertheless, the theme of holistic mission based on the incarnation has been clearly developed in several WCC publications.

The concept of incarnation was integral to the exposition of a holistic evangelism. The idea of holistic evangelism was articulated first at the Mexico CWME conference (1963)[24] and was summed up at Nairobi (1975) after strong statements against reducing the gospel to either personal or corporate dimensions, or to either sin or injustice: "The whole Gospel for the whole person and the whole world" means that we cannot leave any area of human life and suffering without the witness of hope."[25] Mortimer Arias gave a major plenary address at Nairobi on integral evangelism, which "unites sign and word" and addresses the whole person. Such evangelism, he said, is not only integral in content but in form. "True evangelism is incarnate: proclamation in words and deeds in a concrete situation."[26] Here "incarnate" clearly implies a contrast with a gospel that is for the soul only, or communicated in words only. Arias expounded this incarnational evangelism in terms of contextualization, true humanization (anchored in the incarnation), cost and vulnerability, and the life of Christian communities.[27]

As a second example, *Mission and evangelism: An ecumenical affirmation* (commonly abbreviated as ME) was published in 1982 after wide consultation and stands as the most considered official WCC position on mission.[28] It has been widely praised in many circles for its balance. *Mission and evangelism*'s incarnational approach is very strong. It bases the mission of the church on Jesus' commission in John 20:21, "As the Father has sent me, even so I send you" (ME#3, also #28) and says, "Our obedience in mission should be patterned on the ministry and teaching of Jesus' (ME#28). Its holistic approach, linked to the pattern of Jesus' life and ministry, is also evident throughout. For example:

> The lordship of Christ is to be proclaimed to all realms of life. (ME#14)

> The "spiritual Gospel" and the "material Gospel" were in Jesus one Gospel. (ME#33)

> There is no evangelism without solidarity; there is no Christian solidarity that does not involve sharing the knowledge of the kingdom which is God's promise to the poor of the earth. (ME#34)[29]

Mission and evangelism expresses well the incarnational and holistic dimensions of the ecumenical perspective on mission.

A third example can be found in the "Stuttgart Statement" issued at a WCC-sponsored consultation in 1987 where most who attended were ecumenically-involved evangelicals, including leading figures such as Raymond Fung, René Padilla, Vinay Samuel, Ronald Sider and Christopher Sugden.[30] This group's enthusiasm for integral evangelism comes as no surprise when we remember that it was dominated by radical evangelicals. The Stuttgart Statement advocates an "incarnational evangelism" in which proclamation and service are integrated (#6).

We live by the gospel of an incarnate Lord; this implies that the gospel has to become incarnated in ourselves, the "evangelists." This is not to suggest that, in our evangelism, we proclaim ourselves, but that those whom we wish to invite to faith in Christ will invariably look for signs of that faith in us. And what will happen if they do not find these? Does not the credibility of our evangelism, to some extent at least, depend on the authenticity of our own lives? Can we evangelize others without becoming vulnerable ourselves? (#3)

It is worth noting, given that Raymond Fung was a signatory to this statement, that it briefly answers the objection Fung has voiced against an incarnational approach to mission, an objection which acted as a catalyst for this whole study, as we noted in the Introduction.[31] Fung argues that incarnational missiology effectively says "Look at us and you will see Jesus when it should be saying "Look beyond us to Jesus."[32] The Stuttgart Statement suggests, to the contrary, that what is central to incarnational mission is that there is a pattern in God's mission which is also appropriate in Christian mission. The incarnational approach is quite consistent with Christians pointing in humility beyond their own lives.

There is a difference between the ecumenical concept of holistic mission and the evangelical view (at least as represented by John Stott and the Lausanne movement), even though both groups use phrases similar to "the whole church taking the whole gospel to the whole world."[33] The evangelical view sees verbal proclamation and social action as closely related but ultimately distinct, like the two blades of a pair of scissors or the two wings of a bird.[34] The ecumenical concept of holism is thoroughgoing, seeing Christian witness to the kingdom as one task for one vision, taking place in both word and deed, for liberation at all levels of human existence.

Self-emptying Mission, and Good News to the Poor

Of equal prominence to the emphasis on holistic mission has been the call for solidarity with the poor in a spirit of self-emptying after the manner of Jesus. Three elements have been linked in WCC documents: Good News to the poor, kenosis, and following the pattern of Jesus' mission.

Although from its inception the WCC has given great attention to world poverty and human development, it is since 1980, broadly following the directions of liberation theology, that it has clearly said that a "preferential option for the poor" is an integral aspect of mission and evangelism. The

Melbourne CWME conference articulated in detail Jesus' identification with the poor, the privileged role of the poor in the church, the fact that the gospel is particularly good news to the poor, and the belief that the relationship between the church and the poor is the yardstick by which to judge the authenticity of Christian mission.[35] Surveying the WCC emphasis on the poor would be a major undertaking, but our purpose here is to illustrate the way the ecumenical emphasis on the poor is often linked to the incarnation, especially to the self-emptying of Jesus in his incarnation among the poor.

WCC reports and publications have repeatedly based mission on the pattern of Jesus' ministry as seen through the lens of biblical passages such as Philippians 2:6-11 ("Christ Jesus ... emptied himself, taking the form of a slave...."), 2 Corinthians 8:9 ("For your sakes he became poor."), and Luke 4:18-20 ("He has anointed me to bring good news to the poor.").[36] In the ecumenical vision the good news to the world always involves costly obedience on the part of Christians. The following incarnational themes recur: self-emptying love, servanthood, powerlessness, the cross, the poverty of the incarnation, Jesus' solidarity with and compassion for the poor, and his struggle against oppression.[37]

Emilio Castro, director of the CWME from 1973 to 1983, summed up the Melbourne perspective as follows:

> Now ... we have a theological perspective—the Gospel announced to the poor [—] and a vision of God's own missionary style—Jesus emptying himself, going through the cross to the margin of life ... [38]

Mission and evangelism: An ecumenical affirmation speaks at several points of Christ's identification with humanity in general and the poor in particular, and its determinative role in Christian mission. For example:

> The self-emptying of the servant who lived among the people, sharing in their hopes and sufferings, giving his life on the cross for all humanity—this was Christ's way of proclaiming the Good News, and as disciples we are summoned to follow the same way.... Our obedience in mission should be patterned on the ministry and teaching of Jesus. (ME#28)

> Every methodology illustrates or betrays the Gospel we announce. In all communications of the Gospel, power must be subordinate to love. (ME#28)

> The Church of Jesus Christ is called to preach the Good News to the poor following the example of its Lord who was incarnate as poor.... (ME#32)

For the WCC, therefore, as for liberation theologians, the call to solidarity with the poor is based on the ministry of Jesus. This identification with the weak and marginalized is both the content and style of discipleship, determined by the life and crucifixion of Jesus (ME#35). It is a small step from this perspective to the theme that was to emerge in the 1980s in WCC documents, "Mission in Christ's way." While it is a similar theme, it has generated enough significant literature for us to consider it under a separate heading.

Mission in Christ's Way

As early as at the Uppsala assembly in 1968 the WCC spoke of Jesus as the pattern for mission, and this was continued at Melbourne (1980) and in *Mission and evangelism: An ecumenical affirmation* in 1982, as we have noted already.[39] The theme became central when the phrase "Mission in Christ's way" was chosen as part of the title for the 1989 CWME conference at San Antonio. Reflection on the theme began with a consultation in Geneva in 1986, resulting in a group of articles published in the *International Review of Mission*.[40] Lesslie Newbigin wrote a Bible study booklet on the theme (1987).[41] The Stuttgart Consultation with ecumenical evangelicals in 1987 resulted in a book of papers entitled *Proclaiming Christ in Christ's way* (1989) (note the sharpening of the phrase in an evangelical direction).[42] Preparatory study materials on the theme were issued prior to the San Antonio conference,[43] and the proceedings of the conference, containing further reflections on the theme, were published in *The San Antonio Report*.[44]

The main contribution of the theme over the last decade has been to garner a broadening consensus in ecumenical circles for mission's intimate link with the mission of Jesus. Although most of the published reflections only restate previous insights, they have served to highlight the incarnational basis of mission. In the process the WCC has answered some of the critics of its missiology.

Our first few examples of how the theme has been used contribute little that is new. Janet Silman, at the Geneva consultation, said that "our mission as a church today is essentially ... to incarnate God's love and justice in our world."[45] At the same consultation Geevarghese Mar Osthathios briefly spelt out mission in Christ's way as incarnational (concrete, historical and inculturated), cosmic, kenotic, and liberating.[46] Newbigin, in his Bible studies, urged the church to follow in Christ's way by taking the way of the cross, which is to defiantly take on the powers of evil.[47]

At the San Antonio CWME conference itself, "Mission in Christ's way" did not turn out to be a dominant theme, despite being part of the title. The scope of the conference was very wide and references to mission in Christ's way in the section reports were scattered and undeveloped.[48] The Conference moderator, Orthodox bishop Anastasios Yannoulatos of Androussa, added some substantial theological reflection on the theme from a distinctive Orthodox point of view, which we will mention when examining Orthodoxy.[49]

San Antonio understood mission in Christ's way in several senses. The first is sharing the whole gospel as a way of life in word and deed.[50] A second sense is the unity of the church, reflecting the unity of Jesus with the Father.[51] A third view, though the connection is merely asserted, is that "mission in Christ's way must extend to God's creation."[52] The fourth is the call to a costly mission. The opening words of the second section, on "Participating in suffering and struggle," are:

> Participating in suffering and struggle is at the heart of God's mission and God's will for the world. It is central for our understanding of the incarnation, the most glorious example of participation in suffering and struggle. The church is sent in the way of Christ bearing the marks of the cross in the power of the Holy Spirit (cf. John 20:19-23).[53]

The most thorough contribution on the theme has been made by Darrell Guder who draws attention to the broadening consensus on the importance of the incarnation as a guiding principle for evangelistic methodology and mentions briefly most of the major ways of understanding incarnational mission examined in this study.[54] Guder makes several important points.

First, "mission in Christ's way" has come (as we have also shown) from the idea of incarnational evangelism which endeavors to include both proclamation and social action. "It is a genuinely helpful way of thinking, which does not undermine the evangelistic ministry of the church, but rather strengthens it."[55]

Second, Guder points out that what is at issue here is not a discussion of the doctrine of the incarnation but evangelistic methodology. Jesus' divinity and humanity are taken as a starting point and the question missiologists ask is: What is the importance of the incarnation for the way Christians engage in mission?[56]

Third, the term "incarnational," a fairly new word in its adjectival form, tends to refer to mission in which "the communication of the gospel [is] appropriate to its content."[57] Guder traces the use of the term "incarnational witness" to the writing of pioneer ecumenist John Mackay, who in 1964 defined the "incarnational principle" as identifying oneself closely with those around, seeking to overcome outsider status and without condescension becoming (in Mackay's words) "joyously and empathetically involved in their common life and concerns."[58] Guder sums this up as follows:

> [The] humanness of Jesus, and the example of his life, are seen as paradigmatic for the mission activity of the church. In effect, the incarnational approach becomes an ethic of evangelism, based upon the humanity of Christ, whose life and actions are as much the norm of obedient Christian living as are his words.[59]

Fourth, in summary form Guder identifies many of the themes considered in this study, in arguing that the incarnational approach to mission, as a guiding principle or criterion for mission, integrates various dichotomies prevalent in missiology, such as between faith and culture, between Christian traditions, between means and ends in evangelism, between evangelism and doing justice, and between incarnational and atonement-oriented thinking.[60] Guder is by far the clearest contributor in the WCC discussion of what it means to engage in mission in Christ's way.[61]

Incarnational Mission as Inculturation

Along with other Christian traditions ecumenical missiology sees the incarnation as a model of respect for culture and the inculturation of the Good News.

This theme has been present throughout the life of the WCC,[62] and was stated succinctly in *Mission and evangelism: An ecumenical affirmation*, which chose to use the words of the Catholic research seminar SEDOS in 1981 (quoted earlier[63]) to express its view on incarnation and inculturation: "Inculturation has its source and inspiration in the mystery of the incarnation. The Word was made flesh."[64]

Culturally sensitive evangelism is firmly part of the ecumenical perspective. The moderator of the WCC Central Committee, Aram Keshishian, wrote recently that there is now a common ecumenical understanding of mission as sharing in the reconciling ministry of Christ, that is, taking the way of the cross. He identified three dimensions of mission, those of evangelism, service, and dialogue:

> Evangelism means sharing the gospel "in Christ's way" (San Antonio). It implies never dominating the people culturally, religiously, economically, or politically, but sharing the good news in a way that respects the peculiar identity of a given socio-cultural milieu. This missiological concern, which was a predominant one in the assembly, brings the whole question of gospel and culture once again to the forefront of the ecumenical debate.[65]

Keshishian's observations proved accurate because the most recent CWME conference in Salvador (1996) was convened precisely around the theme "Called to one hope: The gospel in diverse cultures." [66]

Evaluative Comments

In evaluating the "ecumenical approach" to incarnational mission we must first recognize the great diversity we find in the WCC and the difficulty of discerning directions from references here and there in official publications.

The WCC has received sustained criticism from various quarters, including from Orthodox and evangelical WCC member churches, for alleged imbalance between doctrinal and social concerns, and between evangelism and social action.

Our study, though not exhaustive, at least indicates that some of the more strident criticisms of the WCC, from evangelicals in particular, are unfounded. Donald McGavran, for example, divides evangelism from social action and then argues strenuously that evangelism is primary. He charges the WCC with being concerned only for structural change and forgetting personal conversion.[67] There is a strong consensus in ecumenical missiology, however, (as well as among radical evangelicals) that no wedge must be driven between evangelism and social action. In our survey we have uncovered repeated concern for a genuinely holistic approach to mission anchored in an incarnational perspective.

Evangelical criticisms such as these at least serve to remind the WCC that it must avoid the danger of being reductionist in the name of being holistic. It must not let the pendulum swing so far from merely verbal evangelism that mission becomes merely "lifestyle evangelism" or "presence" alone, except in the extreme circumstances where Christians feel restricted to such measures.

What we have found and documented in our survey of ecumenical missiology is that the WCC developed a helpful stress on the mission of God, then suffered some loss of direction (particularly in the role of the church in mission), and has regained its focus with an emphasis on an incarnational style in mission. In its earlier period it rightly emphasized mission as *God's*, in and for the world. This discovery, however, involved certain dangers, including leaving the visible church out of the equation and reducing the gospel to social, political, and economic dimensions. Its recovery of missiological focus has led it back to a stress on mission following the pattern of Jesus, that is, to a sharper focus on incarnational style. It has recovered its ecclesiological base for mission without being smug about the church. All of this has taken place in a clearly trinitarian framework in which the incarnating mission of God comes to a climax in Jesus Christ and is carried on in the power of the Holy Spirit in the world today.

Eastern Orthodox Mission Theology

There has been a renewal of Orthodox missiology in the last two or three decades, helped by the Orthodox Studies Desk of the WCC Commission on World Mission and Evangelism, which has sponsored several consultations and publications in order to stimulate missiological reflection in the Orthodox churches and generate dialogue among WCC members.[68] There is much to learn from the Orthodox approach to mission, although it is foreign to a modern Western mind, based as it is on Hellenistic philosophy and patristic theology and not having seriously encountered either the Reformation or the European Enlightenment.

The Orthodox view of mission flows from its overall theology, and in particular from its view of the church. Each aspect of its missiology is only an angle on a unified vision.

Orthodox theology is **cosmic and mystical**, in that it accepts in full metaphysical terms the mystery of God's cosmic plan of redemption, the center of the Christian faith. It looks towards the trinitarian God from whom flows love enough to draw humanity into God. At the same time it looks towards the world which is in the process of being gathered into God's gracious reality, with humanity being restored to God's likeness through the activity of the Holy Spirit in making the presence of Christ real today. Christians, having beheld God's glory in the liturgy of the church, "partake in a mission that has one end in view: the recapitulation of all in Christ, and their participation in the divine glory." [69]

Orthodox missiology is centered on the **love of God** and sees history as a series of epiphanies of God's creative and loving nature, culminating in the incarnation of Jesus Christ.[70] Christian mission is thereby linked immediately to the incarnation, for as love motivated God to send Jesus, so the missionary is called to go out in love to the world.[71]

Incarnation is central to Orthodox missiology, in a number of ways. Although trinitarian in overall shape, Orthodox missiology is classically christocentric. The "Christ" center, however, is focused in the life of the church. Christ is seen as real in the eucharist.

Thus the **church** plays a central role, in fact "ecclesiology determines missiology," because "the church is the aim of mission."[72] Established at Pentecost as a divine-human reality which acts as an icon of the kingdom of God, the institutional church is indispensable, "a visible manifestation ... of the presence of Christ in our life which is part of the Gospel message."[73] Hence mission is calling people to become part of the church.

Following directly from this, mission takes place in the context of **worship and liturgy**. "Preaching the Gospel ... and liturgical celebration are integral parts of the same acts of Christian witness."[74] The rhythm of gathering Christians in to partake of the glory of God and then sending them out to radiate that presence in daily life is nourished and shaped in liturgy, with a strength of emphasis which is hard to understand outside the Orthodox tradition. This perspective, along with the others just mentioned (and the language style which is common), is captured in the following statement by Orthodox representatives at a consultation in Neapolis in 1988:

> In the eucharistic celebration every local church experiences the fullness of the church catholic and prepares itself to address the world through words and deeds of love. The church gathers into one body the whole creation and the joy and the sufferings of all people as it stands in the presence of God in the eucharistic act of praise, thanksgiving and intercession. This inward movement of gathering into one body is

accompanied by the outward movement of going forth in mission and service to God's creation. Together, these movements constitute the church's witness to the crucified and risen Christ in whom the unity and love of the Triune God is manifested in a unique way.... Therefore, the church, the people of God in the communion of the Holy Spirit, is missionary in its very being, ever proceeding and ever gathering, pulsating with God's all-embracing love and unity. The church, as the presence of the kingdom of God in the world, illuminates in one single reality the glory of God and the eschatological destiny of creation.[75]

There are four ways in which Orthodox missiology can be considered incarnational. They are to do with theosis, eucharistic mission, the quality of Christian lives, and inculturation.

Christ's Humanity for Our Divinity

Drawing on Irenaeus, Athanasius, Gregory of Nazianzus and other early fathers the Orthodox churches emphasize that God became human so that humans could become divine.[76] In this way the incarnation is intimately linked with theosis, the doctrine that humans can participate in God's glory.[77] This mystical union with God is the ultimate goal of salvation and the central theme of Orthodoxy.[78] (Note here how a similar mystical union is also the goal of Moltmann's messianic eschatology.)[79]

Orthodox theologians are careful not to try to express what is beyond articulation and emphasize that theosis is a relative rather than an absolute transformation; it is a growing likeness to God which will be complete in the future.[80] Many words have been used for it, including divinization , transformation, participation, communion and union.[81] In the Greek tradition it is associated with incorruptibility and immortality. It comes both by grace and by co-operation on the part of the Christian.[82] It is not merely an external imitation of Christ through moral effort.[83] It seems to be a counterpart to the Protestant idea of sanctification, and a recent Lutheran-Orthodox dialogue found the two ideas to be much closer than previously thought, the main difference being that Lutherans have much lower expectations of being transformed into the likeness of God during life on this earth.[84]

The first comment to make on this doctrine is that Orthodox Christians expect Christian discipleship to make a real difference in life as a result of participating in the life of Christ. This reflects the similar doctrine of the

Anabaptists, who opposed Luther on this point. Justification and sanctification are actually conjoined in Orthodox thought, so that a transformation in "holiness" or daily living is expected. As an incarnational approach to mission it is much stronger than saying, "Jesus demonstrated love and so we should too." We might put it in the following terms: "Because God has become human and is still really present through the Holy Spirit and in the eucharist, we can respond to God's incarnating love by being daily transformed into Christ's likeness." We will return in the next section to the centrality of the eucharist in this process for Eastern Orthodoxy.

A second comment comes from Anastasios Yannoulatos, at the San Antonio CWME conference in 1989 in his address as the conference moderator. What the church offers the world, he said, is the power of the resurrection, what he calls "celestification" (a synonym for theosis). It is only in this power, in which others can see a ray of God's actual presence in Christian lives, that the church is able actually to engage in mission in Christ's way. In other words, only in the process of theosis, conforming to the divine nature through Christ, are Christians able to go about "incarnational mission," that is, mission enabled by the continuing incarnation. We have here an example of the second dimension of incarnational mission outlined in chapter 3, that of mission in the power and presence of the risen Christ; in fact, theosis is probably the strongest form of this second dimension, suggesting that we act in God's power because we increasingly participate in divinity ourselves.

Re-oriented by the Eucharist for Mission

The Orthodox churches see the eucharist as the pre-eminent missionary event in the life of the church. Its link to incarnational mission is substantial, but is essentially the same as that between theosis and incarnational mission.

We need not go into detail in explaining the Orthodox perspective on the inseparability of liturgy and life,[85] and the role of "the liturgical witness to the transcendent dimension of reality."[86] In summary, the liturgy is seen (1) to contain the *motivation* for mission (the redemptive presence of Christ), (2) to be the *method* of mission (proclaiming the gospel in worship, interceding for the world, and sending worshippers out into the world equipped), and (3) to be the *goal* of mission (ultimately to have the world worshipping and sharing in the eucharistic mystery).[87] The Orthodox tradition sees no wall between the altar and the cosmos. The "Eucharist is the meeting point of the fallen world with the world to come.... Eternity runs through time." [88]

Eucharistic mission is incarnational for the same reason that the doctrine of theosis leads to incarnational mission. Orthodox missiologists argue that worshippers are changed in worship and translate that new life into daily mission.[89] The incarnational presence of Christ in the liturgy and particularly in the eucharist (called "the Liturgy") proceeds to the witness of the Church in the world, as from one movement seamlessly to another. Ion Bria calls this second movement the "liturgy after the Liturgy," drawing on the literal meaning of "liturgy" as "the work of the people," in this case mission. There is a double movement in the liturgy, an assembling in which the "cosmos is becoming ecclesia," re-orienting the participants' entire human existence; and a sending into the world rènewed by the Eucharist.[90] In this way "the mission of the Church rests upon the radiating and transforming power of the liturgy." [91]

Mission Through Word and Presence

In reflecting on the theme "Your kingdom come," chosen for the Melbourne CWME conference to be held in 1980, a group of Orthodox theologians expressed clearly what comes through repeatedly in Orthodox writing, namely that mission occurs largely through the quality of the lives of Christians who embody their message:

> If the missionary proclamation of the Gospel of the Kingdom is to reach human hearts, there must be a palpable and real correspondence between the Word preached in the power and joy of the Holy Spirit and the actual life of the preacher and of the Christian community.... The love of Christians is the very substance as well as the radiance of the Gospel.[92]

Listing the central emphases of Orthodox witness, Yannoulatos points to the inner genuineness and the dynamic significance of each believer's holy life, which contributes to the radiation of the gospel.[93] An Orthodox consultation in Bucharest in 1974 said in its report that the church needs to recover the method of the early church, whose quality of life was such that unbelievers were strongly attracted by its power and beauty and longed for its source.[94] Perhaps due to persecution or minority status, the Orthodox approach to mission has often taken the shape of "presence" evangelism, in which Orthodox believers attempt to live alongside others and influence them by their lives; it amounts to deeds without words, rather than the integration of deeds and words.[95]

The types of activities listed as "gospel deeds" or "visibly manifesting the life of Christ in our lives" cover those we have mentioned in other traditions, activities such as whole family life, love for neighbour, service, social and political engagement, solidarity with the poor, and support for human rights. They also include some which are distinctive to the Orthodox view of "holiness" or "divinization," including asceticism (such as fasting), evangelical poverty, lives modeled on saints and martyrs, and as we have mentioned, the celebration of the eucharist.[96]

This emphasis on embodiment draws again on the idea of theosis and the presence of Christ in Christian believers. It shows how the second dimension of incarnational mission (Jesus as presence) leads to the first dimension (Jesus as pattern); the two are inseparable. The third dimension permeates even here, however. We see a quiet confidence that the outgoing cosmic love of God will radiate through the lives of believers by virtue of their Christ-filled presence. The church, for all its centrality, is only a co-operating agent in the ongoing mission of God.

Incarnation as Translation and Inculturation

In a recent full length treatment of Orthodox missiology James Stamoolis discerns three methods of mission in the Orthodox tradition, one being the "presence approach" mentioned above and another being the political approach, relying on government assistance. The third is the one which Stamoolis judges to be the most considered and most successful over the whole of Christian history, and which he labels the incarnational approach. It is characterized chiefly by the use of the people's own language for scripture and liturgy, and the employment of indigenous clergy. It amounts to using the incarnation as the basis for inculturation, as other Christian traditions have also done:

> The Living Word became Incarnate; thus the written word must also become incarnate.... As Christ translated God's thoughts to humankind, the missionary in turn translates them into another language to fulfill the gospel commission.[97]

Commentators often attribute the success of Orthodoxy in the first centuries and the medieval period to its translation of the holy writings (scripture, liturgy, theology, lives of the saints) into the vernacular, even to the point of pioneering the written form of oral languages. The same can be said for training indigenous clergy and becoming embedded in local culture, though foreign authority in the form of bishops has remained common.[98]

Going even further than local language, clergy and culture, the Orthodox vision was that the missionary must live in a manner that communicates Christ's life, becoming one flesh with those with whom the gospel was being shared. There is even an expectation that "a new 'incarnation' will take place."[99] Illustrating the third dimension of incarnational mission, the Orthodox view here is that the ongoing incarnation of God reaches into each new situation and period.

A non-colonialist mission style, therefore, has been part of the Orthodox vision for mission, and Western missions have only recently learned to follow the "honored spirit of indigenization of the Orthodox faith in reference to national cultures." [100]

Evaluative Comments

The main area in which Orthodox Christianity's approach to incarnational mission invites some criticism is in its very high view of the church, which is identified so closely with God's power and purposes that it seems to render the church immune to self-criticism or the reforming principle. The church is described by one writer as "a holy nation, a kingdom of priests, a people perfected in the unity of God [and] an icon of the Trinitarian God."[101] Another writer, Alexander Schmemann says:

In and through the Church the Kingdom of God is made already present, is communicated to [humanity]. And it is this eschatological, God-given fullness of Church (not any theory of mediation) that constitutes the root of the ecclesiological "absolutism" of Eastern Orthodoxy.[102]

A third example comes from Vladimir Lossky: "The Church is the center of the universe, the sphere in which its destinies are determined."[103]

Not only does this approach stand in some tension with the self-emptying approach of Jesus and an awareness of human fallibility, but it carries with it the danger of always seeing mission as a matter of inviting others to the center where Christians already stand. The provocative idea of Bonhoeffer that Jesus' mode of existence was "for others" and, indeed, "for us," raises the question of whether a centrifugal model of mission (directed outwards) rather than a centripetal one (directed towards the center) might follow the spirit of the incarnation more faithfully. A centrifugal model would help to avoid the dangers of becoming inward-looking in mission, under-emphasizing service in the world, and accepting the passivity of lay members of the church.[104]

The centrality of the church tends to lead to a human-centered vision of salvation, which is disappointing because there are resources within the Orthodox perspective for including the restoration of the environment.

We might also comment that some of the strengths of Eastern Orthodoxy, for example, its ancient roots and stability in theology, can also be weaknesses in communicating readily to modern minds, including those in "Orthodox" ethnic groups dispersed around the world. Comparing its christology to our criteria for a contemporary incarnational christology (outlined in chapter 3), we note that Orthodoxy is, for the most part, uncompromisingly metaphysical, rather than metaphorical. Moreover, it still uses Hellenistic substance terms to understand God and humanity. Finally, its christology is "from above." Orthodox theologians may well reply that the modern mind is part of the human problem, of course. It is a challenge, nevertheless, to communicate incarnationally (that is, in embodied witness) a message which is articulated using a culture that stretches back two millennia.

What other traditions can learn from the Orthodox churches, however, is the way in which a large and cosmic vision sustains mission. For the Orthodox the embodiment of the message of Christ in Christian mission flows from a cosmic and trinitarian vision which is sustained in worship and which involves the real transformation of the believer into the likeness of God. In the words of a statement from an Orthodox consultation held in Paris in 1978:

> The only goal of the Church's mission, in the last analysis, is to manifest the presence of Christ and his love in the life of Christians both individually and in their love for one another, as well as in their witness in the world by their life, actions, and love.[105]

Eastern Orthodox missiology exhibits aspects of all three dimensions of incarnational mission (outlined in chapter 3) in a remarkably comprehensive vision. As an example of the **third** dimension, Orthodox missiology holds a powerful cosmic vision in which God is the author of mission and is virtually defined in terms of overflowing and incarnating love. History is a series of divine epiphanies, of which the incarnation is the climax, and the goal of God's incarnating mission is the gathering up of all reality in Christ to participate in the divine glory. The extension of the incarnation in the inculturation of faith in different cultural forms is a part of this vision. The **second** dimension is equally strong. Not only is the church the continuation of the incarnation, but mission simply consists of participation in Christ (theosis), largely through participation in the eucharist and then, in "holiness," engaging in normal daily living. There is very little talk of human effort in Orthodox missiology, as the eucharist plays a mystical role in Christian transformation, enabling us to be conformed to Christ. The **first** dimension is emphasized less, but is represented by mission through word and presence, and the embodiment of the Christian message.

This brings us to the end of our study of the third dimension of incarnational mission, God's incarnating dynamic, which has been found to be particularly strong (generally speaking) in Catholicism, the ecumenical movement and Eastern Orthodoxy. It also concludes the critical survey of various Christian traditions and their many perspectives on incarnational mission.

PART THREE

CONTOURS OF AN
INCARNATIONAL MISSIOLOGY

CHAPTER 10

TOWARDS AN INCARNATIONAL MISSIOLOGY

We are now in a position to bring together many of the ideas we have encountered so far and to outline the contours of an adequate incarnational missiology.

In doing so, we will begin by arguing that authentic Christian mission is incarnational in its overall character.

The second and major task of the chapter will be to attempt to answer the question, "What shape should incarnational mission take if it is to do justice to God's incarnating mission most fully revealed in the incarnation of Jesus Christ?"

To talk of "contours," "shape" and "dimensions" is to recognize the enormous variety within incarnational missiologies; hence the need for a detailed and critical survey. In searching for the contours of an adequate incarnational missiology we also assume that some ways of delineating incarnational mission are better than others, on theological criteria which we can state, at least in general terms. If one dimension of incarnational mission is over-emphasized or another neglected, the result is not usually total error but distortion, or theological imbalance.

In the light of these assumptions the task is to develop a model of incarnational mission which avoids the theological and missiological pitfalls we have identified so far. The main tools we will use are the three-dimensional model of incarnational mission suggested as a perspective in chapter 3 and the insights gained in our critical survey of incarnational themes in various Christian traditions. We will argue for incarnational mission as following Jesus, living in the presence of Christ and joining the cosmic, incarnating mission of God. As well as noting the strengths of each of these interrelated dimensions, we will discuss some of the ways in which incarnational mission can become distorted if one is over-emphasized or neglected.

As a third task, this chapter will briefly discuss implications for the practice of mission. Our primary purpose has been to develop an incarnational *missiology*, which is the reflective aspect of the praxis of incarnational mission; it is an attempt to think clearly and theologically about the importance of incarnation and *the* incarnation for mission. It is fitting that we also signal the practical directions that incarnational *mission* might take.

Christian Mission Is Incarnational

The central defining idea of incarnational missiology is the claim that, when understood properly, Christian mission is decisively influenced by both the content and the method of God's saving activity towards creation. The content of the good news of salvation is inseparable from the method of its communication. It is that, for the salvation of the world, the divine Word became incarnate in Jesus Christ, who lived in vulnerable love, died, was raised and lives today, discernible in the Spirit of God active among us. Incarnational missiology argues that the mission of the church ought to be shaped and empowered by the *missio Dei*, God's incarnational mission. The adjective "incarnational" draws attention to the congruence between the "what" and the "how" of God's saving action and points towards a similar congruence in Christian mission.[1] This insistence on embodying the message being proclaimed is central to all types of incarnational missiology, whether they emphasize following Jesus in discipleship, living in the presence of Christ or joining God in a mission of enfleshment.

Our survey shows there is a wide consensus among missiologists from a variety of Christian traditions that mission should be shaped and empowered by God's incarnating dynamic and, in particular, by the incarnation. In chapter 3 we identified voices from both evangelicalism and the World Council of Churches arguing that all Christian mission ought to be incarnational.[2] The survey shows that we could easily add to these voices many representatives from Anabaptism, radical evangelicalism, liberation theology, Roman Catholicism, Anglo-Catholicism and Eastern Orthodoxy. Moreover, if we consider three of the largest Christian groupings, evangelicalism (including radical evangelicalism), Roman Catholicism, and the ecumenical movement, the evidence from our survey is that this consensus has been growing in the last three or four decades.

The consensus is not complete, however. There are many forms of mission we could label as "non-incarnational." They form the backdrop to this study of the nature of incarnational mission. What characterizes them is a lack of congruence between the gospel message and the manner in which it is proclaimed. Let us briefly consider a list of these types of mission. (In doing so, we would only venture to call a style of mission non-incarnational where the following emphases are very strong or held in imbalance.)

i   Mission as *proclamation* alone.

ii   Mission as merely *"presence."* These first two sever the connection between word and deed, selecting one or the other.

iii *Uncontextualized mission*, which sees the Christian message as "above culture" or entirely transcultural.

iv   *Triumphalistic* mission, emphasizing only God's conquering power. This form of mission in effect bypasses the birth, life and death of Jesus and focuses only on his resurrection power, uninterpreted by the cross.

v   Mission from a position of *power and wealth* rather than self-emptying, vulnerability and even poverty. This form of mission, similar to the last, fails to take into account the specific social location and teaching of Jesus (summed up in Philippians 2:6-11).

vi   Mission as *"gathering-in"* rather than "going-out." This form of mission invites others to join the church on Christian terms in a church-centered existence. John Taylor, drawing on the incarnation, argues against this type of mission, saying that mission always involves being sent, and you can only be sent from where you are to somewhere else, whether speaking geographically or figuratively.[3]

vii A focus merely on the *liturgy* of the church rather than going out to the world and engaging deeply in the life of the wider community. This is a common example of the previous type.

viii *Individualistic* mission, rather than mission emerging from and sustained by the messianic community.

ix An over-emphasis on communicating *doctrine* at the expense of offering a new relationship. This form of mission sees the primary task to be persuading others to believe certain propositions rather than inviting others to enter a new reality in relationship to Christ and the Christian community.

x *Mass-media-centered* mission at the expense of personal engagement.

xi Merely *professional and program-oriented* mission at the expense of relationship and whole-of-life involvement.

This list is derived by noting forms of mission which lack some of the central characteristics of incarnational mission we have repeatedly uncovered in our survey: the integration of word and deed; an awareness of Jesus' identification with his culture and people, and personal style of mission-through-relationship; an emphasis on Jesus' humility and suffering; and a call to costly discipleship in the whole of life. Most of these aspects of incarnational mission are linked to following Jesus as the pattern for mission, what we have called the first dimension of incarnational mission. Nevertheless, the call for Christians to demonstrate in their lives the message they proclaim also draws on what we have called the second dimension of incarnational mission, that is, being empowered to grow in conformity to Christ.

The near consensus we have identified stops at agreeing that mission ought to be incarnational. There is no agreement on exactly what such mission means, as our survey has shown. There is constructive work to be done. This leads us to our main task in this chapter, which is to outline the shape of an adequate incarnational missiology.

The Contours of an Incarnational Missiology

The central argument of this study is that God's movement toward creation in enfleshment, from creation and throughout history but climactically in Jesus Christ, is the ultimate framework and basis of Christian mission and also the central shaping and empowering factor. It is also our aim to clarify and delineate the ways in which incarnational thinking does legitimately shape missiology and the practice of mission. It is our contention that incarnational missiology is theologically balanced when its several dimensions are acknowledged and kept in mind, but not when one incarnational emphasis dominates to the neglect of others.

In making the argument we first reflected on the various meanings of "incarnation" and "the incarnation," discussed the biblical roots of incarnational christology, and argued for a set of directions which viable contemporary incarnational christologies need to take (chapters 2 and 3). We noted that to do this is to begin further back than most missiologists, who assume a doctrine of the incarnation and bring it to bear on their missiological reflections. We then suggested a threefold perspective through which to view understandings of incarnational mission (chapter 3), a perspective we will now develop further. In the middle section of the study (chapters 4 to 9) we examined in some detail the varied uses of the incarnation in the missiological literature. We noted along the way some of the strengths and weaknesses of various emphases in incarnational mission. All of this leads us to complete the argument by outlining, in the light of the critical survey, the contours of an adequate incarnational missiology.

We will now outline our suggested threefold perspective on incarnational mission, discuss its strengths as an approach to mission (against the background of suggested criteria for an adequate missiology), and list some dangers of neglecting any one dimension.

Incarnational Missiology in Threefold Perspective

We have argued that mission can be labeled incarnational in the sense of (1) being patterned on the incarnation, (2) being enabled by the continuing power of the incarnation, and (3) joining the ongoing incarnating mission of God.

Now we return to this framework to summarize the findings of our survey and show how these three dimensions appear in the various traditions. What we can also show, arising from this summary, is that these three dimensions are closely interrelated, and thus need to be held together in an adequate incarnational missiology.

An outline: The first dimension of incarnational mission we discussed is **the following of Jesus**. This vision of incarnational mission emphasizes costly discipleship which involves a whole-of-life response in christopraxis. It pursues holistic mission, which integrates word and deed. It sees mission as being patterned on the life and teaching of Jesus, including solidarity with the poor, a life of vulnerable love, and a socio-religious challenge to the status quo which is likely to lead to suffering (the way of the cross). In examining this tradition we rejected the view of some writers that discipleship is a matter of merely imitating Christ. We took this view on the grounds that it is in danger of perfectionism, "mere exemplarism" and Pelagianism.

The second dimension is incarnational mission as **participation in Christ**. This complements the first dimension by emphasizing the continuing presence and initiative of the risen Christ through the Holy Spirit, without which discipleship is impossible. The metaphor of the church as the body of Christ expresses the view that the church in some sense embodies Christ today, though we rejected the stronger form of this belief, which sees the church without qualification as the continuing incarnation of Christ in the world. If mission as following Jesus emphasizes the cost, mission as participating in Christ (or conforming to Christ) emphasizes grace. Eastern Orthodoxy expresses the transformation which occurs as Christians live in Christ in terms of being drawn into the likeness to God or deified (theosis).

The third dimension is incarnational mission as **joining God's incarnating mission**. This dimension sees God continually reaching out to the universe and becoming embodied in many ways in it, particularly in the life of humanity. It is a panentheistic vision, in which God is immanent in creation and yet is transcendent to it. It is also a sacramental vision in which we discern the divine in the material and the human. The incarnating dynamic of God, therefore, is seen to begin in creation. It is also seen definitively in God's redemptive self-emptying in Jesus Christ. It moves toward eschatological consummation, when the creator will fully indwell creation. God's mission of enfleshment, meanwhile, is revealed to be the basis for inculturation, for God has assumed specific cultural form in Jesus

Christ but also sacramentally in all cultures. In considering this emphasis we noted that it would be a narrow view of incarnation if it referred only to God's "turn to the world" and it neglected the challenge to culture represented in the cross and Jesus' prophetic teaching. Overall, this third dimension provides the basic view of reality in which the incarnation is a natural expression of God's outgoing and incarnating nature.

How the dimensions appear in missiological traditions: We found these three dimensions of incarnational mission in varying strengths in each of the traditions we surveyed. There is no neat pattern, and we allowed each tradition to speak for itself without trying to force it into a predetermined framework.

In the first three traditions we surveyed the first dimension is dominant, though the others are still found. In *Anabaptist* thought discipleship is dominant, with incarnational mission as participation in Christ appearing as a subordinate theme, at times only being paid lip service and at other times an integral part of Anabaptist thinking. We found a similar approach among *radical evangelicals*, except that the role of the Holy Spirit and grace (the second dimension) features more strongly, and radical evangelicals recognize God's incarnating dynamic and the importance of contextualization (third dimension). In the Latin American *liberation theology* we considered, all three dimensions of incarnational mission figured, with the first dominating. Contrary to this pattern, liberation theologian Choan-Seng Song, with his theology of God's universal mission of enfleshment, is our strongest representative of the third dimension of incarnational mission.

The individual theologian *Jürgen Moltmann* was included because he so clearly articulates the second dimension: mission as God's gracious initiative and Christ as the criterion and enabling power of the church's mission. His thought acts as a bridge between christopraxis (first dimension) and a cosmic and eschatological perspective (third dimension), both of which are articulated in his missiology as well. We thus find all three dimensions in Moltmann, who articulates the second most helpfully of all the representatives we surveyed.

In the last four groupings we surveyed, the third dimension of incarnational mission is the strongest. In *Catholicism* (including Roman Catholicism and Anglo-Catholicism) we found a strong sacramental perspective and a view of incarnation as the basis for inculturation. The idea of the church as the continuing incarnation (second dimension) is also strong. *Roman Catholicism* since the Second Vatican Council has increasingly seen the incarnation as the pattern for mission (adding the first dimension). Perhaps the influences of liberation theology are discernible in this trend. *Anglo-Catholicism* makes its own contribution in emphasizing God's immanence in creation and culture, and therefore seeing incarnational mission as life-affirming and largely this-worldly (third dimension). In the *World Council of Churches* we found the first and third dimensions to be strong, in urging the church to express solidarity with the poor ("mission in Christ's way") and join the wider incarnating mission of God in the world. Finally, in *Eastern Orthodoxy* we found the second dimension (theosis, and Christ's eucharistic presence in the church as the continuing incarnation) and the third (sacramentalism and God's cosmic mission) to be very strong, with a muted but discernible emphasis on the integration of word and deed (first dimension).

The dimensions interrelated: The three dimensions of incarnational mission are interrelated in many ways. Considering five of these ways helps us to see that the approach to incarnational mission being argued here is one perspective, though threefold in nature.

First, as suggested in chapter 3, this threefold perspective can be seen as loosely trinitarian in structure, linked to the activity of God the Son, God the Spirit and God the Father (or Creator).[4] Just as the trinity is an attempt to express a threefold understanding of the one God, so also incarnational mission is a unity even if we see it through different lenses and discern three dimensions.

Second, we also suggested that incarnation and *the* incarnation serve in the three dimensions as the model for mission, the power for mission, and the ultimate basis for mission.[5] In each case, though in different ways, incarnation inspires mission.

Third, the three dimensions focus on different aspects of the incarnation of Jesus Christ. The discipleship tradition concentrates on Jesus' *life and death*. It has a strong theology of the cross. The "presence of Christ" dimension emphasizes the *resurrection* and the power of the risen Christ today. The third dimension sees incarnation in terms of God's immanence and movement toward humanity, therefore focusing on the *birth* of Jesus as the center of the incarnation. Speaking only of *the* incarnation for a moment, we can see that if we take it to include the birth, life, death, and resurrection of Jesus Christ (a position we argued for in chapter 2) an incarnational mission needs to include all three dimensions. As the incarnation of Christ includes his birth, life, death, and resurrection, so incarnational mission includes following Jesus, participation in Christ, and joining God's incarnating mission.

Fourth, looked at in temporal terms, the three aspects of incarnational mission tend to focus in turn on the time of *Jesus of Nazareth*, the age of the *church* since, and on the whole span of *cosmic history*, with a strong future focus evident in the third. The first two need to be situated within the third for a complete view. Conversely, from a Christian perspective, cosmic history is to be interpreted by the incarnation. This makes a similar point to the previous paragraph. Just as these three periods in time are part of one framework from the perspective of God's mission, so incarnational mission needs all three aspects, which interpret each other and provide a balance.

The final way in which we can see the complementary nature of the three dimensions is by noting how they most naturally fit slightly different uses of the "incarnation" word family. Incarnational mission involves not only following an *incarnational* style. It also means experiencing the power of *the incarnation* continued today and thus discerning *incarnation* as an ongoing activity of God (or alternatively, discerning God's *incarnating* dynamic). What is indicated here linguistically reflects the conceptual interrelationship of the three dimensions of incarnational missiology.

What we have seen, then, through the findings of our survey, is the strong interdependence of the three dimensions of incarnational missiology. We have found them to be mutually interpretive, and on this basis we contend that an adequate incarnational missiology must include all three dimensions. Furthermore, when all three dimensions are included appropriately, incarnational missiology has many important strengths.

Its Missiological Strengths

No missiologist has yet proposed a set of criteria for measuring the adequacy of a missiological approach, to this writer's knowledge.[6] One of the reasons may be that missiology still struggles to define itself as a discipline.[7] In fact it tends to see itself as a multi-disciplinary enterprise, including disciplines such as biblical studies, history, systematic theology, various social sciences and inter-religious studies. A unitary set of criteria may be difficult to formulate in what is arguably closer to a field (drawing on many disciplines) than a discipline itself.[8]

This study, however, has been a venture in the theology of mission, the part of missiology which draws more on systematic theology than on many of the other disciplines listed. We can therefore turn for help to theologians who reflect on criteria for an adequate theology.[9] The central questions for any theology are also relevant for any theology of mission: Does it faithfully interpret the Christian tradition, particularly scriptural revelation?[10] Does it successfully address contemporary human existence?[11] Does it articulate Christian experience?[12] Is it intelligible and coherent?[13] Does it lead to transformative praxis?[14] We will suggest briefly how the incarnational missiology outlined here meets these criteria. In doing so we will illustrate some of the strengths of the incarnational missiology sketched above.

It faithfully interprets the Christian tradition: The first criterion for a theology of mission is how well it interprets the central symbols of the Christian faith as derived from scripture, tradition and theology. Incarnational missiology is not adventurous or radical in this respect. It stands in the classic tradition, taking the incarnation, in a trinitarian context, as the central factor in understanding the mission of the church. It emphasizes certain theological themes, but none of them is new in itself. We have discussed central issues such as the role of the Holy Spirit, the immanence and transcendence of God, the relationship between creation and redemption, the role of grace, the church as the body of Christ, the centrality of the cross, the resurrection power of Christ and the missiological imperative to integrate word and deed. What is distinctive about incarnational missiology is not its novel interpretation of Christian doctrine but its conviction that God's transforming presence will make a significant difference in what happens in mission and its insistence that the shape of Jesus' own mission is normative.

It addresses contemporary human existence: The second criterion complements the first and is often seen as the second of two foci in theology, expressible as text and context, or message and existence.[15] If it is important for theology it is even more so for missiology that its approach not only is faithful to the Christian witness but also resonates with human existence in its variety and addresses the human condition. Incarnational missiology clearly meets this criterion in the way it seeks to engage deeply with human culture and to address the whole person in the manner of Jesus and in the power of Christ. As an impulse for inculturation, incarnational missiology not only addresses what is common to all human existence (the need for life in God) but leads to mission which "takes flesh" in different forms according to different places, times, and cultures.

Consider briefly two vital contemporary global issues. One strong theme of incarnational mission is liberation of the poor. Based on the manner of the incarnation, mission responds to one of the most pressing aspects of the human condition, that of oppression, poverty, marginalization and dehumanization in many forms. The incarnation affirms the dignity of humanity and the importance of all dimensions of life in the meaning of salvation.

Another pressing aspect of human existence is our growing awareness of an environmental crisis. There is a growing number of theologians and missiologists who argue that the mission of God involves the whole creation.[16] For a start, there is an intrinsic interconnectedness in the whole of creation which binds humanity to its environment. We are directly and intimately connected to the whole universe through our material existence.[17] Karl Rahner writes, "Through bodiliness the whole world belongs to me from the start in everything that happens."[18] Furthermore, the third dimension of incarnational mission insists that God's incarnating dynamic shows itself from the beginning of creation. It links the incarnate Word with the beginnings of the cosmos and connects the saving work of Jesus Christ with the evolutionary presence of Divine Wisdom in all creation, from distant galaxies to sub-atomic events.[19] Although we cannot develop this connection, incarnational missiology can be the platform for the inclusion of environmental concern in the scope of Christian mission, as the cosmic dimensions of God's self-expression in the material universe are explored.[20]

It articulates Christian experience: Part of the task of theology is to make sense of religious experience. As mentioned earlier, the personal journey of this writer led to questioning the theology of "heroic discipleship" taught in some evangelical circles, because it did not match the reality of the Christian life. If incarnational missiology sees discipleship only as trying to be like Jesus, it fails this criterion, which is that theology must articulate the transformation offered to Christians by the forgiving and liberating love of God in Jesus Christ.

Theology is a second-order activity, reflecting on religious experience, whether it be mystical or miraculous, aesthetic or moral, dramatic or seemingly mundane, in solitude or in a group. Liberation theologians rightly insist that theology is reflection on committed praxis. In other words, only for those who "through the day" are walking the way of Jesus is there integrity in "stopping at sundown" and thinking about the meaning of God. This criterion applies both to individual Christian experience and to the worshipping life of the church.

At the individual level, in recognizing the importance of the presence of the risen Christ in incarnational mission (the second dimension above) the incarnational missiology we have outlined follows the New Testament in speaking of the work of the Spirit of Christ within the life of Christians (e.g. Rom 8:9-11, 1 Cor 1:24, 6:19, Gal 2:20). It articulates what Christians have always claimed to experience, new life in God through Jesus Christ.

The criterion operates at the level of Christian community as well. The incarnational vision has always been close to the center of the worshipping, praying and eucharistic life of the church. We noted the particular contribution of Eastern Orthodoxy to the intimate relationship between the eucharist, the incarnational presence of Christ, and Christian mission.[21] From a congregational perspective, for Christ to be "incarnate" in the Christian community is for faith to be expressed in communal life and worship. As the body of Christ heals, upholds, inspires, challenges and teaches—as Christians are being saved, we might say—Christ is present. Thus worship and community life are two of the missionary dimensions of the church. The gradual "incarnation of Christ" in the Christian community is an important part of incarnational mission.

It leads to transformative praxis: The criterion that theology should directly foster practical Christian living complements the preceding criterion, that theology should articulate what is experienced or lived out already. Taken together the two criteria add up to a call for praxis (in the sense of a dialectical rhythm of action and reflection in the cause of transforming the world), where theology reflects on and then feeds back into daily life and experience.

At its simplest this criterion expresses the time-honored call to discern the quality of people and belief-systems by their fruits (Mt 7:16-20; Lk

6:43-44). "Theology ... cannot be justified on the basis of what it says, so much as on the basis of what people *do* on the basis of what it says.'[22]

The central strength of incarnational missiology is that by its very nature it fosters the embodiment of the message Christians proclaim. It more than meets the criterion of leading to transformative praxis. It argues that the very meaning of mission is a following of Jesus which consists of divine empowering and incarnating response. One of its central notions is that of christopraxis, the "practice of Christ." As Frederick Herzog puts it: "God in Christ walks us into a new selfhood that we can call christopraxis."[23]

There is no guarantee of this outcome. Theology can only ever point to a new reality; it cannot actually cause it. Incarnational missiology acknowledges the dependence of Christians on the gracious activity of God in enabling mission to occur. The history of Christian mission is full of examples of the church obscuring rather than "incarnating" Christ. Nevertheless, the actual embodiment of the message proclaimed is the goal which incarnational missiology seeks.

It is intelligible and coherent: As John Macquarrie points out, reason has many functions, some of which cannot easily be set out.[24] Nevertheless, the requirement that theology be intelligible and coherent amounts in practice to insisting that it try to make sense of life as we experience it, constructing pictures of reality (or sets of models) which fit best at this point.[25]

From our finite perspective we need to acknowledge how little we can really understand of God. Mystery is central to theology. Christians believe that we only understand as much as we do because God is self-revealing, so our dependence on God is central. Moreover, because we "know only in part" (1 Cor 13:9, 12) we cannot eliminate contradictions completely. At times we may embrace them as "paradoxes" and find they lead to further insight. At other times we become frustratingly aware that our models are inadequate as ways of understanding reality.

Overall, in complex ways beyond the scope of this discussion, reason (or one version of rationality or another)[26] plays an important part in the adequacy of all attempts to view the world and its meaning.[27]

The approach to incarnational missiology we take in this study can only commend itself as a whole. It is offered in the belief that it makes sense of the mission to which Christians are called.

Our claim that incarnational missiology "adds up" is based on the series of continuities we have argued for throughout. There is a continuity between God's incarnating activity (from creation) and the incarnation. In turn, we are invited to be part of God's incarnating mission. This has the potential for linking God's transforming activity at the personal, social, global and cosmic levels. Second, there is a continuity between Jesus of Nazareth and the risen Christ, present today in the Spirit. This means there is not a radical discontinuity between Jesus and Christians seeking to follow him. Third, there is a continuity between Christian faith and Christian practice, a theme we have expanded on at length.

We need to acknowledge that incarnational missiology sometimes does not translate successfully into incarnational mission, and that Christian failure always puts a question mark against any understanding of the activity of God. In this context of ambiguity we can only commend incarnational missiology, arguing that its coherence and intelligibility are partly a matter of faith. To see things this way is to expect God to act among us, becoming visible in Christian lives.

Summing up the strengths of the incarnational missiology we have outlined, it faithfully interprets Christian revelation and tradition, addresses contemporary human existence, articulates Christian experience, leads to transformative praxis, and is intelligible and coherent.

Potential Dangers to Be Avoided

The shape of incarnational mission is distorted if any of the dimensions we have outlined are over-emphasized or neglected. We will consider here some of the potential theological dangers of incarnational missiology: erring on the side of ecclesiocentrism; reductionism in its view of Jesus Christ; christocentrism; legalism; and pride.

Excessive ecclesiocentrism: On the one hand, it is appropriate to see mission as the task of the church and as a corporate responsibility. We argued that Paul's image of the church as the body of Christ expresses well how the risen Christ seeks to be embodied in the church as its animating principle.[28] Without limiting God's mission to the activity of the church we have affirmed the church's central role in mission. We noted critically how the World Council of Churches played down the role of the church in the nineteen-sixties and seventies, and noted approvingly how several traditions such as Anabaptism, radical evangelicalism and liberation theology make much of Christian community in mission.

On the other hand, there are theological dangers in the much stronger view which sees the church as perpetuating the incarnation, or extending it through history. This type of ecclesiology is common in Catholicism and Eastern Orthodoxy, and there has been a heightened awareness in these traditions in recent decades that Christians should not absolutize the church or see it as beyond criticism.

Theologically, the central danger is that of conflating christology and ecclesiology. Jürgen Moltmann pinpoints it well when he insists that Christ has a critical and liberating relationship with the church as its head, its power, and its criterion.[29] We have argued that it is better to say that the church continues the mission of Jesus in his risen power than to say that the church is Christ incarnate in the world today.[30] The former expresses the inspiration and function of the church whereas the latter claims a guaranteed metaphysical status.

An excessive ecclesiocentrism in mission can lead to the belief that the church is incorruptible or infallible. In seeing the church as the continuing bearer of the incarnation it can look backwards too much as guardian of God's treasure and can neglect the anticipation of the radically new. It can lead to complacency with the church or a sense that the church is the sole locus of God's activity, at the expense of the world. It can reduce the vision of the kingdom of God to the dimensions of the visible church rather than seeing the church as only a sign of the kingdom, pointing beyond itself to much greater things.[31] Finally, it can see the church itself as the goal of mission rather than its means. Incarnating mission is not about transforming the entire world into one universal church, but about invoking, in solidarity with Christ, the coming of God's kingdom in and for the world.[32]

To avoid this danger in incarnational missiology Christians need to remember Moltmann's insistence that the church is only the church when it continues the ongoing incarnating activity of God by embodying the lordship of Christ.[33] This leads to elements of incarnational mission such as an incarnational lifestyle, solidarity with the poor, public apostleship and so on, labelled by Moltmann as a "worldly, bodily and hence also a political Christ-mysticism."[34] In this way the high claim that Christ continues to be incarnate in the church is qualified by acknowledging that Christ is a mystery beyond the church and is incarnate only insofar as he is embodied in the actual life of the church.

Emphasizing only a part of the incarnation: In discussing the meaning of "the incarnation" we chose to include the birth, life, teaching, death and resurrection of Jesus Christ.[35] There is a sense in which these interconnected events interpret each other backwards in Christian theology, with the resurrection casting a new light on the cross and so on. The theological reason for insisting on the unity of these elements of the incarnation is that when one attracts all the focus, theological imbalance occurs.

We noted at various points earlier that if the incarnation refers only to Jesus' birth a certain romanticism can creep in, involving a strong world-affirming temper but without tools for a prophetic challenge to society. Incarnation is then merely God's turn to the world, without God's judging, forgiving and transforming activity in Jesus Christ. While redemption and creation are properly seen as closely connected, they can, on this view, be reduced to the one notion. This is a particular danger in Anglo-Catholic incarnational missiology, for example.[36]

If by the incarnation we mean (merely) the life and teaching of Jesus, we face the danger of exemplarism, in which Jesus is simply our example or hero, and ethics is simply the attempt to pattern our lives on the way of Jesus.[37] This is a particular danger in traditions such as Anabaptism, radical evangelicalism and liberation theology. We will return to this when discussing legalistic discipleship.

These dangers are avoided if the three dimensions of incarnational missiology are held together. As we noted above, an emphasis on the incarnating dynamic of God leads to a focus on Jesus' birth. The discipleship tradition focuses on the life and death of Jesus. An emphasis on the presence of Christ focuses on the resurrection.[38] Each needs to be complemented by and interpreted by the others for a balanced incarnational missiology.

Radical christocentrism: Another danger is to emphasize the call to follow Jesus of Nazareth without sufficiently recognizing the trinitarian context in which we understand Jesus Christ.

It can lead to exemplarism, in which Jesus remains merely a human hero but without the power (other than by inspiration) to save humanity.[39]

We avoid this danger by remembering the second dimension of incarnational mission, living in the power of the risen presence of Christ. This immediately leads us to speak of God the Father raising Jesus Christ the Son and being present to us in the Holy Spirit.

Even a double emphasis on Jesus of Nazareth (first dimension of incarnational mission) and the risen Christ (second dimension) can lead to a radical christocentrism in which the saving activity of God is reduced to the incarnation. At its extreme this could lead to a form of christomonism, where all reality is seen as ultimately the reality of Christ. We have argued (using the third dimension) that God's activity from creation and until the consummation of God's saving purposes is incarnational in character, revealing the nature of God to be outgoing and tending to be embodied in God's creation. The incarnation, on this view, is the centerpiece and climax of God's saving activity, but God is more than Jesus Christ and salvation history is not reducible to the incarnation alone.

In this way we have argued for incarnational mission to be set against a backdrop of incarnational theology.[40] We are advocating a strongly christocentric view of mission, but in a trinitarian framework. It is trinitarian thought that makes the whole idea of the incarnation possible, as it speaks of God's saving action both through Jesus and today through the Spirit.

Legalistic or heroic discipleship: If incarnational mission is understood only as the imitation of Christ, mission is in danger of being assessed by external behavior and will ultimately be an impossible dream. Such a vision lacks a sense of mission as an overflow of grace in the life of Christians. Incarnational mission solely as following the pattern of Jesus can become legalistic. Costly discipleship taken to its extreme can become perfectionist, or even masochistic. These tendencies run counter to the gospel; they deaden and crush the human spirit.

We noted the current debate among Mennonites on this very issue, sparked by Stephen Dintaman, who accuses many Anabaptists of espousing a form of heroic discipleship in which only spiritual giants are capable of engaging in incarnational mission.[41] This is a potential danger in the Christian groups keenest to engage an incarnational mission but without the balancing resources of worship and sacramental encounter. Unless incarnational mission is a participation in Christ it can fall into a burdened activism, always striving but always conscious of failings. Such constant striving often leads to fatigue and "burn-out."

As we have mentioned in the two previous dangers, the critical factor here is the presence of the risen Christ. We can express it in terms of grace, the work of the Holy Spirit, or the empowering presence of Christ. The focus on a human response to the incarnation needs to be balanced by a focus on the initiative of God in transforming Christians. The term "imitation of Christ" is not as helpful as "conformity to Christ," which hints at human and divine initiatives complementing each other.

This is not to soften the call to embody Christ in daily life. Incarnational mission by its very nature calls the church to walk the path towards better reflecting the character of Jesus Christ. We have repeatedly pointed to the cost of discipleship, the need to demonstrate concretely that we follow Jesus to the place of the poor, and the need to integrate evangelism and social action. There is no pulling back from an understanding of incarnational mission that involves a deliberate and committed human response to the call of Jesus.

The dangers of legalism and heroic discipleship are avoided, however, by recognizing that incarnational mission involves not only a style and pattern of mission but also the transforming grace which empowers that response.

Christians pointing to themselves instead of God: Incarnational mission is sometimes reduced to "living out" the gospel, at the expense of putting Christian faith into words. Earlier in this chapter we included "mission as presence" in our list of non-incarnational forms of mission because it does not involve a holistic or integral approach. There is always a danger for the emphasis of incarnational mission on embodiment to drift in this direction and to lead to a neglect of evangelism.[42] We noted, for example, that Orlando Costas often uses "incarnational mission" to mean a Christian lifestyle *rather than* words.[43] By implication such an approach to mission says to the world, "Look at our lives and you will see Jesus," rather than, "Look beyond us to Jesus." [44]

We have argued that incarnational mission need not succumb to this danger. Mission is incarnational because the gospel is incarnational, but this does not mean that Christians proclaim themselves. It means that non-Christians have a right to expect tangible signs of the transformation that Christians proclaim as a reality.[45] Within this context, "incarnational ministry ... does not draw attention to itself, but points to Christ. Just as Jesus directed the attention of his hearers to the Father, we as his witnesses are to point people toward [God]." [46]

This danger is not entirely avoided by Christians "humbly" giving credit to God for renewing them. This can still sound unctuous to others and can raise questions about who is responsible for the many deep failings Christians still exhibit. Nonetheless, part of the joyous claim of incarnational theology is that God is pleased to include us in God's redemptive mission. In perspective, incarnational mission does celebrate God's presence and activity in and through human agents.

One way to avoid the pride which can be a danger in incarnational mission is to insist on the integration of words and deeds. Wherever possible and appropriate, mission should involve a combination of christlike action and verbal witness to the experience of grace which undergirds and enables Christian mission.

Another important way to avoid pride is to openly recognize that the church consistently fails to carry out incarnational mission. "Christlikeness," like so many ideals, is more a direction Christians need to follow than a state anyone can claim. Christians should perhaps use language such as "incarnational mission" among themselves but not as part of the way the church presents itself to the world. This is not a matter of being less than open; rather it acknowledges that incarnational mission is the path to which the church is called but not the standard it claims to have reached.

We have now outlined the contours of an adequate incarnational missiology and discussed its strengths and potential dangers. The key to ensuring a balance in the contours has been to keep in mind the various dimensions of incarnational mission, following Jesus as our pattern, living in the presence of Christ, and joining the ongoing incarnating mission of God. This chapter will conclude with comments on some of the practical implications of incarnational missiology for mission.

Practical Implications for Mission

The practical directions implied by an incarnational missiology have already been signaled throughout the argument so far, but there is value in drawing them together in a sketch of what the life of Christians and churches engaged in incarnational mission might look like.

The first factor is the reality of transforming faith in the lives of Christians. Incarnational mission involves sharing through daily life what Christians experience. The starting point of effective mission (directed outwards) is **inward transformation**. Incarnational missiology insists that Christ is risen and present today, making people whole.

This reality expresses itself in **transformed relationships** within Christian communities. Incarnational mission is mission in community. Congruence is the key to incarnational mission, and evangelism properly takes place in the context of a measure of congruence between the message proclaimed and the life demonstrated in the Christian community. In ethical terms Christians are on a journey towards love and justice between people. Therefore a "community of the incarnation" will practice forgiveness, conflict resolution, inclusion of the marginalized, reciprocal rather than hierarchical relationships, and justice in decision-making and resource-sharing. A community embodying wholeness will also know how to worship meaningfully, celebrate joys, share suffering, express its own creativity, appreciate beauty, make music, laugh and cry. Mission will be seen as the task of the whole church, not just of its leadership—all Christians are called to incarnational mission.

Central to incarnational mission is **compassionate engagement** with the world in the manner of Jesus. The church will respond to those around it, especially the poor, needy, oppressed, and marginalized. Mission will take place incidentally, as Christians live, work, and play in the world. It will also take place intentionally, as the church responds in service, welfare, and the seeking of justice. The gospel is only experienced when it takes historical root and makes a real difference. Every transformation in the direction of love and justice in every dimension of society, both private and public, is an element of the coming of the kingdom of God. Mission will sometimes be gentle and tender, and at other times prophetic and challenging. At times the church will sponsor its own programs, and at other times it will work with like-minded groups in coalition. At times the church will build on cultural foundations, and at other times it will confront cultures, governments and institutions.

Part of this engagement will be the **articulation of Christian faith** in conversation with others. In incarnational mission the church not only embodies the Good News but also points to the source of the transformation and the compassion which the church demonstrates. On the one hand, evangelism will take place embedded in a credible lifestyle, and on the other hand, social transformation will be linked, where possible and appropriate, to the source and pattern of Christian mission, Jesus Christ. Because incarnational mission follows the pattern of Jesus, mission will generally be dialogical in character, deeply respecting the other and listening before proclaiming. There will be a quiet confidence that, ultimately, truth is one and therefore not to be feared. Thus incarnational mission is not in tension with dialogue with those of other religious beliefs. Its christocentric approach is not one-eyed dogmatism but the commitment to walk the way Jesus Christ walks.

Openness to different expressions of Christian faith, especially in cross-cultural situations, will be a mark of incarnational mission. Incarnational mission will seek ongoing **contextualization** of the Good News, searching for languages and forms in which to express it clearly.[47]

A commitment to incarnational mission, at the practical level, is almost the opposite to the nominal Christianity which dominates Western countries. Rather than being a small factor in life, **faith will be the central and normative factor** in life in incarnational mission.

Incarnational mission is **outwardly focused** and deeply engaged in the world, in contrast to the inward-looking life of those Christian churches which revolve completely around the gathered life of their members.

Finally, incarnational mission is **not merely a style** of mission but an understanding of mission which sees it as following the pattern of the mission of Jesus, enabled by the risen power of Christ present today, and a small part of the ongoing incarnating mission of God. Not only will incarnational missiology lead to incarnational mission (reflection leading to action). Incarnational mission will also issue in fresh incarnational missiology and theology (action leading to reflection). We would expect that engagement in incarnational mission will lead to further knowledge of God and articulation of God's presence and purposes in various contexts and cultures.

CHAPTER 11

CONCLUSION AND PROSPECTS

I t remains to summarize the study (which has argued for the *theological* importance of incarnation in mission) and to comment that, on *sociological* grounds as well, incarnational mission is particularly apt in Australian society today. These two criteria together fill out the argument that incarnational mission is of central *missiological* importance. We will finish by mentioning some topics for further research suggested by this study.

Theologically Central

We began with the questions: What do missiologists mean by incarnational mission? Why does it occur so frequently in missiological literature but with so little analysis and clarity of definition? Is there a way of viewing incarnational mission which is theologically defensible and missiologically relevant?

We argued (in chapter 2) that the ongoing process of God's embodiment in creation is an important context for the unique event of the incarnation, which is a unity including the birth, life, death and resurrection of Jesus Christ. We examined some biblical and theological issues involved in incarnational christology and argued for the relevance and viability of the doctrine of the incarnation as a model for understanding God's action in Jesus Christ, who was human and divine. At a minimum, this allows missiology to validly draw upon the doctrine of the incarnation. Going further (chapter 3), we suggested seven dimensions of a contemporary incarnational christology, which inform the rest of the study.

We outlined a framework for classifying and understanding the variety of meanings given to incarnational mission in the literature (chapter 3), a framework whose usefulness was borne out in later argument. It sees incarnational mission as having three meanings or dimensions: Jesus as the pattern for mission; the incarnation and Christ's risen presence as the enabling power for mission; and God's incarnating dynamic as the ultimate foundation for mission. We recognized that on systematic grounds these might have been presented in a different order, but the "opening out" of the meaning of incarnational mission from "style" to "presence" and then to a cosmic understanding reflected the personal journey of this writer.

A detailed critical survey of Christian traditions and theologians who were selected for the frequency of the incarnational motif and grouped roughly according to their strongest emphases demonstrated several things (chapters 4 to 9):

i   The incarnational theme in missiology is pervasive and used with a wide variety of meanings.

ii Most traditions emphasize one dimension of incarnational mission to the potential neglect of others.

iii Some themes, such as the integration of word and deed, the necessity of solidarity with the poor, and the need to inculturate the gospel, occur almost universally and represent a virtual consensus among missiologists who draw on the incarnational motif.

We concluded (in chapter 10) that God's movement toward creation in enfleshment, from creation and throughout history but climactically in Jesus Christ, is the overall framework of Christian mission and also properly the central shaping and empowering factor. The adjective "incarnational" draws attention to the congruence between the "what" and the "how" of God's saving action and points toward a similar congruence in Christian mission. This approach leads to emphases such as self-emptying, integration of words and deeds in christopraxis, Good News to the poor, a theology of the cross, the church as the body of Christ, the presence of Christ, the affirmation of creation, and the importance of the gospel assuming different cultural expressions.

When incarnational missiology holds its various dimensions in balance it not only is theologically defensible but has many commendable strengths. We now add a further argument to these conclusions, suggesting that incarnational missiology is particularly appropriate in the Australian context.

Suited to Contemporary Australia

Incarnational mission is not only theologically central but also a highly relevant form of mission. Various sociological factors make this particularly true in contemporary Australian society, for example, and bear mentioning in brief, although it is beyond our scope to treat these themes in detail.

Theologically all three dimensions of incarnational mission are essential for a balanced and vital mission. The feature of incarnational mission which speaks most effectively to society, however, is the integration of word and deed, in other words, the credibility earned for the gospel by its demonstration in transformed lives and engagement in all aspects of the wider community. The central theme of incarnational mission is embodiment, whether we express it in terms of "the Word taking flesh," christopraxis, costly discipleship, or allowing the gospel to be inculturated. The directions of this "bearing in our bodies the life of Christ" are consistently towards public friendship, solidarity with the poor, compassion, and justice. Compared to merely verbal forms of evangelism incarnational mission strives in the power of Christ for the embodied word (or Word).

In a Skeptical Society

Christian mission needs to be incarnational in the face of the skepticism often observed in Australian society.[1] It is popularly accepted that Australians are skeptical towards organized religion, "high" culture and intellectual pursuits. Compared to those in other cultures, Australians do not pay great respect to authority figures and tend to cut down "tall poppies."[2] These features were part of a romantic image of white bushmen on the frontier of settlement in the nineteenth century. Even though some have questioned its historical basis and even though the legend excludes Aborigines, women, city-dwellers, the upper-classes and non-British immigrants, this stereotype has made its way into the center of the national psyche.[3]

Australians are not generally atheistic or lacking a sense of the spiritual,[4] but tend to be skeptical of organized religion, its ritual and its hierarchy. Recent research suggests that most Australians believe in a higher being but stop short of organizing their beliefs or committing themselves to the practice of religion.[5] Sitting between a religiously committed minority on one extreme and an atheistic minority on the other is a large majority of Australians who are nominally Christian or who are religiously uncommitted. Some pursue non-Christian religions or New Age beliefs, but most do not develop an integrated and alternative meaning system.[6]

In this context it is practical Christianity that is highly regarded. For example, Archbishop Peter Hollingworth (the "Bishop of the Poor") gains wide media respect for his commitment to "a fair go." The Salvation Army also enjoys remarkable public support for "Christianity with its sleeves rolled up." In contrast, New South Wales parliamentarian Rev. Fred Nile divides public opinion deeply and even attracts ridicule for trying to impose conservative Christian standards on Australian society. American televangelists have never succeeded in Australia as they have done in the United States.

Incarnational mission, therefore, has great relevance, because through it the Good News is demonstrated and embodied. The message takes flesh as the church engages in society. "Religious words," of which Australians are generally sceptical, are interpreted against the background of love made visible. Incarnational mission is likely to lead to some of the traits Australians value alongside skepticism: challenging authority, opposing hierarchical structures, defending the "underdog," and rallying to the cause of the poor.[7] In following Jesus, Australian Christians may even end up critical of traditional religious structures themselves. As David Millikan argues, "on occasions Jesus even suggested that the majority of people outside [the temple/church] had a less fettered access to God than those whose life was bound up with the details of church law and doctrine." [8]

In a Post-Christian Society

Incarnational mission is especially urgent in a society which can increasingly be labelled post-Christian or secular. It is arguable that Australia and New Zealand, like many European countries, lead the way in this trend, ahead of Britain and Canada and well ahead of the United States.

Australia can only inaccurately claim the term "post-Christian" because few would argue that it has ever been Christian by any measure. If we use the term "secular," we would need to reject its general dictionary meaning in favor of a more careful sociological use. It does not mean "unrelated to the religious, spiritual or sacred,"[9] but refers to the declining public, cultural, and political influence of religion.[10] Alan Gilbert's definition of the "post-Christian" society applies to Australia fairly well:

> A post-Christian society is not one from which Christianity has departed, but one in which it has become marginal. It is a society where to be irreligious is to be normal, where to think and act in secular terms is to be conventional.[11]

We could add that it is a society in which the Christian heritage is lost to general culture, a society where most people do not know the Bible nor understand Christian history, doctrine, and practice.

Mission in post-Christian society takes place in an open religious marketplace. Christianity vies with other religious options and has to explain itself from the beginning. The context is more like that of the apostolic era than the era of Christendom.[12] Post-Christian paganism, however, may even be more resistant than pre-Christian paganism. Because of this, argues Lesslie Newbigin, communicating the gospel to modern Western culture is the greatest missionary challenge of our time.[13]

In a context like this, incarnational mission is essential. Verbal evangelization on its own will struggle to influence people because Christianity is seen as yesterday's religion. What will arouse interest is a distinctive shared life and the integration of words and deeds.[14] This amounts to local congregations living by a different story from the people alongside them, embodying the challenge that the church proclaims.[15] In a secular culture "the church should start where people really are, 'incarnate itself' in this culture and change it from within."[16]

In a Postmodern Society

For similar reasons incarnational mission is a highly appropriate approach to mission in the context of postmodernity.[17]

It is not our task to characterise postmodernism here.[18] It is a complex social and theoretical phenomenon, still unfolding and attracting very different analyses. The modern era began with great optimism and yet its emphasis on reason, objectivity, science, technology, progress, and the individual has led to disenchantment, fragmentation, and alienation.[19] It is in reaction to these deep contradictions of late modernity that the profusion of postmodern perspectives have arisen. They question all the main tenets of the Enlightenment. This often includes rejecting the foundations of science, comprehensive frameworks of meaning, and the emphasis on an objective understanding of reality. A new mood is evident in many places, from literary theory and architectural style to styles of entertainment and ways of conducting personal relationships. Among other things there is a new emphasis on community, relationships, the local, the marginalized, pluralism, ecology, irony, playfulness, story, image, virtual reality, and the indeterminacy of language. At the personal level, the reaction against meta-narratives (comprehensive worldviews) is often matched by a reduced sense of history and pessimism about the possibility for change.

How Christian theology needs to respond to postmodernism is a complex issue, which will affect missiology. We cannot discuss here which elements of postmodern society can be embraced and which need to be rejected. Incarnational mission, however, is crucial in turbulent social conditions such as we are experiencing. Consider several dimensions of its importance in postmodernity.

People are less open to Christian apologetics which focus on reasons for God's existence, because of their suspicion of meta-narratives. On the other hand living out the gospel message in an incarnational manner speaks to the postmodern condition effectively. Communally-based perspectives are respected more than they have been in a predominantly individualistic culture; Hugh Mackay calls this movement in Australian society "back to the tribe."[20] Incarnational mission offers integration in a fragmented world. The postmodern generation values relationships highly. The telling of stories in credible contexts counts more than the arguing of propositions. Elements of the incarnational approach, such as a prophetic suspicion of power games and a commitment to listen to voices from the margins, suit the spirit of the times. Incarnational mission above all bears witness in daily life to hope, love, and justice in an age which struggles to believe in them and in a generation which teeters on the edge of meaninglessness and hopelessness. In this sense Christian mission stands firmly against the spirit of the age. Nevertheless it also draws on aspects of postmodern culture which resonate with the Good News, and genuinely engages with postmodernity in order to express and live that Good News. In doing so it demonstrates the dynamic of inculturation by both identifying with and yet challenging postmodern culture.

We have noted how suited incarnational mission is for an Australian society which is often labelled sceptical, post-Christian and postmodern. This makes it not just theologically important but also sociologically relevant.

Looking Forward

There are several areas where this study suggests directions for the future.

First, our brief consideration of incarnational christology suggests the need for further work to be done in developing a contemporary christology which takes the incarnation seriously as well as the metaphorical nature of religious language. Many writers sense difficulties in the language of the incarnation when taken literally and yet there are few who have successfully reinterpreted it in a way which speaks to contemporary Christians.

Second, this study has often referred to the integration of word and deed in Christian mission, but has not been able to explore the challenges of pursuing holistic mission in practice. When is it appropriate to witness verbally if one is in the middle of expressing love for one's neighbour? How does co-operation with governments or non-Christian partners limit the integration of evangelism and social action? How does one address the discomfort many Christians feel about offering interpretations of day-to-day expressions of Christian love, or giving Christian reasons for campaigning for policies which can be defended purely on the grounds of justice? Holistic mission, in other words, is more easily argued for than practiced. Christians in mission would be served well if some of its challenges were explored.[21]

Third, the idea of theosis, central to Eastern Orthodox thinking, has hardly been considered in Western Christian theology, and could be fruitful to explore.[22] There could be some fruitful comparisons made between theosis and related notions such as sanctification and christlikeness, as we suggested in our consideration of Orthodox missiology.[23]

The fourth comment is in the way of a prediction. Missiology can expect a convergence in the understanding of incarnational mission across the Christian traditions. This study has shown that, in various but related ways, different types of missiology understand mission as shaped and empowered by the incarnation. The areas of overlap have been as remarkable as the differences. In researching this topic it has become obvious that missiologists from different traditions associate together and refer to each other's writings. Some of the convergence that many perceive to be occurring between evangelical, ecumenical and Roman Catholic thought (to take just three groupings) is evident in missiology and particularly in incarnational missiology, as this study has shown.

This study aims to be a contribution to such an ongoing discussion of incarnational missiology. It is to be hoped that in furthering mutual understanding of the central source and shaping factor of Christian mission this study will in a modest way stimulate the work of Christians in embodying Christ in the world.

Our consideration of incarnational mission has not only demonstrated how important the idea is in a range of missiological traditions. It has suggested that the incarnation provides the enabling power for mission as well as the pattern for mission. Even more foundational, the incarnating dynamic of God from the beginning of creation is the ultimate framework and basis for our understanding of incarnational mission as co-operating in God's mission of embodiment in creation. As Jürgen Moltmann puts it, "Embodiment is the end of all God's works," and therefore is the appropriate goal for Christian mission as well.[24]

NOTES

Chapter 1

1. Ann Wilkinson-Hayes, "A letter to the churches," *Mainstream: Baptists for life and growth* No. 51 (1994): 3.
2. Jude Tiersma, "What does it mean to be incarnational when we are not the Messiah?', in *God so loves the city: Seeking a theology for urban mission*, eds. Charles Van Engen and Jude Tiersma (Monrovia, CA: MARC, 1994), 11.
3. James Wm. McClendon, Jr, *Biography as theology: How life stories can remake today's theology* (Nashville: Abingdon, 1974), 39, 188-190; George W Stroup, *The promise of narrative theology* (London: SCM, 1981), 85; Gabriel Fackre, "Narrative theology: An overview," *Interpretation* 37 (1983): 348-349.
4. In faxed correspondence from Raymond Fung to Ross Langmead, dated February 28, 1995.
5. Correspondence from Raymond Fung, February 28, 1995.
6. For example, Andreas J Köstenberger, "The challenge of a systematized biblical theology of mission: Missiological insights from the Gospel of John," *Missiology* 23 (1995): 455; Harriet Hill, "Incarnational ministry: A critical examination," *Evangelical Missions Quarterly* 26 (1990): 201.
7. See pp. 224-227 below.
8. Don S Browning, *A fundamental practical theology: Descriptive and strategic proposals* (Minneapolis: Fortress, 1991), 36.
9. David J Bosch, *Transforming mission: Paradigm shifts in theology of mission* (Maryknoll: Orbis, 1991), 8-9; Johannes Blauw, *The missionary nature of the church: A survey of the biblical theology of mission* (Grand Rapids: Eerdmans, 1962), 10.

10. For example, Roman Catholicism recovered the emphasis at the Second Vatican Council. See "Ad Gentes (Decree on the Missionary Activity of the Church)', in *The documents of Vatican II*, ed. Walter M Abbott (London: Geoffrey Chapman, 1966), p. 585, #2.

11. Max Stackhouse, *Apologia: Conceptualization, globalization, and mission in theological education* (Grand Rapids: Eerdmans, 1988), 189.

12. For example on p. 226-227 below.

13. For a definition of praxis, see p. 50 below.

14. Charles Gore, ed. *Lux Mundi: A series of studies in the religion of the incarnation*, 15th ed. (London: John Murray, 1904).

15. See brief or indirect references in Elisabeth Schüssler Fiorenza, *In memory of her: A feminist theological reconstruction of Christian origins*, 2nd ed. (London: SCM, 1995), 343-351; Denise L Carmody, *Christian feminist theology: A constructive interpretation* (Oxford: Blackwell, 1995), 182-187, 208-211; Patricia Wilson-Kastner, *Faith, feminism, and the Christ* (Philadelphia: Fortress, 1983), 94-116; Elizabeth A Johnson, *Consider Jesus: Waves of renewal in Christology* (New York: Crossroad, 1994), 62; Daphne Hampson, *Theology and feminism* (Oxford: Basil Blackwell, 1990), 154-155.

16. We draw on McFague's metaphorical theology below (See pp. 36-39 below). Sallie McFague, *The body of God: An ecological theology* (London: SCM, 1993), 159-195.

17. Rosemary Radford Ruether, *Sexism and God-talk: Toward a feminist theology* (Boston: Beacon, 1983), 126.

18. Elizabeth A Johnson, *She who is: The mystery of God in feminist discourse* (New York: Crossroad, 1992); Elisabeth Schüssler Fiorenza, *Jesus: Miriam's child, Sophia's prophet: Critical issues in feminist christology* (New York: Continuum, 1995); Schüssler Fiorenza, *In memory of her*; Sandra M Schneiders, *Women and the Word: The gender of God in the New Testament and the spirituality of women* (New York: Paulist Press, 1986), 50-62.

19. Hampson, *Theology and feminism*, 155. See p. 57 below.

20. Elisabeth Moltmann-Wendel, *I am my body: New ways of embodiment* (London: SCM, 1994); Ruether, *Sexism and God-talk*, 74-75; Sallie McFague, *Models of God: Theology for an ecological, nuclear age* (London: SCM, 1987), 74.

21. See pp. 95, 98, 197 below.

22. See chap. 5 and p.197 below.

23. See chap. 5 throughout.

24. These two traditions which emerged from the cradle of the European Reformation are sometimes broadly and jointly called "Reformed." We follow here a narrower use: The Reformed tradition followed Calvin and Zwingli rather than Luther where they differed, and includes so-called "Reformed churches," Presbyterianism and Congregationalism. Martin H

Cressey, "Reformed/Presbyterian churches," in *Dictionary of the ecumenical movement*, eds. Nicholas Lossky et al. (Geneva: World Council of Churches, 1991), 851-853.

25. Martin Luther, "The freedom of the Christian," in *Luther's Works, Vol. 31: Career of the Reformer, I*, ed. Harold J Grim (Philadelphia: Fortress, 1957 [1520]), 368-371.

26. Darrell L Guder, *Be my witnesses: The church's mission, message, and messengers* (Grand Rapids: Eerdmans, 1985), 18-22.

27. James A Scherer, *Gospel, church and kingdom: Comparative studies in world mission theology* (Minneapolis: Augsburg, 1987), 51-92

28. Scherer, *Gospel, church and kingdom*.

29. See chap. 7 below.

30. Guder, *Be my witnesses*; Darrell L Guder, "Incarnation and the church's evangelistic mission," *International Review of Mission* 83 (1994): 417-428.

31. Robert C Linthicum, *City of God, city of Satan: A biblical theology of the church* (Grand Rapids: Zondervan, 1991); Robert C Linthicum, *Empowering the poor* (Monrovia, CA: MARC, 1991).

32. On the theology of human embodiment see James B Nelson, *Body theology* (Louisville: Westminster/John Knox Press, 1992); James B Nelson, *Embodiment: An approach to sexuality and Christian theology* (Minneapolis: Augsburg, 1978); Moltmann-Wendel, *I am my body*; John Y Fenton, ed. *Theology and body* (Philadelphia: Westminster, 1974).

33. Nelson, *Embodiment*, 36.

34. Margaret R Miles, *The image and practice of holiness: A critique of the classic manuals of devotion* (London: SCM, 1988), 24-25; Nelson, *Embodiment*, 19; McFague, *Models of God*, 71.

35. Moltmann-Wendel, *I am my body*, 103.

Chapter 2

1. Karl Barth, *Church Dogmatics*, vol. IV.1 (Edinburgh: T & T Clark, 1956), 5.

2. Maurice Wiles, "A survey of the issues in the *Myth* debate," in *Incarnation and myth: The debate continued*, ed. Michael Goulder (London: SCM, 1979), 3.

3. George John Hoynacki, "'And the word was made flesh' —Incarnations in religious traditions," *Asia Journal of Theology* 7 (1993): 12.

4. Thomas J Hopkins, *The Hindu religious tradition* (Encino, CA: Dickenson, 1971), 92.

5. Francis X D'Sa, "Christian incarnation and Hindu avatara," *Concilium* (2 1993): 77-85; Hoynacki, "'And the word was made flesh'," 20-26.

6. Hoynacki, "'And the word was made flesh'," 26-27.

7. Manabu Waida, "Incarnation," in *The encyclopedia of religion,* ed. Mircea Eliade, (New York: Macmillan, 1987), 7:156.

8. Choan-Seng Song, "The divine mission of creation," in *Asian Christian theology: Emerging themes,* ed. Douglas J Elwood, Rev. ed. (Philadelphia: Westminster, 1980), 189.

9. John Macquarrie, "Incarnation," in *The Blackwell Encyclopedia of modern Christian thought,* ed. Alister E McGrath (Oxford: Blackwell, 1993), 269; "Incarnation," in Gerald O'Collins and Edward G Farrugia, eds., *A concise dictionary of theology* (New York: Paulist, 1991), 103; Brian Hebblethwaite, "Incarnation—the essence of Christianity," in *The incarnation: Collected essays in christology,* by Brian Hebblethwaite (Cambridge: Cambridge University Press, 1987), 1-2; Brian Hebblethwaite, "Incarnation," in *A new handbook of Christian theology,* eds. Donald W Musser and Joseph L Price (Nashville: Abingdon, 1992), 251.

10. For example, J H Walgrave, "Incarnation and atonement," in *The incarnation: Ecumenical studies in the Nicene-Constantinopolitan Creed, A.D. 381,* ed. Thomas F Torrance (London: Handsel Press, 1981), 148.

11. James D G Dunn, "Incarnation," in *The Anchor Bible dictionary,* ed. David Noel Freeman (New York: Doubleday, 1992), 3:404; James D G Dunn, *Unity and diversity in the New Testament: An inquiry into the character of earliest Christianity,* 2nd ed. (London: SCM, 1990), 223.

12. Jean Daniélou, *The salvation of the nations* (Notre Dame, IN: University of Notre Dame Press, 1962), 33. See p. 165 below.

13. David J Bosch, *Transforming mission: Paradigm shifts in theology of mission* (Maryknoll: Orbis, 1991), 512-513.

14. For example, Karl Rahner, "Incarnation," in *Encyclopedia of theology: A concise Sacramentum Mundi,* ed. Karl Rahner (London: Burns & Oates, 1975), 691; Darrell L Guder, "Incarnation and the church's evangelistic mission," *International Review of Mission* 83 (1994): 420.

15. For example, James D G Dunn, *Christology in the making: An inquiry into the origins of the doctrine of the incarnation,* 2nd ed. (London: SCM, 1989), 262, 265; Geoffrey W H Lampe, *God as Spirit* (Oxford: Oxford University Press, 1977), chap. 4.

16. John Macquarrie, *Jesus Christ in modern thought* (London: SCM, 1990), 22.

17. Rudolf Bultmann, "The Christological confession of the World Council of Churches," in *Essays: philosophical and theological,* by Rudolf Bultmann (London: SCM, 1955), 286.

18. In this avoidance we follow John Macquarrie, "The concept of a Christ-event," in *God incarnate: Story and belief,* ed. A E Harvey (London: SPCK, 1981), 79; Macquarrie, *Jesus Christ in modern thought,* 19-23.

19. We could arguably add Sophia (Wisdom) or Agapé (Love) to the list of divine subjects.

20. To say that "incarnational" is metaphorical here is not to imply that "the incarnation" was used literally in the preceding discussion (see p. 36-37 below). It is just a "more obviously metaphorical" use when applied to the church and its mission.

21. John Macquarrie, *Principles of Christian theology*, Rev. ed. (London: SCM, 1977), 269.

22. Norman Pittenger, *The Word incarnate: A study of the doctrine of the person of Christ* (London: Nisbet, 1959), 192.

23. Justin Martyr, "Apology," in *The Apostolic Fathers: Justin Martyr and Irenaeus*, The Ante-Nicene Fathers: Translation of the writings of the Fathers down to A.D. 325, ed. A Cleveland Coxe, Rev. ed., (Grand Rapids: Eerdmans, ca. 1962), 1:xlvi; Athanasius, "De Incarnatione Verbi Dei [On the Incarnation of the Word]," in *St Athanasius: Select works and letters*, A select library of Nicene and Post-Nicene Fathers of the Christian church, 2nd series, eds. Philip Schaff and Henry Wace, vol. 4 (Grand Rapids: Eerdmans, n.d.), #41.

24. Hans-Georg Gadamer, *Truth and method* (London: Sheed and Ward, 1975), 377-387.

25. William Gray, "The myth of the Word discarnate," *Theology* 88 (1985): 115.

26. Gray, "The myth of the Word discarnate," 116.

27. We will take "transcendence" to be a metaphor expressing a view of God as surpassing humanity or the cosmos in excellence, infinity, holiness or even independence, often put in terms of being "beyond" or "above." We will take "immanence" to metaphorically express a view of God as intimately present in the universe (and humanity in particular), often put in terms of "indwelling" creation, being "within," or found "in the depth of life." Both terms are needed to articulate the Christian understanding of God.

28. Macquarrie, *Jesus Christ in modern thought*, 380.

29. Charles Hartshorne, *Omnipotence and other theological mistakes* (Albany, NY: State University of New York, 1984), 44.

30. Lampe, *God as Spirit*, 23.

31. Choan-Seng Song, *Christian mission in reconstruction: An Asian analysis* (Maryknoll: Orbis, 1977), 51.

32. Song, *Christian mission in reconstruction*, 51-53.

33. James D G Dunn, *Christology in the making: An inquiry into the origins of the doctrine of the incarnation*, 2nd ed. (London: SCM, 1989). See also Dunn, "Incarnation." Other studies include Millard J Erickson, *The Word became flesh: A contemporary incarnational christology* (Grand Rapids: Baker, 1991), 17-39; Brian O McDermott, *Word become flesh: Dimensions of Christology* (Collegeville, MN: The Liturgical Press, 1993); and Gerald O'Collins, *Christology: A biblical, historical, and systematic study of Jesus Christ* (Oxford: Oxford University Press, 1995).

34. The writer(s) of John's gospel will be called "John" for convenience's sake, not to assert that any particular person was the author or main author.

35. Notwithstanding the eagerness to find more direct connections by Balmer H Kelly, "Word of promise: The incarnation in the Old Testament," *Ex Auditu* 7 (1991): 19-27.

36. Dunn, *Christology in the making*, xii. His findings are summarized in Dunn, "Incarnation," 3:397-404.

37. See, for example, Dunn's answers to critics and a listing in his footnotes of the critical discussion attending his first edition, in Dunn, *Christology in the making*, xvii-xxvi.

38. Dunn, *Christology in the making*, 55-56.

39. We do not need to decide here whether Dunn successfully makes the case for denying that passages such as Rom 8:3, 1 Cor 8:6, 15:45-47, 2 Cor 8:9, Gal 4:4-5, Phil 2:6-11 and Col 1:15-20 clearly imply an incarnational christology involving the doctrine of a pre-existent Son.

40. Dunn, *Christology in the making*, 262.

41. Dunn, *Christology in the making*, 164.

42. Dunn, *Christology in the making*, 228-230.

43. Dunn, *Christology in the making*, 253.

44. Dunn, *Christology in the making*, 230-239.

45. Dunn, "Incarnation," 3:404.

46. Erickson, *The Word became flesh*, 457-461.

47. C H Dodd, *The interpretation of the Fourth Gospel* (Cambridge: Cambridge University Press, 1953), 285.

48. Dunn, *Christology in the making*, 58-59.

49. Dunn, *Christology in the making*, 263.

50. Dunn, *Christology in the making*, 256.

51. Dunn, *Christology in the making*, 265.

52. Dunn, *Christology in the making*, 266-267.

53. See pp. 36-39 below.

54. See p. 16 above.

55. Macquarrie, *Jesus Christ in modern thought*, 116-117.

56. J N D Kelly, *Early Christian doctrines*, 4th ed. (London: Adam & Charles Black, 1968), 289-301.

57. Macquarrie, *Jesus Christ in modern thought*, 99, 105.

58. Macquarrie, *Jesus Christ in modern thought*, 117. In the New Testament the word appears only once in a variant manuscript of 1 Jn 4:17. William F Arndt and F Wilbur Gingrich, *A Greek-English lexicon of the New Testament and other early Christian literature*, 4th ed. (Chicago: University of Chicago Press, 1957), ἐνανθρωπέω, 261.

59. Alexander Sand, "σαρξ, σαρκος, η, *sarx*, flesh," in *Exegetical Dictionary of the New Testament*, eds. Horst Balz and Gerhard Schneider (Grand Rapids: Eerdmans, 1990-1993), 3:230.

60. For word studies see Eduard Schweizer, Friedrich Baumgärtel and Rudolf Meyer, "σαρξ," in *Theological Dictionary of the New Testament* [abbreviated as *TDNT*], eds. Gerhard Kittel and Gerhard Friedrich (Grand Rapids: Eerdmans, 1964-1976), 7:98-151; Sand, "σαρξ, σαρκος, η, *sarx*, flesh"; S Vernon McCasland, "Flesh in the NT," in *The interpreter's dictionary of the Bible*, ed. George Arthur Buttrick (Nashville: Abingdon, 1962), 2:276-277; Marianne Meye Thompson, *The humanity of Jesus in the Fourth Gospel* (Philadelphia: Fortress, 1988), chap. 2; John A T Robinson, *The body: A study in Pauline theology* (London: SCM, 1952), 17-26.

61. Günther Bornkamm, *Paul* (London: Hodder & Stoughton, 1971), 133; Schweizer, Baumgärtel and Meyer, "σαρξ," *TDNT* 7:135; Sand, "σαρξ, σαρκος, η, *sarx*, flesh," 231; Kenneth Grayston, "Flesh, fleshly, carnal," in *A theological word book of the Bible*, ed. Alan Richardson (London: SCM, 1950), 84; Herman Ridderbos, *Paul: An outline of his theology* (London: SPCK, 1977), 64-67.

62. Such as Elizabeth Harris, *Prologue and Gospel: The theology of the Fourth Evangelist*, Journal for the Study of the New Testament, Supplement Series, 107 (Sheffield, UK: Sheffield Academic Press, 1994), 12-16, 195; Ernst Käsemann, "The structure and purpose of the Prologue to John's Gospel," in *New Testament questions of today,* by Ernst Käsemann (London: SCM, 1969), 138-139; Udo Schnelle, *Antidocetic christology in the Gospel of John: An investigation of the place of the Fourth Gospel in the Johannine School* (Minneapolis: Fortress, 1992), 211-212; Dodd, *The interpretation of the Fourth Gospel*, 285; Simon Ross Valentine, "The Johannine Prologue—a microcosm of the Gospel," *The Evangelical Quarterly* 68 (1996): 292, 303.

63. Many scholars consider this passage to have been added to John's Gospel.

64. Raymond E Brown, *The Gospel according to John: Introduction, translation and notes*, 2 vols. (Garden City, NY: Doubleday, 1966), 1:13, 31.

65. Ernst Käsemann, *The Testament of Jesus: A study of the gospel of John in the light of Chapter 17* (London: SCM, 1968), 66.

66. Käsemann, *The Testament of Jesus*, 70. Docetism (from the Greek *dokeo*, I seem) is the christological heresy that the humanity of Jesus Christ was only apparent and that he was a divine being only dressed up as a man.

67. Käsemann, "The structure and purpose of the Prologue to John's Gospel," 161.

68. Käsemann, "The structure and purpose of the Prologue to John's Gospel," 163.

69. Rudolf Bultmann, *The Gospel of John: A commentary* (Oxford: Basil Blackwell, 1971), 62, 141.

70. Bultmann, *The Gospel of John*, 63.
71. Rudolf Bultmann, *Theology of the New Testament*, 2 vols. (London: SCM, 1955), 2:66.
72. Dunn, *Christology in the making*, throughout but summarized 251-268.
73. Whereas Gnosticism describes a religious movement of the 2nd and 3rd centuries, gnostic tendencies are found earlier, including: cosmic dualism, valuing spirit over the flesh; a distinction between a transcendent God and a more immediate Creator; humanity being marked by possessing a divine spark; and salvation coming through divine knowledge (*gnosis*). Docetism was a tendency of Christian gnosticism. R McL Wilson, "Gnosticism," in *A new dictionary of Christian theology*, eds. Alan Richardson and John Bowden (London: SCM, 1983), 226-230; Dodd, *The interpretation of the Fourth Gospel*, 97-114. John's Gospel does show some limited Christian gnostic tendencies, which may have prompted the clarifying passages in 1 John 1:1-3 and 4:3, which are strongly anti-docetic. Dunn, *Unity and diversity in the New Testament*, 298-305; Bultmann, *The Gospel of John*, 7-9; Macquarrie, *Jesus Christ in modern thought*, 102-105; R Alan Culpepper, "1-2-3 John," in *The General Letters: Hebrews, James, 1-2 Peter, Jude, 1-2-3 John*, ed. Gerhard Krodel, Rev. & enlarged ed. (Minneapolis: Fortress, 1995), 131.
74. Schnelle, *Antidocetic christology in the Gospel of John*, 222; Dunn, *Unity and diversity in the New Testament*, 300; Bultmann, *Theology of the New Testament*, 2:41-42; Robert Kysar, *The Fourth Evangelist and his Gospel: An examination of contemporary scholarship* (Minneapolis: Augsburg, 1975), 190; Macquarrie, *Jesus Christ in modern thought*, 104.
75. Dunn, *Unity and diversity in the New Testament*, 301; Kysar, *The Fourth Evangelist and his Gospel*, 191.
76. Valentine, "The Johannine Prologue," 295.
77. Kysar, *The Fourth Evangelist and his Gospel*, 159.
78. Thompson, *The humanity of Jesus in the Fourth Gospel*, 51-52.
79. Dunn, *Christology in the making*, 265.
80. Sarah Coakley, *Christ without absolutes: A study of the Christology of Ernst Troeltsch* (Oxford: Clarendon Press, 1988), 104-106.
81. Lampe, *God as Spirit*, not considered by Coakley.
82. Gerald O'Collins, *Christology: A biblical, historical, and systematic study of Jesus Christ* (Oxford: Oxford University Press, 1995).
83. Brian Hebblethwaite, *The incarnation: Collected essays in christology* (Cambridge: Cambridge University Press, 1987).
84. D M MacKinnon, "The relation of the doctrines of the incarnation and the trinity," in *Creation, Christ and culture: Studies in honor of T F Torrance*, ed. Richard W A McKinney (Edinburgh: T & T Clark, 1976), 92-107.
85. Alister E McGrath, *Understanding Jesus: Who Jesus Christ is and why he matters* (Grand Rapids: Academie, 1987).

86. Norman Anderson, *The mystery of the incarnation* (London: Hodder and Stoughton, 1978).
87. George Carey, *God incarnate* (Leicester, UK: Inter-Varsity Press, 1977).
88. Stephen T Davis, "Jesus Christ: Savior or guru?," in *Encountering Jesus: A debate on christology*, ed. Stephen T Davis (Atlanta: John Knox, 1988), 39-59.
89. Millard J Erickson, *The Word became flesh: A contemporary incarnational christology* (Grand Rapids: Baker, 1991).
90. Vernon White, *Atonement and incarnation: An essay in universalism and particularity* (Cambridge: Cambridge University Press, 1991).
91. James Moulder, "Is a Chalcedonian christology coherent?," *Modern Theology* 2 (1986): 285-307.
92. "The Chalcedonian definition of the faith," in *Creeds, councils and controversies: Documents illustrative of the history of the Church, A.D. 337-461*, ed. J Stevenson (London: SPCK, 1966), 337; J N D Kelly, *Early Christian doctrines*, 4th ed. (London: Adam & Charles Black, 1968), 339-341.
93. Barth, *Church Dogmatics*. IV.1:133.
94. Kelly, *Early Christian doctrines*, 342-343; "The Definition of Chalcedon," in *The Oxford dictionary of the Christian church*, eds. F L Cross and E A Livingstone, 2nd ed. (London: Oxford University Press, 1974), 263. Monophysitism is the exception, rejecting Chalcedon's talk of two natures.
95. George W Stroup, III, "Chalcedon revisited," *Theology Today* 35 (1978): 56-57.
96. G W H Lampe, "The essence of Christianity: A personal view," *The Expository Times* 87 (1976): 134.
97. Norman Hook, *Christ in the twentieth century: A Spirit Christology* (London: Lutterworth, 1968), 49-53; Stroup, "Chalcedon revisited," 56; Friedrich Schleiermacher, *The Christian faith*, ed. H R Mackintosh and J S Stewart (Edinburgh: T & T Clark, 1928 [1830]), 394.
98. Schleiermacher, *The Christian faith*, 391-395.
99. Stroup, "Chalcedon revisited," 63.
100. J Denny Weaver, "A believers' church christology," *The Mennonite Quarterly Review* 57 (1983): 113.
101. Hick, *The metaphor of God incarnate*, 10. Hick uses Coakley's list to help to characterize his own position.
102. John Hick, "Jesus and the world religions," in *The myth of God incarnate*, ed. John Hick (London: SCM, 1977), 178; John Hick, "An inspiration christology for a religiously plural world," in *Encountering Jesus: A debate on christology*, ed. Stephen T Davis (Atlanta: John Knox, 1988), 18; Hick, *The metaphor of God incarnate*, ix.

103. Maurice Wiles, "Christianity without incarnation?," in *The myth of God incarnate*, ed. John Hick (London: SCM, 1977), 1-10; Wiles, "A survey of the issues in the *Myth* debate."

104. Michael Goulder, "The two roots of the Christian myth," in *The myth of God incarnate*, ed. John Hick (London: SCM, 1977), 85; Michael Goulder, "Paradox and mystification," in *Incarnation and myth: The debate continued*, ed. Michael Goulder (London: SCM, 1979), 58.

105. Don Cupitt, "The Christ of Christendom," in *The myth of God incarnate*, ed. John Hick (London: SCM, 1977), 145; Don Cupitt, *The debate about Christ* (London: SCM, 1979); Don Cupitt, "Jesus and the meaning of "God" ," in *Incarnation and myth: The debate continued*, ed. Michael Goulder (London: SCM, 1979), 39-40.

106. Dennis Nineham, "Epilogue," in *The myth of God incarnate*, ed. John Hick (London: SCM, 1977), 202-203.

107. John Bowden, *Jesus: The unanswered questions* (London: SCM, 1988), 90.

108. John Hick, ed. *The myth of God incarnate* (London: SCM, 1977).

109. Among the contributions to the debate were Michael Green, ed. *The truth of God incarnate* (London: Hodder and Stoughton, 1977); George Carey, *God incarnate* (Leicester, UK: Inter-Varsity Press, 1977); Michael Goulder, ed. *Incarnation and myth: The debate continued* (London: SCM, 1979).

110. Wiles, "Christianity without incarnation?," 5-6.

111. Frances Young, "A cloud of witnesses," in *The myth of God incarnate*, ed. John Hick (London: SCM, 1977), 18.

112. Frances Young, "Two roots or a tangled mass?," in *The myth of God incarnate*, ed. John Hick (London: SCM, 1977), 101-102; Wiles, "Christianity without incarnation?," 4.

113. Young, "A cloud of witnesses," 24-28.

114. Wiles, "Christianity without incarnation?," 8.

115. Hick, "Jesus and the world religions," 178.

116. Karl Rahner, *Theological investigations*, vol. 4 (London: Darton, Longman & Todd, 1974), 11-113; William V Dych, *Karl Rahner* (London: Geoffrey Chapman, 1992), 67; Macquarrie, *Jesus Christ in modern thought*, 306.

117. Leonardo Boff and Clodovis Boff, *Salvation and liberation: In search of a balance between faith and politics* (Maryknoll: Orbis, 1984), 58; Leonardo Boff, *Jesus Christ liberator: A critical Christology for our time* (Maryknoll: Orbis, 1978), 189-199.

118. Edward Schillebeeckx, *Jesus: An experiment in christology* (New York: Crossroad, 1979), 666-667; McDermott, *Word become flesh*, 275-276.

119. Hans Küng, *On being a Christian* (London: Collins, 1977), 130-132, 448-450.

120. Walter Kasper, *Jesus the Christ* (London: Burns & Oates, 1976), 237-238.

121. McDermott, *Word become flesh*, 273, 281. One must infer his position indirectly.

122. Jürgen Moltmann, *The way of Jesus Christ: Christology in messianic dimensions* (London: SCM, 1990), 46-55.

123. Wolfhart Pannenberg, *Jesus—God and man* (London: SCM, 1968), 283-293.

124. Macquarrie, *Jesus Christ in modern thought*, 375-386; Macquarrie, *Principles of Christian theology* , 294-300.

125. Norman Pittenger, *The Word incarnate: A study of the doctrine of the person of Christ* (London: Nisbet, 1959), 86-88, 237; Norman Pittenger, *Christology reconsidered* (London: SCM, 1970), 5-6.

126. John Cobb, *Christ in a pluralistic age* (Philadelphia: Westminster, 1975), 158-159, 167-173.

127. D M Baillie, *God was in Christ: An essay on incarnation and atonement* (London: Faber and Faber, 1956), 130-131, 152.

128. Lampe, *God as Spirit*, 132-136.

129. John A T Robinson, *The human face of God* (London: SCM, 1973), 35, 114, 116 note 67, 209-211.

Chapter 3

1. Janet Martin Soskice, *Metaphor and religious language* (Oxford: Clarendon, 1985), 15.

2. Max Black, "More about metaphor," in *Metaphor and thought*, ed. Andrew Ortony (Cambridge: Cambridge University Press, 1979), 19-43; Max Black, *Models and metaphors* (Ithaca, NY: Cornell University Press, 1962); I A Richards, *The philosophy of rhetoric* (London: Oxford University Press, 1936); Soskice, *Metaphor and religious language*, 46.

3. Eberhard Jüngel, "Metaphorical truth. Reflections on theological metaphor as a contribution to a hermeneutics of narrative theology," in *Theological essays*, by Eberhard Jüngel (Edinburgh: T & T Clark, 1989), 16-71.

4. Ian G Barbour, *Myths, models and paradigms: The nature of scientific and religious language* (London: SCM, 1974), 30-42.

5. Barbour, *Myths, models and paradigms*, 44; Soskice, *Metaphor and religious language*, 50, 55; Sallie McFague, *Metaphorical theology: Models of God in religious language* (London: SCM, 1983), 67. A model is an enduring and systematically developed metaphor, a step closer to a theory. A model can also be non-linguistic. But it is closely tied in meaning to metaphor: thinking of one thing or state of affairs in terms of another.

6. Barbour, *Myths, models and paradigms*, 38.

7. Black, "More about metaphor," 40.

8. Soskice, *Metaphor and religious language*, 141.

9. Suzanne Langer, *Philosophy in a new key* (New York: Mentor, 1948), 114; cited in Frank B Dilley, *Metaphysics and religious language* (New York: Columbia University Press, 1964), 88.

10. Jüngel, "Metaphorical truth," 60.

11. Soskice, *Metaphor and religious language*, 140.

12. John Macquarrie, *Jesus Christ in modern thought* (London: SCM, 1990), 116. MacCormac points out that to take a metaphor literally always leads to absurdity. Earl R MacCormac, *Metaphor and myth in science and religion* (Durham, NC: Duke University Press, 1976), 73.

13. Evans finds four main meanings of myth, and argues that it is dangerous to call the incarnation a myth unless it is clear that a myth is seen as a story which can express historical and metaphysical truth. C Stephen Evans, "The incarnational narrative as myth and history," *Christian Scholar's Review* 23 (1994): 387-407.

14. John Hick, *The metaphor of God incarnate* (London: SCM, 1993), 104.

15. H A Williams explores in a fascinating way three ways in which to understand God's presence in Jesus, using the metaphors of intimate communion between people, the integrating effect of successful psycho-analysis on a subject, and the Jungian ideas of archetypes and a transpersonal unconscious. H A Williams, "Incarnation: Model and symbol," *Theology* 79 (1976): 10-15.

16. McFague, *Metaphorical theology*, 13, 23.

17. Barbour, *Myths, models and paradigms*, 28.

18. MacCormac, *Metaphor and myth in science and religion*, 74.

19. Norman Pittenger, "The incarnation in Process theology," *Review and Expositor* 71 (1974): 45, 48. Among process christologies are Norman Pittenger, *The Word incarnate: A study of the doctrine of the person of Christ* (London: Nisbet, 1959); John Cobb, *Christ in a pluralistic age* (Philadelphia: Westminster, 1975); Theodore M Snider, *The divine activity: An approach to incarnational theology* (New York: Peter Lang, 1990); Russell Pregeant, *Christology beyond dogma: Matthew's Christ in process hermeneutic* (Philadelphia: Fortress, 1978); David R Griffin, *A process christology* (Philadelphia: Fortress, 1973); Daniel Day Williams, *The Spirit and the forms of love* (Digswell Place, Herts.: James Nisbet, 1968), chaps. 8 & 9.

20. Norman Pittenger, *Christology reconsidered* (London: SCM, 1970).

21. Pittenger, "The incarnation in Process theology," 48.

22. Cobb, *Christ in a pluralistic age*, 75, 138-139.

23. John B Cobb, "Christ beyond creative transformation," in *Encountering Jesus: A debate on christology*, ed. Stephen T Davis (Atlanta: John Knox, 1988), 147.

24. Pittenger, "The incarnation in Process theology," 49.

25. Macquarrie, *Jesus Christ in modern thought*, 363.

26. For example, Brian O McDermott, *Word become flesh: Dimensions of Christology* (Collegeville, MN: The Liturgical Press, 1993), 26.

27. Gerald O'Collins, *Christology: A biblical, historical, and systematic study of Jesus Christ* (Oxford: Oxford University Press, 1995), 17.

28. Macquarrie, *Jesus Christ in modern thought*, 373.

29. Macquarrie, *Jesus Christ in modern thought*, 375.

30. Macquarrie, *Jesus Christ in modern thought*, 376.

31. Wolfhart Pannenberg, *Jesus—God and man* (London: SCM, 1968), 291.

32. Jürgen Moltmann, *The way of Jesus Christ: Christology in messianic dimensions* (London: SCM, 1990), 69.

33. Moltmann, *The way of Jesus Christ*, 69. So does George W Stroup, III, "Chalcedon revisited," *Theology Today* 35 (1978): 62.

34. James D G Dunn, *Jesus and the Spirit: A study of the religious and charismatic experience of Jesus and the first Christians as reflected in the New Testament* (London: SCM, 1975).

35. Keith Ward, "Incarnation or inspiration—A false dichotomy?," *Theology* 80 (1977): 251-255.

36. James D G Dunn, "Incarnation," in *The Anchor Bible dictionary*, ed. David Noel Freeman (New York: Doubleday, 1992), 3:398; Norman Hook, "A Spirit Christology," *Theology* 75 (1972): 229.

37. See for example, Geoffrey W H Lampe, *God as Spirit* (Oxford: Oxford University Press, 1977); G W H Lampe, "The essence of Christianity: A personal view," *The Expository Times* 87 (1976): 132-137; Roger Haight, "The case for Spirit Christology," *Theological Studies* 53 (1992): 257-287; Norman Hook, *Christ in the twentieth century: A Spirit Christology* (London: Lutterworth, 1968); Hook, "A Spirit Christology," 226-232; Paul W Newman, *A Spirit christology: Recovering the biblical paradigm of Christian faith* (Lanham, MD: University Press of America, 1987); Walter Kasper, *Jesus the Christ* (London: Burns & Oates, 1976), 250-252; John A T Robinson, *The human face of God* (London: SCM, 1973). Donald Baillie's "paradox-of-grace" christology is similar as well: D M Baillie, *God was in Christ: An essay on incarnation and atonement* (London: Faber and Faber, 1956).

38. Lampe, *God as Spirit*, 208.

39. Lampe, *God as Spirit*, 23-24.

40. For example, Haight, "The case for Spirit Christology," 276-277; Hook, "A Spirit Christology," 229; Lampe, *God as Spirit*, 13; Robinson, *The human face of God*, 146-147.

41. Hick, *The metaphor of God incarnate*, 106-111. The same point is made by John Bowden, *Jesus: The unanswered questions* (London: SCM, 1988), 86-90.

42. Pittenger, *The Word incarnate*, 215-235; Philip J Rosato, "Spirit Christology: Ambiguity and promise," *Theological Studies* 38 (1977): 423-449; Kasper, *Jesus the Christ*, 249. Haight and Hook affirm an "economic trinity" but not an "immanent trinity": Haight, "The case for Spirit Christology," 284-285; Hook, *Christ in the twentieth century*, 76-79.

43. Lampe, *God as Spirit*, 228; David Brown, *The divine trinity* (London: Duckworth, 1985), 165.

44. Moltmann, *The way of Jesus Christ*, 69-72.

45. Moltmann, *The way of Jesus Christ*, 73-94.

46. Augustine of Hippo, "De Trinitate [On the holy trinity]," in *St Augustin: On the holy trinity, Doctrinal treatises, Moral treatises*, A select library of the Nicene and Post-Nicene Fathers of the Christian church, 1st series, ed. Philip Schaff, vol. 3 (Grand Rapids: Eerdmans, 1956 [400-416]), books IX & X, pp. 125-143.

47. Pittenger, *The Word incarnate*, 231; Hans Küng, *On being a Christian* (London: Collins, 1977), 476.

48. Jürgen Moltmann, *The trinity and the kingdom of God: The doctrine of God* (Minneapolis: Fortress, 1993), 174-176; Richard Bauckham, *The theology of Jürgen Moltmann* (Edinburgh: T & T Clark, 1995), 173-175.

49. Haight, "The case for Spirit Christology," 284.

50. Darrell L Guder, *Be my witnesses: The church's mission, message, and messengers* (Grand Rapids: Eerdmans, 1985), 24.

51. Karl Rahner, "Incarnation," in *Encyclopedia of theology: A concise Sacramentum Mundi*, ed. Karl Rahner (London: Burns & Oates, 1975), 690.

52. We here define soteriology, the study of the saving work of Jesus Christ, as a part of (or, as we here suggest, a permeating dimension of) christology, the study of Jesus Christ.

53. George Newlands, "Soteriology," in *A new dictionary of Christian theology*, eds. Alan Richardson and John Bowden (London: SCM, 1983), 546.

54. Philip Melancthon, "*Loci communes theologici* [Fundamental theological themes, 1521]," in *Melancthon and Bucer*, The Library of Christian Classics, vol. 19, ed. Wilhelm Pauck (London: SCM, 1969), 21-22.

55. Guder, *Be my witnesses*, 25.

56. Guder, *Be my witnesses*, 18.

57. Darrell L Guder, "Incarnation and the church's evangelistic mission," *International Review of Mission* 83 (1994): 420.

58. John Stott, *The contemporary Christian: An urgent plea for double listening* (Leicester, UK: Inter-Varsity Press, 1992), 358.

59. World Council of Churches Commission on World Mission and Evangelism, *Your will be done: Mission in Christ's way: Study material and biblical reflection* (Geneva: World Council of Churches, 1988); cited in Guder, "Incarnation and the church's evangelistic mission," 419.

60. Athol Gill, *Life on the road: The gospel basis for a messianic lifestyle* (Homebush West, NSW: Lancer, 1989).

61. Guder, *Be my witnesses*, 10-11.

62. Dietrich Bonhoeffer, *The cost of discipleship* (London: SCM, 1959), 35-39.

63. Brennan Hill, *Jesus, the Christ: Contemporary perspectives* (Mystic, CN: Twenty-third Publications, 1991), 52.

64. Guder, *Be my witnesses*, 47.

65. Allan W Loy, "Praxis: Karl Marx's challenge to Christian theology," *St Mark's Review* No. 113 (Mar 1983): 7-14, 24.

66. Marcus J Borg, *Jesus in contemporary scholarship* (Valley Forge, PA: Trinity Press International, 1994), 97-126.

67. Viv Grigg, "The urban poor: Prime missionary target," *Evangelical Review of Theology* 11 (1987): 261-272.

68. Leonardo Boff and Clodovis Boff, *Liberation theology: From dialogue to confrontation* (San Francisco: Harper & Row, 1986), 30.

69. Leonardo Boff and Clodovis Boff, *Introducing liberation theology* (Tunbridge Wells, UK: Burns & Oates, 1987), 44-45.

70. Bruce Milne, "'Even so send I you': An expository and theological reflection on John 20:21," in *Mission to the world: Essays to celebrate the 50th anniversary of the ordination of George Raymond Beasley-Murray to the Christian ministry*, ed. Paul Beasley-Murray (Didcot, UK: Baptist Historical Society, 1991), 49; Andreas J Köstenberger, "The challenge of a systematized biblical theology of mission: Missiological insights from the Gospel of John," *Missiology* 23 (1995): 454.

71. Dietrich Bonhoeffer, *Letters and papers from prison* (London: Fontana, 1959), 381.

72. Thorwald Lorenzen, *Resurrection and discipleship: Interpretive models, biblical reflections, theological consequences* (Maryknoll: Orbis, 1996), 220.

73. John Howard Yoder, *The politics of Jesus*, 2nd ed. (Grand Rapids: Eerdmans, 1994), 95.

74. Eldin Villafañe, *Seek the peace of the city: Reflections on urban ministry* (Grand Rapids: Eerdmans, 1995), 14.

75. Frank Rees, "The community of the servant: A critical development of a contemporary image of the church," Thesis (Theol.M.), Melbourne College of Divinity, 1980, 169.

76. Rees, "The community of the servant," 190.

77. "Theology and implications of radical discipleship," in *Let the earth hear his voice: International Congress on World Evangelization, Lausanne, Switzerland*, ed. J D Douglas (Minneapolis: World Wide Publications, 1975), 1294.

78. Sallie McFague, *The body of God: An ecological theology* (London: SCM, 1993), xi.

79. See p. 179 below.
80. Leonardo Boff, *The Lord's Prayer: The prayer of integral liberation* (Melbourne: Dove Communications, 1983), 2.
81. Choan-Seng Song, *Christian mission in reconstruction: An Asian analysis* (Maryknoll: Orbis, 1977), 51-82.
82. Song, *Christian mission in reconstruction*, 217.
83. Baillie, *God was in Christ*, 94-98; Macquarrie, *Jesus Christ in modern thought*, 245-250.
84. Song, *Christian mission in reconstruction*, 72-76.
85. Whiteman, Darrell. "Contextualization: The theory, the gap, the challenge." *International Bulletin of Missionary Research* 21 (1997): 6.
86. Guder, *Be my witnesses*, 47.

Chapter 4

1.   We will use "Anabaptist" to refer both to the sixteenth-century Anabaptist movement and to current expressions of the tradition, the context making its reference clear. The terms "the Radical Reformation" and "the left wing of the Reformation" tend to refer to a wider group of radicals which includes the Anabaptists. George Huntston Williams, *The Radical Reformation*, 3rd ed. (Kirksville, MO: Sixteenth Century Journal Publishers, 1992), 15-18, 1298-1303; Roland Bainton, "The left wing of the Reformation," *Journal of Religion* 21 (1941): 124-134.
2.   J Denny Weaver, *Becoming Anabaptist: The origin and significance of sixteenth-century Anabaptism* (Scottdale, PA: Herald, 1987), 19; C Arnold Snyder, *Anabaptist history and theology: An introduction* (Kitchener, Ontario: Pandora Press, 1995), 1.
3.   Weaver, *Becoming Anabaptist*, 23.
4.   Snyder, *Anabaptist history and theology*, 1; Williams, *The Radical Reformation*, 1208; "Smyth, John," in *The Oxford dictionary of the Christian church*, eds. F L Cross and E A Livingstone, 2nd ed. (London: Oxford University Press, 1974), 1284.
5.   Weaver, *Becoming Anabaptist*, 20.
6.   Guy F Hershberger, "Introduction," in *The recovery of the Anabaptist vision*, ed. Guy F Hershberger (Scottdale, PA: Herald, 1957), 1; Snyder, *Anabaptist history and theology*, 56-60, 146-150.
7.   Harold S Bender, *The Anabaptist vision* (Scottdale, PA: Herald, 1944), 13; The paper is also found in Guy F Hershberger, ed. *The recovery of the Anabaptist vision* (Scottdale, PA: Herald, 1957), 29-54.
8.   Bender, *The Anabaptist vision*, 16.
9.   Bender, *The Anabaptist vision*, 11.

10. Walter Klaassen, "Sixteenth-century Anabaptism: A vision valid for the twentieth century?," *The Conrad Grebel Review* 7 (1989): 241-242.

11. James Stayer, Werner Packull, and Klaus Deppermann, "From monogenesis to polygenesis: The historical discussion of Anabaptist origins," *The Mennonite Quarterly Review* 49 (1975): 83-121; Klaassen, "Sixteenth-century Anabaptism," 242.

12. John Howard Yoder, "Orientation in midstream: A response to the responses," in *Freedom and discipleship: Liberation theology in Anabaptist perspective*, ed. Daniel S Schipani (Maryknoll: Orbis, 1989), 162.

13. Williams, *The Radical Reformation*, 15.

14. Walter Klaassen, "Anabaptism," in *The Mennonite encyclopedia, Vol. 5*, eds. Cornelius J Dyck and Dennis D Martin (Scottdale, PA: Herald, 1990), 24.

15. J A Oosterbaan, "The reformation of the Reformation: Fundamentals of Anabaptist theology," *The Mennonite Quarterly Review* 51 (1977): 182.

16. Oosterbaan, "The reformation of the Reformation," 87.

17. Calvin Redekop, "The community of scholars and the essence of Anabaptism," *The Mennonite Quarterly Review* 67 (1993): 429.

18. Redekop, "The community of scholars and the essence of Anabaptism," 436-437.

19. S F Pannebecker, "Missions, Foreign Mennonite," in *The Mennonite encyclopedia*, eds. Harold S Bender and C Henry Smith, vol. 3 (Scottdale, PA: Mennonite Publishing House, 1957), 712.

20. Neal Blough, "Messianic mission and ethics: Discipleship and the good news," in *The transfiguration of mission: Biblical, theological and historical foundations*, ed. Wilbert R Shenk (Scottdale, PA: Herald, 1993), 179; J D Graber, "Anabaptism expressed in missions and social service," in *The recovery of the Anabaptist vision*, ed. Guy F Hershberger (Scottdale, PA: Herald, 1957), 152-153.

21. Littell, "The Anabaptist theology of mission," 18.

22. Graber, "Anabaptism expressed in missions and social service," 152, 154, 161-163.

23. Larry Miller, "The church as messianic society: Creation and instrument of transfigured mission," in *The transfiguration of mission: Biblical, theological and historical foundations*, ed. Wilbert R Shenk (Scottdale, PA: Herald, 1993), 145.

24. Robert L Ramseyer, "The Anabaptist vision and our world mission, 1," in *Anabaptism and mission*, ed. Wilbert R Shenk (Scottdale, PA: Herald, 1984), 184.

25. Harry Huebner, "Discipleship," in *The Mennonite encyclopedia, Vol. 5*, eds. Cornelius J Dyck and Dennis D Martin (Scottdale, PA: Herald, 1990), 238.

26. J Denny Weaver, "Which way for Mennonite theology?," *Gospel Herald*, 23 Jan 1996, 3.

27. Bender, *The Anabaptist vision*, 20.
28. Bender, *The Anabaptist vision*, 21.
29. Bender, *The Anabaptist vision*, 21.
30. Bender, *The Anabaptist vision*, 33.
31. J Lawrence Burkholder, "The Anabaptist vision of discipleship," in *The recovery of the Anabaptist vision*, ed. Guy F Hershberger (Scottdale, PA: Herald, 1957), 136.
32. Burkholder, "The Anabaptist vision of discipleship," 137.
33. Burkholder, "The Anabaptist vision of discipleship," 137.
34. Burkholder, "The Anabaptist vision of discipleship," 136.
35. Burkholder, "The Anabaptist vision of discipleship," 136.
36. Oosterbaan, "The reformation of the Reformation," 182.
37. John H Elliott, "Backward and forward 'In his steps': Following Jesus from Rome to Raymond and beyond. The tradition, redaction, and reception of 1 Peter 2:18-25," in *Discipleship in the New Testament*, ed. Fernando F Segovia (Philadelphia: Fortress, 1985), 201.
38. Elliott, "Backward and forward 'In his steps'," 201.
39. E J Tinsley, "The imitation of Christ," in *A new dictionary of Christian theology*, eds. John Bowden and Alan Richardson (London: SCM, 1983), 285.
40. W Michaelis, "μιμέομαι, μιμητής, συμμιμητής," in *Theological Dictionary of the New Testament*, eds. Gerhard Kittel and Gerhard Friedrich (Grand Rapids: Eerdmans, 1964-1976), 4:659-674.; William S Kurz, "Kenotic imitation of Paul and of Christ in Philippians 2 and 3," in *Discipleship in the New Testament*, ed. Fernando F Segovia (Philadelphia: Fortress, 1985), 103. Other examples are example Karl Rahner, Josef Fuchs and Charles E Curran: Karl Rahner, *Spiritual exercises* (New York: Herder & Herder, 1965), 115; Josef Fuchs, *Natural law: A theological investigation* (New York: Sheed and Ward, 1965); Josef Fuchs, *Moral demands and personal obligations* (Washington, DC: Georgetown University Press, 1993), 120; Charles E Curran, *A new look at Christian morality* (London: Sheed and Ward, 1969), 12, 21; Charles E Curran, *Directions in fundamental moral theology* (Notre Dame: University of Notre Dame Press, 1985), 6, 11; William C Spohn, *What are they saying about scripture and ethics?* (New York: Paulist Press, 1984), 41-50.
41. One exception is Jeremy Moiser, "Dogmatic thoughts on imitation of Christ," *Scottish Journal of Theology* 30 (1977): 201-213. Moiser picks up the Platonic idea of participation in the context of mimesis and links it positively with Christian concepts of participating in Christ.
42. Alister E McGrath, "In what way can Jesus be a moral example for Christians?," *Journal of the Evangelical Theological Society* 34 (1991): 297.

43. G B Kerferd, "Mimesis," in *The encyclopedia of philosophy*, ed. Paul Edwards (New York: Macmillan, 1967), 5:335.
44. Tinsley, "Imitation of Christ," 208.
45. Tinsley, "Imitation of Christ," 208.
46. Thomas á Kempis, *The imitation of Christ* (Harmondsworth, Msex: Penguin, 1952 [1418]).
47. Margaret R Miles, *The image and practice of holiness: A critique of the classic manuals of devotion* (London: SCM, 1988), 22-26.
48. James Gustafson, *Christ and the moral life* (New York: Harper, 1968), 176; Leo Sherley-Price, "Introduction," in *The imitation of Christ*, by Thomas á Kempis, translated by Leo Sherley-Price (Harmondsworth, Msex: Penguin, 1952 [1418]), 12.
49. Kempis, *The imitation of Christ*, #1.25, p. 66.
50. Charles Monroe Sheldon, *In his steps* (Grand Rapids: Zondervan, 1967 [1896]).
51. Elliott, "Backward and forward 'In his steps'," 184; Sherley-Price, "Introduction," 11.
52. For example, Gustafson, *Christ and the moral life*, 43-44, 156; Elliott, "Backward and forward 'In his steps'," 200-201; Spohn, *What are they saying about scripture and ethics?*, 89.
53. John Howard Yoder, *The politics of Jesus: Vicit agnus noster*, 2nd ed. (Grand Rapids: Eerdmans, 1994), 4 note 7.
54. Alister McGrath's critique of the exemplarism of liberal theology follows these lines. McGrath, "In what way can Jesus be a moral example for Christians?," 289-298.
55. "Pelagianism," in *The Oxford dictionary of the Christian church*, eds. F L Cross and E A Livingstone, 2nd ed., (London: Oxford University Press, 1974), 1058.
56. Ian Hazlett, ed. *Early Christianity: Origins and evolution to AD600* (London: SPCK, 1991), 316.
57. Bender, *The Anabaptist vision*, 13, 18, 33.
58. Stephen F Dintaman, "The spiritual poverty of the Anabaptist vision," *The Conrad Grebel Review* 10 (1992): 205.
59. Dintaman, "The spiritual poverty of the Anabaptist vision," 205.
60. Dintaman, "The spiritual poverty of the Anabaptist vision," 205-208, also appearing in Mennonite weekly magazine *The Gospel Herald*, 23 Feb 1993, 1-3. See also much of the Winter 1995 edition of *The Conrad Grebel Review*, namely: Arnold Snyder, "The Anabaptist vision: Theological perspectives (Editorial)," iii-vii; Stephen F Dintaman, "Reading the reactions to 'The spiritual poverty of the Anabaptist vision'," 2-10; J Lorne Peachey, "Few articles rival this one: Responses to Dintaman in The Gospel Herald," 10-14; Richard Showalter, "'The spiritual poverty of the Anabaptist vision': An

assessment," 14-18; and Mitchell Brown, "Blessed are the spiritually poor: Reflections on Dintaman's 'The spiritual poverty of the Anabaptist vision'," 18-22.

61. Dintaman, "The spiritual poverty of the Anabaptist vision," 206-207.

62. Dintaman, "Reading the reactions to 'The spiritual poverty of the Anabaptist vision'," 6.

63. Cornelius J Dyck, "The Anabaptist understanding of the good news," in *Anabaptism and mission*, ed. Wilbert R Shenk, (Scottdale, PA: Herald, 1984), 29. See also Alan F Kreider, "'The servant is not greater than his master': The Anabaptists and the suffering church," *The Mennonite Quarterly Review* 58 (1984): 5-29, where it is argued that renewal and radicalism were inseparable in the Anabaptist martyrs.

64. Dyck, "The Anabaptist understanding of the good news," 30.

65. Driver, *Understanding the atonement for the mission of the church*, 250-251.

66. Dintaman, "The spiritual poverty of the Anabaptist vision," 205.

67. Kreider, "'The servant is not greater than his master'," 5-29.

68. John Howard Yoder, *The politics of Jesus: Vicit agnus noster*, 2nd ed. (Grand Rapids: Eerdmans, 1994). See also John Howard Yoder, ed. *The legacy of Michael Sattler*, Classics of the Radical Reformation, No. 1 (Scottdale, PA: Herald, 1973), and John Howard Yoder, *The royal priesthood: Essays ecclesiological and ecumenical*, ed. Michael G Cartwright (Grand Rapids: Eerdmans, 1994).

69. Weaver, *Becoming Anabaptist*, 116.

70. Yoder, *The politics of Jesus*, 2, 11.

71. Yoder, *The politics of Jesus*, 53.

72. Yoder, *The politics of Jesus*, 95.

73. Yoder, *The politics of Jesus*, 95.

74. Yoder, *The politics of Jesus*, 113.

75. Yoder, *The politics of Jesus*, 115-127.

76. Yoder, *The politics of Jesus*, 185.

77. Yoder, *The politics of Jesus*, 131.

78. Yoder, *The politics of Jesus*, 132-133. He is referring to Anthony Tyrell Hanson, *The paradox of the cross in the thought of St Paul* (Sheffield: JSOT Press, 1987), and A E Harvey, *Strenuous commands: The ethic of Jesus* (London: SCM, 1990), especially 169-189.

79. Yoder, *The politics of Jesus*, 226-227.

80. See, for example: Weaver, "Discipleship redefined: Four sixteenth century Anabaptists" ; J Denny Weaver, "A believers' church christology," *The Mennonite Quarterly Review* 57 (1983): 112-131; Weaver, *Becoming Anabaptist*; J Denny Weaver, "Atonement for the non-Constantinian church," *Modern Theology* 6 (1990): 307-323; J Denny Weaver, "Christology in historical perspective," in *Contemporary Anabaptist perspectives*, ed. Erland

Waltner (Newton, KN: Faith & Life, 1990), 83-105; J Denny Weaver, "Christus Victor, ecclesiology, and christology," *The Mennonite Quarterly Review* 68 (1994): 277-290; J Denny Weaver, "Narrative theology in an Anabaptist-Mennonite context," *The Conrad-Grebel Review* 12 (1994): 171-188; J Denny Weaver, "The Anabaptist vision: A historical or a theological future?," *The Conrad Grebel Review* 13 (1995): 69-86; Weaver, "Which way for Mennonite theology?."

81. Weaver, *Becoming Anabaptist*, 48, 51, 63, 111, 118, 133-135, 140.
82. Weaver, *Becoming Anabaptist*, 118.
83. Weaver, *Becoming Anabaptist*, 63. He does note that the early German Anabaptist Pilgram Marpeck followed Hans Denck and Hans Hut in stressing that the new life of the Christian is a gift of God's grace, appropriated by faith.
84. Weaver, *Becoming Anabaptist*, 132.
85. Weaver, "Discipleship redefined," 256.
86. Weaver, "Discipleship redefined," 264-265.
87. Weaver, "Discipleship redefined," 267, translated by Weaver from Walter Fellmann, ed., *Hans Denck Schriften, II. Teil Religiöse Schriften* (Gütersloh: Bertelsmann, 1956), 45.
88. For example Weaver, "Which way for Mennonite theology?" ; Weaver, "A believers' church christology," 128-129.
89. Weaver, "A believers' church christology," 128, 130.
90. Weaver, "A believers' church christology," 128.
91. James Moffatt, *Grace in the New Testament* (London: Hodder and Stoughton, 1931), 396.
92. Roger Haight, *The experience and language of grace* (Dublin: Gill and Macmillan, 1979), 6.
93. Haight, *The experience and language of grace*, 7.
94. E J Yarnold, "Grace," in *A new dictionary of Christian theology*, eds. Alan Richardson and John Bowden (London: SCM, 1983), 244-245.
95. Alvin J Beachy, *The concept of grace in the Radical Reformation* (Nieuwkoop, Holland: B. de Graaf, 1977), 29-30. It was ironic given that Luther fought against Agricola on the same issue in about 1539; see Gabriel Fackre, "Antinomianism," in *A new dictionary of Christian theology*, eds. Alan Richardson and John Bowden (London: SCM, 1983), 27; and Martin Luther, "Against the Antinomians," in *Luther's Works, Vol. 47, The Christians in society, IV*, ed. Franklin Sherman (Philadelphia: Fortress, 1971), 107-119.
96. Hans Denck, *Was geredt sei, dass die Schrift sagt [1526] Quellen und Forschungen zur Reformationsgeschichte, Vol. 24*, Part 2, 57-58; cited in Beachy, *The concept of grace in the Radical Reformation*, 30.

97. Balthasar Hubmaier, "Freedom of the will, I," in *Balthasar Hubmaier: Theologian of Anabaptism*, eds. H Wayne Pipkin and John H Yoder (Scottdale, PA: Herald, 1989 [1524]), 426-448.

98. Menno Simons, "Reply to Gellius Faber, 1554," *The complete writings of Menno Simons, c.1496-1561* (Mennonite Publishing House: Scottdale, PA, 1956), 631; cited in Beachy, *The concept of grace in the Radical Reformation*, 33.

99. Beachy, *The concept of grace in the Radical Reformation*. See a summary of his argument in Alvin Beachy, "The grace of God as understood by five major Anabaptist writers," *The Mennonite Quarterly Review* 37 (1963): 5-33.

100. Beachy, *The concept of grace in the Radical Reformation*, 5.

101. Robert Friedmann, *The theology of Anabaptism: An interpretation* (Scottdale, PA: Herald, 1973), 27.

102. Menno Simons, "The new birth," *The complete writings of Menno Simons, c.1496-1561* (Mennonite Publishing House: Scottdale, PA, 1956), 95; cited in Beachy, *The concept of grace in the Radical Reformation*, 77.

103. Beachy, *The concept of grace in the Radical Reformation*, 153.

104. John Driver, *Understanding the atonement for the mission of the church* (Scottdale, PA: Herald, 1986), 103, 193, 250. While Driver says that grace is important, through the Holy Spirit, he only suggests that grace is the motivation for responding to God in covenantal discipleship; he fails to develop the dimension of enablement. Grace is hardly mentioned in his full-sized work on the atonement.

105. C Norman Kraus, *Jesus Christ our Lord: Christology from a disciple's perspective* (Scottdale, PA: Herald, 1987), 180, 227, 236-245. "Grace" does not appear in Kraus's index, but concepts such as "God's gracious love" and "solidarity in Christ" are central for him.

106. Cornelius J Dyck, "Jesus Christ our Lord in historical Anabaptist perspective," in *A disciple's Christology: Appraisals of Kraus's Jesus Christ our Lord*, ed. Richard A Kauffman (Elkhart, IN: Institute of Mennonite Studies, 1989), 47-48.

107. Friedmann, *The theology of Anabaptism*, 27, 91-98. He sees grace as an endowment, an illumination, and a "charisma," and argues that Anabaptism is a theology of grace, but defined very differently from Protestantism.

108. Klaassen, "Sixteenth-century Anabaptism," 247.

109. Snyder, *Anabaptist history and theology*, 380, 384.

110. J C Wenger, *What Mennonites believe*, Rev. ed. (Scottdale, PA: Herald, 1991), 17.

111. Snyder, "The Anabaptist vision: Theological perspectives (Editorial)," v. See p. 70 above.

112. See p. 65 above.

113. Yoder, *The politics of Jesus*, 130.

114. Yoder, *The politics of Jesus*, 115-126.
115. Donald B Kraybill, *The upside-down kingdom*, 2nd ed. (Scottdale , PA: Herald, 1990).
116. Yoder, *The politics of Jesus*, 127-128.
117. José Gallardo, "Ethics and mission," in *Anabaptism and mission*, ed. Wilbert R Shenk (Scottdale, PA: Herald, 1984), 141.
118. Yoder, *The politics of Jesus*, 187.
119. Spohn, *What are they saying about scripture and ethics?*, 105.
120. Spohn, *What are they saying about scripture and ethics?*, 104.
121. Yoder, *The politics of Jesus*, 96.
122. For example. John Driver, "Messianic evangelization," in *The transfiguration of mission: Biblical, theological and historical foundations*, ed. Wilbert Shenk (Scottdale, PA: Herald, 1993), 216.
123. Yoder, *The politics of Jesus*; Driver, *Understanding the atonement for the mission of the church*. Three of the very few references in Driver are found on 35, 231 and 251. The resurrection figures more strongly in John Driver, "Messianic evangelization," esp. 216.
124. Kraus, *Jesus Christ our Lord*, esp. 88-91; Wilbert R Shenk, ed., *The transfiguration of mission: Biblical, theological and historical foundations* (Scottdale, PA: Herald, 1993), esp. David A Shank's chapter on "Jesus the messiah: Messianic foundation of mission," 37-82, see 47, 70-71.
125. Thorwald Lorenzen, *Resurrection and discipleship: Interpretive models, biblical reflections, theological consequences* (Maryknoll: Orbis, 1996), 245.
126. José Míguez Bonino, "On discipleship, justice and power," in *Freedom and discipleship: Liberation theology in Anabaptist perspective*, ed. Daniel S Schipani (Maryknoll: Orbis, 1989), 132.
127. Bonino, "On discipleship, justice and power," 132.
128. C Arnold Snyder, "The relevance of Anabaptist nonviolence for Nicaragua today," in *Freedom and discipleship: Liberation theology in Anabaptist perspective*, ed. Daniel S Schipani (Maryknoll: Orbis, 1989), 113.
129. Snyder, *Anabaptist history and theology*, 225.
130. Snyder, "The relevance of Anabaptist nonviolence for Nicaragua today," 123; from Lotzer's writings, found in Alfred Goetze, ed., *Sebastian Lotzers Schriften* (Leipzig: Teubner, 1902), 33.
131. Snyder, *Anabaptist history and theology*, 227.
132. Ronald J Sider, "Evangelicalism and the Mennonite tradition," in *Evangelicalism and Anabaptism*, ed. C Norman Kraus (Scottdale, PA: Herald, 1979), 166.
133. Driver, "Messianic evangelization," 200-212.
134. Driver, "Messianic evangelization," 216.

135. Linford Stutzman, *With Jesus in the world: Mission in modern, affluent societies* (Scottdale, PA: Herald, 1992). Stutzman's argument is found in summary form in Linford Stutzman, "An incarnational approach to mission in modern, affluent societies," *Urban Mission* 8.5 (May 1991): 35-43 (also appearing in *Mission Focus* 18.1 (1990): 6-11).
136. Stutzman, *With Jesus in the world*, 18.
137. Stutzman, *With Jesus in the world*, 40.
138. Stutzman, *With Jesus in the world*, 45-57.
139. Stutzman, *With Jesus in the world*, 57.
140. Stutzman, *With Jesus in the world*, 58-86.
141. Stutzman, *With Jesus in the world*, 95.
142. Stutzman, *With Jesus in the world*, 95-122.
143. Ronald J Sider, "Mennonites and the poor: Toward an Anabaptist theology of liberation," in *Freedom and discipleship: Liberation theology in Anabaptist perspective*, ed. Daniel S Schipani (Maryknoll: Orbis, 1989), 85. See also Sider's comments in Sider, "Evangelicalism and the Mennonite tradition," 166.
144. Donald F Durnbaugh, *The believers' church: The history and character of radical Protestantism* (New York: Macmillan, 1968). Durnbaugh includes groups such as the Quakers, the early Methodists and Baptists, the Church of the Brethren and the Disciples of Christ.
145. James Leo Garrett, ed., *The concept of the believers' church* (New York: Macmillan, 1969), 5; cited in David A Shank, "Anabaptists and mission," in *Anabaptism and mission*, ed. Wilbert R Shenk (Scottdale, PA: Herald, 1984), 221.
146. Driver, *Understanding the atonement for the mission of the church*, 186.
147. Hans Kasdorf, "The Anabaptist approach to mission," in *Anabaptism and mission*, ed. Wilbert R Shenk (Scottdale, PA: Herald, 1984), 69.
148. Miller, "The church as messianic society," 149-150.
149. See for example Wilbert R Shenk, "The culture of modernity as a missionary challenge," in *The good news of the kingdom: Mission theology for the third millennium*, eds. Charles Van Engen, Dean S Gilliland, and Paul Pierson (Maryknoll: Orbis, 1993), 197; Blough, "Messianic mission and ethics," 180; Kasdorf, "The Anabaptist approach to mission," 64.
150. Shenk, "The relevance of a Messianic missiology for mission today," 32.
151. Driver, *Understanding the atonement for the mission of the church*, 35.
152. Wilbert Shenk, "The relevance of a Messianic missiology for mission today," in *The transfiguration of mission: Biblical, theological and historical foundations*, ed. Wilbert Shenk (Scottdale, PA: Herald, 1993), 32.
153. See p. 6 above.
154. See pp. 36-47 above.

155. John Howard Yoder, ed., *The Schleitheim Confession* (Scottdale, PA: Herald, 1973), 11-12.
156. Snyder, "The relevance of Anabaptist nonviolence for Nicaragua today," 119.
157. Beachy, *The concept of grace in the Radical Reformation*, 79-86, 178.
158. Bonino, "On discipleship, justice and power," 136.
159. Jürgen Moltmann, "Political discipleship of Christ today," in *Communities of faith and radical discipleship: Jürgen Moltmann and others*, ed. G McLeod Bryan (Macon, GA: Mercer University Press, 1986), 17.
160. H Richard Niebuhr, *Christ and culture* (New York: Harper, 1951), 45-82.
161. Charles Scriven, *The transformation of culture: Christian social ethics after H Richard Niebuhr* (Scottdale, PA: Herald, 1988), 44.
162. See Niebuhr, *Christ and culture*, 190-229.
163. Scriven, *The transformation of culture*, 193, 194.
164. Beachy, *The concept of grace in the Radical Reformation*, 179.
165. Dietrich Bonhoeffer, *Ethics* (London: SCM, 1955), 103-104.
166. Beachy, *The concept of grace in the Radical Reformation*, 179.
167. Burkholder, "The Anabaptist vision of discipleship," 149-150.
168. Burkholder, "The Anabaptist vision of discipleship," 151.
169. See pp. 82-85 above.
170. Klaassen, "Sixteenth-century Anabaptism," 247.
171. See pp. 71-75 above.
172. See p. 73 above.
173. See p. 70 above.
174. Dintaman, "Reading the reactions to 'The spiritual poverty of the Anabaptist vision'," 2.

Chapter 5

1. Orlando E Costas, *Christ outside the gate: Mission beyond Christendom* (Maryknoll: Orbis, 1982), 13. Costas (1942-1987) was a Puerto Rican who taught in Costa Rica and in the USA. As director of the Latin American Evangelical Center for Pastoral Studies (CELEP), Costas developed an evangelism program which involved ministry to the whole person. He was an influential voice in the Lausanne movement and in the Latin American Theological Fraternity.
2. "Theology and implications of radical discipleship," in *Let the earth hear his voice: International Congress on World Evangelization, Lausanne, Switzerland*, ed. J D Douglas (Minneapolis: World Wide Publications, 1975), 1294-1296. The word "and" in the title is present on the contents page but missing in the heading of the article itself.

3. "Third World" is used in this study to refer collectively to countries which are politically non-aligned, less economically-developed, and have a low standard of living; most are from Africa, South and Central America, and South East Asia. It is difficult to find a neutral term for such countries, also referred to as "the South" and "the two-thirds world."

4. Guillermo Cook, *The expectation of the poor: Latin American basic ecclesial communities in Protestant perspective* (Maryknoll: Orbis, 1985).

5. Emilio Núñez, "Evangelical theology and praxis for Latin America," *Evangelical Review of Theology* 11 (1987): 107-119; Emilio Núñez, "Towards an evangelical Latin American theology," *Evangelical Review of Theology* 7 (1983): 123-131.

6. For example, John Driver, *Understanding the atonement for the mission of the church* (Scottdale, PA: Herald, 1986); John Driver, "The kingdom of God," and "Messianic evangelization," in *The transfiguration of mission: Biblical, theological and historical foundations*, ed. Wilbert Shenk (Scottdale, PA: Herald, 1993), 83-105 and 199-219.

7. For example, Vinay Samuel and Albrecht Hauser, eds., *Proclaiming Christ in Christ's way: Studies in integral evangelism* (Oxford: Regnum, 1989); Vinay Samuel and Chris Sugden, "Evangelism and social responsibility—a biblical study on priorities," in *In word and deed: Evangelism and social responsibility*, ed. Bruce J Nicholls (Exeter: Paternoster, 1982), 189-214; Vinay Samuel and Chris Sugden, eds., *Evangelism and the poor: A third world study guide*, Rev. ed. (Bangalore: Partnership in Mission-Asia, 1983); Vinay Samuel and Chris Sugden, *Sharing Jesus in the two-thirds world*, The papers of the first Conference of Evangelical Mission Theologians from the Two-thirds World, Bangkok, Mar 1982 (Grand Rapids: Eerdmans, 1983); Vinay Samuel and Chris Sugden, eds., *The church in response to human need* (Oxford: Regnum, 1987); Vinay Samuel and Chris Sugden, "God's intention for the world," in *The church in response to human need*, eds. Vinay Samuel and Chris Sugden (Oxford: Regnum, 1987), 128-160.

8. Jim Wallis, *The call to conversion* (Tring, Herts., UK: Lion, 1981); Jim Wallis, *Agenda for biblical people*, 2nd ed. (San Francisco: Harper & Row, 1984); Jim Wallis, *The soul of politics: A practical and prophetic vision for change* (London: Fount, 1994).

9. Donald B Kraybill, *The upside-down kingdom*, 2nd ed. (Scottdale, PA: Herald, 1990).

10. Richard J Mouw, *Political evangelism* (Grand Rapids: Eerdmans, 1973).

11. George Williamson, "Politics is the law," in *Communities of faith and radical discipleship: Jürgen Moltmann and others*, ed. G McLeod Bryan (Macon, GA: Mercer University Press, 1986), 71-104.

12. Wes Michaelson, "Evangelicalism and radical discipleship," in *Evangelicalism and Anabaptism*, ed. C Norman Kraus (Scottdale, PA: Herald, 1979), 63-82.

13. See, for example, representatives in the following collections of essays: Samuel and Sugden, *Sharing Jesus in the two-thirds world*; Samuel and Hauser, eds., *Proclaiming Christ in Christ's way*; and William A Dyrness, ed., *Emerging voices in global Christian theology* (Grand Rapids: Zondervan, 1994).

14. Athol Gill, *Life on the road: The gospel basis for a messianic lifestyle* (Homebush West, NSW: Lancer, 1989); Athol Gill, *The fringes of freedom: Following Jesus, living together, working for justice* (Homebush West, NSW: Lancer, 1990).

15. Thorwald Lorenzen, *Resurrection and discipleship: Interpretive models, biblical reflections, theological consequences* (Maryknoll: Orbis, 1996).

16. John Smith, *Advance Australia where?* (Homebush West: ANZEA, 1988); John Smith, *Cutting edge* (Tunbridge Wells, UK: Monarch, 1992).

17. Charles Ringma, *Catch the wind* (Sutherland, NSW: Albatross, 1994).

18. Dave Andrews, *Can you hear the heartbeat?* (London: Hodder & Stoughton, 1989); Dave Andrews, *Building a better world* (Sutherland, NSW: Albatross, 1996).

19. Martyn Newman, *Liberation theology is evangelical* (Melbourne: Mallorn, 1990).

20. Viv Grigg, *Companion to the poor*, Rev. ed. (Monrovia, CA: MARC, 1990); Viv Grigg, *Cry of the urban poor* (Monrovia, CA: MARC, 1992); Viv Grigg, "Church of the poor," in *Discipling the city: A comprehensive approach to urban mission*, ed. Roger S Greenway, 2nd ed. (Grand Rapids: Baker, 1992), 159-170.

21. Michael Duncan, *Mission: The incarnational approach*, The Journey Series, No. 2 (Christchurch, NZ: Servants to Asia's Urban Poor, 1991); Michael Duncan, *Costly mission: Following Christ into the slums* (Monrovia, CA: MARC, 1996).

22. Dorothy Harris, "Incarnation as relocation among the poor," *Evangelical Review of Theology* 18 (1994): 117-127.

23. Christopher Marshall, *Kingdom come: The kingdom of God in the teaching of Jesus*, 2nd ed. (Auckland: Impetus, 1993).

24. Colin Marchant, *Signs in the city* (London: Hodder & Stoughton, 1985); Colin Marchant, *Shalom my friends: Building God's kingdom together* (Basingstoke, UK: Marshall Pickering, 1988).

25. John Gladwin, *God's people in God's world: Biblical motives for social involvement* (Leicester, UK: Inter-Varsity Press, 1979).

26. David Sheppard, *Bias to the poor* (London: Hodder & Stoughton, 1983).

27. Jim Punton, *The Messiah people: Punton Papers, Vol. 1*, eds. Paul Grant and Raj Patel (Birmingham, UK: Hot Iron Press, 1993).

28. Pat Dearnley and Pete Broadbent, "Jesus Christ, the life of the city?," *Churchman* 97 (1983): 41-54.

29. D W Bebbington, "Evangelicalism," in *The Blackwell encyclopedia of modern Christian thought*, ed. Alister E McGrath (Oxford: Blackwell, 1993), 183; R V Pierard, "Evangelicalism," in *Evangelical dictionary of theology*, ed. Walter A Elwell (Grand Rapids: Baker, 1984), 379-382.

30. Ronald J Sider and John R W Stott, *Evangelism, salvation and social justice*, Grove Booklet on Ethics No. 16 (Bramcote, Notts.: Grove Books, 1979), 9.

31. Ronald J Sider, *One-sided Christianity? Uniting the church to heal a lost and broken world* (Grand Rapids: Zondervan, 1993), 39-41.

32. Sider, *One-sided Christianity?*, 160-173.

33. John Stott, *The contemporary Christian: An urgent plea for double listening* (Leicester, UK: Inter-Varsity Press, 1992), 337-360.

34. Writers such as Ched Myers, David Batstone, Alfred Krass and Mortimer Arias are examples of those who are not clearly evangelicals.

35. Ched Myers, *Who will roll away the stone? Discipleship queries for first world Christians* (Maryknoll: Orbis, 1994), xxx-xxxi.

36. Michael Westmoreland-Smith, Glen Stassen, and David P Gushee, "Disciples of the incarnation," *Sojourners*, May 1994, 26.

37. See, for example, C René Padilla, "Liberation theology: An appraisal," in *Freedom and discipleship: Liberation theology in Anabaptist perspective*, ed. Daniel S Schipani (Maryknoll: Orbis, 1989), 34-50; Orlando E Costas, *The church and its mission: A shattering critique from the Third World* (Wheaton, IL: Tyndale, 1974), 219-264; Newman, *Liberation theology is evangelical*, 83-95.

38. Myers, *Who will roll away the stone?*, xx, xxii.

39. Michaelson, "Evangelicalism and radical discipleship," 68-69; Lorenzen, *Resurrection and discipleship*, 233; Samuel Escobar and John Driver, *Christian mission and social justice* (Scottdale, PA: Herald, 1978), 112.

40. Michaelson, "Evangelicalism and radical discipleship," 75-76.

41. Orlando E Costas, "A radical evangelical contribution from Latin America," in *Christ's lordship and religious pluralism*, eds. Gerald H Anderson and Thomas F Stransky (Maryknoll: Orbis, 1981), 134.

42. Orlando E Costas, *Liberating news: A theology of contextual evangelization* (Grand Rapids: Eerdmans, 1989), 10.

43. Costas, *Liberating news*, 11.

44. Ched Myers, *Binding the strong man: A political reading of Mark's story of Jesus* (Maryknoll: Orbis, 1988), 106.

45. Costas, "A radical evangelical contribution from Latin America," 133-134.

46. Myers, *Binding the strong man*, 7; citing Dorothy Sölle.

47. Robert MacAfee Brown, "Foreword," in *From conquest to struggle: Jesus of Nazareth in Latin America,* by David Batstone (Albany: State University of New York Press, 1991), xi.

48. Mortimer Arias, *Announcing the reign of God: Evangelization and the subversive memory of Jesus* (Philadelphia: Fortress, 1984), 52.

49. Orlando E Costas, *The integrity of mission: The inner life and outreach of the church* (San Francisco: Harper & Row, 1979), 9.

50. Samuel Escobar, "The Gospel and the poor," in *Christian mission and social justice,* by Samuel Escobar and John Driver (Scottdale, PA: Herald, 1978), 54.

51. Gill, *Life on the road,* 31.

52. Smith, *Advance Australia where?,* 258.

53. Luther E Smith Jr, *Intimacy and mission: Intentional community as crucible for radical discipleship* (Scottdale, PA: Herald, 1994), 22.

54. "Theology and implications of radical discipleship," 1295.

55. Third Latin American Congress on Evangelism, "The whole gospel from Latin America for all peoples," in *New directions in mission and evangelization, 2: Theological foundations,* eds. James A Scherer and Stephen B Bevans (Maryknoll: Orbis, 1994), #III.5, p. 197.

56. Samuel Escobar, "Evangelism and man's search for freedom, justice and fulfillment," in *Let the earth hear his voice: International Congress on World Evangelization, Lausanne, Switzerland,* ed. J D Douglas (Minneapolis: World Wide Publications, 1975), 309.

57. Grigg, *Cry of the urban poor,* 10.

58. Gill, *The fringes of freedom,* 7.

59. Gladwin, *God's people in God's world,* 102.

60. Gladwin, *God's people in God's world,* 102, 35.

61. Gladwin, *God's people in God's world,* 11, 35.

62. Costas, *Christ outside the gate,* 15.

63. Duncan, *Mission: The incarnational approach,* 7.

64. Costas, *The integrity of mission,* 22-23.

65. Kraybill, *The upside-down kingdom,* 270.

66. Gill, *The fringes of freedom,* 34.

67. Gill, *The fringes of freedom,* 10.

68. Costas, *Christ outside the gate,* 15.

69. Lorenzen, *Resurrection and discipleship,* 301.

70. "Theology and implications of radical discipleship," 1294.

71. Lorenzen, *Resurrection and discipleship,* 205.

72. Lorenzen, *Resurrection and discipleship,* 223.

73. Lorenzen, *Resurrection and discipleship,* 218.

74. Lorenzen, *Resurrection and discipleship,* 318.

75. Costas, *Christ outside the gate,* 13.

76. Costas, *Christ outside the gate*, 16.

77. Costas, *Christ outside the gate*, 92.

78. Michaelson, "Evangelicalism and radical discipleship," 64. See, for instance, the views of Arthur P Johnston, "The kingdom in relation to the church and the world," in *In word and deed: Evangelism and social responsibility*, ed. Bruce J Nicholls (Exeter: Paternoster, 1985), 128. But note that the Manila Manifesto of the second Lausanne Congress includes many radical evangelical emphases, reflecting their involvement in the Lausanne movement, "The Manila Manifesto: Calling the whole church to take the whole gospel to the whole world," in *The whole gospel for the whole world: Story of Lausanne II Congress on World Evangelization, Manila 1989*, ed. Alan Nichols (Ventura, CA: Regal, 1989), #2, #4, #8, pp. 113, 115-116, 120.

79. Costas, *Christ outside the gate*, 16.

80. Marshall, *Kingdom come*, 93.

81. Kraybill, *The upside-down kingdom*, 21.

82. Kraybill, *The upside-down kingdom*, 28.

83. Kraybill, *The upside-down kingdom*, 29.

84. Kraybill, *The upside-down kingdom*, 30.

85. Costas, *Christ outside the gate*, 13.

86. Mortimer Arias and Alan Johnson, *The Great Commission: Biblical models for evangelism* (Nashville: Abingdon, 1992), 82.

87. Michaelson, "Evangelicalism and radical discipleship," 65; Samuel Escobar, "The return of Christ," in *The new face of evangelicalism: An international symposium on the Lausanne Covenant*, ed. C René Padilla (London: Hodder & Stoughton, 1976), 263.

88. Costas, "A radical evangelical contribution from Latin America," 133.

89. Escobar, "The return of Christ," 261.

90. "Theology and implications of radical discipleship," 1294.

91. "Theology and implications of radical discipleship," 1295.

92. See, for example, Sallie McFague, *Models of God: Theology for an ecological, nuclear age* (London: SCM, 1987), 19.

93. Costas, *The integrity of mission*, 9.

94. Timothy Chester, *Awakening to a world of need: The recovery of evangelical social concern* (Leicester, UK: Inter-Varsity Press, 1993), 89.

95. For example, Gill, *Life on the road*, 31; Gill, *The fringes of freedom*, 25.

96. "Theology and implications of radical discipleship," 1294.

97. Costas, "A radical evangelical contribution from Latin America," 143.

98. Escobar, "The return of Christ," 263; C René Padilla, "Introduction," in *The new face of evangelicalism: An international symposium on the Lausanne Covenant*, ed. C René Padilla (London: Hodder & Stoughton, 1976), 12.

99. Myers, *Who will roll away the stone?*, xxiii.

100. Tom Sine, *Wild hope* (Dallas: Word Publishing, 1991), 261.

101. Costas, *The church and its mission*, 74.
102. Myers, *Binding the strong man*, 456.
103. Wallis, *Agenda for biblical people*, 68.
104. Clark H Pinnock, "A call for the liberation of North American Christians," in *Evangelicals and liberation*, ed. Carl E Armerding (Grand Rapids: Baker, 1977), 129; Smith, *Advance Australia where?*, 258; Viv Grigg, "Sorry! The frontier moved," *Urban Mission* 4.4 (Mar 1987): 12-25, 21.
105. Gill, *Life on the road*, 84.
106. Gill, *The fringes of freedom*, 41-46.
107. "Holism," in *The Macquarie Dictionary*, 2nd ed. (Macquarie University, NSW: The Macquarie Library, 1989), 841.
108. Chester, *Awakening to a world of need*, 125; Bruce Bradshaw, *Bridging the gap: Evangelism, development and shalom* (Monrovia, CA: MARC, 1993), iii-iv, 16-19 (Bradshaw is World Vision's Director of Holistic Development Research); John Steward, *Biblical holism and the missionary mandate* (Sydney: Sydney Center for World Mission, 1995) (Steward until recently trained staff for World Vision Australia); Stott, *The contemporary Christian*, 337-355.
109. Costas, *The integrity of mission*, xii-xiii.
110. Alan Nichols, ed., *The whole gospel for the whole world: Story of Lausanne II Congress on World Evangelization, Manila 1989* (Ventura, CA: Regal, 1989), 110.
111. Bradshaw, *Bridging the gap*, 12, 16-17.
112. Alfred C Krass, *Five lanterns at sundown: Evangelism in a chastened mood* (Grand Rapids: Eerdmans, 1978), 84.
113. Padilla, "Evangelism and the world," 130.
114. Third Latin American Congress on Evangelism, "The whole gospel from Latin America for all peoples," #3, p. 197.
115. Stott, *The contemporary Christian*, 337-355.
116. Stott, *The contemporary Christian*, 340-341.
117. Stott, *The contemporary Christian*, 343-349.
118. "The Manila Manifesto," #4, p. 115.
119. Stott, *The contemporary Christian*, 355.
120. Sider, *One-sided Christianity?*, 183.
121. Sider, *One-sided Christianity?*, 193.
122. Costas, *The church and its mission*, 138.
123. Costas, *The church and its mission*, 309.
124. Costas, *The integrity of mission*, xiii.
125. Costas, *The church and its mission*, 140.
126. C René Padilla, *Mission between the times: Essays on the kingdom* (Grand Rapids: Eerdmans, 1985), 169. Padilla cites the phrase "embodied question mark" from John Poulton, *People under pressure* (London: Lutterworth,

1973), 112.
127. Costas, *A shattering critique from the Third World*, 140-141.
128. Costas, *The church and its mission*, 247.
129. Costas, *The church and its mission*, 71, 247.
130. Costas, *The integrity of mission*, 23.
131. Costas, *The integrity of mission*, 59.
132. Costas, *Christ outside the gate*, 13.
133. A highly positive evaluation of Costas' holism, however, is given by Priscilla Pope-Levison, *Evangelization from a liberation perspective* (New York: Peter Lang, 1991), 140.
134. Lorenzen, *Resurrection and discipleship*, 229.
135. Dearnley and Broadbent, "Jesus Christ, the life of the city?," 47.
136. Costas, *Christ outside the gate*, 13.
137. Andrews, *Can you hear the heartbeat?*.
138. Duncan, *Costly mission*.
139. Grigg, *Companion to the poor*.
140. Marchant, *Signs in the city*.
141. Punton, *The Messiah people*.
142. Ringma, *Catch the wind*.
143. Ronald J Sider, *Rich Christians in an age of hunger*, Rev. ed. (London: Hodder & Stoughton, 1990).
144. Smith, *Advance Australia where?*.
145. Wallis, *Agenda for biblical people*.
146. Harris, "Incarnation as relocation among the poor," 117-127.
147. Harris, "Incarnation as relocation among the poor," 118; Grigg, "Sorry! The frontier moved," 20-21.
148. Robert C Linthicum, *Empowering the poor* (Monrovia, CA: MARC, 1991), 35; Ray Bakke, *The urban Christian: Effective ministry in today's urban world* (Downers Grove, IL: InterVarsity Press, 1987), 158-159; Ron Browning, *Down and under: Discipleship in an Australian setting* (Melbourne: Spectrum, 1986), 64-65; Eldin Villafañe, *Seek the peace of the city: Reflections on urban ministry* (Grand Rapids: Eerdmans, 1995), 38; Jude Tiersma, "What does it mean to be incarnational when we are not the Messiah?," in *God so loves the city: Seeking a theology for urban mission*, eds. Charles Van Engen and Jude Tiersma (Monrovia, CA: MARC, 1994), 9; David Claerbaut, *Urban ministry* (Grand Rapids: Zondervan, 1983), 24; John Vincent, *Into the city* (London: Epworth, 1982), 14-17; Manuel Ortiz, "Being disciples: Incarnational Christians in the city," in *Discipling the city: A comprehensive approach to urban mission*, ed. Roger S Greenway, 2nd ed. (Grand Rapids: Baker, 1992), 85.
149. Sheppard, *Bias to the poor*, 10; Sider argues the same way, in Sider, *Rich Christians in an age of hunger*, 54-60.

150. John Howard Yoder, *The politics of Jesus: Vicit agnus noster*, 2nd ed. (Grand Rapids: Eerdmans, 1994), 95.
151. Lorenzen, *Resurrection and discipleship*, 217.
152. Gill, *The fringes of freedom*.
153. Arias, *Announcing the reign of God*, 6.
154. Sine, *Wild hope*, 266; he cites Stanley A Hauerwas and William H Willimon, *Resident aliens* (Nashville: Abingdon, 1989), 44-45.
155. Smith, *Intimacy and mission*, 22.
156. Costas, *Liberating news*, 24-25.
157. Costas, *Christ outside the gate*, 13.
158. Costas, *Christ outside the gate*, 14.
159. Padilla, *Mission between the times*, 83.
160. Padilla, *Mission between the times*, 103.
161. For example, Costas, *Christ outside the gate*, 15.
162. See pp. 36-47 above.

Chapter 6

1. Jon Sobrino, *Spirituality of liberation: Toward political holiness* (Maryknoll: Orbis, 1988), 136. (The first sentence, not italicized here, is italicized in Sobrino's book because it functions as an in-text sub-heading.)
2. Deane William Ferm, *Third world liberation theologies: An introductory survey* (Maryknoll: Orbis, 1986), 1; Leonardo Boff and Clodovis Boff, *Introducing liberation theology* (Tunbridge Wells, UK: Burns & Oates, 1987), 28-29.
3. The incarnational theme does not appear strongly in feminist missiology as we noted on p. 10. We have chosen not to examine other liberation theologies, such as African or African-American theology, so it is beyond our competence to comment on the extent to which incarnation is important in their missiology.
4. Leonardo Boff, *Jesus Christ liberator: A critical Christology for our time* (Maryknoll: Orbis, 1978), first published in Portuguese in 1972; Jon Sobrino, *Christology at the crossroads: A Latin American approach* (London: SCM, 1978), first published in Spanish in 1976; Jon Sobrino, *Jesus the liberator: A historical-theological reading of Jesus of Nazareth* (Tunbridge Wells, UK: Burns & Oates, 1994), first published in Spanish in 1991.
5. For example, Julio Lois, "Christology in the theology of liberation," in *Mysterium Liberationis: Fundamental concepts of liberation theology*, eds. Ignacio Ellacuría and Jon Sobrino (Maryknoll: Orbis, 1993), 190 note 3, who regards Boff and Sobrino as more representative of liberation christology than Juan Luis Segundo, for instance; Laverne A Rutschman, "Anabaptism and liberation theology," in *Freedom and discipleship: Liberation theology in*

Anabaptist perspective, ed. Daniel S Schipani (Maryknoll: Orbis, 1989), 62; Sobrino, *Jesus the liberator*, 272; and Donald E Waltermire, *The liberation christologies of Leonardo Boff and Jon Sobrino: Latin American contributions to contemporary christology* (Lanham, MD: University Press of America, 1994), vii.

6. Ferm, *Profiles in liberation*, 124-128; Leonardo Boff, *The path to hope: Fragments from a theologian's journey* (Maryknoll: Orbis, 1993), vi-vii; Leonardo Boff, *Ecology and liberation: A new paradigm* (Maryknoll: Orbis, 1995), cover notes.

7. Sobrino, *Jesus the liberator*, 7 & cover notes; Ferm, *Profiles in liberation*, 184-188.

8. Lists of major themes are to be found in Boff and Boff, *Introducing liberation theology*, 49-63; Leonardo Boff and Clodovis Boff, *Liberation theology: From dialogue to confrontation* (San Francisco: Harper & Row, 1986), 24-30; Roger Haight, *An alternative vision: An interpretation of liberation theology* (New York: Paulist Press, 1985), 44-47; and Robert McAfee Brown, *Theology in a new key* (Philadelphia: Westminster, 1978), 60-74.

9. José Míguez Bonino, "On discipleship, justice and power," in *Freedom and discipleship: Liberation theology in Anabaptist perspective*, ed. Daniel S Schipani (Maryknoll: Orbis, 1989), 132.

10. Leonardo Boff, *Faith on the edge: Religion and marginalized existence* (San Francisco: Harper & Row, 1989), 132.

11. Sobrino, *Christology at the crossroads*, 256.

12. Sobrino, *Christology at the crossroads*, 391.

13. Boff, *Jesus Christ liberator*, 46. See also Bonino, "On discipleship, justice and power," 133.

14. Francisco Moreno Rejón, "Fundamental moral theology in the theology of liberation," in *Mysterium Liberationis: Fundamental concepts of liberation theology*, eds. Ignacio Ellacuría and Jon Sobrino (Maryknoll: Orbis, 1993), 214.

15. Sobrino, for example, distinguishes "practice" from "praxis." Sobrino, *Jesus the liberator*, 87, 160-161.

16. Allan W Loy, "Praxis: Karl Marx's challenge to Christian theology," *St Mark's Review* No. 113 (Mar 1983): 7-14, 24.

17. Marcello de C. Azevedo, "Basic ecclesial communities," in *Mysterium Liberationis: Fundamental concepts of liberation theology*, eds. Ignacio Ellacuría and Jon Sobrino (Maryknoll: Orbis, 1993), 651 note 2.

18. Jon Sobrino, "Systematic christology: Jesus Christ, the absolute mediator of the reign of God," in *Mysterium Liberationis: Fundamental concepts of liberation theology*, eds. Ignacio Ellacuría and Jon Sobrino (Maryknoll: Orbis, 1993), 448.

19. Sobrino, *Spirituality of liberation*, 4.
20. Jon Sobrino, *The true church and the poor* (London: SCM, 1985), 270.
21. Sobrino, *The true church and the poor*, 271; Sobrino, *Spirituality of liberation*, 51-52.
22. Boff and Boff, *Liberation theology*, 1.
23. Boff and Boff, *Introducing liberation theology*, 1-2.
24. Cited without source given, in Sobrino, *Spirituality of liberation*, 43-44.
25. Boff, *Jesus Christ liberator*, 64-72.
26. Sobrino, *Spirituality of liberation*, 51.
27. Leonardo Boff, "Images of Jesus in Brazilian liberal Christianity," in *Faces of Jesus: Latin American christologies*, ed. José Míguez Bonino (Maryknoll: Orbis, 1984), 13.
28. Jon Sobrino, "Central position of the reign of God in liberation theology," in *Mysterium Liberationis: Fundamental concepts of liberation theology*, eds. Ignacio Ellacuría and Jon Sobrino (Maryknoll: Orbis, 1993), 378; Sobrino, *Jesus the liberator*, 55.
29. Sobrino, *Christology at the crossroads*, 59.
30. Leonardo Boff, *Liberating grace* (Maryknoll: Orbis, 1979), 3.
31. Boff, *Liberating grace*, 118-119.
32. Boff, *Jesus Christ liberator*, 221.
33. Jon Sobrino, "Spirituality and the following of Jesus," in *Mysterium Liberationis: Fundamental concepts of liberation theology*, eds. Ignacio Ellacuría and Jon Sobrino (Maryknoll: Orbis, 1993), 693; Sobrino, *Christology at the crossroads*, 262-263.
34. Sobrino, *Spirituality of liberation*, 21-22.
35. Sobrino, "Spirituality and the following of Jesus," 680.
36. René Padilla, "Christology and mission in the two thirds world," in *Sharing Jesus in the two-thirds world: Evangelical Christologies from the contexts of poverty, powerlessness and religious pluralism*, eds. Vinay Samuel and Chris Sugden (Grand Rapids: Eerdmans, 1983), 28.
37. Lois, "Christology in the theology of liberation," 173.
38. Leonardo Boff, *Passion of Christ, passion of the world: The facts, their interpretations and their meanings, yesterday and today* (Maryknoll: Orbis, 1988), 11.
39. Boff, *Jesus Christ liberator*, 279; also Boff, *Faith on the edge*, 131-132.
40. Boff, *Jesus Christ liberator*, 37.
41. Boff, *Jesus Christ liberator*, 13, 37.
42. Boff, *Jesus Christ liberator*, 40.
43. James M Dawsey, "The biblical authority of the poor," *The Expository Times* 101 (1990): 295-298.
44. Sobrino, *Christology at the crossroads*, 2-9.
45. Sobrino, *Christology at the crossroads*, 352.

46. Jon Sobrino, *Jesus in Latin America* (Maryknoll: Orbis, 1987), 65-66.
47. John Macquarrie, *Jesus Christ in modern thought* (London: SCM, 1990), 363. Both are indebted to Karl Rahner's transcendental anthropology.
48. Boff, *Jesus Christ liberator*, 194-199; Leonardo Boff, *New evangelization: Good news to the poor* (Maryknoll: Orbis, 1991), 73-74.
49. Leonardo Boff, *The Lord's Prayer: The prayer of integral liberation* (Melbourne: Dove Communications, 1983), 1-3.
50. Boff, "Images of Jesus in Brazilian liberal Christianity," 26.
51. Boff, *Ecology and liberation*, 61.
52. Boff, *The Lord's Prayer*, 2.
53. Boff, *The path to hope*, 63.
54. Boff, *The Lord's Prayer*, 2.
55. Boff, "Images of Jesus in Brazilian liberal Christianity," 27.
56. Boff, *Ecology and liberation*, 150-151. See also Boff, *Jesus Christ liberator*, 266.
57. Boff and Boff, *Liberation theology*, 26.
58. Sobrino, *The true church and the poor*, 150; Sobrino, *Spirituality of liberation*, 136; Jon Sobrino, "Communion, conflict, and ecclesial solidarity," in *Mysterium Liberationis: Fundamental concepts of liberation theology*, eds. Ignacio Ellacuría and Jon Sobrino (Maryknoll: Orbis, 1993), 622.
59. Boff and Boff, *Liberation theology*, 30.
60. Boff and Boff, *Introducing liberation theology*, 44-45.
61. Sobrino, "Communion, conflict, and ecclesial solidarity," 623.
62. Jon Sobrino, "The economics of ecclesia: A poor church is a church rich in compassion," in *New visions for the Americas: Religious engagement and social transformation*, ed. David Batstone (Minneapolis: Fortress, 1993), 93.
63. Sobrino, *Spirituality of liberation*, 136.
64. For example Sobrino, *Jesus the liberator*, 179.
65. Boff, *Jesus Christ liberator*, 272-278.
66. Boff, *Faith on the edge*, 142; Boff, *Jesus Christ liberator*, 59-60.
67. Boff, *Ecology and liberation*, 151.
68. Lois, "Christology in the theology of liberation," 183.
69. Sobrino, *Christology at the crossroads*, 210.
70. Sobrino, *Jesus the liberator*, 244.
71. Sobrino, *Jesus the liberator*, 254, 264.
72. Cited repeatedly by Sobrino. For example Sobrino, *Spirituality of liberation*, 44, 86; Jon Sobrino, *Archbishop Romero: Memories and reflections* (Maryknoll: Orbis, 1990), 38; Sobrino, "Spirituality and the following of Jesus," 695; and Sobrino, "The economics of ecclesia," 85-86.
73. Sobrino, "Spirituality and the following of Jesus," 695; see also Sobrino, "Communion, conflict, and ecclesial solidarity," 625.

74. Leonardo Boff, *When theology listens to the poor* (San Francisco: Harper & Row, 1988), 25-26.
75. Leonardo Boff, *Ecclesiogenesis: The base communities reinvent the church* (London: Collins, 1986), 22.
76. Boff, *Jesus Christ liberator*, 199.
77. Boff, *Jesus Christ liberator*, 205.
78. Boff, *Jesus Christ liberator*, 205.
79. Boff, *Jesus Christ liberator*, 40. Boff does say that in the resurrection the incarnation is complete (201). He seems to mean that in the resurrection Christ's work is done, but the unfolding of its implications continues.
80. Leonardo Boff, *Church, charism and power: Liberation theology and the institutional church* (London: SCM, 1985), 144.
81. Boff, *Church, charism and power*, 147.
82. Boff, *When theology listens to the poor*, 33; see also Boff, *Faith on the edge*, 106.
83. Boff, *Ecclesiogenesis*, 21.
84. Sobrino, "Communion, conflict, and ecclesial solidarity," 620.
85. Boff and Boff, *Introducing liberation theology*, 59; Sobrino, *Spirituality of liberation*, 132.
86. Sobrino, *The true church and the poor*, 270.
87. Sobrino, *Spirituality of liberation*, 139.
88. Boff, *New evangelization*, 75; Juan Ramón Moreno, "Evangelization," in *Mysterium Liberationis: Fundamental concepts of liberation theology*, eds. Ignacio Ellacuría and Jon Sobrino (Maryknoll: Orbis, 1993), 573.
89. Priscilla Pope-Levison, *Evangelization from a liberation perspective* (New York: Peter Lang, 1991), 167.
90. For example Boff, *Ecclesiogenesis*, 18 ("taking flesh"); Boff, *New evangelization*, 36, 71 ("incarnate ... in cultures"); Sobrino, *Spirituality of liberation*, 3 ("incarnation ... in culture and society").
91. Even more frequent than these, but not directly relevant to our study, is the charge that liberation theologians reduce salvation to socio-economic liberation. This charge is only sustainable by ignoring their repeated insistence that salvation is multi-dimensional and contains both historical and eschatological dimensions, e.g. Boff, *Jesus Christ liberator*, 60; Leonardo Boff, *New evangelization*, 77.
92. For example, Michael L Cook, "Jesus from the other side of history: Christology in Latin America," *Theological Studies* 44 (1983): 272-274; Arthur F McGovern, *Liberation theology and its critics: Toward an assessment* (Maryknoll: Orbis, 1989), 75-80; Ched Myers, *Binding the strong man: A political reading of Mark's story of Jesus* (Maryknoll: Orbis, 1988), 464; Russell Pregeant, "Christological groundings for liberation praxis," *Modern Theology* 5 (1989): 115-116; Fernando Segovia, "A response to Fr.

Sobrino," in *Theology and discovery: Essays in honor of Karl Rahner, S.J.*, ed. William J Kelly (Milwaukee, WI: Marquette University Press, 1980), 223.

93. Sobrino, *Christology at the crossroads*, 91-95, 365.

94. Myers, *Binding the strong man*, 465; see also Cook, "Jesus from the other side of history," 273.

95. Sobrino, *Christology at the crossroads*, 322-323.

96. Boff, *Jesus Christ liberator*, 37. An example of a New Testament scholar who is sceptical of our ability to uncover the historical Jesus but still assumes a "reliable continuity" between Jesus and the Synoptic Gospels is Myers, *Binding the strong man*, 21-31.

97. Sobrino, *Jesus the liberator*, 45, 50, 51.

98. Todd Saliba Speidell, "The incarnation as the hermeneutical criterion for liberation and reconciliation," *Scottish Journal of Theology* 40 (1987): 252.

99. Boff, *Jesus Christ liberator*, 221.

100. Sobrino, "Spirituality and the following of Jesus," 693; Sobrino, *Christology at the crossroads*, 262-263.

101. Ignacio Ellacuría, *Freedom made flesh: The mission of Christ and his church* (Maryknoll: Orbis, 1976), 132, 140.

102. Ferm, *Profiles in liberation*, 107-111; Choan-Seng Song, *Christian mission in reconstruction: An Asian analysis* (Maryknoll: Orbis, 1977), cover notes; Choan-Seng Song, *Jesus and the reign of God* (Minneapolis: Fortress, 1993), cover notes.

103. Choan-Seng Song, *Third-eye theology: Theology in formation in Asian settings*, 2nd ed. (Maryknoll: Orbis, 1990); Choan-Seng Song, *Tell us our names: Story theology from an Asian perspective* (Maryknoll: Orbis, 1979).

104. The three volumes are: Choan-Seng Song, *Jesus, the crucified people* (New York: Crossroad, 1990), see xi for details of the trilogy; Choan-Seng Song, *Jesus and the reign of God* (Minneapolis: Fortress, 1993); Choan-Seng Song, *Jesus in the power of the Spirit* (Minneapolis: Fortress, 1994).

105. Choan-Seng Song, "Taiwan: Theology of the incarnation," in *Asian voices in Christian theology*, ed. Gerald H Anderson (Maryknoll: Orbis, 1976), 147-160; Song, *Christian mission in reconstruction*.

106. Song, *Christian mission in reconstruction*, 51, 272; Song, "Taiwan: Theology of the incarnation," 156.

107. Song, *Christian mission in reconstruction*, 71.

108. Song, *Christian mission in reconstruction*, chap. 2, 51-82. He refers to the Prologue in John's Gospel, making the same point, also in Song, *Jesus, the crucified people*, x; Song, *Third-eye theology*, 112; Song, *Jesus and the reign of God*, 78; C S Song, "Jesus Christ—The life of the world—An Asian meditation," *East Asia Journal of Theology* 1 (1983): 119.

109. Song, *Christian mission in reconstruction*, 51-52.

110. Song, *Christian mission in reconstruction*, 53.

111. Song, *Christian mission in reconstruction*, 53.
112. Song, "Taiwan: Theology of the incarnation," 156.
113. Song, "Taiwan: Theology of the incarnation," 156, 158; Song, *Christian mission in reconstruction*, 217.
114. Song, *Christian mission in reconstruction*, 158.
115. Song, *Christian mission in reconstruction*, 53.
116. Song, *Christian mission in reconstruction*, 54.
117. Song, *Christian mission in reconstruction*, 55.
118. Song, *Christian mission in reconstruction*, 66, 72-76.
119. Song, *Christian mission in reconstruction*, 76; see Dietrich Bonhoeffer, *Letters and papers from prison*, ed. Eberhard Bethge, Enlarged ed. (London: SCM, 1971), 382-383.
120. Song, *Christian mission in reconstruction*, 30, 56-57, 64-65.
121. Song, *Christian mission in reconstruction*, 57.
122. Song, *Christian mission in reconstruction*, 57-60.
123. Song, *Christian mission in reconstruction*, 86.
124. Song, *Christian mission in reconstruction*, 83.
125. Song, *Christian mission in reconstruction*, 100.
126. Song, *Christian mission in reconstruction*, 87.
127. Song, *Christian mission in reconstruction*, 87.
128. Song, *Christian mission in reconstruction*, 215-222.
129. Song, *Christian mission in reconstruction*, 219-221.
130. Song, *Third-eye theology*, 218.
131. Song, *Christian mission in reconstruction*, 219-221.
132. Song, *Jesus, the crucified people*, 31,122. See Jürgen Moltmann, *The crucified God: The cross of Christ as the foundation and criticism of Christian theology* (London: SCM, 1974).
133. Song, *Jesus, the crucified people*, 169.
134. Shusaka Endo, *The samurai* (New York: Vintage Books, 1982).
135. Endo, *The samurai*, 122; quoted in Song, *Jesus, the crucified people*, 221.
136. Song, *Jesus, the crucified people*, 223.
137. Song, *Jesus, the crucified people*, 215.
138. Song, *Jesus and the reign of God*, 9.
139. Song, *Third-eye theology*, 182
140. Song, *Jesus, the crucified people*, x. Song has put the three parts of John 1:14, one by one, on the inner cover of each of the three parts of his trilogy *The cross in the lotus world*.
141. See p. 124 above.

Chapter 7

1.   Richard Bauckham, "Jürgen Moltmann," in *The modern theologians: An introduction to Christian theology in the twentieth century*, ed. David F Ford,

2nd ed. (Oxford: Blackwell, 1997), 209-210; Christopher Morse, "Jürgen Moltmann," in *A handbook of Christian theologians*, eds. Martin E Marty and Dean G Peerman, Enlarged ed., (Nashville: Abingdon, 1984), 661. See also Roger E Olson, "Is Moltmann the evangelicals' ally?," *Christianity Today* 37 (11 Jan 1993): 32.

2. Jürgen Moltmann, *Theology of hope: On the ground and the implications of a Christian eschatology* (London: SCM, 1967); Jürgen Moltmann, *The crucified God: The cross of Christ as the foundation and criticism of Christian theology* (London: SCM, 1974); Jürgen Moltmann, *The church in the power of the Spirit: A contribution to messianic ecclesiology* (London: SCM, 1977).

3. Jürgen Moltmann, *The trinity and the kingdom of God: The doctrine of God* (London: SCM, 1981), xi.

4. Moltmann, *The trinity and the kingdom of God*, xi.

5. Jürgen Moltmann, *The trinity and the kingdom: The doctrine of God* (Minneapolis: Fortress, 1993), first published in English in 1981 (London: SCM); Jürgen Moltmann, *God in creation: An ecological doctrine of creation* (London: SCM, 1985); Jürgen Moltmann, *The way of Jesus Christ: Christology in messianic dimensions* (London: SCM, 1990); Jürgen Moltmann, *The Spirit of life: A universal affirmation* (London: SCM, 1992); and Jürgen Moltmann, *The coming of God: Christian eschatology* (London: SCM, 1996).

6. Don Schweitzer, "The consistency of Jürgen Moltmann's theology," *Studies in Religion/Sciences Religieuses* 22 (1993): 197-208; Morse, "Jürgen Moltmann," 663.

7. Particularly *The way of Jesus Christ* and *The church in the power of the Spirit*.

8. Moltmann, *Theology of hope,* 95-138.

9. Moltmann, *Theology of hope,* 17.

10. Moltmann, *Theology of hope,* 16.

11. For example Moltmann, *The way of Jesus Christ,* xiii.

12. Bauckham, "Jürgen Moltmann," 300.

13. Moltmann, *The crucified God,* 200-219.

14. Moltmann, *The crucified God,* 2, 24, 204.

15. Moltmann, *The crucified God,* 200-290.

16. Jürgen Moltmann, *The trinity and the kingdom: The doctrine of God* (Minneapolis: Fortress, 1993), 64, 75.

17. Moltmann, *The trinity and the kingdom,* 157.

18. Moltmann, *The trinity and the kingdom,* viii-ix; Richard J Bauckham, "Moltmann's messianic christology," *Scottish Journal of Theology* 44 (1991): 520-522.

19. Moltmann, *The way of Jesus Christ,* 272.

20. Moltmann, *The way of Jesus Christ*, xiii.
21. Moltmann, *The crucified God*, 5; Morse, "Jürgen Moltmann," 668.
22. Moltmann, *The crucified God*, 325-329, 338 note 1; Moltmann, *The church in the power of the Spirit*, 16.
23. Moltmann, *Theology of hope*, 19.
24. Moltmann, *Theology of hope*, 21-22.
25. Moltmann, *Theology of hope*, 225.
26. Moltmann, *The church in the power of the Spirit*, 10.
27. Moltmann, *The church in the power of the Spirit*, 75.
28. Moltmann, *The church in the power of the Spirit*, 5; Jürgen Moltmann, *The future of creation* (London: SCM, 1979), 106.
29. Moltmann, *The church in the power of the Spirit*, 6.
30. Moltmann, *The church in the power of the Spirit*, 11.
31. Moltmann, *The church in the power of the Spirit*, 76.
32. Moltmann, *The church in the power of the Spirit*, 93.
33. Moltmann, *The church in the power of the Spirit*, 98.
34. Moltmann, *The church in the power of the Spirit*, 104.
35. Moltmann, *The church in the power of the Spirit*, 108-114; Moltmann, *The future of creation*, 107; Jürgen Moltmann, *The open church: Invitation to a messianic lifestyle* (London: SCM, 1978), 64-81.
36. Moltmann, *The church in the power of the Spirit*, 109.
37. Moltmann, *The church in the power of the Spirit*, 114-121; Moltmann, *The open church*, 50-63.
38. See p. 67 above.
39. Moltmann, *The church in the power of the Spirit*, 123-132.
40. Moltmann, *The church in the power of the Spirit*, 123.
41. Moltmann, *The church in the power of the Spirit*, 132.
42. Moltmann, *The church in the power of the Spirit*, 132.
43. Moltmann, *The church in the power of the Spirit*, 132.
44. Moltmann, *The church in the power of the Spirit*, 6, 10, 20, 35.
45. Moltmann, *God in creation*, 226.
46. Moltmann, *God in creation*, 227.
47. Moltmann, *God in creation*, 227.
48. Moltmann, *God in creation*, 245.
49. Moltmann, *God in creation*, 245-246.
50. Moltmann, *The way of Jesus Christ*, 260-261.
51. Moltmann, *God in creation*, 246.
52. Moltmann, *The way of Jesus Christ*, xiv.
53. Moltmann uses christopraxis as a synonym for discipleship, and compares its use to the way in which liberation theologians advocate orthopraxis over orthodoxy, differing, however, in that he does not give christopraxis priority over christology. Moltmann, *The way of Jesus Christ*, 41, 348 note 6.

54. Moltmann, *The way of Jesus Christ*, 42.
55. Moltmann, *The way of Jesus Christ*, 42-43.
56. Moltmann, *The way of Jesus Christ*, 43.
57. For this see William C Spohn, *What are they saying about scripture and ethics?* (New York: Paulist, 1984).
58. Moltmann, *The way of Jesus Christ*, 118.
59. Moltmann, *The way of Jesus Christ*, 118, 357 note 66.
60. Moltmann, *The way of Jesus Christ*, 118-119.
61. Moltmann, *The church in the power of the Spirit*, 20.
62. Moltmann, *The trinity and the kingdom*, viii-ix. See for example Moltmann, *The church in the power of the Spirit*, 20, and Moltmann, *The Spirit of life*, 9-10.
63. I owe this insight to a conversation with Frank Rees.
64. Bauckham, "Moltmann's messianic christology," 527.
65. Richard John Neuhaus, "Moltmann vs. monotheism," *Dialog* 20 (1981): 239-243; Olson, "Is Moltmann the evangelicals' ally?," 32; Ted Peters, "Trinity Talk: Part 1," *Dialog* 26 (1987): 46; J P Mackey, "Doctrine of the Trinity," in *A new dictionary of Christian theology*, eds. Alan Richardson and John Bowden (London: SCM, 1983), 588.
66. Moltmann, *The trinity and the kingdom*, viii.
67. Peters, "Trinity Talk: Part 1," 46.
68. Moltmann, *The trinity and the kingdom*, 149-150.
69. Moltmann, *The trinity and the kingdom*, 144.
70. William C Placher, *Narratives of a vulnerable God: Christ, theology and scripture* (Louisville, KY: Westminster John Knox, 1994), 67-73. A similar explanation of divine perichoresis, or mutual indwelling, is given by Daniel L Migliore, *Faith seeking understanding: An introduction to Christian theology* (Grand Rapids: Eerdmans, 1991), 70.
71. Colin Gunton, *The one, the three and the many: God, creation and the culture of modernity* (Cambridge: Cambridge University Press, 1993), 210-231.
72. Catherine Mowry Lacugna, *God for us: The trinity and Christian life* (San Francisco: Harper, 1991), 243-250.
73. Wolfhart Pannenberg, *Systematic theology*, vol. 1 (Grand Rapids: Eerdmans, 1991), 300-336.
74. Leonardo Boff, *Trinity and society* (Tunbridge Wells, UK: Burns & Oates, 1988), 118-120.
75. Cornelius Plantinga, Jr, "Social trinity and tritheism," in *Trinity, incarnation and atonement: Philosophical and theological essays*, eds. Ronald J Feenstra and Cornelius Plantinga, Jr (Notre Dame: University of Notre Dame Press, 1989), 21-47; Cornelius Plantinga, Jr, "Gregory of Nyssa and the social analogy of the trinity," *The Thomist* 50 (1986): 325-352.

76. David Brown, *The divine trinity* (London: Duckworth, 1985), 272-301.
77. Migliore, *Faith seeking understanding*, 66-72.
78. John L Gresham, Jr, "The social model of the trinity and its critics," *Scottish Journal of Theology* 46 (1993): 342-343.
79. Moltmann, *The crucified God*, 25.
80. Moltmann, *The crucified God*, 25.
81. Moltmann, *The church in the power of the Spirit*, 116-118.
82. Moltmann, *The church in the power of the Spirit*, 120-121.
83. Moltmann, *The open church*, 60-63.
84. Moltmann, *God in creation*, 8-19.
85. Moltmann, *The trinity and the kingdom*, ix; Moltmann, *God in creation*, xii; Moltmann, *The way of Jesus Christ*, 119; Moltmann, *The Spirit of life*, xii.
86. Moltmann, *The way of Jesus Christ*, 119.
87. Moltmann, *The church in the power of the Spirit*, 224-225, 314-317.
88. Morse, "Jürgen Moltmann," 673. See also Richard J Bauckham, *Moltmann: Messianic theology in the making* (Basingstoke, UK: Marshall Morgan and Scott, 1987), 45.
89. See p. 67 above.
90. Moltmann, *The church in the power of the Spirit*, 73.
91. Moltmann, *The church in the power of the Spirit*, 124.
92. Moltmann, *The church in the power of the Spirit*, 124.
93. Pius XII, *Mystici Corporis Christi* (London: Catholic Truth Society, 1944), #51, p. 32.; cited in Moltmann, *The church in the power of the Spirit*, 72.
94. Moltmann, *The church in the power of the Spirit*, 72.
95. Moltmann, *The church in the power of the Spirit*, 72.
96. Bauckham, "Jürgen Moltmann," 307.
97. Morse, "Jürgen Moltmann," 675.
98. Bauckham, "Jürgen Moltmann," 308.
99. John Macquarrie, "Today's word for today: I. Jürgen Moltmann," *Expository Times* 92 (Oct 1980): 5; Richard Bauckham, *The theology of Jürgen Moltmann* (Edinburgh: T & T Clark, 1995), 25.
100. Macquarrie, "Today's word for today," 5.
101. Peters, "Trinity Talk: Part 1," 46.
102. Macquarrie, "Today's word for today," 6.
103. This covers six of the seven requirements, ignoring "Christology from above and below" ; we have already noted his rejection of these terms.
104. Moltmann, *God in creation*, 245-246.
105. Moltmann, *The way of Jesus Christ*, 41.
106. Moltmann, *The way of Jesus Christ*, xiv.
107. Moltmann, *The way of Jesus Christ*, 119.

Chapter 8

1. We readily acknowledge that in three of the four traditions grouped here under the third dimension of incarnational mission (Roman Catholicism, Anglo-Catholicism and Eastern Orthodoxy) the idea of the church as the continuation of the incarnation is very strong. We noted in chapter 3 that this notion sits halfway between the second and third dimensions anyway.
2. The term "catholic" (with a lower-case "c") refers to a property of the true church, its universality or catholicity, its extension through all the world. Timothy G McCarthy, *The Catholic tradition: Before and after Vatican II, 1878-1993* (Chicago: Loyola University Press, 1994), 91.
3. Richard McBrien, *Catholicism*, 3rd ed. (Nth Blackburn, Vic.: CollinsDove, 1994), 5.
4. McBrien, *Catholicism*, 9.
5. McBrien, *Catholicism*, 12.
6. McBrien, *Catholicism*, 13.
7. McBrien, *Catholicism*, 10. See p. 179 below.
8. Mary Motte, "Issues in Protestant-Roman Catholic discussions of theology of mission," in *The good news of the kingdom: Mission theology for the third millennium*, eds. Charles Van Engen, Dean S Gilliland, and Paul Pierson (Maryknoll: Orbis, 1993), 120.
9. Avery Dulles, "The meaning of Catholicism: Adventures of an idea," in *The reshaping of Catholicism: Current challenges in the theology of church* (San Francisco: Harper & Row, 1988), 51-74.
10. Johann Adam Möhler, *Symbolism; or, Exposition of the doctrinal differences between Catholics and Protestants as evidenced by their symbolic writings* (New York: E Dunigan, 1844), 333; cited in Dulles, "The meaning of Catholicism," 60.
11. James A Scherer, *Gospel, church and kingdom: Comparative studies in world mission theology* (Minneapolis: Augsburg, 1987), 196.
12. Marie-Joseph Le Guillou, "Mission as an ecclesiological theme," *Concilium* No. 13: 44.
13. Le Guillou, "Mission as an ecclesiological theme," 44.
14. Jean Daniélou, *Christ and us* (London: Mowbray, 1961), 157.
15. Jean Daniélou, *The salvation of the nations* (Notre Dame: University of Notre Dame Press, 1962), 59.
16. Daniélou, *Christ and us*, 207.
17. Daniélou, *Christ and us*, 208.
18. Daniélou, *Christ and us*, 164.
19. Daniélou, *Christ and us*, 182, 206.
20. Daniélou, *Christ and us*, 235-236.

21. "Lumen Gentium (Dogmatic Constitution on the Church)," in *The documents of Vatican II*, ed. Walter M Abbott (London: Geoffrey Chapman, 1966), #7, p. 22, abbreviated as LG#7.

22. Jean Daniélou, *The salvation of the nations* (Notre Dame: University of Notre Dame Press, 1962). First published in French in 1949. See a good summary of it in Charles L Chaney, "An introduction to the missionary thought of Jean Daniélou," *Occasional Bulletin from the Missionary Research Library* 17.5 (May 1966): 1-10.

23. Jean Daniélou, *The Lord of history: Reflections on the inner meaning of history* (London: Longmans, 1958), 44.

24. Daniélou, *The salvation of the nations*, 47-48.

25. Daniélou, *The salvation of the nations*, 48-49.

26. Daniélou, *The salvation of the nations*, 65.

27. Daniélou, *The salvation of the nations*, 50.

28. Daniélou, *The salvation of the nations*, 60, 62.

29. Daniélou, *The salvation of the nations*, 59-60.

30. Daniélou, *The salvation of the nations*, 54, 58, 59.

31. Daniélou, *The salvation of the nations*, 50-52.

32. Daniélou, *The salvation of the nations*, 52.

33. See pp. 26-27 above.

34. Daniélou, *The salvation of the nations*, 55.

35. Aidan Nichols, *Yves Congar* (London: Geoffrey Chapman, 1989), 7-8.

36. Yves Congar, "Reflections on being a theologian," *New Blackfriars* 62.736 (1981): 409; cited in Nichols, *Yves Congar*, 8.

37. Found, amongst other places, in Walter M Abbott, ed., *The documents of Vatican II* (London: Geoffrey Chapman, 1966), at pp. 14-101, 199-308, and 584-630 respectively. Referred to in the text hereafter by abbreviation and followed by document section numbers, e.g. GS#12.

38. Some of the headings are adapted from some of those used in David J Bosch, *Transforming mission: Paradigm shifts in theology of mission* (Maryknoll: Orbis, 1991), 372-380.

39. Bosch, *Transforming mission*, 372.

40. W Richey Hogg, "Vatican II's *Ad Gentes*: A twenty-year retrospective," *International Bulletin of Missionary Research* 9 (1985): 152.

41. Eugene L Smith, "A response [to *Ad Gentes*]," in *The documents of Vatican II*, ed. Walter M Abbott (London: Geoffrey Chapman, 1966), 631.

42. Thomas F Stransky, "From Vatican II to *Redemptoris Missio*: A development in the theology of mission," in *The good news of the kingdom: Mission theology for the third millennium*, eds. Charles Van Engen, Dean S Gilliland, and Paul Pierson (Maryknoll: Orbis, 1993), 137.

43. Bosch, *Transforming mission*, 373, citing the view of Robrecht Michiels.

44. Abbott, ed., *The documents of Vatican II*, 24 note 27. The image is taken up in the opening paragraphs of *Gaudium et Spes* (GS#3) in order to echo the advances made in *Lumen Gentium*. See also its use in GS#11.

45. "Unitatis Redintegratio (Decree on Ecumenism)," in *The documents of Vatican II*, ed. Walter M Abbott (London: Geoffrey Chapman, 1966), #6, p. 350.

46. Bosch, *Transforming mission*, 374.

47. See p. 162 above.

48. See p. 179 below.

49. Avery Dulles, "The basic teaching of Vatican II," in *The reshaping of Catholicism: Current challenges in the theology of church*, by Avery Dulles (San Francisco: Harper & Row, 1988), 29; Walbert Bühlmann, *With eyes to see: Church and world in the third millennium* (Maryknoll: Orbis, 1990), 10-11; Aylward Shorter, *Toward a theology of inculturation* (Maryknoll: Orbis, 1988), 197, 270.

50. See pp. 186, 189 below.

51. Dulles, "The basic teaching of Vatican II," 19-33.

52. Robert J Schreiter, "Changes in Roman Catholic attitudes toward proselytism and mission," in *New directions in mission and evangelization, 2: Theological foundations*, eds. James A Scherer and Stephen B Bevans (Maryknoll: Orbis, 1994), 117.

53. Synod of Bishops Third General Assembly (October 26 1974), "Evangelization of the modern world," in *The gospel of peace and justice: Catholic social teaching since Pope John*, ed. Joseph Gremillion (Maryknoll: Orbis, 1976), 593-598.

54. Pope Paul VI, *Evangelii Nuntiandi [On evangelization in the modern world]* (Homebush, NSW: Society of St Paul, 1976). Hereafter abbreviated as EN.

55. See SEDOS, ed., *Foundations of mission theology* (Maryknoll: Orbis, 1972); and Mary Motte and Joseph R Lang, eds., *Mission in dialogue: The SEDOS research seminar on the future of mission, March 8-19, 1981, Rome, Italy* (Maryknoll: Orbis, 1982). Also William Jenkinson and Helen O'Sullivan, eds., *Trends in mission: Toward the third millennium. Essays in celebration of twenty-five years of SEDOS* (Maryknoll: Orbis, 1991).

56. Latin American Episcopal Council (CELAM), *Medellín, 1968: The church in the present day transformation of Latin America*, 2 vols. (Washington, DC: U.S. Catholic Conference, 1968); Third General Conference of Latin American Bishops, *Puebla: Evangelization at present and in the future of Latin America. Conclusions* (Middlegreen, UK: St Paul Publications, 1980).

57. *Common witness: A study document of the joint working group of the Roman Catholic Church and the World Council of Churches* (Geneva: World Council of Churches, 1981).

58. John Paul II, *Redemptoris Missio: The permanent validity of the church's missionary mandate* (Homebush, NSW: St Paul Publications, 1991). Hereafter abbreviated as RM.

59. Gerald A Arbuckle, *Earthing the gospel: An inculturation handbook for the pastoral worker* (Maryknoll: Orbis, 1990), 17; Shorter, *Toward a theology of inculturation*, 11.

60. Shorter, *Toward a theology of inculturation*, 13-14.

61. Aloysius Pieris, "The problem of universality and inculturation with regard to patterns of theological thinking," *Concilium* (6 1994): 70.

62. Enda McDonagh, "The missionary task after Vatican II," in *The church is mission*, eds. Enda McDonagh et al. (London: Geoffrey Chapman, 1969), 17.

63. "Agenda for future planning, study, and research in mission [from the SEDOS Research Seminar on the Future of Mission, Rome, March 1981]," in *Trends in mission: Toward the third millennium. Essays in celebration of twenty-five years of SEDOS*, eds. William Jenkinson and Helen O'Sullivan (Maryknoll: Orbis, 1991), #29, p. 404.

64. Avery Dulles, *The dimensions of the church: A postconciliar reflection* (Westminster, MD: Newman Press, 1967), 52.

65. Johannes Schütte, "Why engage in missionary work?," in *Foundations of mission theology*, ed. SEDOS (Maryknoll: Orbis, 1972), 45.

66. Cited in Shorter, *Toward a theology of inculturation*, 211.

67. Cited in Shorter, *Toward a theology of inculturation*, 247.

68. Walbert Bühlmann, *The coming of the Third Church: An analysis of the present and future of the Church* (Slough, UK: St Paul Publications, 1976), 287; Walbert Bühlmann, "My pilgrimage in mission," *International Bulletin of Missionary Research* 10 (1986): 99.

69. Third General Conference of Latin American Bishops, *Puebla*, #400, p. 93.

70. Donal Dorr, "New challenges—new hopes," in *A new missionary era*, ed. Padraig Flanagan (Maryknoll: Orbis, 1982), 14.

71. Anthony J Gittins, *Gifts and strangers: Meeting the challenge of inculturation* (New York: Paulist, 1989), x, 49.

72. Robert Hardawiryana, "Mission in Asia: Theological perspectives," in *Towards an Asian theology of mission*, eds. Michael T Seigel and Leonardo N Mercado (Manila: Divine Word Publications, 1995), 24, 45.

73. Shorter, *Toward a theology of inculturation*, 79.

74. Shorter, *Toward a theology of inculturation*, 81-82; Aylward Shorter, *Evangelization and culture* (London: Geoffrey Chapman, 1994), 35.

75. Shorter, *Toward a theology of inculturation*, 82-87; Aylward Shorter, *Revelation and its interpretation* (London: Geoffrey Chapman, 1983), 248; Shorter, *Evangelization and culture*, 35-36.

76. Shorter, *Toward a theology of inculturation*, 81-82.

77. See pp. 17-19 above.

78. See p. 165 above.
79. Shorter, *Revelation and its interpretation*, 248; Shorter, *Evangelization and culture*, 35.
80. Shorter, *Toward a theology of inculturation*, 82.
81. Shorter, *Revelation and its interpretation*, 233-234.
82. James H Kroeger, "Sent to witness—with enthusiasm," *African Ecclesial Review* 33 (1991): 290; Aloysius Pieris, "Whither new evangelism?," *Pacifica* 6 (1993): 328.
83. Hardawiryana, "Mission in Asia: Theological perspectives," 45.
84. Barbara Hendricks, "Mission in service of God's reign," in *Mission in the nineteen 90s*, eds. Gerald H Anderson, James M Phillips, and Robert T Coote (Grand Rapids: Eerdmans, 1991), 28.
85. Bernard J Lonergan, *Method in theology* (London: Darton, Longman & Todd, 1972), 73.
86. Lonergan, *Method in theology*, 362.
87. Avery Dulles, *Models of the church*, 2nd ed. (New York: Image, 1987), 222, 224.
88. Schütte, "Why engage in missionary work?," 45.
89. Gittins, *Gifts and strangers*, ix.
90. Jacob Kavunkal, "Ministry and mission," in *New directions in mission and evangelization, 2: Theological foundations*, eds. James A Scherer and Stephen B Bevans (Maryknoll: Orbis, 1994), 92-94.
91. Third General Conference of Latin American Bishops, *Puebla*, #1134, p. 178.
92. See our discussion of liberation theology's treatment of Good News to the poor in chap. 6 (p. 125).
93. Third General Conference of Latin American Bishops, *Puebla*, #192-193, p. 61.
94. Mary Motte, "The poor: Starting point for mission," in *Mission in the 1990s*, eds. Gerald H Anderson, James M Phillips, and Robert T Coote (Grand Rapids: Eerdmans, 1991), 52; see similarly Maria Arlinda Rodriguez, "Living with the poor in Brazil: 1. 'Insertion': A new way of being a religious missionary," in *Trends in mission: Toward the third millennium*, eds. William Jenkinson and Helen O'Sullivan (Maryknoll: Orbis, 1991), 216-220.
95. Joachim G Piepke, "Incarnation in cultural context," *Indian Missiological Review* 12 (1990): 48-49; Robert J Schreiter, "Mission into the third millennium," *Missiology* 18 (1990): 7; Andrew Hamilton, "What has Asia to do with Australia: Reflections on the theology of Aloysius Pieris," *Pacifica* 3 (1990): 310 (summarizing Pieris' view); Pieris, "Whither new evangelism?," 333.
96. Jon Sobrino, *The true church and the poor* (London: SCM, 1985), 150.
97. Pieris, "Whither new evangelism?," 333.
98. McBrien, *Catholicism*, 9-10.

99. Baptism, Confirmation, Eucharist, Penance, Marriage, Holy Orders, and the Anointing of the Sick (McBrien, *Catholicism*, 1250).

100. Anselm Prior, "Equipping the people of God for Christian witness—A Roman Catholic account," *International Review of Mission* 83 (1994): 58; McBrien, *Catholicism*, 10; Dulles, *Models of the church*, 68.

101. Henri de Lubac, *Catholicism* (London: Burns & Oates, 1950), 29; Dulles, *Models of the church*, 63; Prior, "Equipping the people of God for Christian witness," 58.

102. Edward Schillebeeckx, *Christ the sacrament of the encounter with God* (New York: Sheed & Ward, 1963).

103. For example, LG#9, #48, AG#5, GS#42. Timothy McCarthy calls it a major theme of Vatican II (McCarthy, *The Catholic tradition*, 98).

104. See p. 169 above.

105. McBrien, *Catholicism*, 13.

106. Prior, "Equipping the people of God for Christian witness," 69.

107. McCarthy, *The Catholic tradition*, 87.

108. Dulles, *Models of the church*, 68.

109. McCarthy, *The Catholic tradition*, 89; McBrien, *Catholicism*, 10.

110. Dulles, *Models of the church*, 74-75.

111. Dulles, *Models of the church*, 28.

112. Charles Gore, ed., *Lux Mundi: A series of studies in the religion of the incarnation*, 15th ed. (London: John Murray, 1904 (1889)).

113. For example, Alister E McGrath, "Anglicanism," in *The Blackwell Encyclopedia of modern Christian thought*, ed. Alister E McGrath (Oxford: Blackwell, 1993), 4; G P Mellick Belshaw, "The religion of the incarnation," *Anglican Theological Review* 76 (1994): 432.

114. H D Weidner, "Editor's introduction," in John Henry Newman, *The via media of the Anglican church* [1889 ed.], ed. H D Weidner (Oxford: Clarendon Press, 1990), xv; Bernard M G Reardon, *From Coleridge to Gore: A century of religious thought in Britain* (London: Longman, 1971), 455.

115. McGrath, "Anglicanism," 3.

116. Owen Chadwick, *The Victorian church: Part Two, 1860-1901*, 2nd ed. (London: SCM, 1987), 2.

117. Reardon, *From Coleridge to Gore*, 433.

118. Trevor Williams, "Protestant theology: Britain," in *The Blackwell Encyclopedia of Modern Christian Thought*, ed. Alister E McGrath (Oxford: Blackwell, 1993), 483. See also Reardon, *From Coleridge to Gore*, 430.

119. Geoffrey Rowell, "Historical retrospect: Lux Mundi 1889," in *The religion of the incarnation: Anglican essays in commemoration of Lux Mundi*, ed. Robert Morgan (Bristol: Bristol Classical Press, 1989), 216.

120. George Carey, "Revitalizing the Catholic tradition," in *Living tradition: Affirming Catholicism in the Anglican church*, ed. Jeffrey John (London: Darton, Longman and Todd, 1992), 17-28; W S F Pickering, *Anglo-Catholicism: A study in religious ambiguity* (London: SPCK, 1989), 17-26, 121-123.

121. Williams, "Protestant theology: Britain," 483. He distinguishes three types of immanentist theology: incarnationalism, immanentalism and mysticism (482).

122. Aidan Nichols, *The panther and the hind: A theological history of Anglicanism* (Edinburgh: T & T Clark, 1993), 137.

123. Aubrey Moore, "The Christian doctrine of God," in *Lux Mundi: A series of studies in the religion of the incarnation*, ed. Charles Gore, 15th ed. (London: John Murray, 1904), 76.

124. Cited without locating it, in J R Illingworth, "The incarnation and development," in *Lux Mundi: A series of studies in the religion of the incarnation*, ed. Charles Gore, 15th ed. (London: John Murray, 1904), 136.

125. Alisdair Heron, "The person of Christ," in *Keeping the faith: Essays to mark the centenary of Lux Mundi*, ed. Geoffrey Wainwright (Philadelphia: Fortress, 1988), 99.

126. For example, Arthur Lyttleton, "The atonement," in *Lux Mundi: A series of studies in the religion of the incarnation*, ed. Charles Gore, 15th ed. (London: John Murray, 1904), 201, 226; Reardon, *From Coleridge to Gore*, 433.

127. Belshaw, "The religion of the incarnation," 437; Heron, "The person of Christ," 122; Nichols, *The panther and the hind*, 137; Williams, "Protestant theology: Britain," 483. Possible exceptions to this neglect are Lyttleton, "The atonement," 228; and Charles Gore, "The Holy Spirit and inspiration," in *Lux Mundi: A series of studies in the religion of the incarnation*, ed. Charles Gore, 15th ed. (London: John Murray, 1904), 234.

128. Heron, "The person of Christ," 122-123.

129. Illingworth, "The incarnation and development," 155.

130. Cited without source, in Carey, "Revitalizing the Catholic tradition," 19.

131. J K Mozley, *The doctrine of the incarnation* (London: The Unicorn Press, 1936), 166.

132. Mozley, *The doctrine of the incarnation*, 161.

133. Pickering, *Anglo-Catholicism*, 121.

134. W J H Campion, "Christianity and politics," in *Lux Mundi: A series of studies in the religion of the incarnation*, ed. Charles Gore, 15th ed. (London: John Murray, 1904), 338.

135. Robert Ottley, "Christian ethics," in *Lux Mundi: A series of studies in the religion of the incarnation*, ed. Charles Gore, 15th ed. (London: John Murray, 1904), 380.

136. Campion, "Christianity and politics," 323, 325, 334, 336.

137. See for example, the work of Trevor Huddleston in Africa. Trevor Huddleston, *Naught for your comfort* (London: Collins, 1956); Deborah Duncan Honoré, ed. *Trevor Huddleston: Essays on his life and work* (Oxford: Oxford University Press, 1988).

138. Charles Gore, *The incarnation of the Son of God* (London: John Murray, 1891), 203-206, 211-212.

139. Belshaw, "The religion of the incarnation," 432-443.

140. Belshaw, "The religion of the incarnation," 433.

141. Belshaw, "The religion of the incarnation," 443.

142. Belshaw, "The religion of the incarnation," 443.

143. McGrath, "Anglicanism," 4; Pickering, *Anglo-Catholicism*, 134.

144. Duncan Forrester, "Christianity and politics," in *Keeping the faith: Essays to mark the centenary of Lux Mundi*, ed. Geoffrey Wainwright (Philadelphia: Fortress, 1988), 250. David Nicholls goes further and charges the *Lux Mundi* group with being naïve and failing to see how much they were part of the establishment. David Nicholls, "Christianity and politics," in *The religion of the incarnation: Anglican essays in commemoration of Lux Mundi*, ed. Robert Morgan (Bristol: Bristol Classical Press, 1989), 172-188.

145. Illingworth, "The incarnation and development," 155.

146. H Richard Niebuhr, *Christ and culture* (New York: Harper, 1951), 115.

147. Niebuhr, *Christ and culture*, 110.

148. Illingworth, "The incarnation and development," 155.

149. Gore, *The incarnation of the Son of God*, 219. An even stronger view is found in W Lock, "The church," in *Lux Mundi: A series of studies in the religion of the incarnation*, ed. Charles Gore, 15th ed. (London: John Murray, 1904), 289. See similar views in George S Hendry, *The gospel of the incarnation* (London: SCM, 1959), 153.

150. Bosch, *Transforming mission*, 500.

151. Carl Braaten, *The flaming center: A theology of the Christian mission* (Philadelphia: Fortress, 1977), 50.

152. See p. 147 above.

Chapter 9

1. Nicholas Lossky, "Orthodoxy," "Eastern Orthodoxy," and "Oriental Orthodox churches," in *Dictionary of the ecumenical movement*, eds. Nicholas Lossky et al. (Geneva: World Council of Churches, 1991), 764-768, 311-313, 755-757.

2. Lossky, "Eastern Orthodoxy," 312.

3. Jean Stromberg, ed., *Mission and evangelism: An ecumenical affirmation* (New York: National Council of the Churches of Christ in the USA (NCCC), 1982); appearing also in *International Review of Mission* 71 (1982): 427-451;

and in *New directions in mission and evangelization, 1: Basic statements, 1974-1991*, eds. James A Scherer and Stephen B Bevans (Maryknoll: Orbis, 1992), 36-51. Frederick R Wilson, ed., *The San Antonio Report: Your will be done: Mission in Christ's way* (Geneva: World Council of Churches, 1990).

4. Darrell L Guder, "Incarnation and the church's evangelistic mission," *International Review of Mission* 83 (1994): 417.

5. David J Bosch, *Transforming mission: Paradigm shifts in theology of mission* (Maryknoll: Orbis, 1991), 390.

6. The predecessor of the CWME.

7. Rodger C Bassham, *Mission theology: 1948-1975. Years of worldwide creative tension, ecumenical, evangelical and Roman Catholic* (Pasadena: William Carey Library, 1979), 167-168; James A Scherer, *Gospel, church and kingdom: Comparative studies in world mission theology* (Minneapolis: Augsburg, 1987), 94-98; Christopher Yates, *Christian mission in the twentieth century* (Cambridge: Cambridge University Press, 1994), 163-164.

8. J C Hoekendijk, "The church in missionary thinking," *International Review of Missions* 41 (1952): 332-334. See also his later book, J C Hoekendijk, *The church inside out* (London: SCM, 1966).

9. Wilhelm Andersen, *Towards a theology of mission: A study of the encounter between the missionary enterprise and the church and its theology* (London: SCM, 1955), 49.

10. Andersen, *Towards a theology of mission*, 40.

11. Andersen, *Towards a theology of mission*, 47.

12. Andersen, *Towards a theology of mission*, 51.

13. Andersen, *Towards a theology of mission*, 49.

14. Andersen, *Towards a theology of mission*, 49, 51.

15. Priscilla Pope-Levison, "Evangelism in the WCC: From New Delhi to Canberra," in *New directions in mission and evangelization, 2: Theological foundations*, eds. James A Scherer and Stephen B Bevans (Maryknoll: Orbis, 1994), 133; Scherer, *Gospel, church and kingdom*, 94.

16. Pope-Levison, "Evangelism in the WCC," 127; Philip Potter, "Evangelism and the World Council of Churches," *The Ecumenical Review* 20 (1968): 176; Paul Löffler, "The confessing community: Evangelism in ecumenical perspective," *International Review of Mission* 66 (1977): 339, 341.

17. Pope-Levison, "Evangelism in the WCC," 126.

18. Donald A McGavran, "New mission: A systematic reinterpretation of the concepts of mission," and "The current conciliar theology of mission," in *Contemporary theologies of mission*, by Arthur F Glasser and Donald A McGavran (Grand Rapids: Baker, 1983), 47-61, 62-81; John Stott, "Response to Bishop Mortimer Arias ['That the world may believe']," *International Review of Mission* 65 (1976): 30-33.

19. McGavran, "The current conciliar theology of mission," 67-68; various critics cited in Bassham, *Mission theology*, 96.

20. World Council of Churches, *Bangkok Assembly 1973: Minutes and report of the Assembly of the Commission on World Mission and Evangelism of the World Council of Churches, December 31, 1972 and January 9-12, 1973* (Geneva: World Council of Churches, 1973), 89.

21. WCC, *Bangkok Assembly 1973*, 88.

22. WCC, *Bangkok Assembly 1973*, 87.

23. WCC, *Bangkok Assembly 1973*, 89.

24. Martin Lehmann-Habeck, "Wholistic evangelism: A WCC perspective," *International Review of Mission* 73 (1984): 7.

25. David M Paton, ed., *Breaking barriers: Nairobi 1975. The official report of the fifth assembly of the World Council of Churches, Nairobi, 23 November-10 December, 1975* (London: SPCK, 1976), Report of Section 1, #18, #19, p. 45.

26. Mortimer Arias, "That the world may believe," *International Review of Mission* 65 (1976): 18.

27. Arias, "That the world may believe," 19-23.

28. Stromberg, ed., *Mission and evangelism*. Hereafter referred to in the text as ME, followed by document section numbers, e.g. ME#12.

29. Other clear examples are found in ME #5, #6, #11 to #17, #26, #28, #30, #32.

30. "Statement of the Stuttgart Consultation on Evangelism," in *Proclaiming Christ in Christ's way: Studies in integral evangelism*, eds. Vinay Samuel and Albrecht Hauser (Oxford: Regnum, 1989), 212-225; it also appears, excluding only the final paragraph, as World Council of Churches CWME, "Stuttgart Consultation (Stuttgart, 1987)," in *New directions in mission and evangelization, 1: Basic statements, 1974-1991*, eds. James A Scherer and Stephen B Bevans (Maryknoll: Orbis, 1992), 65-72.

31. See p. 4 above.

32. In lectures given in January 1993 on "Evangelism in the modern world," at Whitley College, Melbourne.

33. See "The Lausanne Covenant," in *Let the earth hear his voice: International Congress on World Evangelization, Lausanne, Switzerland, Official reference volume*, ed. J D Douglas (Minneapolis: World Wide Publications, 1975), #6, p. 5; the chapter headings of Alan Nichols, ed., *The whole gospel for the whole world: Story of Lausanne II Congress on World Evangelization, Manila 1989* (Ventura, CA: Regal, 1989); and the history of the phrase in the WCC in Arias, "That the world may believe," 13-14, 17.

34. John Stott, *The contemporary Christian: An urgent plea for double listening* (Leicester, UK: Inter-Varsity Press, 1992), 340; *Evangelism and social responsibility: An evangelical commitment*, Grand Rapids Report No.21, Consultation on the Relationship between Evangelism and Social

Responsibility (CRESR) (Wheaton: Lausanne Committee on World Evangelization and the World Evangelical Fellowship, 1982), 23.

35.   *Your kingdom come: Mission perspectives. Report on the World Conference on Mission and Evangelism, Melbourne, Australia, 12-25 May 1980* (Geneva: World Council of Churches, 1980), particularly: Plenary presentations, Section 1, pp. 83-119; Section reports, Section 1, pp. 171-178; and Emilio Castro's "Reflection after Melbourne," pp. 225-234. For a good summary of Melbourne see Scherer, *Gospel, church and kingdom*, 141-145.

36.   For example, WCC, *Bangkok Assembly 1973*, 88; *Your kingdom come*: Section reports, I.#1, I.#2, III.#4, Canaan Banana, "Good news to the poor," 104, Geevarghese Mar Osthathios, "The gospel of the kingdom and the crucified and risen lord," 50; *Common witness: A study document of the joint working group of the Roman Catholic Church and the World Council of Churches* (Geneva: World Council of Churches, 1981), #16, p. 13; ME#7; and Eka Darmaputera, "Your will be done—Mission in Christ's way," *International Review of Mission* 75 (1986): 432-433.

37.   Lehmann-Habeck, "Wholistic evangelism: A WCC perspective," 12.

38.   Emilio Castro, "Reflections after Melbourne," in *Your kingdom come: Mission perspectives. Report on the World Conference on Mission and Evangelism, Melbourne, Australia, 12-25 May 1980* (Geneva: World Council of Churches, 1980), 234.

39.   Pope-Levison, "Evangelism in the WCC," 131.

40.   "Your will be done—Mission in Christ's way [Selections from a CWME consultation]," *International Review of Mission* 75 (1986): 423-454.

41.   Lesslie Newbigin, *Mission in Christ's way: A gift, a command, an assurance* (Geneva: World Council of Churches, 1987).

42.   Vinay Samuel and Albrecht Hauser, eds., *Proclaiming Christ in Christ's way: Studies in integral evangelism* (Oxford: Regnum, 1989).

43.   World Council of Churches Commission on World Mission and Evangelism, *Your will be done: Mission in Christ's way: Study material and biblical reflection* (Geneva: World Council of Churches, 1988).

44.   Wilson, ed. *The San Antonio Report.*

45.   Janet Silman, "Your will be done—Mission in Christ's way," *International Review of Mission* 75 (1986): 436.

46.   Geevarghese Mar Osthathios, "Your will be done—Mission in Christ's way," *International Review of Mission* 75 (1986): 440-443.

47.   Newbigin, *Mission in Christ's way*, 27.

48.   Wilson, ed. *The San Antonio Report*, 27-28, 37, 46, 54.

49.   Anastasios of Androussa, "Address of the Conference Moderator," in *The San Antonio Report: Your will be done: Mission in Christ's way*, ed. Frederick R Wilson (Geneva: World Council of Churches, 1990), 100-114.

50.   Wilson, ed. *The San Antonio Report*, 23-24.

51. Wilson, ed. *The San Antonio Report,* I.#9-10, p. 27.
52. Wilson, ed. *The San Antonio Report,* III.#12, p. 54.
53. Wilson, ed. *The San Antonio Report,* II.#1, p. 37. See also II.#22, p. 46.
54. Guder, "Incarnation and the church's evangelistic mission," 417-428.
55. Guder, "Incarnation and the church's evangelistic mission," 418.
56. Guder, "Incarnation and the church's evangelistic mission," 419.
57. Guder, "Incarnation and the church's evangelistic mission," 420.
58. John A Mackay, *Ecumenics: The science of the church universal* (Englewood Cliffs: Prentice-Hall, 1964), 173; cited in Guder, "Incarnation and the church's evangelistic mission," 420-421.
59. Guder, "Incarnation and the church's evangelistic mission," 422.
60. Guder, "Incarnation and the church's evangelistic mission," 422-425.
61. See also his book on the theme of incarnational witness: Darrell L Guder, *Be my witnesses: The church's mission, message, and messengers* (Grand Rapids: Eerdmans, 1985), and Darrell L Guder, *The continuing conversion of the church* (Grand Rapids, Eerdmans, 2000).
62. For example, WCC, *Bangkok Assembly 1973,* I.A.#6-7, pp. 72-74; Paton, ed. *Breaking barriers: Nairobi 1975,* I.#21-25, pp. 45-46; Michael Kinnamon, ed., *Signs of the Spirit: Official report, World Council of Churches, Seventh Assembly, Canberra, Australia, 7-20 February 1991* (Geneva: World Council of Churches, 1991), 93, 102.
63. See p 174 above.
64. ME#26, quoting from "Agenda for future planning, study, and research in mission [from the SEDOS Research Seminar on the Future of Mission, Rome, March 1981]," to be found, among other places, in *Trends in mission: Toward the third millennium. Essays in celebration of twenty-five years of SEDOS,* eds. William Jenkinson and Helen O'Sullivan (Maryknoll: Orbis, 1991), #29, p. 404.
65. Aram Keshishian, "Central Committee, 1991: Report of the Moderator," *The Ecumenical Review* 44 (1992): 116.
66. Gerald H Anderson, "Another world mission conference: What impact?," *International Bulletin of Missionary Research* 20 (1996): 145.
67. McGavran, "The current conciliar theology of mission," 62-81.
68. See, for example, Georges Tsetsis, ed. *Orthodox thought: Reports of Orthodox consultations organized by the World Council of Churches, 1975-1982* (Geneva: World Council of Churches, 1983).
69. Anastasios Yannoulatos, "Discovering the Orthodox missionary ethos," in *Martyria/mission: The witness of the Orthodox churches today,* ed. Ion Bria (Geneva: World Council of Churches, 1980), 21.
70. James J Stamoolis, *Eastern Orthodox mission theology today* (Maryknoll: Orbis, 1986), 10.
71. Stamoolis, *Eastern Orthodox mission theology today,* 82.

72. Ion Bria, "Introduction," in *Martyria/mission: The witness of the Orthodox churches today*, ed. Ion Bria (Geneva: World Council of Churches, 1980), 8.

73. Bria, "Introduction," 8.

74. Bria, "Introduction," 9.

75. "Final report of CWME consultation of Eastern Orthodox and Oriental Orthodox churches, Neapolis, 1988," in *New directions in mission and evangelization, 1: Basic statements, 1974-1991*, eds. James A Scherer and Stephen B Bevans (Maryknoll: Orbis, 1992), 235-236.

76. Daniel B Clendenin, "Partakers of divinity: The orthodox doctrine of theosis," *Journal of the Evangelical Theological Society* 37 (1994): 371; Daniel B Clendenin, *Eastern Orthodox Christianity: A Western perspective* (Grand Rapids: Baker, 1994), 120.

77. James Stamoolis, "Eastern Orthodox mission theology," *International Bulletin of Missionary Research* 8 (1984): 60.

78. "The evangelistic witness of Orthodoxy today [Report No. 4 from the Orthodox consultation on Confessing Christ Today, Bucharest, 1974]," in *Mission trends No. 2: Evangelization*, eds. Gerald H Anderson and Thomas F Stransky (New York: Paulist, 1975), #1.b, p. 268; also appears as "Confessing Christ today: Reports of groups at a consultation of Orthodox theologians," *International Review of Mission* 64 (1975): 74-94, Report No. 4 on 86-92; and "The evangelistic witness of Orthodoxy today [Report No. 4 from the Orthodox consultation on Confessing Christ Today, Bucharest, 1974]," in *Martyria/mission: The witness of the Orthodox churches today*, ed. Ion Bria (Geneva: World Council of Churches, 1980), 224-230.

79. Jürgen Moltmann, *God in creation: An ecological doctrine of creation* (London: SCM, 1985), 225-229. See p. 148 above.

80. Clendenin, "Partakers of divinity," 373.

81. Clendenin, "Partakers of divinity," 374.

82. Clendenin, "Partakers of divinity," 376-377.

83. "Christ 'in us' and Christ 'for us' in Lutheran and Orthodox theology," in *Salvation in Christ: A Lutheran-Orthodox dialogue*, eds. John Meyendorff and Robert Tobias (Minneapolis: Augsburg, 1992), 19.

84. "Christ 'in us' and Christ 'for us'," 19, 24.

85. Bria, "Introduction," 10.

86. "Final report of CWME consultation, Neapolis, 1988," 236.

87. Stamoolis, *Eastern Orthodox mission theology today*, 88-102; Ion Bria, ed. *Go forth in peace: Orthodox perspectives on mission* (Geneva: World Council of Churches, 1986), 17-23.

88. George Khodre, "The Church as the privileged witness of God," in *Martyria/mission: The witness of the Orthodox churches today*, ed. Ion Bria (Geneva: World Council of Churches, 1980), 31.

89. Yannoulatos, "Discovering the Orthodox missionary ethos," 27.

90. Ion Bria, "The liturgy after the Liturgy," *International Review of Mission* 67 (1978): 87-88.
91. Bria, "The liturgy after the Liturgy," 88.
92. "Your kingdom come [Working document from an Orthodox consultation, Paris, September 1978]," *International Review of Mission* 68 (1979): 143.
93. Yannoulatos, "Discovering the Orthodox missionary ethos," 26.
94. "The evangelistic witness of Orthodoxy today," 271-272.
95. Stamoolis, *Eastern Orthodox mission theology today*, 61, 74-80.
96. Clendenin, "Partakers of divinity," 378; "The evangelistic witness of Orthodoxy today," 272; "Final report of CWME consultation, Neapolis, 1988," 236-237; John Meyendorff, "The Orthodox church and mission: Past and present perspectives," in *Mission trends No. 1: Crucial issues in mission today*, eds. Gerald H Anderson and Thomas F Stransky (New York: Paulist, 1974), 63; Dumitru Staniloae, "Witness through "holiness" of life," in *Martyria/mission: The witness of the Orthodox churches today*, ed. Ion Bria (Geneva: World Council of Churches, 1980), 49; "Your kingdom come [Working document from an Orthodox consultation, Paris, September 1978]," 144; Bria, ed. *Go forth in peace*, 39-40.
97. Stamoolis, *Eastern Orthodox mission theology today*, 62.
98. Stamoolis, *Eastern Orthodox mission theology today*, 61-70.
99. Efthimios Stylios, "The missionary as an imitator of Christ," *Porefthendes* 5 (1963): 8-10; cited in Stamoolis, *Eastern Orthodox mission theology today*, 62. See also Bria, ed. *Go forth in peace*, 56-63.
100. "The evangelistic witness of Orthodoxy today," 272-273.
101. Khodre, "The Church as the privileged witness of God," 31.
102. Alexander Schmemann, *Church, world, mission: Reflections on Orthodoxy in the West* (Crestwood, NY: St Vladimir's Seminary Press, 1979), 212.
103. Vladimir Lossky, *The mystical theology of the Eastern Church* (Cambridge, UK: James Clarke, 1991 (1944)), 178.
104. Lossky, "Orthodoxy," 768.
105. "Your kingdom come, Paris, 1978," 144.

Chapter 10

1. See p. 47 above.
2. See p. 47 above.
3. John V Taylor, "My pilgrimage in mission," *International Bulletin of Missionary Research* 17 (1993): 59.
4. See p. 58 above.
5. See p. 58 above.

6.   The closest is Schreiter's set of criteria for a successfully contextualized theology. Robert J Schreiter, *Constructing local theologies* (Maryknoll: Orbis, 1985), 117-121.

7.   James A Scherer, "Missiology as a discipline and what it includes," in *New directions in mission and evangelization 2: Theological foundations*, eds. James A Scherer and Stephen B Bevans (Maryknoll: Orbis, 1994), 179-184.

8.   *Disciplines*, characterized by distinctive concepts, relationships between concepts, central claims, and ways of testing those claims, are sometimes distinguished in philosophy of education from *fields*, which are united by a common, often practical, interest, and which draw on several disciplines. Paul H Hirst, "Liberal education and the nature of knowledge," in *Knowledge and the curriculum: A collection of philosophical papers*, by Paul H Hirst (London: Routledge & Kegan Paul, 1974), 44-46.

9.   Among those who offer criteria for adequate models or approaches in theology are: Avery Dulles, *Models of the church*, 2nd ed. (New York: Image, 1987), 25-26; Langdon Gilkey, *Message and existence: An introduction to Christian theology* (Minneapolis: Seabury Press, 1979), 7-20; Peter C Hodgson, *Winds of the Spirit: A constructive Christian theology* (Louisville: Westminster John Knox, 1994), 19-30; Jeffery Hopper, *Understanding modern theology II: Reinterpreting Christian faith for changing worlds* (Philadelphia: Fortress, 1987), 100-124; Sallie McFague, *Metaphorical theology: Models of God in religious language* (London: SCM, 1983), 136-144; John Macquarrie, *Principles of Christian theology*, Rev. ed. (London: SCM, 1977), 4-17; Daniel L Migliore, *Faith seeking understanding: An introduction to Christian theology* (Grand Rapids: Eerdmans, 1991), 10-13; Schubert Ogden, "What is theology?," in *Readings in Christian theology*, eds. Peter C Hodgson and Robert H King (Philadelphia: Fortress, 1985), 15-30; Schreiter, *Constructing local theologies*, 117-121; (assessing a christology:) M Thomas Thangaraj, *The crucified guru: An experiment in cross-cultural christology* (Nashville: Abingdon, 1994), 144-151.

10. Gilkey, *Message and existence*, 7; Hodgson, *Winds of the Spirit*, 19-24; Macquarrie, *Principles of Christian theology*, 6-12; Ogden, "What is theology?," 17-19; Migliore, *Faith seeking understanding*, 10-11; Schreiter, *Constructing local theologies*, 119-120; Thangaraj, *The crucified guru*, 146-147.

11. Gilkey, *Message and existence*, 7; Hodgson, *Winds of the Spirit*, 25-26; Macquarrie, *Principles of Christian theology*, 12-13; Ogden, "What is theology?," 19-20; Migliore, *Faith seeking understanding*, 12.

12. Macquarrie, *Principles of Christian theology*, 5-6; Schreiter, *Constructing local theologies*, 118-119; Thangaraj, *The crucified guru*, 148.

13. Macquarrie, *Principles of Christian theology*, 13-17; McFague, *Metaphorical theology*, 140-143; Schreiter, *Constructing local theologies*, 118; Thangaraj, *The crucified guru*, 144-145.

14. Migliore, *Faith seeking understanding*, 12-13; Schreiter, *Constructing local theologies*, 119; Thangaraj, *The crucified guru*, 145-146.

15. Gilkey, *Message and existence*, 7, citing Albrecht Ritschl without locating the source; Ogden, "What is theology?," 17-19.

16. For example, among theologians, Sallie McFague, *Models of God: Theology for an ecological, nuclear age* (London: SCM, 1987); John Macquarrie, *Jesus Christ in modern thought* (London: SCM, 1990), 307; Jürgen Moltmann, *God in creation: An ecological doctrine of creation* (London: SCM, 1985), xi-xv, 1-19; Wolfhart Pannenberg, *Toward a theology of nature: Essays on science and faith* (Louisville: Westminster/John Knox, 1993).

   Among missiologists: Donald E Messer, *A conspiracy of goodness: Contemporary images of Christian mission* (Nashville: Abingdon, 1992), 45-66, 79-90; The World Council of Churches Commission on World Mission and Evangelism (CWME), in Frederick R Wilson, ed. *The San Antonio Report: Your will be done: Mission in Christ's way* (Geneva: World Council of Churches, 1990), 52-68.

   The missiology of David Bosch is notable for the absence of ecological themes; for example, David J Bosch, *Transforming mission: Paradigm shifts in theology of mission* (Maryknoll: Orbis, 1991). In our survey we noted our disagreement with Choan-Seng Song, who is one writer who concentrates almost exclusively on humanization as the goal of God's enfleshment. See p. 169 above.

17. Denis Edwards, *Jesus and the cosmos* (Homebush, NSW: St Paul Publications, 1991), 107.

18. Karl Rahner, "The body in the order of salvation," in *Theological investigations, Vol. 17: Jesus, man and the church,* by Karl Rahner (London: Darton, Longman & Todd, 1962), 71-89, 87.

19. Denis Edwards, *Jesus the Wisdom of God: An ecological theology* (Homebush, NSW: St Paul's, 1995), 69.

20. Among those who explore this aspect of incarnational missiology are Edwards, *Jesus the Wisdom of God*; Karl Rahner, *Foundations of Christian faith* (New York: Seabury Press, 1978); and Moltmann, *God in creation*.

21. See p. 249 above.

22. Gareth Jones, *Critical theology: Questions of truth and method* (Cambridge: Polity Press, 1995), 202.

23. Frederick Herzog, *God-walk: Liberation shaping dogmatics* (Maryknoll: Orbis, 1988), 92.

24. Macquarrie, *Principles of Christian theology*, 13-16.

25. McFague, *Metaphorical theology*, 143.

26. Alisdair MacIntyre, *Whose justice? Which rationality?* (London: Duckworth, 1988).

27. Basil Mitchell, *The justification of religious belief* (London: Macmillan, 1973).

28. See p. 187 above.

29. Jürgen Moltmann, *The church in the power of the Spirit: A contribution to messianic ecclesiology* (London: SCM, 1977), 73.

30. See p. 187 above.

31. See p. 187 above.

32. Philip J Rosato, "The mission of the Spirit within and beyond the church," in *To the wind of God's Spirit: Reflections on the Canberra theme*, ed. Emilio Castro (Geneva: World Council of Churches, 1990), 21.

33. Moltmann, *The church in the power of the Spirit*, 5-6.

34. Moltmann, *The church in the power of the Spirit*, 93.

35. See p. 19 above.

36. See p. 183 above.

37. See p. 67-69 above.

38. See p. 222 above.

39. Discussed above in the context of Anabaptism (p. 67-69).

40. See pp. 20, 44-45 above.

41. See p. 70 above.

42. For example, incarnational mission in the inner city is defined as "physical presence" in Eugene Rubingh, "Mission in an urban world," *Evangelical Review of Theology* 11 (1987): 378.

43. See p. 109-110 above.

44. We noted earlier that Raymond Fung levels this objection against all incarnational missiology (pp. 4, 197 above).

45. See p. 197 above.

46. Darrell L Guder, *Be my witnesses: The church's mission, message, and messengers* (Grand Rapids: Eerdmans, 1985), 32.

47. Not all cross-cultural missionaries are convinced that the incarnational model is possible or effective when Westerners go to tribal situations. As Harriet Hill argues, taken simply to mean "complete identification," incarnational mission is unrealistic, dishonest, and unsustainable (Harriet Hill, "Incarnational ministry: A critical examination," *Evangelical Missions Quarterly* 26 (1990): 198). Missionaries have health cover, guaranteed income and regular furlough for a start. But, as Kenneth McElhanon argues in reply, incarnational mission is still the only viable model. We can move in the direction of incarnational mission, without aiming for "identification" but instead removing barriers and considering ourselves as sharing one humanity with those of very different cultural backgrounds (Kenneth McElhanon, "Don't give up on the incarnational model," *Evangelical Missions Quarterly*

27 (1991): 390-393).

Chapter 11

1. For example, Veronica Brady, *A crucible of prophets: Australians and the question of God* (Sydney: Theological Explorations, 1981), 1; David Millikan, "Christianity and Australian identity," in *The shape of belief: Christianity in Australia today*, eds. Dorothy Harris, Douglas Hynd and David Millikan (Homebush West, NSW: Lancer, 1982), 37-38.
2. Russel Ward, *The Australian legend*, 2nd ed. (Oxford: OUP, 1966 (1958)), 1-2.
3. A critical stance is taken towards both the historical basis and usefulness of the legend in Richard White, *Inventing Australia: Images and identity, 1688-1980* (St Leonards, NSW: Allen & Unwin, 1981); James Walter, "Defining Australia," in *Images of Australia: An introductory reader in Australian studies*, eds. Gillian Whitlock and David Carter (St Lucia, Qld: University of Queensland Press, 1992), 7-22; and Graeme Davidson, "Inventing Australia," in *Images of Australia: An introductory reader in Australian studies*, eds. Gillian Whitlock and David Carter (St Lucia, Qld: University of Queensland Press, 1992), 191-204.
4. Tony Kelly, *A new imagining: Towards an Australian spirituality* (Melbourne: Collins Dove, 1990), 1-24.
5. Peter Bentley, 'Tricia Blombery and Philip Hughes, *Faith without the church? Nominalism in Australian Christianity* (Melbourne: Christian Research Association, 1992), 44-49, 70-109; Gary D Bouma and Beverly R Dixon, *The religious factor in Australian life* (Melbourne: MARC Australia, 1986), 166-167.
6. Bentley, Blombery and Hughes, *Faith without the church?*, 102.
7. Gordon Dicker, "Kerygma and Australian culture: The case of the Aussie battler," in *Toward theology in an Australian context*, ed. Victor C Hayes (Bedford Park, SA: The Australian Association for the Study of Religions, 1979), 50.
8. David Millikan, *The sunburnt soul: Christianity in search of an Australian identity* (Homebush West, NSW: Lancer, 1981), 108.
9. *The Macquarie Dictionary*, 2nd ed. (Macquarie University, NSW: The Macquarie Library, 1991), 1587.
10. Bryan Wilson, "Secularization," in *A new dictionary of Christian theology*, eds. Alan Richardson and John Bowden (London: SCM, 1983), 535.
11. Alan D Gilbert, *The making of post-Christian Britain: A history of the secularization of modern society* (London: Longmans, 1980), ix. We need to take "irreligious" here to mean "not committed to organized religion," as discussed above.

12. Loren B Mead, *The once and future church: Reinventing the congregation for a new mission frontier* (New York: The Alban Institute, 1991), 8-29.

13. Lesslie Newbigin, *Foolishness to the Greeks: The gospel and Western culture* (Grand Rapids: Eerdmans, 1986), 20.

14   Lesslie Newbigin, "Evangelism in the context of secularization," in *A word in season: Perspectives on Christian world missions,* by Lesslie Newbigin (Grand Rapids: Eerdmans, 1994), 152-155.

15. Brian Carrell, "The Christian faith in a post-Christian society," *Evangelical Review of Theology* 18 (1994): 357.

16   Klaas Runia, "The challenge of the modern world to the church," *Evangelical Review of Theology* 18 (1994): 314-316.

17. We use postmodernity to refer to the set of social trends and postmodernism to refer to new cultural and intellectual sensibilities, though the two overlap. In this we follow David Lyon, *Postmodernity* (Minneapolis: University of Minnesota Press, 1994), 7; and Hans Bertens, *The idea of the postmodern: A history* (London: Routledge, 1995), 5-10.

18. For introductions to postmodernism, see Lyon, *Postmodernity*; Bertens, *The idea of the postmodern*; Patricia Waugh, "Introduction," in *Postmodernism: A reader*, ed. Patricia Waugh (London: Edward Arnold, 1992), 1-10; David Harvey, *The condition of postmodernity: An enquiry into the origins of cultural change* (Oxford: Blackwell, 1989).

Introductions from a theological perspective: Stanley J Grenz, *A primer on postmodernism* (Grand Rapids: Eerdmans, 1996); Walter Brueggemann, *Texts under negotiation: The Bible and postmodern imagination* (Minneapolis: Fortress, 1993), 1-25; Millard J Erickson, *The Word became flesh: A contemporary incarnational christology* (Grand Rapids: Baker, 1991), 305-315; Thomas Finger, "Modernity, postmodernity—What in the world are they?," *Transformation* 10.4 (Oct-Dec 1993): 20-26; James B Miller, "The emerging postmodern world," in *Postmodern theology: Christian faith in a pluralist world,* ed. Frederic B Burnham (San Francisco: Harper & Row, 1989), 1-19; Craig Van Gelder, "A great new fact of our day: America as a mission field," *Missiology* 19 (1991): 409-418.

19. R Detweiler, "Postmodernism," in *The Blackwell Encyclopedia of modern Christian thought,* ed. Alister E McGrath (Oxford: Blackwell, 1993), 456.

20. Hugh Mackay, *Reinventing Australia: The mind and mood of Australia in the 90s* (Sydney: Angus & Robertson, 1993), 262.

21. The only study on this question known to me concentrates on mission in tribal contexts: Bruce Bradshaw, *Bridging the gap: Evangelism, development and shalom* (Monrovia, CA: MARC, 1993).

22. An article by Daniel Clendenin is the only source I came across from outside Eastern Orthodoxy: Daniel B Clendenin, "Partakers of divinity: The orthodox doctrine of theosis," *Journal of the Evangelical Theological Society* 37

(1994): 365-379.
23. See p. 205 above.
24 Jürgen Moltmann, *God in creation: An ecological doctrine of creation* (London: SCM, 1985), 244-245. He attributes the slogan to Friedrich Oetinger, but without locating its source.

BIBLIOGRAPHY

Abbott, Walter M, ed. *The documents of Vatican II*. London: Geoffrey Chapman, 1966.

"Ad Gentes (Decree on the Missionary Activity of the Church)." In *The documents of Vatican II*, ed. Walter M Abbott. London: Geoffrey Chapman, 1966. 584-630.

"Agenda for future planning, study, and research in mission [from the SEDOS Research Seminar on the Future of Mission, Rome, March 1981]." In *Trends in mission: Toward the third millennium. Essays in celebration of twenty-five years of SEDOS*, eds. William Jenkinson and Helen O"Sullivan. Maryknoll: Orbis, 1991. 399-414.

Anastasios of Androussa. "Address of the Conference Moderator." In *The San Antonio Report: Your will be done: Mission in Christ"s way*, ed. Frederick R Wilson. Geneva: World Council of Churches, 1990. 100-114.

Andersen, Wilhelm. *Towards a theology of mission: A study of the encounter between the missionary enterprise and the church and its theology*. London: SCM, 1955.

Anderson, Gerald H. "Another world mission conference: What impact?." *International Bulletin of Missionary Research* 20 (1996): 145.

Anderson, Gerald H, ed. *Asian voices in Christian theology*. Maryknoll: Orbis, 1976.

Anderson, Gerald H and Thomas F Stransky, eds. *Christ's lordship and religious pluralism*. Maryknoll: Orbis, 1981.

Anderson, Gerald H and Thomas F Stransky, eds. *Mission trends No.1: Crucial issues in mission today*. New York: Paulist, 1974.

Anderson, Gerald H, James M Phillips and Robert T Coote, eds. *Mission in the Nineteen-90s*. Grand Rapids: Eerdmans, 1991.

Anderson, Norman. *The mystery of the incarnation.* London: Hodder and Stoughton, 1978.

Andrews, Dave. *Building a better world.* Sutherland, NSW: Albatross, 1996.

———. *Can you hear the heartbeat?* London: Hodder & Stoughton, 1989.

Arbuckle, Gerald A. *Earthing the gospel: An inculturation handbook for the pastoral worker.* Maryknoll: Orbis, 1990.

Arias, Mortimer. *Announcing the reign of God: Evangelization and the subversive memory of Jesus.* Philadelphia: Fortress, 1984.

———. "That the world may believe." *International Review of Mission* 65 (1976): 13-26.

Arias, Mortimer and Alan Johnson. *The Great Commission: Biblical models for evangelism.* Nashville: Abingdon, 1992.

Armerding, Carl E, ed. *Evangelicals and liberation.* Grand Rapids: Baker, 1977.

Arndt, William F and F Wilbur Gingrich. *A Greek-English lexicon of the New Testament and other early Christian literature.* 4th ed. Chicago: University of Chicago Press, 1957.

Augustine of Hippo. "De Trinitate [On the holy trinity]." In *St Augustin: On the holy trinity, Doctrinal treatises, Moral treatises,* A select library of the Nicene and Post-Nicene Fathers of the Christian church, 1st series, ed. Philip Schaff. Vol. 3 [400-416 CE]. Grand Rapids: Eerdmans, 1956. 1-228.

Azevedo, Marcello de C. "Basic ecclesial communities." In *Mysterium Liberationis: Fundamental concepts of liberation theology,* eds. Ignacio Ellacuría and Jon Sobrino. Maryknoll: Orbis, 1993. 636-653.

Baillie, D M. *God was in Christ: An essay on incarnation and atonement.* London: Faber and Faber, 1956.

Bainton, Roland. "The left wing of the Reformation." *Journal of Religion* 21 (1941): 124-134.

Bakke, Ray. *The urban Christian: Effective ministry in today's urban world.* Downers Grove, IL: InterVarsity Press, 1987.

Balz, Horst and Gerhard Schneider, eds. *Exegetical Dictionary of the New Testament.* 3 vols. Grand Rapids: Eerdmans, 1990-1993.

Banana, Canaan. "Good news to the poor." In *Your kingdom come: Mission perspectives. Report on the World Conference on Mission and Evangelism, Melbourne, Australia, 12-25 May 1980,* Geneva: World Council of Churches, 1980. 104-119.

Barbour, Ian G. *Myths, models and paradigms: The nature of scientific and religious language.* London: SCM, 1974.

Barth, Karl. *Church Dogmatics.* Vol. IV.1. Edinburgh: T & T Clark, 1956.

Bassham, Rodger C. *Mission theology: 1948-1975. Years of worldwide creative tension, ecumenical, evangelical and Roman Catholic.* Pasadena: William Carey Library, 1979.

Batstone, David. *From conquest to struggle: Jesus of Nazareth in Latin America.* Albany: State University of New York Press, 1991.

Bauckham, Richard. "Jürgen Moltmann." In *The modern theologians: An introduction to Christian theology in the twentieth century,* ed. David F Ford. 2nd ed., Oxford: Blackwell, 1997. 209-224.

_____. *Moltmann: Messianic theology in the making.* Basingstoke, UK: Marshall Morgan and Scott, 1987.

_____. "Moltmann's messianic christology." *Scottish Journal of Theology* 44 (1991): 519-531.

_____. *The theology of Jürgen Moltmann.* Edinburgh: T & T Clark, 1995.

Beachy, Alvin J. *The concept of grace in the Radical Reformation.* Nieuwkoop, Holland: B. de Graaf, 1977.

_____. "The grace of God as understood by five major Anabaptist writers." *The Mennonite Quarterly Review* 37 (1963): 5-33.

Beasley-Murray, Paul, ed. *Mission to the world: Essays to celebrate the 50th anniversary of the ordination of George Raymond Beasley-Murray to the Christian ministry.* Didcot, UK: Baptist Historical Society, 1991.

Bebbington, D W. "Evangelicalism." In *The Blackwell encyclopedia of modern Christian thought,* ed. Alister E McGrath. Oxford: Blackwell, 1993. 183-186.

Belshaw, G P Mellick. "The religion of the incarnation." *Anglican Theological Review* 76 (1994): 432-443.

Bender, Harold S. *The Anabaptist vision.* Scottdale, PA: Herald, 1944. Also found in *The recovery of the Anabaptist vision,* ed. Guy F Hershberger. Scottdale, PA: Herald, 1957. 29-54.

Bender, Harold S and C Henry Smith (vols. 1-4), Cornelius J Dyck and Dennis D Martin (vol. 5), eds. *The Mennonite encyclopedia.* 5 vols. Scottdale, PA: Mennonite Publishing House (Herald), 1955-1959 and 1990.

Bentley, Peter, 'Tricia Blombery and Philip Hughes. *Faith without the church? Nominalism in Australian Christianity.* Melbourne: Christian Research Association, 1992.

Bertens, Hans. *The idea of the postmodern: A history.* London: Routledge, 1995.

Black, Max. *Models and metaphors.* Ithaca, NY: Cornell University Press, 1962.

_____. "More about metaphor." In *Metaphor and thought,* ed. Andrew Ortony. Cambridge: Cambridge University Press, 1979. 19-43.

Blauw, Johannes. *The missionary nature of the church: A survey of the biblical theology of mission.* Grand Rapids: Eerdmans, 1962.

Blough, Neal. "Messianic mission and ethics: Discipleship and the good news." In *The transfiguration of mission: Biblical, theological and historical foundations,* ed. Wilbert R Shenk. Scottdale, PA: Herald, 1993. 178-198.

Boff, Leonardo. *Church, charism and power: Liberation theology and the institutional church.* London: SCM, 1985.

_____. *Ecclesiogenesis: The base communities reinvent the church.* London: Collins, 1986.

_____. *Ecology and liberation: A new paradigm.* Maryknoll: Orbis, 1995.

_____. *Faith on the edge: Religion and marginalized existence.* San Francisco: Harper & Row, 1989.

_____. "Images of Jesus in Brazilian liberal Christianity." In *Faces of Jesus: Latin American christologies,* ed. José Míguez Bonino. Maryknoll: Orbis, 1984. 9-29.

_____. *Jesus Christ liberator: A critical Christology for our time.* Maryknoll: Orbis, 1978.

_____. *Liberating grace.* Maryknoll: Orbis, 1979.

_____. *The Lord's Prayer: The prayer of integral liberation.* Melbourne: Dove Communications, 1983.

_____. *New evangelization: Good news to the poor.* Maryknoll: Orbis, 1991.

_____. *Passion of Christ, passion of the world: The facts, their interpretations and their meanings, yesterday and today.* Maryknoll: Orbis, 1988.

_____. *The path to hope: Fragments from a theologian's journey.* Maryknoll: Orbis, 1993.

_____. *Trinity and society.* Tunbridge Wells, UK: Burns & Oates, 1988.

_____. *When theology listens to the poor.* San Francisco: Harper & Row, 1988.

Boff, Leonardo and Clodovis Boff. *Introducing liberation theology.* Tunbridge Wells, UK: Burns & Oates, 1987.

Boff, Leonardo and Clodovis Boff. *Liberation theology: From dialogue to confrontation.* San Francisco: Harper & Row, 1986.

Boff, Leonardo and Clodovis Boff. *Salvation and liberation: In search of a balance between faith and politics.* Maryknoll: Orbis, 1984.

Bonhoeffer, Dietrich. *The cost of discipleship.* London: SCM, 1959.

_____. *Ethics.* London: SCM, 1955.

_____. *Letters and papers from prison.* Ed. Eberhard Bethge. Enlarged ed. London: SCM, 1971.

Bonino, José Míguez. "On discipleship, justice and power." In *Freedom and discipleship: Liberation theology in Anabaptist perspective,* ed. Daniel S Schipani. Maryknoll: Orbis, 1989. 131-138.

Bonino, José Míguez, ed. *Faces of Jesus: Latin American christologies.* Maryknoll: Orbis, 1984.

Borg, Marcus J. *Jesus in contemporary scholarship.* Valley Forge, PA: Trinity Press International, 1994.

Bornkamm, Günther. *Paul.* London: Hodder & Stoughton, 1971.

Bosch, David J. *Transforming mission: Paradigm shifts in theology of mission.* Maryknoll: Orbis, 1991.

Bouma, Gary D and Beverly R Dixon. *The religious factor in Australian life.* Melbourne: MARC Australia, 1986.

Bowden, John. *Jesus: The unanswered questions*. London: SCM, 1988.

Braaten, Carl. *The flaming center: A theology of the Christian mission*. Philadelphia: Fortress, 1977.

Bradshaw, Bruce. *Bridging the gap: Evangelism, development and shalom*. Monrovia, CA: MARC, 1993.

Brady, Veronica. *A crucible of prophets: Australians and the question of God*. Sydney: Theological Explorations, 1981.

Bria, Ion. "The liturgy after the Liturgy." *International Review of Mission* 67 (1978): 86-90.

Bria, Ion, ed. *Go forth in peace: Orthodox perspectives on mission*. Geneva: World Council of Churches, 1986.

Bria, Ion, ed. *Martyria/mission: The witness of the Orthodox churches today*. Geneva: World Council of Churches, 1980.

Brown, David. *The divine trinity*. London: Duckworth, 1985.

Brown, Mitchell. "Blessed are the spiritually poor: Reflections on Dintaman's 'The spiritual poverty of the Anabaptist vision'." *The Conrad Grebel Review* 13 (1995): 18-22.

Brown, Raymond E. *The Gospel according to John: Introduction, translation and notes*. 2 vols. Garden City, NY: Doubleday, 1966.

Brown, Robert MacAfee. "Foreword." In *From conquest to struggle: Jesus of Nazareth in Latin America*, by David Batstone. Albany: State University of New York Press, 1991. ix-xi.

_____. *Theology in a new key: Responding to liberation themes*. Philadelphia: Westminster, 1978.

Browning, Don S. *A fundamental practical theology: Descriptive and strategic proposals*. Minneapolis: Fortress, 1991.

Browning, Ron. *Down and under: Discipleship in an Australian setting*. Melbourne: Spectrum, 1986.

Brueggemann, Walter. *Texts under negotiation: The Bible and postmodern imagination*. Minneapolis: Fortress, 1993.

Bryan, G McLeod, ed. *Communities of faith and radical discipleship: Jürgen Moltmann and others*. Macon, GA: Mercer University Press, 1986.

Bühlmann, Walbert. *The coming of the Third Church: An analysis of the present and future of the Church*. Slough, UK: St Paul Publications, 1976.

_____. "My pilgrimage in mission." *International Bulletin of Missionary Research* 10 (1986): 104-105.

_____. *With eyes to see: Church and world in the third millennium*. Maryknoll: Orbis, 1990.

Bultmann, Rudolf. "The Christological confession of the World Council of Churches." In *Essays: philosophical and theological*, by Rudolf Bultmann. London: SCM, 1955. 271-290.

_____. *Theology of the New Testament*. 2 vols. London: SCM, 1955.

_____. *The Gospel of John: A commentary.* Oxford: Basil Blackwell, 1971.

Burkholder, J Lawrence. "The Anabaptist vision of discipleship." In *The recovery of the Anabaptist vision,* ed. Guy F Hershberger. Scottdale, PA: Herald, 1957. 135-151.

Burnham, Frederic B, ed. *Postmodern theology: Christian faith in a pluralist world.* San Francisco: Harper & Row, 1989.

Campion, W J H. "Christianity and politics." In *Lux Mundi: A series of studies in the religion of the incarnation,* ed. Charles Gore. 15th ed., London: John Murray, 1904 (1889). 318-339.

Carey, George. *God incarnate.* Leicester, UK: Inter-Varsity Press, 1977.

_____. "Revitalizing the Catholic tradition." In *Living tradition: Affirming Catholicism in the Anglican church,* ed. Jeffrey John. London: Darton, Longman and Todd, 1992. 17-28.

Carmody, Denise L. *Christian feminist theology: A constructive interpretation.* Oxford: Blackwell, 1995.

Carrell, Brian. "The Christian faith in a post-Christian society." *Evangelical Review of Theology* 18 (1994): 354-358.

Castro, Emilio. "Reflections after Melbourne." In *Your kingdom come: Mission perspectives. Report on the World Conference on Mission and Evangelism, Melbourne, Australia, 12-25 May 1980,* Geneva: World Council of Churches, 1980. 225-234.

"The Chalcedonian definition of the faith." In *Creeds, councils and controversies: Documents illustrative of the history of the Church, A.D. 337-461,* ed. J Stevenson. London: SPCK, 1966. 334-338.

Chadwick, Owen. *The Victorian church: Part Two, 1860-1901.* 2nd ed. London: SCM, 1987.

Chaney, Charles L. "An introduction to the missionary thought of Jean Daniélou." *Occasional Bulletin from the Missionary Research Library* 17.5 (May 1966): 1-10.

Chester, Timothy. *Awakening to a world of need: The recovery of evangelical social concern.* Leicester, UK: Inter-Varsity Press, 1993.

"Christ 'in us' and Christ 'for us' in Lutheran and Orthodox theology." In *Salvation in Christ: A Lutheran-Orthodox dialogue,* eds. John Meyendorff and Robert Tobias. Minneapolis: Augsburg, 1992. 15-33.

Claerbaut, David. *Urban ministry.* Grand Rapids: Zondervan, 1983.

Clendenin, Daniel B. *Eastern Orthodox Christianity: A Western perspective.* Grand Rapids: Baker, 1994.

_____. "Partakers of divinity: The orthodox doctrine of theosis." *Journal of the Evangelical Theological Society* 37 (1994): 365-379.

Coakley, Sarah. *Christ without absolutes: A study of the Christology of Ernst Troeltsch.* Oxford: Clarendon, 1988.

Cobb, John B. "Christ beyond creative transformation." In *Encountering Jesus: A debate on christology*, ed. Stephen T Davis. Atlanta: John Knox, 1988. 141-158.

_____. *Christ in a pluralistic age.* Philadelphia: Westminster, 1975.

"Confessing Christ today: Reports of groups at a consultation of Orthodox theologians." *International Review of Mission* 64 (1975): 74-94.

Congar, Yves. "Reflections on being a theologian." *New Blackfriars* 62 (1981): 405-409.

Cook, Guillermo. *The expectation of the poor: Latin American basic ecclesial communities in Protestant perspective.* Maryknoll: Orbis, 1985.

Cook, Michael L. "Jesus from the other side of history: Christology in Latin America." *Theological Studies* 44 (1983): 258-287.

Costas, Orlando E. *Christ outside the gate: Mission beyond Christendom.* Maryknoll: Orbis, 1982.

_____. *The church and its mission: A shattering critique from the Third World.* Wheaton, IL: Tyndale, 1974.

_____. *The integrity of mission: The inner life and outreach of the church.* San Francisco: Harper & Row, 1979.

_____. *Liberating news: A theology of contextual evangelization.* Grand Rapids: Eerdmans, 1989.

_____. "A radical evangelical contribution from Latin America." In *Christ's lordship and religious pluralism*, eds. Gerald H Anderson and Thomas F Stransky. Maryknoll: Orbis, 1981. 133-156.

Cressey, Martin H. "Reformed/Presbyterian churches." In *Dictionary of the ecumenical movement*, eds. Nicholas Lossky et al. Geneva: World Council of Churches, 1991. 851-853.

Cross, F L and E A Livingstone, eds. *The Oxford dictionary of the Christian church.* 2nd ed. London: Oxford University Press, 1974.

Culpepper, R Alan. "1-2-3 John." In *The General Letters: Hebrews, James, 1-2 Peter, Jude, 1-2-3 John*, ed. Gerhard Krodel. Rev. & enlarged ed., Minneapolis: Fortress, 1995. 110-144.

Cupitt, Don. "The Christ of Christendom." In *The myth of God incarnate*, ed. John Hick. London: SCM, 1977. 133-147.

_____. *The debate about Christ.* London: SCM, 1979.

_____. "Jesus and the meaning of "God"." In *Incarnation and myth: The debate continued*, ed. Michael Goulder. London: SCM, 1979. 31-40.

Curran, Charles E. *Directions in fundamental moral theology.* Notre Dame: University of Notre Dame Press, 1985.

_____. *A new look at Christian morality.* London: Sheed and Ward, 1969.

Daniélou, Jean. *Christ and us.* London: Mowbray, 1961.

_____. *The Lord of history: Reflections on the inner meaning of history.* London: Longmans, 1958.

_____. *The salvation of the nations.* Notre Dame: University of Notre Dame Press, 1962.

Darmaputera, Eka. "Your will be done—Mission in Christ's way." *International Review of Mission* 75 (1986): 432-434.

Davidson, Graeme. "Inventing Australia." In *Images of Australia: An introductory reader in Australian studies,* eds. Gillian Whitlock and David Carter. St Lucia, Qld: University of Queensland Press, 1992. 191-204.

Davis, Stephen T. "Jesus Christ: Savior or guru?." In *Encountering Jesus: A debate on christology,* ed. Stephen T Davis. Atlanta: John Knox, 1988. 39-59.

Davis, Stephen T, ed. *Encountering Jesus: A debate on christology.* Atlanta: John Knox, 1988.

Dawsey, James M. "The biblical authority of the poor." *The Expository Times* 101 (1990): 295-298.

de Lubac, Henri. *Catholicism.* London: Burns & Oates, 1950.

Dearnley, Pat and Pete Broadbent. "Jesus Christ, the life of the city?." *Churchman* 97 (1983): 41-54.

Detweiler, R. "Postmodernism." In *The Blackwell Encyclopedia of modern Christian thought,* ed. Alister E McGrath. Oxford: Blackwell, 1993. 456-461.

Dicker, Gordon. "Kerygma and Australian culture: The case of the Aussie battler." In *Toward theology in an Australian context,* ed. Victor C Hayes. Bedford Park, SA: The Australian Association for the Study of Religions, 1979. 46-52.

Dilley, Frank B. *Metaphysics and religious language.* New York: Columbia University Press, 1964.

Dintaman, Stephen F. "Reading the reactions to 'The spiritual poverty of the Anabaptist vision'." *The Conrad Grebel Review* 13 (1995): 2-10.

_____. "The spiritual poverty of the Anabaptist vision." *The Conrad Grebel Review* 10 (1992): 205-208.

Dodd, C H. *The interpretation of the Fourth Gospel.* Cambridge: Cambridge University Press, 1953.

Dorr, Donal. "New challenges—new hopes." In *A new missionary era,* ed. Padraig Flanagan. Maryknoll: Orbis, 1982. 9-20.

Douglas, J D, ed. *Let the earth hear his voice: International Congress on World Evangelization, Lausanne, Switzerland.* Minneapolis: World Wide Publications, 1975.

Driver, John. "The kingdom of God." In *The transfiguration of mission: Biblical, theological and historical foundations,* ed. Wilbert R Shenk. Scottdale, PA: Herald, 1993. 83-105.

_____. "Messianic evangelization." In *The transfiguration of mission: Biblical, theological and historical foundations,* ed. Wilbert Shenk. Scottdale, PA: Herald, 1993. 199-219.

_____. *Understanding the atonement for the mission of the church.* Scottdale, PA: Herald, 1986.

D'Sa, Francis X. "Christian incarnation and Hindu avatara." *Concilium* (2 1993): 77-85.

Dulles, Avery. "The basic teaching of Vatican II." In *The reshaping of Catholicism: Current challenges in the theology of church*, by Avery Dulles. San Francisco: Harper & Row, 1988. 19-33.

_____. *The dimensions of the church: A postconciliar reflection*. Westminster, MD: Newman Press, 1967.

_____. "The meaning of Catholicism: Adventures of an idea." In *The reshaping of Catholicism: Current challenges in the theology of church*, by Avery Dulles. San Francisco: Harper & Row, 1988. 51-74.

_____. *Models of the church*. 2nd ed. New York: Image, 1987.

Duncan, Michael. *Costly mission: Following Christ into the slums*. Monrovia, CA: MARC, 1996.

_____. *Mission: The incarnational approach*. The Journey Series, No. 2. Christchurch, NZ: Servants to Asia"s Urban Poor, 1991.

Dunn, James D G. *Christology in the making: An inquiry into the origins of the doctrine of the incarnation*. 2nd ed. London: SCM, 1989.

_____. "Incarnation." In *The Anchor Bible dictionary*, ed. David Noel Freeman. New York: Doubleday, 1992. 3:397-404.

_____. *Jesus and the Spirit: A study of the religious and charismatic experience of Jesus and the first Christians as reflected in the New Testament*. London: SCM, 1975.

_____. *Unity and diversity in the New Testament: An inquiry into the character of earliest Christianity*. 2nd ed. London: SCM, 1990.

Durnbaugh, Donald F. *The believers' church: The history and character of radical Protestantism*. New York: Macmillan, 1968.

Dych, William V. *Karl Rahner*. London: Geoffrey Chapman, 1992.

Dyck, Cornelius J. "The Anabaptist understanding of the good news." In *Anabaptism and mission*, ed. Wilbert R Shenk. Scottdale, PA: Herald, 1984. 24-39.

_____. "*Jesus Christ our Lord* in historical Anabaptist perspective." In *A disciple's Christology: Appraisals of Kraus's Jesus Christ our Lord*, ed. Richard A Kauffman. Elkhart, IN: Institute of Mennonite Studies, 1989. 42-49.

Dyrness, William A, ed. *Emerging voices in global Christian theology*. Grand Rapids: Zondervan, 1994.

Edwards, Denis. *Jesus and the cosmos*. Homebush, NSW: St Paul Publications, 1991.

_____. *Jesus the Wisdom of God: An ecological theology*. Homebush, NSW: St Paul"s, 1995.

Edwards, Paul, ed. *The encyclopedia of philosophy*. 8 vols. New York: Macmillan, 1967.

Eliade, Mircea, ed. *The encyclopedia of religion.* 16 vols. New York: Macmillan, 1987.

Ellacuría, Ignacio. *Freedom made flesh: The mission of Christ and his church.* Maryknoll: Orbis, 1976.

Ellacuría, Ignacio and Jon Sobrino, eds. *Mysterium Liberationis: Fundamental concepts of liberation theology.* Maryknoll: Orbis, 1993.

Elliott, John H. "Backward and forward 'In his steps': Following Jesus from Rome to Raymond and beyond. The tradition, redaction, and reception of 1 Peter 2:18-25." In *Discipleship in the New Testament,* ed. Fernando F Segovia. Philadelphia: Fortress, 1985. 184-208.

Elwell, Walter A, ed. *Evangelical dictionary of theology.* Grand Rapids: Baker, 1984.

Elwood, Douglas J, ed. *Asian Christian theology: Emerging themes.* Rev. ed. Philadelphia: Westminster, 1980.

Endo, Shusaka. *The samurai.* New York: Vintage Books, 1982.

Erickson, Millard J. *The Word became flesh: A contemporary incarnational christology.* Grand Rapids: Baker, 1991.

Escobar, Samuel. "Evangelism and man's search for freedom, justice and fulfillment." In *Let the earth hear his voice: International Congress on World Evangelization, Lausanne, Switzerland,* ed. J D Douglas. Minneapolis: World Wide Publications, 1975. 303-326.

_____. "The Gospel and the poor." In *Christian mission and social justice,* by Samuel Escobar and John Driver. Scottdale, PA: Herald, 1978. 36-56.

_____. "The return of Christ." In *The new face of evangelicalism: An international symposium on the Lausanne Covenant,* ed. C René Padilla. London: Hodder & Stoughton, 1976. 255-264.

Escobar, Samuel and John Driver. *Christian mission and social justice.* Scottdale, PA: Herald, 1978.

Evangelism and social responsibility: An evangelical commitment. Grand Rapids Report No.21, Consultation on the Relationship between Evangelism and Social Responsibility (CRESR). Wheaton: Lausanne Committee on World Evangelization and the World Evangelical Fellowship, 1982.

"The evangelistic witness of Orthodoxy today [Report No. 4 from the Orthodox consultation on Confessing Christ Today, Bucharest, 1974]." In *Martyria/mission: The witness of the Orthodox churches today,* ed. Ion Bria. Geneva: World Council of Churches, 1975. 224-230.

Evans, C Stephen. "The incarnational narrative as myth and history." *Christian Scholar"s Review* 23 (1994): 387-407.

Fackre, Gabriel. "Antinomianism." In *A new dictionary of Christian theology,* eds. Alan Richardson and John Bowden. London: SCM, 1983. 27.

_____. "Narrative theology: An overview." *Interpretation* 37 (1983): 340-350.

Feenstra, Ronald J and Cornelius Plantinga, Jr, eds. *Trinity, incarnation and atonement: Philosophical and theological essays.* Notre Dame: University of Notre Dame Press, 1989.

Fenton, John Y, ed. *Theology and body.* Philadelphia: Westminster, 1974.

Ferm, Deane William. *Third world liberation theologies: An introductory survey.* Maryknoll: Orbis, 1986.

"Final report of CWME consultation of Eastern Orthodox and Oriental Orthodox churches, Neapolis, 1988." In *New directions in mission and evangelization, 1: Basic statements, 1974-1991,* eds. James A Scherer and Stephen B Bevans. Maryknoll: Orbis, 1992. 232-250.

Finger, Thomas. "Modernity, postmodernity—What in the world are they?." *Transformation* 10.4 (Oct-Dec 1993): 20-26.

Flanagan, Padraic, ed. *A new missionary era.* Maryknoll: Orbis, 1982.

Ford, David F, ed. *The modern theologians: An introduction to Christian theology in the twentieth century.* 2nd ed. Oxford: Blackwell, 1997.

Forrester, Duncan. "Christianity and politics." In *Keeping the faith: Essays to mark the centenary of Lux Mundi,* ed. Geoffrey Wainwright. Philadelphia: Fortress, 1988. 250-273.

Freeman, David Noel, ed. *The Anchor Bible dictionary.* 6 vols. New York: Doubleday, 1992.

Friedmann, Robert. *The theology of Anabaptism: An interpretation.* Scottdale, PA: Herald, 1973.

Fuchs, Josef. *Moral demands and personal obligations.* Washington, DC: Georgetown University Press, 1993.

_____. *Natural law: A theological investigation.* New York: Sheed and Ward, 1965.

Gadamer, Hans-Georg. *Truth and method.* London: Sheed and Ward, 1975.

Gallardo, José. "Ethics and mission." In *Anabaptism and mission,* ed. Wilbert R Shenk. Scottdale, PA: Herald, 1984. 137-157.

Garrett, James Leo, ed. *The concept of the believers' church.* New York: Macmillan, 1969.

"Gaudium et Spes (Pastoral Constitution on the Church in the Modern World)." In *The documents of Vatican II,* ed. Walter M Abbott. London: Geoffrey Chapman, 1966. 199-308.

Gilbert, Alan D. *The making of post-Christian Britain: A history of the secularization of modern society.* London: Longmans, 1980.

Gilkey, Langdon. *Message and existence: An introduction to Christian theology.* Minneapolis: Seabury Press, 1979.

Gill, Athol. *The fringes of freedom: Following Jesus, living together, working for justice.* Homebush West, NSW: Lancer, 1990.

_____. *Life on the road: The gospel basis for a messianic lifestyle.* Homebush West, NSW: Lancer, 1989.

Gittins, Anthony J. *Gifts and strangers: Meeting the challenge of inculturation.* New York: Paulist, 1989.

Gladwin, John. *God's people in God's world: Biblical motives for social involvement.* Leicester, UK: Inter-Varsity Press, 1979.

Glasser, Arthur F and Donald A McGavran. *Contemporary theologies of mission.* Grand Rapids: Baker, 1983.

Goetze, Alfred, ed. *Sebastian Lotzers Schriften.* Leipzig: Teubner, 1902.

Gore, Charles. "The Holy Spirit and inspiration." In *Lux Mundi: A series of studies in the religion of the incarnation,* ed. Charles Gore. 15th ed., London: John Murray, 1904 (1889). 230-266.

_____. *The incarnation of the Son of God.* London: John Murray, 1891.

Gore, Charles, ed. *Lux Mundi: A series of studies in the religion of the incarnation.* 15th ed. London: John Murray, 1904.

Goulder, Michael. "Paradox and mystification." In *Incarnation and myth: The debate continued,* ed. Michael Goulder. London: SCM, 1979. 51-59.

_____. "The two roots of the Christian myth." In *The myth of God incarnate,* ed. John Hick. London: SCM, 1977. 64-86.

Goulder, Michael, ed. *Incarnation and myth: The debate continued.* London: SCM, 1979.

Graber, J D. "Anabaptism expressed in missions and social service." In *The recovery of the Anabaptist vision,* ed. Guy F Hershberger. Scottdale, PA: Herald, 1957. 152-166.

Gray, William. "The myth of the Word discarnate." *Theology* 88 (1985): 112-117.

Grayston, Kenneth. "Flesh, fleshly, carnal." In *A theological word book of the Bible,* ed. Alan Richardson. London: SCM, 1950. 83-84.

Green, Michael, ed. *The truth of God incarnate.* London: Hodder and Stoughton, 1977.

Greenway, Roger S, ed. *Discipling the city: A comprehensive approach to urban mission.* 2nd ed. Grand Rapids: Baker, 1992.

Gremillion, Joseph, ed. *The gospel of peace and justice: Catholic social teaching since Pope John.* Maryknoll: Orbis, 1976.

Grenz, Stanley J. *A primer on postmodernism.* Grand Rapids: Eerdmans, 1996.

Gresham, John L, Jr. "The social model of the trinity and its critics." *Scottish Journal of Theology* 46 (1993): 325-343.

Griffin, David R. *A process christology.* Philadelphia: Fortress, 1973.

Grigg, Viv. "Church of the poor." In *Discipling the city: A comprehensive approach to urban mission,* ed. Roger S Greenway. 2nd ed., Grand Rapids: Baker, 1992. 159-170.

_____. *Companion to the poor.* Rev. ed. Monrovia, CA: MARC, 1990.

_____. *Cry of the urban poor.* Monrovia, CA: MARC, 1992.

_____. "Sorry! The frontier moved." *Urban Mission* 4.4 (Mar 1987): 12-25.

_____. "The urban poor: Prime missionary target." *Evangelical Review of Theology* 11 (1987): 261-272.

Guder, Darrell L. *Be my witnesses: The church's mission, message, and messengers.* Grand Rapids: Eerdmans, 1985.

_____. "Incarnation and the church's evangelistic mission." *International Review of Mission* 83 (1994): 417-428. (Given name misspelt as "Daryl" and "Darrel" on p. 417.)

_____. *The continuing conversion of the church.* Grand Rapids: Eerdmans, 2000.

Gunton, Colin. *The one, the three and the many: God, creation and the culture of modernity.* Cambridge: Cambridge University Press, 1993.

Gustafson, James. *Christ and the moral life.* New York: Harper, 1968.

Haight, Roger. *An alternative vision: An interpretation of liberation theology.* New York: Paulist, 1985.

_____. "The case for Spirit Christology." *Theological Studies* 53 (1992): 257-287.

_____. *The experience and language of grace.* Dublin: Gill and Macmillan, 1979.

Hamilton, Andrew. "What has Asia to do with Australia: Reflections on the theology of Aloysius Pieris." *Pacifica* 3 (1990): 304-322.

Hampson, Daphne. *Theology and feminism.* Oxford: Basil Blackwell, 1990.

Hanson, Anthony Tyrell. *The paradox of the cross in the thought of St Paul.* Sheffield: JSOT Press, 1987.

Hardawiryana, Robert. "Mission in Asia: Theological perspectives." In *Towards an Asian theology of mission,* eds. Michael T Seigel and Leonardo N Mercado. Manila: Divine Word Publications, 1995. 18-50.

Harris, Dorothy. "Incarnation as relocation among the poor." *Evangelical Review of Theology* 18 (1994): 117-127.

Harris, Dorothy, Douglas Hynd and David Millikan, eds. *The shape of belief: Christianity in Australia today.* Homebush West, NSW: Lancer, 1982.

Harris, Elizabeth. *Prologue and Gospel: The theology of the Fourth Evangelist.* Journal for the Study of the New Testament, Supplement Series, 107. Sheffield, UK: Sheffield Academic Press, 1994.

Hartshorne, Charles. *Omnipotence and other theological mistakes.* Albany, NY: State University of New York, 1984.

Harvey, A E. *Strenuous commands: The ethic of Jesus.* London: SCM, 1990.

Harvey, A E, ed. *God incarnate: Story and belief.* London: SPCK, 1981.

Harvey, David. *The condition of postmodernity: An enquiry into the origins of cultural change.* Oxford: Blackwell, 1989.

Hauerwas, Stanley A and William H Willimon. *Resident aliens.* Nashville: Abingdon, 1989.

Hazlett, Ian, ed. *Early Christianity: Origins and evolution to AD600.* London: SPCK, 1991.

Hebblethwaite, Brian. "Incarnation." In *A new handbook of Christian theology*, eds. Donald W Musser and Joseph L Price. Nashville: Abingdon, 1992. 250-254.

_____. *The incarnation: Collected essays in christology*. Cambridge: Cambridge University Press, 1987.

_____. "Incarnation—the essence of Christianity." In *The incarnation: Collected essays in christology*, by Brian Hebblethwaite. Cambridge: Cambridge University Press, 1987. 1-10.

Hendricks, Barbara. "Mission in service of God's reign." In *Mission in the nineteen 90s*, eds. Gerald H Anderson, James M Phillips and Robert T Coote. Grand Rapids: Eerdmans, 1991. 26-30.

Hendry, George S. *The gospel of the incarnation*. London: SCM, 1959.

Heron, Alisdair. "The person of Christ." In *Keeping the faith: Essays to mark the centenary of Lux Mundi*, ed. Geoffrey Wainwright. Philadelphia: Fortress, 1988. 99-123.

Hershberger, Guy F, ed. *The recovery of the Anabaptist vision*. Scottdale, PA: Herald, 1957.

Herzog, Frederick. *God-walk: Liberation shaping dogmatics*. Maryknoll: Orbis, 1988.

Hick, John. "An inspiration christology for a religiously plural world." In *Encountering Jesus: A debate on christology*, ed. Stephen T Davis. Atlanta: John Knox, 1988. 5-22.

_____. "Jesus and the world religions." In *The myth of God incarnate*, ed. John Hick. London: SCM, 1977. 167-185.

_____. *The metaphor of God incarnate*. London: SCM, 1993.

Hick, John, ed. *The myth of God incarnate*. London: SCM, 1977.

Hill, Brennan. *Jesus, the Christ: Contemporary perspectives*. Mystic, CN: Twenty-third Publications, 1991.

Hill, Harriet. "Incarnational ministry: A critical examination." *Evangelical Missions Quarterly* 26 (1990): 196-201.

Hirst, Paul H. "Liberal education and the nature of knowledge." In *Knowledge and the curriculum: A collection of philosophical papers*, by Paul H Hirst. London: Routledge & Kegan Paul, 1974. 30-53.

Hodgson, Peter C. *Winds of the Spirit: A constructive Christian theology*. Louisville: Westminster John Knox, 1994.

Hodgson, Peter C and Robert H King, eds. *Readings in Christian theology*. Philadelphia: Fortress, 1985.

Hoekendijk, J C. "The church in missionary thinking." *International Review of Missions* 41 (1952): 324-336.

_____. *The church inside out*. London: SCM, 1966.

Hogg, W Richey. "Vatican II's *Ad Gentes*: A twenty-year retrospective." *International Bulletin of Missionary Research* 9 (1985): 146-154.

Honoré, Deborah Duncan, ed. *Trevor Huddleston: Essays on his life and work.* Oxford: Oxford University Press, 1988.

Hook, Norman. *Christ in the twentieth century: A Spirit Christology.* London: Lutterworth, 1968.

_____. "A Spirit Christology." *Theology* 75 (1972): 226-232.

Hopkins, Thomas J. *The Hindu religious tradition.* Encino, CA: Dickenson, 1971.

Hopper, Jeffery. *Understanding modern theology II: Reinterpreting Christian faith for changing worlds.* Philadelphia: Fortress, 1987.

Hoynacki, George John. "'And the word was made flesh'—Incarnations in religious traditions." *Asia Journal of Theology* 7 (1993): 12-34.

Hubmaier, Balthasar. "Freedom of the will, I." In *Balthasar Hubmaier: Theologian of Anabaptism*, eds. H Wayne Pipkin and John H Yoder. Scottdale, PA: Herald, 1989 [1524]. 426-448.

Huddleston, Trevor. *Naught for your comfort.* London: Collins, 1956.

Huebner, Harry. "Discipleship." In *The Mennonite encyclopedia, Vol. 5*, eds. Cornelius J Dyck and Dennis D Martin. Scottdale, PA: Herald, 1990. 238-239.

Illingworth, J R. "The incarnation and development." In *Lux Mundi: A series of studies in the religion of the incarnation*, ed. Charles Gore. 15th ed., London: John Murray, 1904 (1889). 132-157.

Jenkinson, William and Helen O'Sullivan, eds. *Trends in mission: Toward the third millennium. Essays in celebration of twenty-five years of SEDOS.* Maryknoll: Orbis, 1991.

John, Jeffrey, ed. *Living tradition: Affirming Catholicism in the Anglican church.* London: Darton, Longman and Todd, 1992.

John Paul II, Pope. *Redemptoris Missio: The permanent validity of the church's missionary mandate.* Homebush, NSW: St Paul Publications, 1991.

Johnson, Elizabeth A. *Consider Jesus: Waves of renewal in Christology.* New York: Crossroad, 1994.

Johnston, Arthur P. "The kingdom in relation to the church and the world." In *In word and deed: Evangelism and social responsibility*, ed. Bruce J Nicholls. Exeter: Paternoster, 1985. 109-134.

Jüngel, Eberhard. "Metaphorical truth. Reflections on theological metaphor as a contribution to a hermeneutics of narrative theology." In *Theological essays*, by Eberhard Jüngel. Edinburgh: T & T Clark, 1989. 16-71.

Justin Martyr. "Apology." In *The Apostolic Fathers: Justin Martyr and Irenaeus*, The Ante-Nicene Fathers: Translation of the writings of the Fathers down to A.D. 325, ed. A Cleveland Coxe. Rev. ed., Vol. 1. Grand Rapids: Eerdmans, ca. 1962. 159-193.

Kasdorf, Hans. "The Anabaptist approach to mission." In *Anabaptism and mission*, ed. Wilbert R Shenk. Scottdale, PA: Herald, 1984. 51-69.

Käsemann, Ernst. "The structure and purpose of the Prologue to John's Gospel." In *New Testament questions of today*, by Ernst Käsemann. London: SCM, 1969. 138-167.

_____. *The Testament of Jesus: A study of the gospel of John in the light of Chapter 17*. London: SCM, 1968.

Kasper, Walter. *Jesus the Christ*. London: Burns & Oates, 1976.

Kauffman, Richard A, ed. *A disciple's Christology: Appraisals of Kraus's Jesus Christ our Lord*. Occasional Papers No. 13. Elkhart, IN: Institute of Mennonite Studies, 1989.

Kavunkal, Jacob. "Ministry and mission." In *New directions in mission and evangelization, 2: Theological foundations*, eds. James A Scherer and Stephen B Bevans. Maryknoll: Orbis, 1994. 87-95.

Kelly, Balmer H. "Word of promise: The incarnation in the Old Testament." *Ex Auditu* 7 (1991): 19-27.

Kelly, J N D. *Early Christian doctrines*. 4th ed. London: Adam & Charles Black, 1968.

Kelly, Tony. *A new imagining: Towards an Australian spirituality*. Melbourne: Collins Dove, 1990.

Kelly, William J, ed. *Theology and discovery: Essays in honor of Karl Rahner, S.J.* Milwaukee, WI: Marquette University Press, 1980.

Kerferd, G B. "Mimesis." In *The encyclopedia of philosophy*, ed. Paul Edwards. New York: Macmillan, 1967. 5:335.

Keshishian, Aram. "Central Committee, 1991: Report of the Moderator." *The Ecumenical Review* 44 (1992): 113-120.

Khodre, George. "The Church as the privileged witness of God." In *Martyria/mission: The witness of the Orthodox churches today*, ed. Ion Bria. Geneva: World Council of Churches, 1980. 30-37.

Kinnamon, Michael, ed. *Signs of the Spirit: Official report, World Council of Churches, Seventh Assembly, Canberra, Australia, 7-20 February 1991*. Geneva: World Council of Churches, 1991.

Kittel, Gerhard and Gerhard Friedrich, eds. *Theological Dictionary of the New Testament*. 10 vols. Transl. Geoffrey W Bromiley. Grand Rapids: Eerdmans, 1964-1976 (German:1933-1973).

Klaassen, Walter. "Anabaptism." In *The Mennonite encyclopedia, Vol. 5*, eds. Cornelius J Dyck and Dennis D Martin. Scottdale, PA: Herald, 1990. 23-26.

_____. "Sixteenth-century Anabaptism: A vision valid for the twentieth century?." *The Conrad Grebel Review* 7 (1989): 241-251.

Köstenberger, Andreas J. "The challenge of a systematized biblical theology of mission: Missiological insights from the Gospel of John." *Missiology* 23 (1995): 445-464.

Krass, Alfred C. *Five lanterns at sundown: Evangelism in a chastened mood*. Grand Rapids: Eerdmans, 1978.

Kraus, C Norman. *Evangelicalism and Anabaptism.* Scottdale, PA: Herald, 1979.
_____. *Jesus Christ our Lord: Christology from a disciple's perspective.* Scottdale, PA: Herald, 1987.

Kraybill, Donald B. *The upside-down kingdom.* 2nd ed. Scottdale, PA: Herald, 1990.

Kreider, Alan F. "'The servant is not greater than his master': The Anabaptists and the suffering church." *The Mennonite Quarterly Review* 58 (1984): 5-29.

Krodel, Gerhard, ed. *The General Letters: Hebrews, James, 1-2 Peter, Jude, 1-2-3 John.* Minneapolis: Fortress, 1995.

Kroeger, James H. "Sent to witness—with enthusiasm." *African Ecclesial Review* 33 (1991): 288-294.

Küng, Hans. *On being a Christian.* London: Collins, 1977.

Kurz, William S. "Kenotic imitation of Paul and of Christ in Philippians 2 and 3." In *Discipleship in the New Testament,* ed. Fernando F Segovia. Philadelphia: Fortress, 1985. 103-126.

Kysar, Robert. *The Fourth Evangelist and his Gospel: An examination of contemporary scholarship.* Minneapolis: Augsburg, 1975.

Lacugna, Catherine Mowry. *God for us: The trinity and Christian life.* San Francisco: Harper, 1991.

Lampe, G W H. "The essence of Christianity: A personal view." *The Expository Times* 87 (1976): 132-137.

Lampe, Geoffrey W H. *God as Spirit.* Oxford: Oxford University Press, 1977.

Langer, Suzanne. *Philosophy in a new key.* New York: Mentor, 1948.

Latin American Episcopal Council (CELAM). *Medellin, 1968: The church in the present day transformation of Latin America.* 2 vols. Washington, DC: U.S. Catholic Conference, 1968.

"The Lausanne Covenant." In *Let the earth hear his voice: International Congress on World Evangelization, Lausanne, Switzerland, Official reference volume,* ed. J D Douglas. Minneapolis: World Wide Publications, 1975. 3-9.

Le Guillou, Marie-Joseph. "Mission as an ecclesiological theme." *Concilium* 3.2 (Mar 1966): 43-67.

Lehmann-Habeck, Martin. "Wholistic evangelism: A WCC perspective." *International Review of Mission* 73 (1984): 7-16.

Linthicum, Robert C. *City of God, city of Satan: A biblical theology of the church.* Grand Rapids: Zondervan, 1991.
_____. *Empowering the poor.* Monrovia, CA: MARC, 1991.

Lock, W. "The church." In *Lux Mundi: A series of studies in the religion of the incarnation,* ed. Charles Gore. 15th ed., London: John Murray, 1904 (1889). 267-295.

Löffler, Paul. "The confessing community: Evangelism in ecumenical perspective." *International Review of Mission* 66 (1977): 339-348.

Lois, Julio. "Christology in the theology of liberation." In *Mysterium Liberationis: Fundamental concepts of liberation theology*, eds. Ignacio Ellacuría and Jon Sobrino. Maryknoll: Orbis, 1993. 168-194.

Lonergan, Bernard J. *Method in theology*. London: Darton, Longman & Todd, 1972.

Lorenzen, Thorwald. *Resurrection and discipleship: Interpretive models, biblical reflections, theological consequences*. Maryknoll: Orbis, 1996.

Lossky, Nicholas. "Eastern Orthodoxy." In *Dictionary of the ecumenical movement*, eds. Nicholas Lossky et al. Geneva: World Council of Churches, 1991. 311-313.

_____. "Oriental Orthodox churches." In *Dictionary of the ecumenical movement*, eds. Nicholas Lossky et al. Geneva: World Council of Churches, 1991. 755-757.

_____. "Orthodoxy." In *Dictionary of the ecumenical movement*, eds. Nicholas Lossky et al. Geneva: World Council of Churches, 1991. 764-768.

Lossky, Nicholas et al., eds. *Dictionary of the ecumenical movement*. Geneva: World Council of Churches, 1991.

Lossky, Vladimir. *The mystical theology of the Eastern Church*. Cambridge, UK: James Clarke, 1991 (1944).

Loy, Allan W. "Praxis: Karl Marx's challenge to Christian theology." *St Mark"s Review* No. 113 (Mar 1983): 7-14, 24.

"Lumen Gentium (Dogmatic Constitution on the Church)." In *The documents of Vatican II*, ed. Walter M Abbott. London: Geoffrey Chapman, 1966. 14-101.

Luther, Martin. "Against the Antinomians." In *Luther"s Works, Vol. 47: The Christians in Society, IV*, ed. Franklin Sherman. Philadelphia: Fortress, 1971 [1540?]. 107-119.

_____. "The freedom of the Christian." In *Luther"s Works, Vol. 31: Career of the Reformer, I*, ed. Harold J Grim. Philadelphia: Fortress, 1957 [1520]. 333-377.

Lyon, David. *Postmodernity*. Minneapolis: University of Minnesota Press, 1994.

Lyttleton, Arthur. "The atonement." In *Lux Mundi: A series of studies in the religion of the incarnation*, ed. Charles Gore. 15th ed., London: John Murray, 1904 (1889). 201-229.

MacCormac, Earl R. *Metaphor and myth in science and religion*. Durham, NC: Duke University Press, 1976.

MacIntyre, Alisdair. *Whose justice? Which rationality?* London: Duckworth, 1988.

Mackay, Hugh. *Reinventing Australia: The mind and mood of Australia in the 90s*. Sydney: Angus & Robertson, 1993.

Mackay, John A. *Ecumenics: The science of the church universal*. Englewood Cliffs: Prentice-Hall, 1964.

Mackey, J P. "Trinity, Doctrine of the." In *A new dictionary of Christian theology*, eds. Alan Richardson and John Bowden. London: SCM, 1983. 581-589.

MacKinnon, D M. "The relation of the doctrines of the incarnation and the trinity." In *Creation, Christ and culture: Studies in honour of T F Torrance,* ed. Richard W A McKinney. Edinburgh: T & T Clark, 1976. 92-107.

The Macquarie Dictionary. 2nd ed. Macquarie University, NSW: The Macquarie Library, 1991.

Macquarrie, John. "The concept of a Christ-event." In *God incarnate: Story and belief,* ed. A E Harvey. London: SPCK, 1981. 69-80.

_____. "Incarnation." In *The Blackwell Encyclopedia of modern Christian thought,* ed. Alister E McGrath. Oxford: Blackwell, 1993. 269-272.

_____. *Principles of Christian theology.* Rev. ed. London: SCM, 1977.

_____. "Today's word for today: I. Jürgen Moltmann." *Expository Times* 92 (Oct 1980): 4-7.

_____. *Jesus Christ in modern thought.* London: SCM, 1990.

"The Manila Manifesto: Calling the whole church to take the whole gospel to the whole world." In *The whole gospel for the whole world: Story of Lausanne II Congress on World Evangelization, Manila 1989,* ed. Alan Nichols. Ventura, CA: Regal, 1989. 110-126.

Marchant, Colin. *Shalom my friends: Building God's kingdom together.* Basingstoke, UK: Marshall Pickering, 1988.

_____. *Signs in the city.* London: Hodder & Stoughton, 1985.

Marshall, Christopher. *Kingdom come: The kingdom of God in the teaching of Jesus.* 2nd ed. Auckland: Impetus, 1993.

Marty, Martin E and Dean G Peerman, eds. *A handbook of Christian theologians.* Nashville: Abingdon, 1984.

McBrien, Richard. *Catholicism.* 3rd ed. Nth Blackburn, Vic.: CollinsDove, 1994.

McCarthy, Timothy G. *The Catholic tradition: Before and after Vatican II, 1878-1993.* Chicago: Loyola University Press, 1994.

McCasland, S Vernon. "Flesh in the NT." In *The Interpreter's Dictionary of the Bible,* ed. George Arthur Buttrick. Nashville: Abingdon, 1962. 2:276-277.

McClendon, James Wm., Jr. *Biography as theology: How life stories can remake today's theology.* Nashville: Abingdon, 1974.

McDermott, Brian O. *Word become flesh: Dimensions of Christology.* Collegeville, MN: The Liturgical Press, 1993.

McDonagh, Enda. "The missionary task after Vatican II." In *The church is mission,* eds. Enda McDonagh et al. London: Geoffrey Chapman, 1969. 7-23.

McDonagh, Enda et al., eds. *The church is mission.* London: Geoffrey Chapman, 1969.

McElhanon, Kenneth. "Don't give up on the incarnational model." *Evangelical Missions Quarterly* 27 (1991): 390-393.

McFague, Sallie. *The body of God: An ecological theology.* London: SCM, 1993.

_____. *Metaphorical theology: Models of God in religious language.* London: SCM, 1983.

_____. *Models of God: Theology for an ecological, nuclear age.* London: SCM, 1987.

McGavran, Donald A. "The current conciliar theology of mission." In *Contemporary theologies of mission*, by Arthur F Glasser and Donald A McGavran. Grand Rapids: Baker, 1983. 62-81.

_____. "New mission: A systematic reinterpretation of the concepts of mission." In *Contemporary theologies of mission*, by Arthur F Glasser and Donald A McGavran. Grand Rapids: Baker, 1983. 47-61.

McGovern, Arthur F. *Liberation theology and its critics: Toward an assessment.* Maryknoll: Orbis, 1989.

McGrath, Alister E. "Anglicanism." In *The Blackwell Encyclopedia of modern Christian thought*, ed. Alister E McGrath. Oxford: Blackwell, 1993. 3-5.

_____. "In what way can Jesus be a moral example for Christians?" *Journal of the Evangelical Theological Society* 34 (1991): 289-298.

_____. *Understanding Jesus: Who Jesus Christ is and why he matters.* Grand Rapids: Academie, 1987.

McGrath, Alister E, ed. *The Blackwell encyclopedia of modern Christian thought.* Oxford: Blackwell, 1993.

McKinney, Richard W A, ed. *Creation, Christ and culture: Studies in honour of T F Torrance.* Edinburgh: T & T Clark, 1976.

Mead, Loren B. *The once and future church: Reinventing the congregation for a new mission frontier.* New York: The Alban Institute, 1991.

Melancthon, Philip. "*Loci communes theologici* [Fundamental theological themes, 1521]." In *Melancthon and Bucer*, The Library of Christian Classics, Vol. 19, ed. Wilhelm Pauck. London: SCM, 1969. 18-152.

Messer, Donald E. *A conspiracy of goodness: Contemporary images of Christian mission.* Nashville: Abingdon, 1992.

Meyendorff, John. "The Orthodox church and mission: Past and present perspectives." In *Mission trends No. 1: Crucial issues in mission today*, eds. Gerald H Anderson and Thomas F Stransky. New York: Paulist, 1974. 59-71.

Meyendorff, John and Robert Tobias, eds. *Salvation in Christ: A Lutheran-Orthodox dialogue.* Minneapolis: Augsburg, 1992.

Michaelis, W. "μιμέομαι, μιμητής, συμμιμητής." In *Theological Dictionary of the New Testament*, eds. Gerhard Kittel and Gerhard Friedrich. Grand Rapids: Eerdmans, 1964-1976. 4:659-674.

Michaelson, Wes. "Evangelicalism and radical discipleship." In *Evangelicalism and Anabaptism*, ed. C Norman Kraus. Scottdale, PA: Herald, 1979. 63-82.

Migliore, Daniel L. *Faith seeking understanding: An introduction to Christian theology.* Grand Rapids: Eerdmans, 1991.

Miles, Margaret R. *The image and practice of holiness: A critique of the classic manuals of devotion.* London: SCM, 1988.

Miller, James B. "The emerging postmodern world." In *Postmodern theology: Christian faith in a pluralist world*, ed. Frederic B Burnham. San Francisco: Harper & Row, 1989. 1-19.

Miller, Larry. "The church as messianic society: Creation and instrument of transfigured mission." In *The transfiguration of mission: Biblical, theological and historical foundations*, ed. Wilbert R Shenk. Scottdale, PA: Herald, 1993. 130-152.

Millikan, David. "Christianity and Australian identity." In *The shape of belief: Christianity in Australia today*, eds. Dorothy Harris, Douglas Hynd and David Millikan. Homebush West, NSW: Lancer, 1982. 29-46.

_____. *The sunburnt soul: Christianity in search of an Australian identity*. Homebush West, NSW: Lancer, 1981.

Milne, Bruce. "'Even so send I you': An expository and theological reflection on John 20:21." In *Mission to the world: Essays to celebrate the 50th anniversary of the ordination of George Raymond Beasley-Murray to the Christian ministry*, ed. Paul Beasley-Murray. Didcot, UK: Baptist Historical Society, 1991. 47-51.

Mitchell, Basil. *The justification of religious belief*. London: Macmillan, 1973.

Moffatt, James. *Grace in the New Testament*. London: Hodder and Stoughton, 1931.

Möhler, Johann Adam. *Symbolism; or, Exposition of the doctrinal differences between Catholics and Protestants as evidenced by their symbolic writings*. New York: E Dunigan, 1844.

Moiser, Jeremy. "Dogmatic thoughts on imitation of Christ." *Scottish Journal of Theology* 30 (1977): 201-213.

Moltmann, Jürgen. *The church in the power of the Spirit: A contribution to messianic ecclesiology*. London: SCM, 1977.

_____. *The coming of God: Christian eschatology*. London: SCM, 1996.

_____. *The crucified God: The cross of Christ as the foundation and criticism of Christian theology*. London: SCM, 1974.

_____. *The future of creation*. London: SCM, 1979.

_____. *God in creation: An ecological doctrine of creation*. London: SCM, 1985.

_____. *The open church: Invitation to a messianic lifestyle*. London: SCM, 1978.

_____. "Political discipleship of Christ today." In *Communities of faith and radical discipleship: Jürgen Moltmann and others*, ed. G McLeod Bryan. Macon, GA: Mercer University Press, 1986. 15-31.

_____. *The Spirit of life: A universal affirmation*. London: SCM, 1992.

_____. *Theology of hope: On the ground and the implications of a Christian eschatology*. London: SCM, 1967.

_____. *The trinity and the kingdom: The doctrine of God*. Minneapolis: Fortress, 1993. First published in English as *The trinity and the kingdom of God*. London: SCM, 1981.

_____. *The way of Jesus Christ: Christology in messianic dimensions.* London: SCM, 1990.

Moltmann-Wendel, Elisabeth. *I am my body: New ways of embodiment.* London: SCM, 1994.

Moore, Aubrey. "The Christian doctrine of God." In *Lux Mundi: A series of studies in the religion of the incarnation,* ed. Charles Gore. 15th ed., London: John Murray, 1904 (1889). 41-81.

Moreno, Juan Ramón. "Evangelization." In *Mysterium Liberationis: Fundamental concepts of liberation theology,* eds. Ignacio Ellacuría and Jon Sobrino. Maryknoll: Orbis, 1993. 564-580.

Morgan, Robert, ed. *The religion of the incarnation: Anglican essays in commemoration of Lux Mundi.* Bristol: Bristol Classical Press, 1989.

Morse, Christopher. "Jürgen Moltmann." In *A handbook of Christian theologians,* eds. Martin E Marty and Dean G Peerman. Enlarged ed., Nashville: Abingdon, 1984. 660-676.

Motte, Mary. "Issues in Protestant-Roman Catholic discussions of theology of mission." In *The good news of the kingdom: Mission theology for the third millennium,* eds. Charles Van Engen, Dean S Gilliland and Paul Pierson. Maryknoll: Orbis, 1993. 119-126.

_____. "The poor: Starting point for mission." In *Mission in the 1990s,* eds. Gerald H Anderson, James M Phillips and Robert T Coote. Grand Rapids: Eerdmans, 1991. 50-54.

Motte, Mary and Joseph R Lang, eds. *Mission in dialogue: The SEDOS research seminar on the future of mission, March 8-19, 1981, Rome, Italy.* Maryknoll: Orbis, 1982.

Moulder, James. "Is a Chalcedonian christology coherent?." *Modern Theology* 2 (1986): 285-307.

Mouw, Richard J. *Political evangelism.* Grand Rapids: Eerdmans, 1973.

Mozley, J K. *The doctrine of the incarnation.* London: The Unicorn Press, 1936.

Musser, Donald W and Joseph L Price, eds. *A new handbook of Christian theology.* Nashville: Abingdon, 1992.

Myers, Ched. *Binding the strong man: A political reading of Mark"s story of Jesus.* Maryknoll: Orbis, 1988.

_____. *Who will roll away the stone? Discipleship queries for first world Christians.* Maryknoll: Orbis, 1994.

Nelson, James B. *Body theology.* Louisville: Westminster/John Knox Press, 1992.

_____. *Embodiment: An approach to sexuality and Christian theology.* Minneapolis: Augsburg, 1978.

Neuhaus, Richard John. "Moltmann vs. monotheism." *Dialog* 20 (1981): 239-243.

Newbigin, Lesslie. "Evangelism in the context of secularization." In *A word in season: Perspectives on Christian world missions,* by Lesslie Newbigin. Grand Rapids: Eerdmans, 1994. 148-157.

_____. *Foolishness to the Greeks: The gospel and Western culture*. Grand Rapids: Eerdmans, 1986.

_____. *Mission in Christ's way: A gift, a command, an assurance*. Geneva: World Council of Churches, 1987.

Newlands, George. "Soteriology." In *A new dictionary of Christian theology*, eds. Alan Richardson and John Bowden. London: SCM, 1983. 546-548.

Newman, Martyn. *Liberation theology is evangelical*. Melbourne: Mallorn, 1990.

Newman, Paul W. *A Spirit Christology: Recovering the biblical paradigm of Christian faith*. Lanham, MD: University Press of America, 1987.

Nicholls, Bruce J, ed. *In word and deed: Evangelism and social responsibility*. Exeter: Paternoster, 1985.

Nicholls, David. "Christianity and politics." In *The religion of the incarnation: Anglican essays in commemoration of Lux Mundi*, ed. Robert Morgan. Bristol: Bristol Classical Press, 1989. 172-188.

Nichols, Alan, ed. *The whole gospel for the whole world: Story of Lausanne II Congress on World Evangelization, Manila 1989*. Ventura, CA: Regal, 1989.

Nichols, Aidan. *The panther and the hind: A theological history of Anglicanism*. Edinburgh: T & T Clark, 1993.

_____. *Yves Congar*. London: Geoffrey Chapman, 1989.

Niebuhr, H Richard. *Christ and culture*. New York: Harper, 1951.

Nineham, Dennis. "Epilogue." In *The myth of God incarnate*, ed. John Hick. London: SCM, 1977. 186-204.

Núñez, Emilio. "Evangelical theology and praxis for Latin America." *Evangelical Review of Theology* 11 (1987): 107-119.

_____. "Towards an evangelical Latin American theology." *Evangelical Review of Theology* 7 (1983): 123-131.

O'Collins, Gerald. *Christology: A biblical, historical, and systematic study of Jesus Christ*. Oxford: Oxford University Press, 1995.

O'Collins, Gerald and Edward G Farrugia, eds. *A concise dictionary of theology*. New York: Paulist, 1991.

Ogden, Schubert. "What is theology?" In *Readings in Christian theology*, eds. Peter C Hodgson and Robert H King. Philadelphia: Fortress, 1985. 15-30.

Olson, Roger E. "Is Moltmann the evangelicals ally?." *Christianity Today* 37 (11 Jan 1993): 32.

Oosterbaan, J A. "The reformation of the Reformation: Fundamentals of Anabaptist theology." *The Mennonite Quarterly Review* 51 (1977): 171-195.

Ortiz, Manuel. "Being disciples: Incarnational Christians in the city." In *Discipling the city: A comprehensive approach to urban mission*, ed. Roger S Greenway. 2nd ed., Grand Rapids: Baker, 1992. 85-98.

Ortony, Andrew, ed. *Metaphor and thought*. Cambridge: Cambridge University Press, 1979.

Osthathios, Geevarghese Mar. "The gospel of the kingdom and the crucified and risen lord." In *Your kingdom come: Mission perspectives. Report on the World Conference on Mission and Evangelism, Melbourne, Australia, 12-25 May 1980*, Geneva: World Council of Churches, 1980. 37-51.

———. "Your will be done—Mission in Christ's way." *International Review of Mission* 75 (1986): 438-443.

Ottley, Robert. "Christian ethics." In *Lux Mundi: A series of studies in the religion of the incarnation*, ed. Charles Gore. 15th ed., London: John Murray, 1904 (1889). 340-381.

Padilla, René. "Christology and mission in the two thirds world." In *Sharing Jesus in the two-thirds world: Evangelical Christologies from the contexts of poverty, powerlessness and religious pluralism*, eds. Vinay Samuel and Chris Sugden. Grand Rapids: Eerdmans, 1983. 12-32.

———. "Evangelism and the world." In *Let the earth hear his voice: International Congress on World Evangelization, Lausanne, Switzerland*, ed. J D Douglas. Minneapolis: World Wide Publications, 1975. 116-146.

———. "Introduction." In *The new face of evangelicalism: An international symposium on the Lausanne Covenant*, ed. C René Padilla. London: Hodder & Stoughton, 1976. 9-16.

———. "Liberation theology: An appraisal." In *Freedom and discipleship: Liberation theology in Anabaptist perspective*, ed. Daniel S Schipani. Maryknoll: Orbis, 1989. 34-50.

———. *Mission between the times: Essays on the kingdom*. Grand Rapids: Eerdmans, 1985.

Padilla, C René, ed. *The new face of evangelicalism: An international symposium on the Lausanne Covenant*. London: Hodder & Stoughton, 1976.

Pannebecker, S F. "Missions, Foreign Mennonite." In *The Mennonite encyclopedia*, eds. Harold S Bender and C Henry Smith. Vol. 3. Scottdale, PA: Mennonite Publishing House, 1957. 712-717.

Pannenberg, Wolfhart. *Jesus—God and man*. London: SCM, 1968.

———. *Systematic theology*. Vol. 1. Grand Rapids: Eerdmans, 1991.

———. *Toward a theology of nature: Essays on science and faith*. Louisville: Westminster/John Knox, 1993.

Paton, David M, ed. *Breaking barriers: Nairobi 1975. The official report of the fifth assembly of the World Council of Churches, Nairobi, 23 November-10 December, 1975*. London: SPCK, 1976.

Paul VI, Pope. *Evangelii Nuntiandi [On evangelization in the modern world]*. Homebush, NSW: Society of St Paul, 1976.

Peachey, J Lorne. "Few articles rival this one: Responses to Dintaman in the *Gospel Herald*." *The Conrad Grebel Review* 13 (1995): 10-14.

Peters, Pam. *The Cambridge Australian English Style Guide*. Cambridge: Cambridge University Press, 1995.

Peters, Ted. "Trinity Talk: Parts 1 & 2." *Dialog* 26 (1987): 44-48, 133-138.

Pickering, W S F. *Anglo-Catholicism: A study in religious ambiguity.* London: SPCK, 1989.

Piepke, Joachim G. "Incarnation in cultural context." *Indian Missiological Review* 12 (1990): 39-52.

Pierard, R V. "Evangelicalism." In *Evangelical dictionary of theology*, ed. Walter A Elwell. Grand Rapids: Baker, 1984. 379-382.

Pieris, Aloysius. "The problem of universality and inculturation with regard to patterns of theological thinking." *Concilium* 6 1994): 70-79.

_____. "Whither new evangelism?." *Pacifica* 6 (1993): 327-334.

Pinnock, Clark H. "A call for the liberation of North American Christians." In *Evangelicals and liberation*, ed. Carl E Armerding. Grand Rapids: Baker, 1977. 128-136.

Pipkin, H Wayne and John H Yoder, eds. *Balthasar Hubmaier: Theologian of Anabaptism.* Scottdale, PA: Herald, 1989.

Pittenger, Norman. *Christology reconsidered.* London: SCM, 1970.

_____. "The incarnation in Process theology." *Review and Expositor* 71 (1974): 43-57.

_____. *The Word incarnate: A study of the doctrine of the person of Christ.* London: Nisbet, 1959.

Pius XII, Pope. *Mystici Corporis Christi.* London: Catholic Truth Society, 1944.

Placher, William C. *Narratives of a vulnerable God: Christ, theology and scripture.* Louisville, KY: Westminster John Knox, 1994.

Plantinga, Cornelius, Jr. "Gregory of Nyssa and the social analogy of the trinity." *The Thomist* 50 (1986): 325-352.

_____. "Social trinity and tritheism." In *Trinity, incarnation and atonement: Philosophical and theological essays*, eds. Ronald J Feenstra and Cornelius Plantinga, Jr. Notre Dame: University of Notre Dame Press, 1989. 21-47.

Pope-Levison, Priscilla. "Evangelism in the WCC: From New Delhi to Canberra." In *New directions in mission and evangelization, 2: Theological foundations*, eds. James A Scherer and Stephen B Bevans. Maryknoll: Orbis, 1994. 126-140.

_____. *Evangelization from a liberation perspective.* New York: Peter Lang, 1991.

Potter, Philip. "Evangelism and the World Council of Churches." *The Ecumenical Review* 20 (1968): 171-182.

Pregeant, Russell. "Christological groundings for liberation praxis." *Modern Theology* 5 (1989): 113-132.

_____. *Christology beyond dogma: Matthew's Christ in process hermeneutic.* Philadelphia: Fortress, 1978.

Prior, Anselm. "Equipping the people of God for Christian witness—A Roman Catholic account." *International Review of Mission* 83 (1994): 57-65.

Punton, Jim. *The Messiah people: Punton Papers, Vol. 1.* Ed. Paul Grant and Raj Patel. Birmingham, UK: Hot Iron Press, 1993.

Rahner, Karl. "The body in the order of salvation." In *Theological investigations, Vol. 17: Jesus, man and the church,* by Karl Rahner. London: Darton, Longman & Todd, 1962. 71-89.

_____. *Foundations of Christian faith.* New York: Seabury Press, 1978.

_____. "Incarnation." In *Encyclopedia of theology: A concise Sacramentum Mundi,* ed. Karl Rahner. London: Burns & Oates, 1975. 690-697.

_____. *Spiritual exercises.* New York: Herder & Herder, 1965.

_____. *Theological investigations.* Vol. 4. London: Darton, Longman & Todd, 1974.

Rahner, Karl, ed. *Encyclopedia of theology: A concise Sacramentum Mundi.* London: Burns & Oates, 1975.

Ramseyer, Robert L. "The Anabaptist vision and our world mission, 1." In *Anabaptism and mission,* ed. Wilbert R Shenk. Scottdale, PA: Herald, 1984. 178-187.

Reardon, Bernard M G. *From Coleridge to Gore: A century of religious thought in Britain.* London: Longman, 1971.

Redekop, Calvin. "The community of scholars and the essence of Anabaptism." *The Mennonite Quarterly Review* 67 (1993): 429-450.

Rees, Frank. "The community of the servant: A critical development of a contemporary image of the church." Thesis (Theol.M.). Melbourne College of Divinity, 1980.

Rejón, Francisco Moreno. "Fundamental moral theology in the theology of liberation." In *Mysterium Liberationis: Fundamental concepts of liberation theology,* eds. Ignacio Ellacuría and Jon Sobrino. Maryknoll: Orbis, 1993. 210-231.

Richards, I A. *The philosophy of rhetoric.* London: Oxford University Press, 1936.

Richardson, Alan, ed. *A theological wordbook of the Bible.* London: SCM, 1950.

Richardson, Alan and John Bowden, eds. *A new dictionary of theology.* London: SCM, 1983.

Ridderbos, Herman. *Paul: An outline of his theology.* London: SPCK, 1977.

Ringma, Charles. *Catch the wind.* Sutherland, NSW: Albatross, 1994.

Robinson, John A T. *The body: A study in Pauline theology.* London: SCM, 1952.

_____. *The human face of God.* London: SCM, 1973.

Rodriguez, Maria Arlinda. "Living with the poor in Brazil: 1. 'Insertion': A new way of being a religious missionary." In *Trends in mission: Toward the third millennium,* eds. William Jenkinson and Helen O'Sullivan. Maryknoll: Orbis, 1991. 216-220.

Rosato, Philip J. "The mission of the Spirit within and beyond the church." In *To the wind of God's Spirit: Reflections on the Canberra theme,* ed. Emilio Castro. Geneva: World Council of Churches, 1990. 21-30.

_____. "Spirit Christology: Ambiguity and promise." *Theological Studies* 38 (1977): 423-449.

Rowell, Geoffrey. "Historical retrospect: Lux Mundi 1889." In *The religion of the incarnation: Anglican essays in commemoration of Lux Mundi*, ed. Robert Morgan. Bristol: Bristol Classical Press, 1989. 205-217.

Rubingh, Eugene. "Mission in an urban world." *Evangelical Review of Theology* 11 (1987): 369-379.

Ruether, Rosemary Radford. *Sexism and God-talk: Toward a feminist theology*. Boston: Beacon, 1983.

Runia, Klaas. "The challenge of the modern world to the church." *Evangelical Review of Theology* 18 (1994): 301-321.

Rutschman, Laverne A. "Anabaptism and liberation theology." In *Freedom and discipleship: Liberation theology in Anabaptist perspective*, ed. Daniel S Schipani. Maryknoll: Orbis, 1989. 51-65.

Samuel, Vinay and Albrecht Hauser. "Proclaiming Christ in Christ's way: Studies in integral evangelism: Introduction." In *Proclaiming Christ in Christ's way: Studies in integral evangelism*, eds. Vinay Samuel and Albrecht Hauser. Oxford: Regnum, 1989. 9-14.

Samuel, Vinay and Albrecht Hauser, eds. *Proclaiming Christ in Christ's way: Studies in integral evangelism*. Oxford: Regnum, 1989.

Samuel, Vinay and Chris Sugden. "Evangelism and social responsibility—a biblical study on priorities." In *In word and deed: Evangelism and social responsibility*, ed. Bruce J Nicholls. Exeter: Paternoster, 1982. 189-214.

_____. "God's intention for the world." In *The church in response to human need*, eds. Vinay Samuel and Chris Sugden. Oxford: Regnum, 1987. 128-160.

_____. *Sharing Jesus in the two-thirds world*. The papers of the first Conference of Evangelical Mission Theologians from the Two-thirds World, Bangkok, March 1982. Grand Rapids: Eerdmans, 1983.

Samuel, Vinay and Chris Sugden, eds. *The church in response to human need*. Oxford: Regnum, 1987.

Samuel, Vinay and Chris Sugden, eds. *Evangelism and the poor: A third world study guide*. Rev. ed. Bangalore: Partnership in Mission-Asia, 1983.

Sand, Alexander. "σαρξ, σαρκος, η *sarx*, flesh." In *Exegetical Dictionary of the New Testament*, eds. Horst Balz and Gerhard Schneider. Grand Rapids: Eerdmans, 1990-1993. 3:230-233.

Scherer, James A. *Gospel, church and kingdom: Comparative studies in world mission theology*. Minneapolis: Augsburg, 1987.

_____. "Missiology as a discipline and what it includes." In *New directions in mission and evangelization 2: Theological foundations*, eds. James A Scherer and Stephen B Bevans. Maryknoll: Orbis, 1994. 173-187.

Scherer, James A and Stephen B Bevans, eds. *New directions in mission and evangelization, 1: Basic statements, 1974-1991*. Maryknoll: Orbis, 1992.

Scherer, James A and Stephen B Bevans, eds. *New directions in mission and evangelization, 2: Theological foundations.* Maryknoll: Orbis, 1994.

Schillebeeckx, Edward. *Christ the sacrament of the encounter with God.* New York: Sheed and Ward, 1963.

_____. *Jesus: An experiment in christology.* New York: Crossroad, 1979.

Schipani, Daniel S, ed. *Freedom and discipleship: Liberation theology in Anabaptist perspective.* Maryknoll: Orbis, 1989.

Schleiermacher, Friedrich. *The Christian faith.* Ed. H R Mackintosh and J S Stewart. Edinburgh: T & T Clark, 1928 [1830].

Schmemann, Alexander. *Church, world, mission: Reflections on Orthodoxy in the West.* Crestwood, NY: St Vladimir"s Seminary Press, 1979.

Schneiders, Sandra M. *Women and the Word: The gender of God in the New Testament and the spirituality of women.* New York: Paulist Press, 1986.

Schnelle, Udo. *Antidocetic christology in the Gospel of John: An investigation of the place of the Fourth Gospel in the Johannine School.* Minneapolis: Fortress, 1992.

Schreiter, Robert J. "Changes in Roman Catholic attitudes toward proselytism and mission." In *New directions in mission and evangelization, 2: Theological foundations*, eds. James A Scherer and Stephen B Bevans. Maryknoll: Orbis, 1994. 113-125.

_____. *Constructing local theologies.* Maryknoll: Orbis, 1985.

_____. "Mission into the third millennium." *Missiology* 18 (1990): 3-12.

Schüssler Fiorenza, Elisabeth. *In memory of her: A feminist theological reconstruction of Christian origins.* 2nd ed. London: SCM, 1995.

_____. *Jesus: Miriam's child, Sophia's prophet: Critical issues in feminist christology.* New York: Continuum, 1995.

Schütte, Johannes. "Why engage in missionary work?." In *Foundations of mission theology*, ed. SEDOS. Maryknoll: Orbis, 1972. 39-50.

Schweitzer, Don. "The consistency of Jürgen Moltmann"s theology." *Studies in Religion/Sciences Religieuses* 22 (1993): 197-208.

Schweizer, Eduard, Friedrich Baumgärtel and Rudolf Meyer. "σαρξ." In *Theological Dictionary of the New Testament*, eds. Gerhard Kittel and Gerhard Friedrich. Grand Rapids: Eerdmans, 1964-1976. 7:98-151.

Scriven, Charles. *The transformation of culture: Christian social ethics after H Richard Niebuhr.* Scottdale, PA: Herald, 1988.

SEDOS, ed. *Foundations of mission theology.* Maryknoll: Orbis, 1972.

Segovia, Fernando F. "A response to Fr. Sobrino." In *Theology and discovery: Essays in honor of Karl Rahner, S.J.*, ed. William J Kelly. Milwaukee, WI: Marquette University Press, 1980. 222-227.

Segovia, Fernando F, ed. *Discipleship in the New Testament.* Philadelphia: Fortress, 1985.

Seigel, Michael T and Leonardo N Mercado, eds. *Towards an Asian theology of mission*. Manila: Divine Word Publications, 1995.

Shank, David A. "Anabaptists and mission." In *Anabaptism and mission*, ed. Wilbert R Shenk. Scottdale, PA: Herald, 1984. 202-228.

_____. "Jesus the Messiah: Messianic foundation of mission." In *The transfiguration of mission: Biblical, theological, and historical foundations*, ed. Wilbert R Shenk. Scottdale, PA: Herald, 1993. 37-82.

Sheldon, Charles Monroe. *In his steps*. Grand Rapids: Zondervan, 1967 [1896].

Shenk, Wilbert R. "The culture of modernity as a missionary challenge." In *The good news of the kingdom: Mission theology for the third millennium*, eds. Charles Van Engen, Dean S Gilliland and Paul Pierson. Maryknoll: Orbis, 1993. 192-199.

_____. "The relevance of a Messianic missiology for mission today." In *The transfiguration of mission: Biblical, theological and historical foundations*, ed. Wilbert R Shenk. Scottdale, PA: Herald, 1993. 17-36.

Shenk, Wilbert R, ed. *Anabaptism and mission*. Scottdale, PA: Herald, 1984.

Shenk, Wilbert R, ed. *The transfiguration of mission: Biblical, theological and historical foundations*. Scottdale, PA: Herald, 1993.

Sheppard, David. *Bias to the poor*. London: Hodder & Stoughton, 1983.

Sherley-Price, Leo. "Introduction." In *The imitation of Christ*, by Thomas á Kempis. Transl. and ed. Leo Sherley-Price. Harmondsworth, Msex: Penguin, 1952 [1418]. 11-25.

Shorter, Aylward. *Evangelization and culture*. London: Geoffrey Chapman, 1994.

_____. *Revelation and its interpretation*. London: Geoffrey Chapman, 1983.

_____. *Toward a theology of inculturation*. Maryknoll: Orbis, 1988.

Showalter, Richard. "'The spiritual poverty of the Anabaptist vision': An assessment." *The Conrad Grebel Review* 13 (1995): 14-18.

Sider, Ronald J. "Evangelicalism and the Mennonite tradition." In *Evangelicalism and Anabaptism*, ed. C Norman Kraus. Scottdale, PA: Herald, 1979. 149-168.

_____. "Mennonites and the poor: Toward an Anabaptist theology of liberation." In *Freedom and discipleship: Liberation theology in Anabaptist perspective*, ed. Daniel S Schipani. Maryknoll: Orbis, 1989. 85-100.

_____. *One-sided Christianity? Uniting the church to heal a lost and broken world*. Grand Rapids: Zondervan, 1993. Also published as *Evangelism and social action*. London: Hodder & Stoughton, 1993.

_____. *Rich Christians in an age of hunger*. Rev. ed. London: Hodder & Stoughton, 1990.

Sider, Ronald J and John R W Stott. *Evangelism, salvation and social justice*. Grove Booklet on Ethics No. 16. Bramcote, Notts.: Grove Books, 1979.

Silman, Janet. "Your will be done—Mission in Christ's way." *International Review of Mission* 75 (1986): 435-438.

Simons, Menno. "Reply to Gellius Faber, 1554." In *The complete writings of Menno Simons, c. 1496-1561*, 3 vols. ed. J C Wenger. Scottsdale, PA: Mennonite Publishing House, 1956. 1:625-781.

Sine, Tom. *Wild hope*. Dallas: Word Publishing, 1991.

Smith, Eugene L. "A response [to *Ad Gentes*]." In *The documents of Vatican II*, ed. Walter M Abbott. London: Geoffrey Chapman, 1966. 631-633.

Smith, John. *Advance Australia where?* Homebush West: ANZEA, 1988.

_____. *Cutting edge*. Tunbridge Wells, UK: Monarch, 1992.

Smith, Luther E, Jr. *Intimacy and mission: Intentional community as crucible for radical discipleship*. Scottdale, PA: Herald, 1994.

Snider, Theodore M. *The divine activity: An approach to incarnational theology*. New York: Peter Lang, 1990.

Snyder, C Arnold. *Anabaptist history and theology: An introduction*. Kitchener, Ontario: Pandora Press, 1995.

_____. "The Anabaptist vision: Theological perspectives (Editorial)." *The Conrad Grebel Review* 13.1 (Winter 1995): iii-vii.

_____. "The relevance of Anabaptist nonviolence for Nicaragua today." In *Freedom and discipleship: Liberation theology in Anabaptist perspective*, ed. Daniel S Schipani. Maryknoll: Orbis, 1989. 112-127.

Sobrino, Jon. *Archbishop Romero: Memories and reflections*. Maryknoll: Orbis, 1990.

_____. "Central position of the reign of God in liberation theology." In *Mysterium Liberationis: Fundamental concepts of liberation theology*, eds. Ignacio Ellacuría and Jon Sobrino. Maryknoll: Orbis, 1993. 350-388.

_____. *Christology at the crossroads: A Latin American approach*. London: SCM, 1978.

_____. "Communion, conflict, and ecclesial solidarity." In *Mysterium Liberationis: Fundamental concepts of liberation theology*, eds. Ignacio Ellacuría and Jon Sobrino. Maryknoll: Orbis, 1993. 615-636.

_____. "The economics of ecclesia: A poor church is a church rich in compassion." In *New visions for the Americas: Religious engagement and social transformation*, ed. David Batstone. Minneapolis: Fortress, 1993. 83-100.

_____. *Jesus in Latin America*. Maryknoll: Orbis, 1987.

_____. *Jesus the liberator: A historical-theological reading of Jesus of Nazareth*. Tunbridge Wells, UK: Burns & Oates, 1994.

_____. *Spirituality of liberation: Toward political holiness*. Maryknoll: Orbis, 1988.

_____. *The true church and the poor*. London: SCM, 1985.

_____. "Spirituality and the following of Jesus." In *Mysterium Liberationis: Fundamental concepts of liberation theology*, eds. Ignacio Ellacuría and Jon Sobrino. Maryknoll: Orbis, 1993. 677-701.

_____. "Systematic christology: Jesus Christ, the absolute mediator of the reign of God." In *Mysterium Liberationis: Fundamental concepts of liberation theology*, eds. Ignacio Ellacuría and Jon Sobrino. Maryknoll: Orbis, 1993. 440-461.

Song, Choan-Seng. *Christian mission in reconstruction: An Asian analysis*. Maryknoll: Orbis, 1977.

_____. "The divine mission of creation." In *Asian Christian theology: Emerging themes*, ed. Douglas J Elwood. Rev. ed., Philadelphia: Westminster, 1980. 177-199.

_____. *Jesus and the reign of God*. Minneapolis: Fortress, 1993.

_____. "Jesus Christ—The life of the world—An Asian meditation." *East Asia Journal of Theology* 1 (1983): 116-123.

_____. *Jesus in the power of the Spirit*. Minneapolis: Fortress, 1994.

_____. *Jesus, the crucified people*. New York: Crossroad, 1990.

_____. "Taiwan: Theology of the incarnation." In *Asian voices in Christian theology*, ed. Gerald H Anderson. Maryknoll: Orbis, 1976. 147-160.

_____. *Tell us our names: Story theology from an Asian perspective*. Maryknoll: Orbis, 1979.

_____. *Third-eye theology: Theology in formation in Asian settings*. 2nd ed. Maryknoll: Orbis, 1990.

Soskice, Janet Martin. *Metaphor and religious language*. Oxford: Clarendon, 1985.

Speidell, Todd Saliba. "The incarnation as the hermeneutical criterion for liberation and reconciliation." *Scottish Journal of Theology* 40 (1987): 249-258.

Spohn, William C. *What are they saying about scripture and ethics?* New York: Paulist, 1984.

Stackhouse, Max. *Apologia: Contextualization, globalization, and mission in theological education*. Grand Rapids: Eerdmans, 1988.

Stamoolis, James J. "Eastern Orthodox mission theology." *International Bulletin of Missionary Research* 8 (1984): 60-63.

_____. *Eastern Orthodox mission theology today*. Maryknoll: Orbis, 1986.

Staniloae, Dumitru. "Witness through 'holiness' of life." In *Martyria/mission: The witness of the Orthodox churches today*, ed. Ion Bria. Geneva: World Council of Churches, 1980. 45-51.

"Statement of the Stuttgart Consultation on Evangelism." In *Proclaiming Christ in Christ's way: Studies in integral evangelism*, eds. Vinay Samuel and Albrecht Hauser. Oxford: Regnum, 1989. 212-225.

Stayer, James, Werner Packull and Klaus Deppermann. "From monogenesis to polygenesis: The historical discussion of Anabaptist origins." *The Mennonite Quarterly Review* 49 (1975): 83-121.

Stevenson, J, ed. *Creeds, councils and controversies: Documents illustrative of the history of the Church, A.D. 337-461.* London: SPCK, 1966.

Steward, John. *Biblical holism and the missionary mandate.* Sydney: Sydney Centre for World Mission, 1995.

Stott, John. *Christian mission in the modern world.* Eastbourne: Kingsway, 1975.

_____. *The contemporary Christian: An urgent plea for double listening.* Leicester, UK: Inter-Varsity Press, 1992.

_____. "Response to Bishop Mortimer Arias ['That the world may believe']." *International Review of Mission* 65 (1976): 30-33.

Stransky, Thomas F. "From Vatican II to *Redemptoris Missio*: A development in the theology of mission." In *The good news of the kingdom: Mission theology for the third millennium*, eds. Charles Van Engen, Dean S Gilliland and Paul Pierson. Maryknoll: Orbis, 1993. 137-147.

Stromberg, Jean, ed. *Mission and evangelism: An ecumenical affirmation.* New York: National Council of the Churches of Christ in the USA (NCCC), 1982. Also found in World Council of Churches. "Mission and evangelism—An ecumenical affirmation." *International Review of Mission* 71 (1982): 427-451.

Stroup, George W, III. "Chalcedon revisited." *Theology Today* 35 (1978): 52-64.

Stroup, George W. *The promise of narrative theology.* London: SCM, 1981.

Stutzman, Linford. "An incarnational approach to mission in modern, affluent societies." *Urban Mission* 8.5 (May 1991): 35-43.

_____. *With Jesus in the world: Mission in modern, affluent societies.* Scottdale, PA: Herald, 1992.

Stylios, Efthimios. "The missionary as an imitator of Christ." *Porefthendes* 5 (1963): 8-10.

Synod of Bishops Third General Assembly (October 26 1974). "Evangelization of the modern world." In *The gospel of peace and justice: Catholic social teaching since Pope John*, ed. Joseph Gremillion. Maryknoll: Orbis, 1976. 593-598.

Taylor, John V. "My pilgrimage in mission." *International Bulletin of Missionary Research* 17 (1993): 59-61.

Thangaraj, M Thomas. *The crucified guru: An experiment in cross-cultural christology.* Nashville: Abingdon, 1994.

"Theology and implications of radical discipleship." In *Let the earth hear his voice: International Congress on World Evangelization, Lausanne, Switzerland*, ed. J D Douglas. Minneapolis: World Wide Publications, 1975. 1294-1296.

Third General Conference of Latin American Bishops. *Puebla: Evangelization at present and in the future of Latin America. Conclusions.* Middlegreen, UK: St Paul Publications, 1980.

Third Latin American Congress on Evangelism. "The whole gospel from Latin America for all peoples." In *New directions in mission and evangelization, 2:*

Theological foundations, eds. James A Scherer and Stephen B Bevans. Maryknoll: Orbis, 1994. 191-198.

Thomas á Kempis. *The imitation of Christ*. Transl. and ed. Leo Sherley-Price. Harmondsworth, Msex: Penguin, 1952 [1418].

Thompson, Marianne Meye. *The humanity of Jesus in the Fourth Gospel*. Philadelphia: Fortress, 1988.

Tiersma, Jude. "What does it mean to be incarnational when we are not the Messiah?" In *God so loves the city: Seeking a theology for urban mission*, eds. Charles Van Engen and Jude Tiersma. Monrovia, CA: MARC, 1994. 7-25.

Tinsley, E J. "The imitation of Christ." In *A new dictionary of Christian theology*, eds. John Bowden and Alan Richardson. London: SCM, 1983. 285-286.

Torrance, Thomas F, ed. *The incarnation: Ecumenical studies in the Nicene-Constantinopolitan Creed, A.D. 381*. London: Handsel Press, 1981.

Tsetsis, Georges, ed. *Orthodox thought: Reports of Orthodox consultations organized by the World Council of Churches, 1975-1982*. Geneva: World Council of Churches, 1983.

Turabian, Kate L, John Grossman and Alice Bennett. *A manual for writers of term papers, theses, and dissertations*. 6th ed. Chicago: University of Chicago Press, 1996.

"Unitatis Redintegratio (Decree on Ecumenism)." In *The documents of Vatican II*, ed. Walter M Abbott. London: Geoffrey Chapman, 1966. 341-366.

Valentine, Simon Ross. "The Johannine Prologue—a microcosm of the Gospel." *The Evangelical Quarterly* 68 (1996): 291-304.

Van Engen, Charles, Dean S Gilliland and Paul Pierson, eds. *The good news of the kingdom: Mission theology for the third millennium*. Maryknoll: Orbis, 1993.

Van Engen, Charles and Jude Tiersma, eds. *God so loves the city: Seeking a theology for urban mission*. Monrovia: MARC/World Vision, 1994.

Van Gelder, Craig. "A great new fact of our day: America as a mission field." *Missiology* 19 (1991): 409-418.

Villafañe, Eldin. *Seek the peace of the city: Reflections on urban ministry*. Grand Rapids: Eeerdmans, 1995.

Vincent, John. *Into the city*. London: Epworth, 1982.

Waida, Manabu. "Incarnation." In *The encyclopedia of religion*, ed. Mircea Eliade. 16 vols.. New York: Macmillan, 1987. 7:156-161.

Wainwright, Geoffrey, ed. *Keeping the faith: Essays to mark the centenary of "Lux Mundi."* London: SPCK, 1988.

Walgrave, J H. "Incarnation and atonement." In *The incarnation: Ecumenical studies in the Nicene-Constantinopolitan Creed, A.D. 381*, ed. Thomas F Torrance. London: Handsel Press, 1981. 148-176.

Wallis, Jim. *Agenda for biblical people*. 2nd ed. San Francisco: Harper & Row, 1984.

_____. *The call to conversion*. Tring, Herts., UK: Lion, 1981.

_____. *The soul of politics: A practical and prophetic vision for change.* London: Fount, 1994.

Walter, James. "Defining Australia." In *Images of Australia: An introductory reader in Australian studies,* eds. Gillian Whitlock and David Carter. St Lucia, Qld: University of Queensland Press, 1992. 7-22.

Waltermire, Donald E. *The liberation christologies of Leonardo Boff and Jon Sobrino: Latin American contributions to contemporary christology.* Lanham, MD: University Press of America, 1994.

Waltner, Erland, ed. *Christology in historical perspective.* Newton, KN: Faith & Life, 1990.

Ward, Keith. "Incarnation or inspiration—A false dichotomy?" *Theology* 80 (1977): 251-255.

Ward, Russel. *The Australian legend.* 2nd ed. Oxford: OUP, 1966 (1958).

Waugh, Patricia, ed. *Postmodernism: A reader.* London: Edward Arnold, 1992.

Weaver, J Denny. "The Anabaptist vision: A historical or a theological future?" *The Conrad Grebel Review* 13 (1995): 69-86.

_____. "Atonement for the nonconstantinian church." *Modern Theology* 6 (1990): 307-323.

_____. *Becoming Anabaptist: The origin and significance of sixteenth-century Anabaptism.* Scottdale, PA: Herald, 1987.

_____. "A believers' church christology." *The Mennonite Quarterly Review* 57 (1983): 112-131.

_____. "Christology in historical perspective." In *Contemporary Anabaptist perspectives,* ed. Erland Waltner. Newton, KN: Faith & Life, 1990. 83-105.

_____. "Christus Victor, ecclesiology, and christology." *The Mennonite Quarterly Review* 68 (1994): 277-290.

_____. "Discipleship redefined: Four sixteenth century Anabaptists." *The Mennonite Quarterly Review* 54 (1980): 255-279.

_____. "Narrative theology in an Anabaptist-Mennonite context." *The Conrad Grebel Review* 12 (1994): 171-188.

_____. "Which way for Mennonite theology?" *Gospel Herald,* 23 Jan 1996, 1-8.

Weidner, H D. "Editor's introduction." In John Henry Newman. *The via media of the Anglican church* [1889 ed.]. ed. H D Weidner. Oxford: Clarendon, 1990. xiii-vxxix.

Wenger, J C. *What Mennonites believe.* Rev. ed. Scottdale, PA: Herald, 1991.

Westmoreland-Smith, Michael, Glen Stassen and David P Gushee. "Disciples of the incarnation." *Sojourners,* May 1994, 26-30.

White, Richard. *Inventing Australia: Images and identity, 1688-1980.* St Leonards, NSW: Allen & Unwin, 1981.

White, Vernon. *Atonement and incarnation: An essay in universalism and particularity.* Cambridge: Cambridge University Press, 1991.

Whiteman, Darrell. "Contextualization: The theory, the gap, the challenge." *International Bulletin of Missionary Research* 21 (1997): 2-7.

Whitlock, Gillian and David Carter, eds. *Images of Australia: An introductory reader in Australian studies.* St Lucia: University of Queensland Press, 1992.

Wiles, Maurice. "Christianity without incarnation?" In *The myth of God incarnate,* ed. John Hick. London: SCM, 1977. 1-10.

_____. "A survey of the issues in the *Myth* debate." In *Incarnation and myth: The debate continued,* ed. Michael Goulder. London: SCM, 1979. 1-12.

Wilkinson-Hayes, Ann. "A letter to the churches." *Mainstream: Baptists for life and growth* (Great Britain) No. 51 (1994): 3-5.

Williams, Daniel Day. *The Spirit and the forms of love.* Digswell Place, Herts.: James Nisbet, 1968.

Williams, George Huntston. *The Radical Reformation.* 3rd ed. Kirksville, MO: Sixteenth Century Journal Publishers, 1992.

Williams, H A. "Incarnation: Model and symbol." *Theology* 79 (1976): 6-18.

Williams, Trevor. "Protestant theology: Britain." In *The Blackwell Encyclopedia of Modern Christian Thought,* ed. Alister E McGrath. Oxford: Blackwell, 1993. 480-486.

Williamson, George. "Politics is the law." In *Communities of faith and radical discipleship: Jürgen Moltmann and others,* ed. G McLeod Bryan. Macon, GA: Mercer University Press, 1986. 71-104.

Wilson, Bryan. "Secularization." In *A new dictionary of Christian theology,* eds. Alan Richardson and John Bowden. London: SCM, 1983. 534-535.

Wilson, Frederick R, ed. *The San Antonio Report: Your will be done: Mission in Christ's way.* Geneva: World Council of Churches, 1990.

Wilson, R McL. "Gnosticism." In *A new dictionary of Christian theology,* eds. Alan Richardson and John Bowden. London: SCM, 1983. 226-230.

Wilson-Kastner, Patricia. *Faith, feminism, and the Christ.* Philadelphia: Fortress, 1983.

World Council of Churches. "Mission and evangelism—An ecumenical affirmation." *International Review of Mission* 71 (1982): 427-451. Also found in Stromberg, Jean, ed. *Mission and evangelism: An ecumenical affirmation.* New York: National Council of the Churches of Christ in the USA (NCCC), 1982.

World Council of Churches Commission on World Mission and Evangelism. *Bangkok Assembly 1973: Minutes and report of the Assembly of the Commission on World Mission and Evangelism of the World Council of Churches, December 31, 1972 and January 9-12, 1973.* Geneva: World Council of Churches, 1973.

World Council of Churches Commission on World Mission and Evangelism. *Your kingdom come: Mission perspectives. Report on the World Conference on*

Mission and Evangelism, Melbourne, Australia, 12-25 May 1980. Geneva: World Council of Churches, 1980.

World Council of Churches Commission on World Mission and Evangelism. *Your will be done: Mission in Christ's way: Study material and biblical reflection.* Geneva: World Council of Churches, 1988.

World Council of Churches CWME. "Stuttgart Consultation (Stuttgart, 1987)." In *New directions in mission and evangelization, 1: Basic statements, 1974-1991,* eds. James A Scherer and Stephen B Bevans. Maryknoll: Orbis, 1992. 65-72.

Yannoulatos, Anastasios. "Discovering the Orthodox missionary ethos." In *Martyria/mission: The witness of the Orthodox churches today,* ed. Ion Bria. Geneva: World Council of Churches, 1980. 20-29.

Yarnold, E J. "Grace." In *A new dictionary of Christian theology,* eds. Alan Richardson and John Bowden. London: SCM, 1983. 244-245.

Yates, Christopher. *Christian mission in the twentieth century.* Cambridge: Cambridge University Press, 1994.

Yoder, John Howard. "Orientation in midstream: A response to the responses." In *Freedom and discipleship: Liberation theology in Anabaptist perspective,* ed. Daniel S Schipani. Maryknoll: Orbis, 1989. 159-168.

_____. *The politics of Jesus: Vicit agnus noster.* 2nd ed. Grand Rapids: Eerdmans, 1994.

_____. *The royal priesthood: Essays ecclesiological and ecumenical.* Ed. Michael G Cartwright. Grand Rapids: Eerdmans, 1994.

Yoder, John Howard, ed. *The legacy of Michael Sattler.* Classics of the Radical Reformation, No. 1. Scottdale, PA: Herald, 1973.

Yoder, John Howard, ed. *The Schleitheim Confession.* Scottdale, PA: Herald, 1973.

Young, Frances. "A cloud of witnesses." In *The myth of God incarnate,* ed. John Hick. London: SCM, 1977. 13-47.

_____. "Two roots or a tangled mass?." In *The myth of God incarnate,* ed. John Hick. London: SCM, 1977. 87-121.

"Your kingdom come [Working document from an Orthodox consultation, Paris, September 1978]." *International Review of Mission* 68 (1979): 139-147.

"Your will be done—Mission in Christ"s way [Selections from a CWME consultation]." *International Review of Mission* 75 (1986): 423-454.

INDEX

A

accommodation, 173
Ad Gentes, 167-72
adaptation, 173
AG (see Ad Gentes)
AMECEA, 174
Anabaptism, 8, 58, 61-92, 96, 99-
    100, 103, 105, 119, 132, 140,
    206, 221, 231
Anabaptist vision, The, 63, 66, 70,
    91
Anderson, Norman, 31
Anderson, Wilhelm, 193
Andrews, Dave, 94, 110
Anglicanism, 33, 182, 193
Anglo-Catholicism, 9, 18, 56, 161-
    62, 182-88, 221, 230
anthropocentrism, 139
antinomianism, 76
Arias, Mortimer, 103, 112, 114,
    196
asceticism, 166, 208
assumptions, 6
Athanasius, 21, 183, 205
atonement, 5, 46, 182-83, 201
Augustine, 45, 76, 158, 183
Auschwitz, 184
Australia, 237, 239-44
avataras, 16

B

Baillie, Donald, 34
Bangkok CWME (1973), 194-95
Barbour, Ian, 39
Barmen Theological Declaration,
    153
Barth, Karl, 15, 31, 42, 64, 155
Batstone, David, 114
Beachy, Alvin, 77, 89
beauty, 148, 234
believers' church, 85
Belloc, Hilaire, 184
Belshaw, Mellick, 185
Bender, Harold, 63, 66, 70, 77, 91
Bernard of Clairvaux, 68
Berrigan, Daniel & Philip, 95
bodhisattvas, 16
body (soma), 26
body of Christ, 9, 12, 53, 74, 85,
    101, 158, 163, 187, 220, 224,
    228, 238
body theology, 12
Boff, Clodovis, 50, 125
Boff, Leonardo, 34, 50, 55, 118-32,
    140, 155
Bonaventure, 72
Bonhoeffer, Dietrich, 49, 52, 76,
    81, 89, 96, 135, 153, 209
Bonino, José Míguez, 82, 88

ABOUT THE AUTHOR

Ross Langmead is Professor of Missiology at Whitley College, the Baptist seminary of Victoria, Australia, and the Director of the School of World Mission in Melbourne. His articles on theology of mission, ecotheology and multicultural mission have appeared in various journals.

Made in the USA
Lexington, KY
23 July 2015